PATRISTIC MONOGRAPH SERIES, NO. 10

PAGAN-CHRISTIAN CONFLICT
OVER MIRACLE IN
THE SECOND CENTURY

by

HAROLD REMUS

The Philadelphia Patristic Foundation, Ltd.

1983

Library of Congress Cataloging in Publication Data

Remus, Harold, 1928—
  Pagan-Christian conflict over miracle in the
second century.

  (Patristic monograph series ; no. 10)
  Bibliography : p.
  Includes indexes.
  1. Miracles — History. I. Title. II. Series.
BL 487.R45 1983   231.7′3   83-6729
ISBN 0-915646-09-9 (pbk.)

Copyright © 1983
The Philadelphia Patristic Foundation, Ltd.
99 Brattle Street, Cambridge, MA 02138

FOR CAROLYN

In Memory--and Gratitude

CONTENTS

INDEXES

PREFACE

That there is more than one way to approach the question of
conflict between pagans and Christians over miracle in the
early centuries of the present era is clear from the extensive secondary literature on "miracle" in this period.
The present study presupposes and draws on these earlier
studies, as is evident from the documentation and the
bibliography. That it focuses especially on social and
cultural aspects does not constitute a claim that such is
the only way or even the best way to approach the question.
It is, rather, an attempt to do justice to factors the
neglect of which has often obscured the nature of such
conflict or made it difficult to understand by divesting it
of flesh and blood (and sweat and tears). Approaching a
topic sociologically, as well as ideologically, does not
minimize the importance of the latter. As Gerd Theissen
has observed (1975b, 156), ideas usually assume importance
only when social groups bestow on them the power to
influence behavior. Sociological and ideological analyses
can be mutually illuminating.

        When this study was conceived some years ago, the
current surge of interest in the social world of early
Christianity was barely beginning. Today, however, one
publication after another offers investigation of various
social aspects of the early Christian movement or applies
sociological theory to it in some way.[1] No full-scale
study, however, has addressed itself to the social and
cultural dimensions of competing miracle claims made by
Christians, on the one hand, and adherents of Greco-Roman
cults, on the other. That such dimensions are important
has been suggested in various studies, however, for example,
in the recognition that a social group will designate its
thaumaturge as "savior," "*theios aner*," or "son of God" and

ix

his or her wonders as "miracle" while outsiders will often
label him or her a "magician" and denigrate the same
wonders as "magic" and belief in them as "superstition."[2]
Geffcken lamented the untidy polemic that resulted because
pagan and Christian opponents often employed the same
weapons against each other while defending opposing positions; however, he failed to explore the implications of
such an observation (see below, p. 105). Harnack expressed
puzzlement that two men of such intellectual prowess as
Celsus and Origen should so mingle superstition and critical acumen in definding the rival deities Asclepius and
Christ (see below, p. 108); he, too, did not pursue the
issue. One important avenue to the understanding of such
argumentation, in which opponents "talk past" each other or
seemingly bypass "logic" to make their points, is sociology
of knowledge. Its use can illuminate conflicts like those
noted above because it invites one to seek out those
motives in assertion and argumentation that are fundamental
but unstated because they are presupposed by members of a
social group as a result of socialization into that group.
The present study draws upon the sociology of knowledge,
and at the appropriate place some of the theoretical aspects
of that discipline are spelled out. Sociology of knowledge
has aptly been characterized as a development and special
application of historical method (see below, pp. 86-87), and
it is in this light that I have understood it and sought to
integrate it with the close textual study that traditionally
belongs to historical method.

Part One of the study addresses to ancient sources
the question of the definition of miracle. Social and
cultural aspects are seen to figure into the definition.
Chapter Four treats, *inter alia*, a troublesome case of
definition: "miracle" vs. "magic." Theoretical considera-
tions deriving from the sociology of knowledge are then set
forth and illustrated from the history of study of miracle.
The ground is thus laid for Part Two, examination of a

complex of conflicts associated with the name of Asclepius
in the second century. Actual cases of Christians squaring
off against pagans, or vice-versa, on the question of
miracle are few in the second century. There are such
instances, however, and where there is not explicit
confrontation, positions taken by various pagans and Christians regarding miracle are, on investigation, seen to be
in conflict. It is in this sense of explicit or implicit
opposition that the word "conflict" is used in the study.
In examining these conflicts I have gone into detail,
tediously so, some may think. However, it is only such
detailed examination, I believe, that can demonstrate the
social and cultural aspects of these differences and
justify (or not) giving attention to these aspects as a
means of illuminating the conflicts.[3]

Several reasons underlie the choice of the second
century. One is the necessity of keeping the study within
reasonable bounds; even so, there had to be a selection of
the sources investigated. Another is that for the second
century the study of miracle is a field less ploughed than
is the first century for which the studies of "miracle in
the New Testament" are rife. Since the second-century
Christian sources generally lie outside the Christian canon
of scripture, the religious commitment that has informed
much of the study of miracle accounts in first-century
Christian sources is not as intrusive in the study of the
second century; the way thus seemed more open to fresh
analysis and perhaps a more dispassionate hearing. Moreover, in the second century Christianity has become a movement of sufficient importance to produce significant
conflict over miracle between pagan and Christian.[4]

I have sought to restrain my propensity for citing
texts in support of claims; had I exercised further
restraint, the manuscript might have been less extensive,
but as one who expects such documentation from others (and
is often disappointed) and wishes to run as he reads (and,

recently, has but limited access to a research library), I
have proceeded on the assumption (not unfounded, I believe)
that there are other souls with such idiosyncrasies.

To some, my efforts in this essay may perhaps
appear as an exercise in naming--the attaching of new
labels to old situations. Even if that were so, the act of
naming is, nonetheless, an art, as is attested by a long
tradition from Adam to Linnaeus to present-day work in
taxonomy. Labeling implies identification; such identification of certain aspects of definitions and conflicts as
"social" and "cultural" contributes, I believe, to understanding of them. Much in this study is not new, but the
whole is, I believe, greater than the sum of its parts.

*   *   *

The subject of this study, accepted as a Ph.D.
dissertation at the University of Pennsylvania in 1981 and
here presented with slight corrections and revisions, grew
out of a long-standing interest both in early Christianity
and the classics. Other responsibilities and interruptions
of various kinds extended the research and writing over a
longer period than expected; I am grateful to my advisor,
Robert A. Kraft, for his patience, but also for his keen
insights and criticism and his unfailing encouragement
during my whole course of doctoral study. To another of my
teachers, Van A. Harvey, I am indebted for valuable
instruction and dialogue in the course of which sociology
of knowledge presented itself to me as of heuristic value
for pursuing the topic. Lively discussions with John Gager
provided insight into sociological perception of ancient
texts. I deeply regret that the late Robert F. Evans was
unable to give the manuscript a critical reading, as we had
planned; the gestation of the topic profited much from his
sound learning. Richard Luecke, from whom I learned so
much--in what, recalled, now seems "an ultimate, dim Thule"

--must also share some of the credit and bear some of the
blame for what these pages set forth. That I have pursued
the topic differently than any of these would have is
clear.

*   *   *

Much of chapter six was published as an article
entitled "Sociology of Knowledge and the Study of Early
Christianity," *Studies in Religion/Sciences Religieuses* 11
(1982), 45-56. Much of chapter four has appeared as
"'Magic or Miracle'? Some Second-Century Instances," *The
Second Century: A Journal of Early Christian Studies* 2
(1982), 127-56. Appendix E, "Plotinus and Gnostic Thaumaturgy," appears as an article with that title in *Laval
théologique et philosophique* 39/1 (1983).

*   *   *

To the staff of the Council on the Study of Religion, at Wilfrid Laurier University, the staff of Wilfrid
Laurier University Press, and my colleagues in the faculty
and administration at Wilfrid Laurier University I am
indebted in ways too numerous to recite. Nancy Stade
deserves special thanks for her care and attention to
detail in preparing the typescript. Finally, I acknowledge
with gratitude a book preparation grant from the Research
Office at Wilfrid Laurier University.

Harold Remus

Wilfrid Laurier University
December 1982

PART ONE

"MIRACLE":
DEMARCATIONS,
EXPLANATIONS, AND
SOCIAL DIMENSIONS

1

A PARADIGM

"To discourse of miracle without defining what one means
by the word miracle," wrote John Locke, "is to make a shew,
but in effect to talk of nothing" (1958b, 79).

Modern studies of miracle in the Greco-Roman world
have often neglected to define miracle or have defined it
only briefly or vaguely or with little attention to ancient
terms and presuppositions. Some of the writers and
scholars of that world and of classical antiquity in
general attempted explicit definitions, but these are
largely along etymological lines--still an uncertain under-
taking--and are often contradicted by usage.[1] Even where
no definitions are attempted, however, there is an awareness, both among learned and unlearned, that certain phenomena and events are set apart from others as unusual, and
that certain of these are so extraordinary as to be explicable only by ascribing them to agency or causation
exceeding or other than human capacity or the agents and
causes familiar in everyday experience. The fact that one
of the first Christian apologists, writing early in the
second century, is at pains to defend certain acts of Jesus
--healings and resurrections--implies an awareness of them
as out of the ordinary and as needing defense (Quadratus,
in Eusebius, *H.E.* 4.3.2). Late in the same century, the
same kinds of unusual phenomena figure in Celsus' attack on
Christianity.

On what bases was something adjudged unusual? What
consensus existed on what constituted the bases of judgment? What degree of inexplicability was necessary before
something was attributed to other than familiar causation?
How is one to account for the differing judgments one finds
in these matters? These questions are pertinent to the

3

question of definition of miracle and are essential to the
discussion of conflict over miracle that is the subject of
this investigation.

A passage in Livy (44.37), concerning a lunar
eclipse, may serve as a paradigm of the issues here. The
Roman legions are drawn up before the Macedonians on the
eve of the decisive battle of Pydna (168 B.C.E.). The
Roman officers are aware that a lunar eclipse is to occur
that night, and in order that it may not terrify or dis-
hearten the soldiers they undertake to instruct them
regarding it. Their spokesman, Gallus, announces that

> in the coming night, in order that no one may take it for a portent
> [*portento*], from the second to the fourth hour of the night, the moon
> will disappear. This, because it occurs in the natural order [*naturali
> ordine*], at set times, it is possible to know beforehand and to pre-
> dict. Therefore, even as, because the rising and setting of the sun
> and the moon are fixed, they [the soldiers] do not marvel that the moon
> now shines in full orb and, now waning, with a little horn, so also
> they ought not to interpret it as a prodigy [*prodigium*] when the moon
> becomes dark because it is hidden by the shadow of the earth (44.37.6-7)

When the eclipse occurs as predicted, Gallus' wisdom seems
to the Roman soldiers almost divine (*prope divina*). In
contrast to the calm in the Roman camp is the uproar among
the Macedonians. Both the interpreters of prodigies and
the soldiers view the eclipse as a dire omen (*triste
prodigium*) portending the fall of their kingdom and the
ruin of their people. There is noisemaking and wailing in
their camp until the moon reappears (44.37.9).

What makes the eclipse a *prodigium* or a *portentum*
for the Macedonians but not for the Romans?

First, a *prodigium* is something that is, at the
least, irregular and unusual, and probably rare and extraordinary. In the natural order (*naturali ordine*) events
occur with regularity and therefore need occasion neither
wonder nor (being anticipated) any surprise. The rising
and setting of the sun and the moon are fixed and therefore
no one marvels (*mirarentur*) at the waxing and waning of the
moon. So also an eclipse occurs at "fixed times" (*statis
temporibus*), when the earth's shadow darkens the moon, thus
enabling one to predict its occurrence. Therefore, argues
Gallus, one should not, by consensus on the meaning of

portentum and *prodigium*, interpret a lunar eclipse as a
prodigium or *portentum*.

Second, a *prodigium* or a *portentum* is not explicable according to the natural order and so is referred to
deity. The Macedonians view the eclipse as a dire message
--*scil*. from the divine--and the Roman soldiers would have
too had they not been given an alternative explanation
prior to the event. The Macedonians' clamor is not mere
noise, it is noisemaking--purposeful activity in support of
the threatened moon goddess (cf. Tacitus, *Ann*. 1.28).
Religion is one of the contexts of *prodigium*, *portentum*,
and *mirari*.

Third, the definition of miracle is socially and
culturally influenced. Gallus is a tribune of the soldiers
of the second legion; in the year just past he has served
as *praetor* (44.37.5). That is, he belongs to the Roman
aristocracy. It is with the permission of the consuls,
also members of the aristocracy, that Gallus undertakes to
instruct the soldiers. The aristocracy, or Livy as their
spokesman, have available to them, because of their wider
knowledge, another option for interpreting an eclipse.[2]
The Roman soldiers (*milites*), on the other hand, and the
Macedonians (Livy does not discriminate among the latter)
have only one explanatory option: the eclipse is divinely
sent and divinely portending. When the Roman soldiers are
presented with an alternative explanation, which is proved
true by the event, then their epithet *divina* is applied to
Gallus' wisdom, now as inexplicable and awesome to them as
the eclipse was previously. Here two cultural traditions,
related to social status and accompanying education,
confront each other. One identifies a lunar eclipse as a
prodigium, the other does not. The decision in the latter
case is conscious and deliberate, according to specific
criteria. In both cases, it is perception--interpretation
--that makes or unmakes a *prodigium*. By definition a
prodigium ceases to be a *prodigium* when it is explicable in
the terms outlined above. Gallus' (or Livy's)[3] prescrip-
tive language--the soldiers "ought not" (*ne . . . debere*)
to interpret the eclipse as a *prodigium*--is motivated by

more than a concern for definition, however. For the
soldiers to regard the eclipse as a *prodigium* would have an
adverse affect on the outcome of the battle, in which the
officers have a great stake. Hence Gallus' lecture in
astromony. He and the consuls are authority figures,[4] and
the soldiers allow themselves to be persuaded--on this one
point and for the moment--into another tradition of knowledge.[5]

   The following pages will seek to demonstrate that
attention to all three of these elements is essential to a
demarcation of "miracle" in pagan and Christian sources
from the second century. To attempt such a demarcation on
the basis of second-century sources is impossible, however,
without reference to prior as well as subsequent traditions
that illuminate them. Yet some principle of selection is
necessary inasmuch as pagan and Christian sources abound in
reports of extraordinary phenomena. Since our concern in
this study is with conflicts over miracle, and these
generally relate in some way to the extraordinary phenomena
recounted in Christian traditions, these kinds of phenomena
will serve as the focal points for this discussion.

   To reduce distortion in understanding, it would be
best, were it not so cumbersome, to treat all three
elements each time an extraordinary phenomenon is taken up.
Instead, the attempt will be made to understand each of the
elements in turn, as with the Livy example, with a synthe-
sis and conclusion coming at the end. In some cases, however, it is impossible to discuss them in isolation from
each other, which means there will be some overlapping.

2
THE ORDINARY AND THE EXTRAORDINARY

As many of the examples in this chapter will indicate, one
may with some justice say that for the Romans, "Die Welt
war voll von Wundern; Unbegreifliches geschah alle Tage im
Himmel und auf Erden" (Lembert, 1905, 21), and that "the
ancients" generally "konnten jedes göttliche Handeln als
Wunder bezeichnen, auch wenn as in natürlichen Bahnen
verlief. Alles, was geschah, konnte als Wunder aufgefasst
werden" (Weinreich, 1909, vii). But such statements are
too undifferentiated and ignore such canons as the ancients
possessed for demarcating the unusual from the usual, the
extraordinary from the ordinary, as well as the differences
in these canons among individuals, groups, and time periods.
The self-conscious use by poets of a literary device known
as "the impossible" (*adynaton*)[1] depends for its effect on
widely held canons of the possible and the impossible, the
ordinary and the extraordinary. Some such canons are
implicit in the works, current in the Greco-Roman period,
consisting simply of accounts of extraordinary phenomena.
Labeled paradoxography by modern scholars,[2] the ancient
titles give a straightforward indication of the nature of
the contents: θαυμάσια, περὶ θαυμασίων, θαυμασίων συναγωγή,
ἱστορίαι θαυμασίαι, παράδοξα, περὶ παραδόξων, ἱστόρικα
παράδοξα, *De admirandis*, and the like. Aulus Gellius
characterizes the phenomena reported as "unheard of" and
"incredible," contained in books "full of marvels and
fictions."[3] The contents, culled from the historians and
from writings with a scientific interest, sometimes with
additions from the author's own experience, report extraordinary phenomena in the whole realm of human experience.
The paradoxographers did not exclude extraordinary phenomena reported for the distant Homeric world of gods and

men, but their chief interest lay in those reported as
presently existing, or as once having existed, in ascer-
tained (or theoretically ascertainable) times and places.

The familiar, everyday world is the background
against which such phenomena stand out as unexpected, rare,
extraordinary. That world may vary from people to people,
so that what one considers ordinary another will experience
as rare and impressive. And within a people, what is
unusual or rare for all may be ascribed to the divine by
some persons but explained by others without reference to
special action of deity. These are matters primarily for
the chapters that follow. Here our concern is to point out
that there were canons of the ordinary among both pagans
and Christians, learned and unlearned, and to indicate some
of these canons.

2.1 Revivification Accounts

The fact that certain kinds of narratives are singled out
for telling implies a world of the ordinary against which
such "miracle stories" stand out as extraordinary. The
happenings are demarcated as extraordinary through specific
terminology (see below, ch. 4), and certain stereotyped
features of the narratives make clear to the audience that
something extraordinary is occurring. Amazement and sometimes fear is the proper reaction of the onlookers.

Narratives of revivification of the dead, a disputed issue between second-century Christians and pagans
and therefore pertinent to our inquiry, may serve as
examples. Against Christian resurrection accounts Celsus
pits accounts of revivification in pagan Greek traditions.[4]
These are stock examples and are found, along with still
others, in various pagan and Christian writers,[5] including
the paradoxographers.[6] The assessment of such accounts,
pagan or Christian, varies in their present settings, from
missionary affirmation to simple reporting to mild disbelief
to rejection. Presupposed in all, however, is that revivification, should such occur, would not be an everyday
affair and would be something worth investigating or
acclaiming or recording or puzzling over.

2.2 The Human Being as a Canon of the Ordinary

One common canon by which something was adjudged extraordinary was the human being as he or she is in the
majority of cases. Consideration of this canon is pertinent
since the figure of Jesus is central to pagan and Christian
conflict over miracle.[7]

Humans come into the world ordinarily through
intercourse of man and woman,[8] attain their full mental
powers slowly,[9] grow to a more or less limited height,[10] and
have an appearance that distinguishes them from animals.[11]
Their capacities are limited (see below, p. 13), and this
distinguishes them from the gods, as does the fact that
they are mortal and, once dead, ordinarily do not return
from the dead.[12] This background of the ordinary is the
necessary foil to accounts of persons more than human, less
than human, or something other than human. Into the latter
two categories would fall persons with deficient parts or
hybrids of humans and animals. However one explained these,
the assessment of them as extraordinary was made on the
basis of physical appearance; that is, the canon of the
ordinary was fairly tight. Into the first category would
fall persons with redundant parts--where, again, visual
comparison with the majority of humans constituted a fairly
tight canon--and persons of more than human nature or capacities. In the case of these last, the canons were looser.
The sources here, covering a long span of time and a
variety of peoples, fall into several groups.[13]

2.2.1 Heroes

The term ἥρως/heros is of broad and varied denotation,
but in most of the cases the individual denoted is distinguished in some way from others, whether these "others" are
humans--as when the term denotes a deity[14]--or are humans
more ordinary than the men and women designated "heroes."
Such men and women were accorded divine honors after death
and from their tomb exerted beneficent or baleful
influence.[15] In time "hero" came to refer to any dead
person, with no necessary connotation of power attaching.[16]
But generally those so honored had been distinguished in

some way in life: as warriors, as persons of great size or
strength, as athletes, healers, rulers, legislators, poets,
philosophers, or in other ways that benefited a community
or brought honor to it.[17] Almost any outstanding characteristic could result in heroization.[18] The Christian
counterparts to these pagan exemplars were the heroes of
the faith, the saints and martyrs, who before their deaths
displayed prophetic powers[19] and worked wonders[20] and,
after death, were potent forces from their tombs or through
their relics.[21] The foil to all these is the ordinary
human, but the canons of judgment are loose, partly, it
would seem, because heroes were beyond the realm of everyday experience: they were minor deities, or persons of the
distant past, or if near at hand, beyond the barrier of
death. These judgments were socially and culturally
influenced and therefore variable, but common to most of
them was the more ordinary human being as the general canon
of measurement.

2.2.2 Rulers

Related to hero cult is the deification of rulers in
Hellenistic and Roman times.[22] As in the case of heroes,
but with political motivations prominent, deification was a
recognition--whether imposed from above or stemming from
below, or both--of some characteristic or attainment beyond
the ordinary, which was deemed beneficent to the subjects.
It may have been military prowess or skill in governing or
even praeternatural powers,[23] or all of these. In
examining the canons of judgment here, one becomes aware of
their social matrices. To rally allies against Xerxes, for
example, the Greek messengers assert that he is no god but
a man.[24] Alexander's fellow Macedonians, accustomed to
selecting a king from their own ranks, generally refuse to
accord him divine honors, while the Persians, for whom
deification was traditional, are ready to do so.[25] The
native Egyptian population should likewise have had no
problem with the Ptolomies' deification of themselves even
before death (cf. Cerfaux and Tondriau, 1956, 208ff.).
Athenians acclaim Demetrius Poliorcetes as a deity near at

hand and ask him to protect their city,[26] while Rhodes, on
the other hand, venerates Ptolemy I because he has saved
them from Demetrius (Tarn and Griffith, 1961, 53).

In Rome, emperors were not officially deified until
after death (e.g., Tacitus, *Ann.* 15.74). The traditional
Roman suspicion of kings and an awareness of their humanity
are reflected in the disclaiming of divine honors by certain
emperors,[27] in ritual reminders of the ruler's humanity,[28]
and in explicit statements of it.[29] Certain emperors, however, were accorded near-divine honors while still living
or claimed them for themselves.[30] The attitude of subjects
to the deity or deification of emperors is difficult to
establish and assess with precision. In general, one might
say that it is a function of the degree to which the
emperor's person and achievements were truly exceptional
and of the subject's personal relation to the emperor. A
seven-day comet that appeared during the funeral games for
Julius Caesar reportedly convinced the people (*volgus*) that
his soul had been taken to heaven (Suetonius, *Jul.* 88); but
it is doubtful that any such wonder could have stayed the
pent-up anger that overflowed at the death of Tiberius
(Suetonius, *Tib.* 75). Martial's and Statius' extravagant
praise of Domitian as divine (Cerfaux and Tondriau, 1956,
357) must be viewed in relation both to the character of
Domitian and their relation to him, no less so than the
probably genuine acclaim of the emperor by the Augustan
poets (ibid., 332-34).

In the provinces, deification of the Roman emperor
while living continued the Hellenistic tradition noted
above (Nilsson, 1961, 384ff.). Dio Chrysostom's discourses
on kingship probably reflect popular feeling in the
provinces when they compare the rule of Zeus and the rule
of a good sovereign.[31] At the same time, voices in the
philosophical tradition stress the emperors' mere humanity
(see Nilsson, 1961, 392-93, and literature cited there).

In Jewish opposition to participation in emperor
cult, according to the extant texts, social and cultural
motives are again evident: patriotism and the Pentateuchal
tradition of prohibition of other gods and images (cf.

Goodenough, 1962, 71-72). Occasionally the claim to
divinity is measured against the emperor's mere humanity.[32]
In Christian texts, there is a general indebtedness to
Judaism both for support of the emperor and for opposition
to the cult of the emperor; in both respects, however, the
emperor's mere humanity is a consistent strain. In the
earlier texts, in which obedience to, and prayer for, the
emperor and other rulers are urged, their humanity is
assumed;[33] on occasion Caesar and God may be explicitly
contrasted (Mk. 12.13-17 par.; *1 Clem.* 60-61). Later, when
participation in emperor cult had become an issue and a
test of loyalty, Christian apologists argued explicitly from
the emperor's humanity evident in his mortality, his
limited capacities, and his placement in office by God
(Justin, *1 Apol.* 1.17; Tertullian, *Apol.* 30-35, with *homo*
as the canon in 30.1-4; 33.3-4; 34.3).

2.2.3 Others

A third group of sources concerns the many reports of
persons not falling in the category of hero or ruler[34] but
yet possessing natures or capacities considered beyond
those of ordinary humans.[35] In the Greco-Roman period
these reports are so numerous and the designation Θεός or
Θεῖος[36] so common that 'άνθρωπος/*homo* would seem to have
been hardly operative as a canon of the ordinary.[37] The
canon does indeed function, as has been indicated; but the
edges are blurred and there are frequent departures from
it; that is, it is a loose canon. It will be pertinent to
our inquiry, and economical, to take the figure of Jesus
as illustrative.[38]

Assertions of the divine origin of an extraordinary
human figure is a common topos in pagan sources (Bieler,
1967, vol. 1, 24ff.). The canon is reproduction in the
ordinary way, which is represented in those Jesus traditions that know nothing of virgin birth or divine paternity
or reject these and in pagan charges of Mary's adultery.[39]
His body is portrayed in some sources as like other men's,
requiring food and rest and experiencing pain and death.
For some pagans this precluded Jesus' deity.[40] On the

other hand, like other extraordinary figures in this third
group, his body is sometimes exempt from the limitations to
which those of ordinary humans are subject,[41] such as
specific gravity,[42] tangibleness or visibility,[43] space,[44]
or mortality.[45] These are traditional characteristics of
deity, and at times Jesus' divine nature is revealed in an
epiphany[46] as well as through special knowledge,[47] speech,[48]
and deeds[49] acclaimed by others as beyond ordinary human
capacities. Jesus' virtue and beneficence also mark him
off from others.[50] Two common attributes of deity or of
divine men in the pagan world, great physical strength and
good looks,[51] are sometimes asserted of Jesus, but there is
also a vigorous tradition to the contrary.[52]

Jesus could thus be viewed as having simply the
same nature as other humans,[53] or as having that nature but
possessing or possessed by extraordinary wisdom or power.
Or he could be regarded as so surpassing the human as to be
placed in the category of divine man or of deity. Various
combinations of these traits, human and divine, were made
in the second century, often with little regard for their
compatability. The looseness of the canon of judgment here
--what is human and what is divine, and what and where are
the boundaries?--meant that conflicts over Jesus' nature
and achievements, between Christian and Christian or between
pagan and Christian, were apt to arise and were not readily
resolvable. Those details in the Jesus story which assert
his common humanity, his powerlessness in the face of assault,
and his resulting degradation also provide fertile ground
for pagan-Christian conflict, as we shall see later (ch. 8).

2.3 Flora and Fauna as Canons of the Ordinary

Even as the ordinary human serves as a canon to demarcate
the extraordinary person, so ordinary plants and animals
are the necessary backdrop to reports of species or behavior
that depart from the ordinary and are sometimes explained
by reference to the divine. Thus stories of a fig tree
that suddenly withers (Mt. 21.19), a palm tree that
obligingly bends to offer its fruit (*Gospel Ps.-Matt.* 20),
and grain that yields extraordinarily (*Inf. Gospel of Thom.*

12) presuppose ordinary trees and grain. Ordinary animals
are presupposed in accounts of a fish with a needed coin in
its mouth (Mt. 17.24-27), animals that worship and carni-
vores that do certain humans no harm (*Gospel Ps.-Matt.* 14,
19), and an ass that performs an exorcism and preaches a
sermon and then returns to its normal wild state (*Acts
Thom.* 74, 78-79, 81). Genetic malformations and reproductions of one species by another are also demarcated as
extraordinary and sometimes attributed to divine intervention (see below, chs. 2.4 and 3.1.1).

 Because flora and fauna differ from region to
region, the canon of the ordinary varies as well, as is
evident from the paradoxographical reports that multiplied
in the Greek world as its horizons expanded through trade,
colonization, military ventures, and exploration. The more
remote the region, the greater the credence apt to be given
to extraordinary flora and fauna,[54] even as the accuracy of
geography was apt to be inversely proportional to the
remoteness of the region being described (see the dis-
cerning remarks of Godley, vol. 2 [1921], xiiff.). The
extraordinary near at hand was more likely to be referred
to the divine than were reports of the extraordinary far
away where, for such regions, it was common enough to be
ordinary (cf. further below, ch. 3).

2.4 Nature as a Canon of the Ordinary

One of the most important canons of the ordinary is
"nature."[55] Byzantine lexicography defined a τέρας as something that is or comes into being παρὰ φύσιν.[56] Ancient
usage bears this out, but *physis* (and *natura*) occur in a
variety of realms of experience, with a variety of meanings
and nuances. Conceptions of departures from nature vary
accordingly.

 In the realm of reproduction, genetic malformations
or reproduction of one species by another are "against
nature" or "transgress nature."[57] As applied to the products of ordinary reproduction, "nature" functions as a
canon of the ordinary, in the case of humans rather as an
equivalent of the *anthropos/homo* canon examined above; that

is, it designates human nature,[58] or the characteristics of
human nature, such as limited capacities, or a determinate
sex,[59] or mortality.[60]   The extraordinary would be something contrary to or exceeding human nature, such as a
change of sex, or a return from the dead, or unexpected or
inexplicable feats.[61]   Applied to individuals or specific
groups, "nature" designates their given disposition or
character.[62]   The extraordinary would be behavior counter
to these.   Insofar as human nature or one's individual
nature is viewed as determined by one's origins--as often
in Greek thought (see Leisegang, 1941)--the canon may be
tight or loose, depending on how one views those origins
and the forces that act upon humans subsequent to their
coming into the world (education is such a force, deity
another, chance and fate still others).

In the theory and practice of Greek medicine, the
concept of nature plays an important role.[63]   The term is
used to designate the normal human condition, that is,
health, while illness or injury is a departure from
nature.[64]   The physician's aim is to return the patient to
nature,[65] and his art is modeled after nature[66]--itself a
healing power[67]--but must also take account of the nature
of humans generally and of the patient individually as well
as of the nature of the disease.[68]   If the illness runs a
normal course, that, too, is "nature" (Leisegang, 1941,
1143).

"Nature" provided Greek physicians with a symbolic
universe and a vocabulary with which to identify and interpret departures from the canon.   These were, thus,
"expected."   But sickness was (and remains) a situation
with loose warrants.   Diagnosis and prognosis were often
erroneous, and treatment mistaken, so that the illness ran
longer than expected,[69] or did not respond to the
physician's treatment,[70] or by its "nature" was beyond
medical help[71] or the person's financial means.[72]   In these
kinds of contingent situations the sick person might turn
to an oracle or to Asclepius or a healer.   The miracle
account was the vehicle for reporting the happy results:

a sudden recovery, beyond ordinary expectation and beyond the physician's art.[73]

"Nature" was also used in both Greek and Latin to designate "the ways things are," the order and regularity in the cosmos. This is a canon of the ordinary relevant to what are commonly called nature miracles. There are several ways in which this canon is expressed.

One is through the adjective "natural." In the Livy narrative in chapter one, *ordo naturalis* designates the regular and expected movements of earth and moon. A *dies naturalis* is a day measured from sunrise to sunset, that is, with reference to something over which humans have no control, namely, nature.[74] Departures from these regularities would be considered extraordinary. Explanation in terms of the natural order, as in the case of the eclipse, would remove them from the category of miracle. Otherwise they might be referred to deity (see further, ch. 3 below).

The word *physikos* is first attested in a signifi-cant way in Aristotle's writings.[75] As a noun it was used by Aristotle and later writers to designate the Ionian (Milesian) and other pre-Socratic philosophers,[76] who wrote books on *physis*[77] which sought to explain the world by reference to its origin and growth (*phy-*), whence it receives its distinctive character (*physis*). *Physis* is contrasted with τύχη and τέχνη.[78] For those things that come into being according to nature (φύσει), their distinc-tive character (φύσιϛ) follows from that origin. Charac-teristic of the Ionians is their reinterpretation of traditional Greek theology in terms of *physis*: the vital forces operative in the process of growth and becoming are termed divine,[79] or they are given the names of traditional Greek gods (see Leisegang, 1941, 1137), to whom reference need not be made in explaining the workings of the cosmos and whose interventions would constitute a disturbance of that order.[80]

With the phrase ἡ φυσικὴ ἐπιστήμη Aristotle desig-nates the science that deals with "a being in which the principle of movement and of the rest is in itself"

(*Metaph.* 1025b.18-21). Using the word *physis* he similarly divides all things according to their αἰτία: "some exist by nature [φύσει], some through other causes [δι' ἄλλαϛ αἰτίαϛ]." In the first category he places animals, plants, and the four elements, because common to them all is that "they have within themselves a principle of movement and rest," whereas other things, such as a bed or a cloak, are fashioned (ἀπὸ τέχνηϛ) and have no such implanted impetus to change (*Phys.* 192b.8-20). As an example of how *physis* functions as a canon, Aristotle cites fire rising, something which is "by nature and according to nature" (φύσει δὲ καὶ κατὰ φύσιν, *Phys.* 192b.36-193a.1). Fire with downward motion,[81] then, would be extraordinary.

Turning specifically to "nature" in the Greco-Roman period, an examination and comparison of Pliny and Seneca is instructive both for their typicality and their idiosyncrasy. Pliny's designation of his work as "libros historiae naturalis" (*N.H.*, Pref., 1) accords with the long philosophical tradition that divided knowledge into physics, ethics, and logic.[82] The genres Pliny contrasts with his own work are only vaguely characterized, as subtle, obscure, and much published (ibid., 14). However, his description of his own subject as "barren material--the nature of things--that is, life, and in its basest part" (ibid., 13), the general thrust of his table of contents (Bk. 1), his efforts to explain many seemingly irregular phenomena so they can be construed as part of that *ordo naturalis* of which Gallus speaks in the Livy narrative discussed in chapter one, indicate that his intention is to treat *naturae opera* (7.179) in the sense, first, of phenomena that are "given"--natural--in contrast to *prodigia*, which cannot be integrated into that order. That he is inconsistent on both counts is partly idiosyncratic[83] and perhaps partly a result of his method of work (described in Pliny the Younger, *Ep.* 3.5) and the fact that, however studious, he was still an amateur.

A comparison with the work on the same subject by the philosopher and his contemporary, Seneca's *Naturales Quaestiones*, shows that both pursue the aim of setting

forth *rerum natura* (*N.Q.* 3, Pref., 1 and 18), providing
explanations that demonstrate its order. Seneca is more
consistent than Pliny in excluding prodigies or, if he
reports them, in offering explanations that integrate them
into the natural order.[84] He is also more consistent in
excluding from his subject matter human creations and
institutions, though it is part of his method to wed
natural science and ethics by drawing moral lessons from
the phenomena he records.

A brief hint of the passion in the tradition of
natural science in which Pliny and Seneca stand is given in
Pliny's discussion of a report that posed a possible conflict with it. If one accepts the report that (in 467
B.C.E.) Anaxagoras of Clazomenae predicted a stone would
fall from the sun, says Pliny, that entails that Anaxagoras'
divination was a greater wonder than the stone itself. And
if one believes that the sun is a stone or that there was
ever a stone in it, then our understanding of the natural
order is undone and all things become confused.[85] One
might call this an "ethics of belief" (Clifford, 1877;
Harvey, 1969, 1970, 1979) with respect to nature as a canon
of the ordinary, though it is not a very rigorous ethic--
Pliny admits that stones (from the sun?) often do fall and
says that he himself has seen one (7.150).[86]

Despite Pliny's inconsistencies and idiosyncrasies,
his positing of nature as a canon of the ordinary is not
atypical. It is attested in Greco-Roman Stoicism,
Platonism, and Peripateticism.[87] In a number of sources it
serves as a measure of the possible.[88] Not even God is
capable of all things, says Pliny in one place,[89] and
citing a number of such impossibilities he concludes that
"the power of nature is what we call 'God.'"[90] In another
passage (2.113) he makes clear that it is the order in
nature which makes it possible to distinguish fortuitous
thunderbolts, which are of no significance (*bruta fulmina
et vana*) because they come from no principle of nature
(*nulla veniant ratione naturae*), from those that are predictive (*faticida*). The latter "come from on high, from fixed
causes and from their own stars,"[91] while the former strike

2. The Ordinary and the Extraordinary / 19

aimlessly at mountains and seas. Aristotle had formulated
the canons here precisely: nature does nothing superfluous
or in vain,[92] and nothing that is "by nature" or "according
to nature" is without order, "for nature is the cause of
order in all things."[93]

Lucretius used the same example of aimless thunderbolts as disproof of their having been hurled by Jupiter.[94]
The god in his poem (1.1ff) is Nature, invoked under the
name of Venus.[95] The equivalence of nature and deity is
widely attested in Greek and Roman sources, explicitly or
implicitly in passages where nature is credited with
granting the gifts or doing the deeds traditionally
ascribed to familiar deities or is addressed in terms
generally applied to those deities (examples from all
periods in Leisegang, 1941).

Nature viewed as deity goes against many traditional
cultic conceptions of deity. A passage from Galen, the
second-century physician, is instructive here.[96] He has
been arguing that the demiurge, who functions for him as
the equivalent of nature (see the exposition and sources in
R. M. Grant, 1952, 12-14), made eyelashes a constant
length, not in obedience to some god (as Moses says), but
because it was better to do so. Moreover, he did not
simply "will" it to be so, without regard to nature,

for if he should wish to make a stone into a man in an instance it
would not be possible. And it is this in which our own opinion, and
that of Plato and of the others among the Greeks who pursue in a
correct way the principles of nature, differs from the opinion of Moses.
For him it is sufficient that God wills to bring order to matter, and
immediately it is so ordered. For he thinks all things are possible
for God, even should he wish to make ashes into a horse or bovine. We,
however, do not see it this way but say, rather, that some things are
impossible by nature [ἀδύνατα φύσει] and that these God does not attempt
but instead chooses that which is best among the possibilities of
becoming.

Several observations may be made on this argument.
First, Galen speaks not just for himself but for others.
Our exposition has suggested who some of those others might
be. Second, there is conflict here, explicitly between
pagan and Jewish viewpoints, but implicitly between pagan
and Christian insofar as the latter may view God as Galen's

Moses does,[97] and the conflict turns on the respective
views of God and nature and the relations between these two.
However, there is, thirdly, a conflict not only between
these groups and viewpoints, but also between pagan and
pagan, and, indeed, between Jew and Jew, and Christian and
Christian. Galen's objections to a God who acts in a dis-
orderly way, counter to nature, could apply equally to
traditional pagan deities. The lines of conflict cut
across pagan and Christian and Jewish lines and are intra-
mural within these groups, between persons schooled in
philosophical thought on the workings of the cosmos and
those adhering to conceptions of its workings traditional
in cultic pieties. Finally, the lines may be blurred, as
happened in healings, for example (see below, ch. 3.2.3),
or by Plutarch who interprets a τέρας/σημεῖον in terms both
of nature and of deity (below, ch. 3.3.1). And, as we
shall see later, some Christians held philosophical conceptions of deity and nature even while affirming Christian
miracle accounts that manifestly derive from settings in
which God was seen as intervening in the regular order that
philosophers called nature.

2.5 "Law(s) of Nature"/"Natural Law" as a Canon of the Ordinary

The terms "law(s) of nature" and "natural law" have their
own development, not unrelated to that of "nature" but yet
distinct enough to require separate treatment. It is also
justified, and complicated, by the fact that the concept of
law(s) of nature or of natural law assumed such an important role in later European history, especially in ethics
but also in the philosophy of science and in popular
thought about science, with the result that in discussions
of miracle these phrases have been employed without much
precision and often without attention to ancient usage.[98]
Only in relatively recent times has there been a consciousness of the need to disentangle ancient from modern usage[99]
and, indeed, to scrutinize the use of the term "laws of
nature" in modern scientific theory and its possible
relation to definition and discussions of miracle.[100]

Several recent studies have helped to place the respective Greek and Latin terms historically.[101] Perhaps the most striking thing about the ancient texts, in contrast to modern usage, is the relative paucity of the terms. The Greek phrase, νόμος φύσεως, is not attested in the extant pre-Socratic sources[102] and until Philo is found barely half a dozen times, though νόμος and φύσεως occur together. The usage is mainly ethical.[103]

In the other passages the content is similar to that of *physis*. Νόμος φύσεως expresses a general "givenness," for example, of numerical relations,[104] or of the functioning of the body,[105] or of the cosmos.[106] In designating the desire to live as νόμος φύσεως, Josephus at the end of the first century C.E. also expresses this givenness;[107] death is κατὰ τὸν τῆς φύσεως νόμον (*BJ* 3.374). The ordinary when measured by this canon would seem to be no different than when measured by *physis* used by itself.

Philo's extant writings contain the term νόμος φύσεως at least thirty times, along with several equivalents (Koester, 1968, 530), and provide further insight into usage in the first century C.E. Like Cleanthes, Philo speaks of God as ruling the cosmos by the laws and statutes of nature.[108] As in Aristotle, *physis* and God are closely linked, if not wholly identified as (commonly) in Stoicism.[109] The Torah, written and unwritten, is given by nature and is the law of nature (references in Koester, 1968, 533-35). This law governs the seasons of the year,[110] reproduction and growth accord with it,[111] and it functions as a canon of the ordinary and the possible.[112]

To attempt a sharp separation in Philo's writings between νόμος φύσεως in the sphere of physics and of ethics is dubious. God achieves his moral purposes with the cooperation of *physis*, in the sense of the material world, which may if necessary depart from its normal state in order to do so.[113] Some of the texts in Philo's portraits of the patriarchs are pertinent here because they deal with Pentateuchal miracle stories.

The patriarchs were, in their persons, "animate[114] and reasoning[115] laws" (ἔμψυχοι καὶ λογικοὶ νόμοι, *Abr*. 5), who "welcomed the following of nature, since they regarded

nature itself, as in fact it is, as the most venerable
statute [Θεσμόν]" (*Abr*. 6). Moses later recorded the laws,
but, says Philo, combined history with them in order that
he might show, "first, that the same father and maker of
the cosmos is in fact also the lawgiver, and, second, that
he who would keep the laws will welcome the following of
nature and will live in accordance with the ordering of the
universe, his deeds being in harmony and concert with his
words and his words with his deeds."[116]

Moses knew what to write because in the theophany
on the mount "he entered, it is said, into the darkness
where God was, that is, into the unformed and unseen and
incorporeal, paradigmatic essence of the existents, per-
ceiving the things invisible to human nature" (*V. Mos.*
1.158). With this Platinic blik (cf. further *V. Mos.* 2.271
and *Abr*. 77), Moses is able to command nature: "each of
the elements obeyed him as a master, altering its natural
property [δύναμιν] and submitting to his commands" (*V. Mos.*
1.156). He is also able to provide explanations of how God
works wonders and why (*V. Mos.* 1.201-02).[117] Here God's
moral purposes and the elements' participation in them
become clear.

An important canon of the ordinary for Philo,
ἰσότης--equality or equity--becomes evident in certain of
these miracle passages. The rebellion of Korah, for
example, so outrages earth and sky that these fundamental
principles of the universe (αἱ τοῦ παντὸς ἀρχαί, *Vit. M.*
2.285) combine to remove all trace of the offenders. The
earth then returns to normal, τὸ ἰσόπεδον (2.287). The
flood and the restoration of the earth afterward are a
repetition in fine of the creation and demonstrate the
ἰσότης that is the divine will for it.[118] Goodenough, who
made a special study of this concept in Philo, relates it
to Pythagoreanism[119] and notes the close relation between
ἰσότης, νόμος, and νόμος φύσεως.[120]

Another equivalent of νόμος φύσεως in Philo is
λόγος φύσεως and ὁ ὀρθὸς τῆς φύσεως λόγος,[121] where again
physics and ethics are intertwined. In introducing various
accounts of how the elements such as fire and water

punished evildoers, Philo refers to Moses' legislation,
saying that its whole purpose was a striving for harmony in
the universe (τῆς τοῦ παντὸς ἁρμονίας) and for accord with
the logos of eternal nature (τῷ λόγῳ τῆς ἀϊδίου φύσεως,
V. Mos. 2.52). In setting as his aim τὸν ὀρθὸν τῆς φύσεως
λόγον, Moses stands in contrast to Balaam, the mercenary,
self-seeking μάντις who only unwillingly performs God's
will (V. Mos. 2.263ff.).

In Greek usage nomos and physis often stand opposed
(see n. 102 of this chapter). In Jewish writings in Greek,
physis appears primarily, and not often, in books composed
originally in Greek (see Koester, 1968, 531), whereas
nomos, of course, occurs abundantly. The bringing together
of nomos and physis in a significant way in Philo is part
of an extremely nuanced mode of thought that enables him to
employ νόμος φύσεως as a canon of the ordinary even while
treating departures from it as reinforcements of that
canon.[122]

In contrast to Philonic usage, νόμος φύσεως occurs
but seldom, and then in an ethical sense, in the extant
second-century Christian sources in Greek (references in
R. M. Grant, 1952, 24). In Latin Christianity, however,
Tertullian sets forth a canon of the ordinary in the
material world when he says that resurrection of the flesh
will be "by divine power and not by natural laws."[123] In
his treatise on the soul Tertullian draws this same
contrast between divine power or freedom and the ordinary
as enunciated by philosophy, which elevates its opinions
into laws of nature.[124]

In Roman literature the ethical usage predomi-
nates.[125] But there is also a sense of law(s) given by
nature and functioning as a canon of the ordinary.
Speaking of how different lands bring forth different
products, Vergil says that in dim antiquity "nature laid
down these laws and eternal covenants for certain
regions."[126] Lucan speaks of a lex aeterna summoning the
sun to its daily course (Phars. 7.1). It is an instance of
the extraordinary when the incantations of a Thessalian
vates prevent the ether from obeying law.[127]

Ethical exhortations to live "according to nature" often left "nature" undefined (see Watson, 1971, 219). Seneca, however, in telling Nero that a ruler's power will not be harmful if it accords *ad naturae legem* gives as an example nature's ordering of the bees' society, where the king bee has no sting.[128] Presumably a king bee with a sting would be a portent. In any case, unusual behavior of bees was often interpreted by the Romans as portentous (references in Krauss, 1930, 115), and Seneca specifies bees' ordinary behavior as a *lex naturae*.

2.6 Seeds of Conflict

Our inventory of canons of the ordinary in the Greco-Roman world is hardly exhaustive. It was noted above (p. 8) that canons of the ordinary are implicit in miracle accounts. Such canons are implicit also in such Greek stories as Persephone and Hades (regularity of the seasons) or Phaethon and Helios (regularity of the sun's daily course, and droughts and extreme cold as exceptional phenomena). They are implied also in the poetic device of *adynata* (above, p. 7), which depend for their effect on the ordinary course of the cosmos even as do the Christian hyperboles or *adynata* about faith moving mountains (Mk. 11.22//Mt. 21.21; Mt. 17.20; 1 Cor. 13.2) or transplanting trees into the sea (Lk. 17.6). When Herodotus reports (2.142) that only four times in over 11,000 years of Egyptian kingship had the sun either risen or set contrary to custom (ἐξ ἠθέων), he presupposes canons of the ordinary. In speaking of comets, Seneca (*N.Q.* 7.1.1-2) summarizes one common canon of the ordinary--frequency and regularity--as well as learned opinion of it:

No one is so slow and dull and bowed to the earth that he is not roused as a result of divine things and stands erect with his whole mind, particularly when some new wonder shines from the sky. For as long as things move along as they are accustomed to do [*solita*], familiarity [*consuetudo*] conceals their greatness. For we are so constituted that everyday things [*cotidiana*], even though deserving of wonder, pass us by, whereas the sight of even very minor things becomes pleasant if these turn out to be unusual [*insolitae*]. Therefore the conjunction of stars with which the beauty of this immense structure is adorned does not draw a crowd; but when something is changed from the customary,[129]

the faces of all are turned up to the sky. The sun does not have a
spectator unless it is in eclipse. No one watches the moon unless it
is in trouble; then cities raise a clamor, then each person makes noise
in accord with empty superstition.[130]

These examples show that among both learned and
unlearned there was a sense of the ordinary and the extraordinary, the regular and the irregular, in the functioning
of the cosmos. Sometimes the consensus was strict enough
to be made the basis of categorical assertion[131] and even
of oaths.[132] Where the consensus was looser, there was
usually some effort made to reduce the area of uncertainty
and inexplicability.[133] The knowledge of the day might
limit such efforts, however--many phenomena could be
neither predicted nor measured. For example, certain
notions about power were commonly held,[134] but since there
was no precise way of measuring force even in physical
phenomena (cf. Nilsson, 1948a, 140), let alone in humans,
discussions of power remained inconclusive, leaving fertile
ground for conflict over what was ordinary and what was
extraordinary and how the extraordinary was to be explained.

Not surprisingly, the range of explanation was
wider for persons of greater education; the differences in
interpreting the eclipse in our paradigm from Livy in the
first chapter is but one example. Within a given society
there are, thus, differences of judgment regarding the
extraordinary and its explanation that root in differences
in socialization within that society. Also unsurprising is
that competing social groups and rival peoples will assert
or deny the extraordinary and offer antithetical explanations of such phenomena, each to its own advantage. In
these explanations the canons of the ordinary are sometimes
shared by both groups but turned against each other; at
other times the canons will differ because the traditions
of knowledge differ.

The next chapter will examine, then, the second
element noted in our paradigm from Livy, explanation of the
extraordinary in the Greco-Roman world, for it is in the
explanation of the extraordinary that miracle is either
asserted or denied. Chapter four will illustrate how

distinctions between ordinary and extraordinary and conflict over these distinctions are reflected in language. The third element in the paradigm, the cultural and social dimensions of demarcation of miracle, will arise in the course of this discussion and will be the subjects of chapters five and six.

3

EXPLANATION OF THE EXTRAORDINARY:

INEXPLICABILITY AND MIRACLE

Puzzling events and phenomena are explained in various ways
in the Greco-Roman world. Where they are not explicable by
reference to the canons of the ordinary, they are commonly
referred to the divine and are designated "miracle" by a
variety of terms (see below, ch. 4). Many times, however,
puzzling phenomena are not referred to deity, or there is
dispute over whether they should receive such reference.
These instances can be divided into (a) those in which
certain phenomena are affirmed as wondrous but yet are not
attributed to deity, i.e., they are not placed in the
category of miracle; (b) those in which puzzling phenomena
are deliberately explained either by reference to canons of
the ordinary or in some way that makes divine reference
superfluous--again there is no miracle; and (c) those in
which a phenomenon is referred to deity (i.e., a miracle
is said to have occurred) even though it could be (or had
been) otherwise explained. The premise shared by proponents and opponents of miracle was that explanation of an
extraordinary phenomenon by reference to deity was intrinsic to "miracle." What they disagreed on was whether or
not a particular phenomenon could or should indeed be
explained without such reference.[1]

3.1 Explanation Without Reference to Deity

A number of sources reporting extraordinary phenomena offer
no explicit explanation of them, either in terms of familiar
causes or by reference to the divine or to praeternatural
or more than human causation or agency. However, their
demarcation of the phenomena through geography or special
circumstances amounts to a tacit kind of explanation. The

phenomena remain wondrous, but lacking the divine reference
they are not "miracles." Thus Herodotus says it was a most
wondrous phenomenon (φάσμα . . . μέγιστον) when rain fell
in Thebes, Egypt, where it had never rained before and
where no rain had fallen since (3.10). But Herodotus does
not attribute this unique event to the divine nor does he
report that the Thebans did so,[2] nor does he offer any
other explanation. During 11,340 years of kingship, the
Egyptians told Herodotus, the sun twice rose where it
customarily sets and twice set where it customarily rises
(2.142; see above, p. 24). Again no explanation of any
kind is offered, though the regularity of the sun's course
is elsewhere reported by Herodotus as the basis of an
Athenian oath (see above, ch. 2, n. 132).

        In the paradoxographical tradition, which was a
(sometimes distant) kin of historiography and scientific
investigation and largely parasitic on these areas of study
(see Ziegler, 1949), extraordinary phenomena are generally
simply recorded, with no attempt at explicit explanation,
or with deity only occasionally appearing as an explanatory
factor.[3] It is a kind of explanation, however, when in
these writings, as in the Herodotus examples, such phenomena are confined to designated (often remote) geographical
areas, to certain times, and to certain categories of
existents. They are thus demarcated from the everyday
experience of the reporters and their readers or hearers.
Several clusters of traditions in the area of reproduction
will serve to illustrate. This area is pertinent to our
investigation in view of use made of them by Christian
authors and the conflicts over the Christian virgin birth
accounts in the second century. To anticipate our conclusions, in these traditions various kinds of explanation
will be observed, since the reporters are so various. Some
of the explanations are of the tacit kind; some, such as
Aristotle's, stand in a tradition of self-conscious explanation of observed phenomena. Common to almost all of them,
however, is the ignoring of the divine as an explanatory
factor. These traditions illustrate the variety of options
available for explanation of puzzling phenomena.

3.1.1 Explanation of Extraordinary Reproduction
Aristotle's effort to systematize and advance knowledge
of reproduction and embryology by devoting a whole treatise
to the subject stands in a tradition of reflection on what
was a concern of all the ancients in many areas of their
lives and at many levels of knowledge.[4] The Roman treatises on farming, each of which devotes careful attention
to breeding, represent a deposit of generations of
experience and lore on the subject.[5] A stock of commonly
accepted beliefs about what was ordinary in reproduction is
the necessary premise of, and foil to, the many traditions
about unusual kinds of reproduction which are our concern
here.[6]

3.1.1.1 Mules' Foaling
The fact that the sterility of mules is mentioned
or discussed in a variety of sources from the pre-Socratic
into the Christian period attests widespread awareness of
the mode of regeneration of this hybrid.[7] So do the
proverbs that derive their force from the unlikelihood of
mules' foaling,[8] as well as the reporting of such foalings
as divine omens.[9] In certain geographical areas, however,
foalings by mules are reported as common.[10] Under such
circumstances, says Varro, there is no portent.[11] Foaling
by a mule, if it was close at hand, was apt to be ascribed
to divine causation, where the report was accepted as
true.[12] In those places where such foaling was reported as
common, no reference to the divine was necessary and none
was offered: it remained an extraordinary event but safely
remote (i.e., remote from the transmitters of the extant
traditions) and in those geographical areas was part of the
order of things. Such explanation by demarcation sufficed.

3.1.1.2 Impregnation by the Wind
Impregnation by the wind is another kind of extraordinary reproduction reported in both pagan and Christian
sources.[13] The tradition for mares is especially well
attested. It is demarcated as extraordinary: implicitly
through the fact that it receives special mention in

discussions of reproduction[14] as well as in other contexts
and explicitly through terminology.[15] The foil is ordinary
reproduction, through coition of mare and stallion,[16] with
the learned tradition going beyond this to give explanations of the process of animal impregnation.[17] This kind
of explanation is lacking in the traditions of wind
impregnation of mares, but other kinds of explanation are
found, incorporating several motifs: the wind-like swift-
ness and nimbleness of horses,[18] the passionate nature of
mares, which causes them to conceive even by the wind,[19]
their fecundity in certain geographical regions (Solinus,
Justinus), the fecund power of the wind.[20] To these demarcations was added demarcation by space, time, and result:
such impregnation of mares occurs in specific geographical
areas,[21] at certain times of the year,[22] with the offspring
surviving only a short time.[23]

The reports about mares were lent plausibility by
accounts of wind impregnations in other species.[24] Only in
poetic accounts is impregnation by the wind ascribed to the
divine. These are set in the remote past or a timeless
present, where the personified wind impregnates mares[25] or
nymphs.[26] In other settings the explanations by demarcation, not all of which are found in any one account, serve
to preserve the common stock of knowledge about *ordinary*
means of reproduction. Christian writers defending the
virgin birth sometimes draw on the traditions of wind
impregnation or self-propagation of species in support of
their case, but ascribe only their own species of partheno-
genesis to the divine. The divinity or divine force of the
air or the wind is doubtless the starting point of these
various traditions (cf. Guthrie's exposition, 1954, 138-43)
and is perhaps an unspoken element in many of them. But
except in the poetic accounts and in the discourse on
providence in the pseudo-Clementine *Recognitions*[27] there is
no explicit reference to deity. Wind impregnation was
considered, rather, as a part--albeit extraordinary--of the
order of things and not something specially worked by the
divine or divinely portending.

3.1.1.3 Superfetation

Superfetation--the simultaneous carrying in the womb of distinct litters or embryos at different stages of development--appears in a variety of sources, pagan and Christian, over many centuries.[28] That it is considered unusual or even extraordinary is shown by terminology[29] as well as by its being singled out for special mention and discussion.

The accounts of superfetation occur in three kinds of contexts:

a. Genetic Malformations

In several texts superfetation is connected with genetic malformations, commonly called τέρατα.

The treatise on superfetation in the Hippocratic corpus[30] ascribes it to incomplete closing of the woman's uterus after impregnation and describes under what conditions such conceptions can come to term. If the superfetations do not develop discrete body members but remain simply flesh (σάρξ), they putrify and are eventually expelled. Whatever persons less schooled in medicine might have made of the birth of such a growth, the thought world of the treatise is far removed from designating them as *terata* or attributing them to the divine.

In *De generatione animalium* Aristotle seems to restrict his discussion of superfetation to multiple births and litters that come successfully to term.[31] But the background of this discussion is his effort, immediately preceding, to find a single cause (see 771a.14ff.) for various kinds of departures from ordinary reproduction, whether these are multiple births in animals that generally bear but a single offspring, or are *terata* (offspring with redundant or deficient parts) in any animal. Thus hens (ἀλέκτορες) are multibearing, not only in that they bear (i.e., lay) frequently, but also in that they have many fetations simultaneously,[32] which is the definition of superfetation. Therefore hens bear many "twins,"[33] i.e., lay many eggs with double yolks. When the yolks are

separated by a membrane, two normal[34] chicks develop; if
not, they become monstrous (τερατώδειϛ), with various
redundant parts (770a.16ff.). Similarly, in viviparous
animals redundant parts occurring παρὰ φύσιν and twins both
have the same cause (τὸ αὐτὸ αἴτιον, 772b.14): surplus
matter (ὕλη) "sets" in the uterus, producing either twins,
which are considered as τερατῶδη because they occur contrary to the majority of cases,[35] or monstrously formed
parts or redundant parts (772b.13ff.), i.e., *terata*. Thus,
in Aristotle's exposition, neither twins nor monstrosities
need to be ascribed to the divine, that is, they need not
function as *terata* to be studied by diviners, because now
the physiological conditions under which they occur have
been explained. Similarly, for Democritus, whose explanation of genetic malformations as the result of superfetation is the starting point of Aristotle's own discussion.[36]

b. Multiple Offspring

Multiple offspring born to human parents
represented another phenomenon for which superfetation
provided an explanation, as was observed already in the
preceding section. Aristotle labeled twins τερατῶδη (in
the sense of "uncommon," as indicated above), and paradoxographical tradition reported uncommon ones indeed,[37] but,
as often, without explanation, either physiological or
theological. Pliny attaches no divine significance to the
birth of triplets; the examples he cites, the Horatii and
the Curiatii, were evidently sufficient to render them not
uncommon for him. Beyond three, however, multiple offspring
are considered *ostenta*--except in places where that is
common, as in Egypt.[38]

Pliny gives examples of twins produced by superfetation, i.e., fraternal twins whose differences were
attributed to different fathers.[39] In certain traditions,
both pagan and Christian, the differences are attributed to
deity. These are the twins one of which has a divine
father and the other a human father: Heracles and Iphicles,
Castor and Pollux, Zethus and Amphion, Romulus and Remus,
Jesus and Judas Thomas.[40]

The Hippocratic treatise on superfetation mentions twins but does not explicitly ascribe them to superfetation. Aristotle does, and gives his usual detailed physiological explanation (*Gen. an.* 773a.33ff.; cf. further 771b.15ff.). Superfetation is simply a special case of regular reproduction.[41] However, only some animals--hares and humans, for example--can bring superfetations to term. This is because their *physis* is such as to meet the conditions necessary for it. In humans, unlike hares, bringing to term can occur, however, only if the second impregnation comes soon after the first,[42] a statement echoed by Pliny (*N.H.* 7.48-49). Superfetation thus viewed accords with the *physis* of the animals in which it occurs and fits into Aristotle's explanation of animal reproduction in general. There is no need to ascribe it to the divine.

c. <u>The Hare</u>
The largest body of texts dealing with superfetation connects it with the well-known fecundity of the hare (λαγώς, δασύπους, πτώξ, *lepus*).[43] Except in Aristotle, no physiological explanation is given. Yet only Herodotus ascribes it to the divine, not as a portent, however, but as part of divine providence (τοῦ θειοῦ ἡ προνοίη): cowardly, edible animals are prolific, so that they will not become extinct, whereas cruel and harmful creatures have few offspring.[44] The remaining sources simply view superfetation as one of the hare's many strange traits,[45] unusual in itself but common among hares. This is a crude form of the careful zoological classification of hares elaborated by Aristotle and, to a lesser extent, by Pliny. Unlike the traditions on wind impregnation of mares, only the earliest source, Herodotus, circumscribes superfetation geographically (Arabia).

Several writings, both pagan and Christian, are acquainted with the tradition of superfetation of hares but are concerned primarily with drawing moral lessons from it. Thus the Oppian poem on hunting interprets the hares' traditional sleeplessness as rooting in the female's unceasing desire to mate with the male, who is himself

drawn by salacious desire (πολύθουρον ἐρώην, 516). "One
after another she gives birth and never--shameless female--
forgets lust; she fulfills whatever desire commands, not
even in the pangs of birth forgetting Aphrodite" (523-25).
No interest is shown in the physiological side of superfetation, and if the poet considers it extraordinary, he
makes no attempt to explain it.

Clement's *Paedagogus*, and perhaps *Barnabas*,[46]
discuss superfetation in connection with the Pentateuchal
prohibition against the eating of the hare.[47] The prohibition is explained as based on the lasciviousness of the
hare, which copulates without restraint and superfetates.
Christians are thereby instructed to avoid indulgence of
sexual appetites and intercourse during pregnancy (*Paed*.
88.3). Clement's comments on the physiology of superfetation in hares are expressed in ethical terms (88.1-2), and
whereas in Aristotle *physis* figures in a physiological
explanation of superfetation, in Clement it functions
ethically. That copulation during pregnancy is wrong is
seen from the fact that *physis* has arranged for the mouth
of the womb to close during pregnancy so that fetation will
not be disturbed (92.3-93.2). Clement thus seems to
preclude superfetation for humans, while for hares he has
given a physiological and ethical explanation. Superfetation is thus an unusual phenomenon but not one requiring
ascription to the divine.[48]

3.1.2 Summary

These various examples make clear that in the Greco-
Roman world and its antecedents much thought was given to
departures from the ordinary and that explanation by
reference to the divine was not an automatic reaction.
There were other modes of explanation, and the choice
varied with the nature and circumstances of the phenomenon
to be explained and the person(s) doing the explaining.
Sometimes the choice was a self-conscious denial of divine
reference that explained away the "miracle," as will be
seen in the next section.

3.2 Explanation Denying Divine Reference

One stream of knowledge in which the wondrousness of an
extraordinary phenomenon is sometimes dispelled by
explaining it in ways that make divine reference gratuitous
is the learned tradition that derives from philosophy and
is represented by philosophers but also by educated persons
generally. As we have observed earlier, this stream of
knowledge constitutes an ethics of belief.

3.2.1 Some Principles of Explanation

A clear example is Cicero's treatment of prodigies and
portents in *De divinatione*.[49] All things, he asserts, can
be explained by reference to natural causes (*naturalemque
rationem omnium*). Nothing happens *fortuito*. "Nothing can
happen without a cause." If no cause can be found, the
thing did not happen. "If something happened that could
have happened, it should not be viewed as a portent.
Therefore, there are no portents."[50]

Earlier in the dialogue the Stoic has given an
example of the kind of "impossibility" for which Cicero
would seek a cause other than the divine. Before Caesar's
assassination the ox he sacrificed turned out to have no
heart. "Now, then," asks the Stoic, "do you think that any
animal which has blood is able to exist without a heart"
(1.52.119)? The expected answer to this exception to
ordinary and scientific canons of viable life[51] is, No--
unless one accepts the premise of the Stoic's argument that
there is a divine power that encompasses the life of
humans, making such things possible and intelligible (1.52.
118). But Cicero does not accept that principle of
explanation. His "one principle" (*una ratio*) is that
"whatever comes into being, whatever it is, necessarily has
a cause in nature, so that even if it should appear
conspicuously contrary to what is customary, yet it cannot
actually be contrary to nature."[52] Neither rarity nor
extraordinariness[53] nor lack of success in finding a
natural cause should deter one from the conviction that
there is such a cause that will dissolve the prodigy and

dispel any terror it may have aroused (*De div*. 2.28.60).
Cicero then proceeds to apply these principles to reports
of various prodigies (for examples, see below, p. 51).

A second-century example of this ethic of belief is
Lucian of Samosata's polemic against Alexander of Abonoteichos. When confronted with reports of unusual phenomena
associated with Alexander, Lucian enunciates the axiom that
one should disbelieve on principle, convinced a priori that
such things are impossible. By giving detailed explanations of how such phenomena might be ascribed to familiar
causes quite within human capacity, Lucian seeks to dispel
the air of divine awe and mystery surrounding Alexander and
his god Glycon (see the detailed discussion in ch. 10
below).

3.2.2 Historians and Explanation

Another tradition of knowledge in which principles of
explanation were enunciated with respect to extraordinary
phenomena is historiography. Greek and Roman historians
were noted, or notorious, for reporting, as Seneca says,
miracula rather than *cotidiana*.[54] However, beginning at
least with Thucydides (cf. 1.21; on Herodotus see App. A
below) some historians take a more critical attitude.
Polybius dissociates himself from the "genealogical way"
(γενεαλογικὸϛ τρόποϛ, 9.1.4) of writing history that deals
in genealogies and myths (τὰϛ γενεαλογίαϛ καὶ μύθουϛ,
9.2.1). He discounts reports of excessively extraordinary
phenomena as naive and impossible (16.12.3-11) and seeks
the causes of events in the human character (see the
references and analysis in Petzold, 1969, 7-8, 11). Only
if events are explicable in no other way is he inclined to
ascribe them to something outside human control.[55] A
similar principle of explanation, akin to those enunciated
by Cicero and by Lucian, is set forth in a Polybius tradition attested in a tenth-century manuscript[56] which
represents his as saying that only after other explanations
have been exhausted will he ascribe extraordinary happenings
to the gods.

Livy's history, in the century after Polybius,

offers an explicit example of such ascription. A lake
rises to an unusual height, "apart from any celestial
waters or any other cause that might exclude the thing from
being a miracle."[57]

Tacitus, writing at the beginning of the second
century C.E., states that it does not comport with the
serious nature of his *Histories* to include fictitious tales
(*fabulosa*) or to entertain his readers with fabrications
(*fictis*) (2.50.4). If an event is well attested, however,
he will not deny it marvelous character or divine
reference.[58] In the case of Nero, however, Tacitus applies
the two canons of morality and non-fulfillment in refusing
to attribute certain *prodigia* to the gods.[59] He makes the
sociological observation that *prodigia* are in his day
reported only in a period of anxiety (*metu*) rather than at
other seasons as well, as in early times (*rudibus saeculis*).
To this mood he attributes the fact that the blocking of
the path of Otho's forces by flood debris "was turned into
a prodigy and an omen of imminent disasters," i.e.,
referred to the divine rather than to "fortuitous or
natural causes."[60]

3.2.3 Physicians and Explanation

Medicine was another tradition of knowledge in which
explanations of extraordinary happenings such as sudden
healings and revivifications often made divine reference
superfluous and thus marked at least some of its practitioners off from practitioners of home and folk medicine[61]
and from the healers of cultic piety. Diodorus Siculus
(4.71.1), in the first century B.C.E., reports the tradition that Asclepius wondrously (παραδόξως) healed persons
regarded as beyond help, so that many were convinced he
made the dead alive again (τῶν τετελευτηκότων ποιεῖν πάλιν
ζῶντας); but in fact he owed his ability to perform these
feats to his medical knowledge (τὴν ἰατρικὴν ἐπιστήμην).
Apuleius, in the second century C.E., relates that the
famous physician Asclepiades (first century B.C.E.) once
"resurrected" a man after close observation revealed that
the "corpse" was still alive and could be revived by certain

drugs.[62] In the *Metamorphoses* (10.11-12) Apuleius also
tells the tale of a revivification of a "corpse" that is in
fact only in a coma induced by a soporific drug dispensed
by a physician who reveals this to the spectators, thus
robbing them of a possible miracle. The same conflict in
the demarcation of miracle is seen in the reports that
Empedocles either raised a woman from the dead (Diogenes
Laertius, 8.67) or merely roused her from a trance (ibid.,
8.60-61, 69).

The conflict is seen also in the polemic of the
writer of *The Sacred Disease*, in the Hippocratic corpus,
against those who labeled epilepsy "sacred" (ἱερῆʃ) or
"divine" (θεῖον) because of its extraordinariness (διὰ τὸ
θαυμάσιαν, ch. 1) and, ascribing its cause to a god (θεῷ,
ch. 4), prescribed incantations and other means quite
inappropriate to a disease with a specific *physis* and a
cause (chs. 5ff.) that would respond to medical treatment
just as other illnesses do.

Diodorus Siculus relates several instances of how
medical explanation was able to dispel the wonder and
horror aroused by persons of dual or uncertain sex or
sudden transitions from one sex to the other.[63] He reports
sudden transitions that parallel the graphic account in
Phlegon (*Mir*. 6.1-4), where the phenomenon baffles physicians and results in the emperor's erecting an altar to
Zeus the Averter. Diodorus Siculus labels "superstitious"
(δεισιδαιμονοῦσιν) those persons and peoples who regard
such happenings as *terata*.[64] *Physis* does not allow true
bisexuals (32.12.1), and Diodorus gives examples of how
persons with medical training calmly provide treatment of
such transitions according to sound medical procedure.

From the side of thaumaturgical healing, the
frequent stressing of physicians' inability to cure the
patient functioned to magnify the healer and the wonder.
But sometimes the lines are blurred. The relation between
medicine and miracle in the Asclepius inscriptions at
Epidaurus, for example, is still a disputed matter.[65]
Menekrates Zeus (fourth century B.C.E.), referred to in the
tradition as a physician[66] who offered healing to the sick

and health to the robust, on into old age, if they followed
his directions,[67] also cured several cases of "the sacred
disease" (epilepsy) and, perhaps because he had succeeded
where others had failed,[68] conceived of himself as Zeus.[69]
In the second century C.E., Aelius Aristides characterizes
Asclepius' healings as beyond medical art (see below, ch. 7,
n. 13), but his physician often employed Aelius' dream
revelations from Asclepius to alleviate his symptoms (see
below, p. 98). The famous second-century physician, Galen,
confesses that he had become a follower of Asclepius after
the god healed him of an abscess (Edelstein, *Asclepius* 1,
T. 458); he also attests that Asclepius healed others who
were gravely ill (ibid., T. 436, 459). These persons and
others whom physicians failed turned elsewhere for healing
that was medically inexplicable--beyond human art, a
miracle worked by "the savior" Asclepius or Jesus or the
like.

3.2.4   Technique as Explanation

As medical technique and the theory related to it could
be used to explain away miracles, so technique generally
could function in the same way. A couple of examples will
serve to illustrate.

Of the many extraordinary events traced to divine
causation in Herodotus' history one in particular shows how
something may be extraordinary and inexplicable--a numinous
occurrence (τέρας)--to some persons but not to others who
understand it in terms of familiar causation. The Phocians,
at war with the Thessalians, whiten some of their soldiers
with gypsum and dispatch them to attack the enemy by night,
killing anyone not identified by the gypsum. The enemy,
thinking it is some praeternatural phenomenon (δόξασαι ἄλλο
τι εἶναι τέρας), take fright (ἐφοβήθησαν) and flee. For
the Phocians, however, there is no τέρας, only a stratagem
and a technique (Herodotus 8.27).

In a number of sources knowledge of technique is
seen as dispelling the inexplicability intrinsic to miracle.
A passage from the *Georgics* is instructive in that Vergil
views the same phenomenon as divinely caused--a miracle--in
one context and the result of human technique in another.
For the farmer whose colony of bees has died out Vergil

gives instructions in the technique (*artem*, 4.315) of
generating bees from the putrid carcass of a bullock.[70]
But Vergil also relates an aetiology of this technique:
the first time this event occurred was at a deity's bidding
and is designated by Vergil as a *monstrum* and "wondrous to
relate" (*dictu mirabile*) (4.554). A *monstrum* that is
repeatable through technique, however, ceases to be a
monstrum.[71]

3.2.5 Stigmatization as Explanation

There are several important clusters of traditions in
which the means of removing an extraordinary phenomenon
from the category of miracle is to attach to it a denigra-
ting label that *eo ipso* denies it divine reference.

In Christian texts a familiar means of achieving
this result, yet often while retaining some or all of the
extraordinary character of a puzzling phenomenon, is to
attribute it to demonic agency.[72] "Demonic" here functions
pejoratively, referring to a malevolent being more than
human yet inferior to the Christian deity.[73] The influence
of Christianity's Jewish roots, with their one supreme
deity opposed by a realm of evil spirits, is evident here.
In pagan usage, on the other hand, daimon/daemon had good
as well as bad connotations, both in traditional piety[74] as
well as in philosophical theology where daimons functioned
not only as the necessary mediators between gods and
humans[75] but also came to fill a role as scapegoats for
some of the objectionable features in traditional theology
(see Nilsson, 1961, 256-57). This latter bears some
affinity with Christian demonizing of various areas of
life. In Christian schemas, however, the mediatorial
functions were performed by Christ, saints and martyrs, and
archons. No niche remained for demons, except to be
exposed as the true identities of the pagan gods (see the
convenient survey of this tradition in the appendix to
Pohlenz, 1909, 140ff.). By ascribing pagan miracles to
demons, Christians thus denied them reference to deity in
the Christian sense. In a later terminology (Aquinas,
Summa c. G. 3/2, 103) they might still be *mirabilia* but

without divine reference would not be *miracula*.

Another way of denying divine reference, one
attested in both pagan and Christian texts, is to characterize the agent of the phenomenon as "false." This charge
is commonly leveled at "prophets" (see BAG, s.v.
ψευδοπροφήτης; LSJ, s.v. ψευδομάντις). Since "prophet" is
a term of broad and varied usage, our examples will be
confined to those instances where the divine reference is
clear, whether in divine possession or in performance of
otherwise inexplicable feats, including prediction of the
future.

These are primarily Christian texts, but the one
major pagan example, Lucian's portrait of Alexander of
Abonoteichos on the Black Sea, is a paradigm of this kind
of dissolution of divine reference. Alexander fakes his
divine ecstasy (*Alex*. 12-13), the epiphany of his oracular
deity (7; 13-17), and his oracles (19-22; 26; 28; 37;
53-54). His claim of wondrous feats are dubious (24; 28;
36; 59), his activity harmful (28; 32; 36; 44-46; 56), his
morals thoroughly corrupt (4-5; 41-42), as accords with a
man driven by greed (6; 8; 23; 50; 54). Lucian therefore
labels him a *pseudomantis*.[76]

On the Christian side comparable portraits are
drawn by two polemics, nearly contemporary with Lucian,
against the Montanist movement, which originated about the
time of Alexander, and again in Asia Minor.[77] Despite
their claims of divine possession,[78] the Montanists are
false prophets[79] whose utterances are spurious[80] as well as
demented,[81] harmful,[82] and deceiving.[83] The Montanists'
morality is reprehensible,[84] and their reported wonders end
in disaster (5.16.14). The writer adds another trait, one
prominent in Christian denigrations of false teachers:
disloyalty to the Christian community.[85] Such error must
be the devil's doing (5.16.9). The divine that is thus
denied the Montanists is found, however, in the councils
assembled to examine and reject the new movement and to
expel its representatives (5.16.10; cf. Kretschmar, 1966,
4-6).

Elements of these developed polemical pieces appear

in other Christian writings of the first and second
centuries: the charges of deceit and harm, of corrupt
motivation and reprehensible or defective behavior, of
inauthentic wonders and predictions, of deficient or
aberrant group loyalty, and of diabolic inspiration.[86]

Related to the labels "demonic" and "false prophet"
as a way of denying divine reference is the term "magician."
Many of the elements already noted appear: deceit, evil
intent, reprehensible behavior, spurious wonders, association with demons. However, "magician" and "magic" were not
always or necessarily pejorative terms, and since an
analysis of them is very complex it will be deferred to the
next chapter.

3.3 Reconciling Explanations: "Saving the Phenomena"

Sometimes extraordinary phenomena that are explicable in
terms of familiar, non-divine phenomena are nonetheless
referred to deity.

3.3.1 "Both-And" Explanations

Plutarch (*Pericles* 6.2-4) relates that a one-horned ram
belonging to Pericles is interpreted by the *mantis* Lampon
as a sign (σημεῖον) from the deity that Pericles would
become sole ruler of Athens but by Anaxagoras, the natural
philosopher (φυσικός), as caused by the shape and location
of the brain in the skull, which he had had cut open.
Plutarch, the philosopher and priest, wants to retain both
interpretations. Lampon's tells one the τέλος of the
phenomenon, what divine message it communicated (τί
σημαίνει)--and, indeed, events vindicated Lampon. Anaxagoras' dissection, on the other hand, disclosed the cause
(τὴν αἰτίαν) of the single horn, "but those who say that
the discovery of the cause is a destruction of the σημεῖον
do not perceive that along with the divine acts[87] they are
thus rejecting humanly contrived symbols: clashings of
gongs, lights of signal fires, and shadows of pointers on
sundials."[88] Plutarch reconciles the two explanations of
the phenomenon, the one affirming and the other denying
divine agency.

In his *Corialanus* Plutarch offers still another
example of both-and explanation.   Reports of sweating,
weeping, and bleeding statues can be attributed to atmos-
pheric moisture; yet the divine (τὸ δαιμόνιον) can use this
to communicate (σημαίνειν) to humans (38.1).   Plutarch then
considers talking statues, which he is unable to explain
except by reference to the divine.   He concedes that sounds
may possibly be heard coming from a statue but not articulate speech, since that is impossible, even for the deity
(τὸν θεόν), "apart from a body functioning and equipped
with vocal parts" (38.2).   Yet where investigation (ἱστορία)
overwhelms us with many and persuasive reports of such
phenomena, the explanation is to be sought in perceptions
that differ from sensation and yet resemble it, such as the
illusion of actually hearing and seeing in dreams (38.3).
This leads Plutarch to argue that the deity's very unlike-
ness to humans means that if he does something they do not
do, this is not beyond reason (παράλογον) (38.3-4).   Here
Plutarch has sought to save the tradition of miracle, with
its divine reference, as well as the philosophical tradition of explaining extraordinary phenomena in a rational
way.

Allegorization is another form of the both-and
mentality: by giving extraordinary phenomena worked by
deity--"miracles"--a meaning other than the literal,
allegory sought to "save the phenomena."[89]   The Stoics, in
accord with their general cordiality to many forms of
traditional cultic piety, became adepts in allegorization.
Their espousal of divination led them into other kinds of
both-and affirmations so that Cicero accuses them of
offering detailed explanations of the natural causes (*vi
naturae*) of thunderbolts while yet maintaining that these
are prophetic (*De div*. 2.19.44; on the philosophical issues
here cf. n. 95 of this chapter).

In Latin literature Pliny provides an example of
the both-and attitude toward extraordinary phenomena.   He
denies specifically that rainbows are divine signs or
miracles (*N.H*. 2.150; see below, p. 52).   Earthquakes he
treats differently.   They are caused by winds,[90] but this

explanation does not make them less calamitous or numinous,
for the peril of a quake resides not only in "the motion
itself, but equally or more in its being an omen [*ostento*]:
never has the city of Rome been shaken when it was not a
premonition [*praenuntiatum*] of some event that was going to
take place" (*N.H.* 2.200). Thus, during the trying times of
the Punic War fifty-seven earthquakes were reported in a
single year (*N.H.* 2.200), and outside Rome a great quake
(*ingens terrarum portentum*) occurred in Cisalpine Gaul the
year before the Roman Social War (2.199).

Pliny also gives a list of indicators that warn of
the approach of earthquakes (*N.H.* 2.192, 195-97; cf.
Aristotle, *Meteor.* 367a-368a). Yet the ability to predict
an earthquake is attributed to divine inspiration (2.191),
and if reports of such predictions are true "how much can
such [prophets] be thought to differ from a god even while
they are living?" (2.192). Pliny's attempts to explain
when earthquakes will occur are too crude to allow accurate
predictions. They contrast with contemporary knowledge of
eclipses, where warrants were much tighter and the accuracy
of prediction allowed one to deny the term *prodigium* or
portentum to the event, as in the Livy example cited in
chapter one. Even were Pliny a more rigorous investigator
and thinker,[91] he would still, in the nature of the case,
not have been able to provide means of accurate prediction.
Given the element of uncertainty remaining, his reaction to
accurate predictions of earthquakes is like that of the
Roman soldiers to Gallus' prediction of the eclipse: such
knowledge is divine.

His explanation of the cause of earthquakes, on the
other hand, he intends to be as fully explanatory, without
reference to the divine, as, say, those offered by Aristotle
or Lucretius (see n. 90 of this chapter). But his reading
of his sources showed him a connection between earthquakes
and subsequent events, and so while he may, to his own
satisfaction,[92] explain earthquakes without reference to
deity he does not attack the *post hoc* argumentation
involved.

3.3.2 Post hoc Explanation (Coincidence)

Such *post hoc* interpretations of what today are commonly
called coincidences occurs in both pagan and Christian
sources and provide further examples of events that in
themselves were common enough to require no explanation or
could be explained without reference to deity and yet,
under certain circumstances, were referred to deity.[93]

Construction of buildings, great or small, simple
or elaborate, required knowledge of construction technique,
and a collapse was explicable in terms of such technique.[94]
But a collapse at a particular time, with great loss of
life, could also be referred to deity (on this subject cf.
Evans-Pritchard, 1937, 69-70). When a roof fell in,
killing all but one of a hundred and twenty boys at school,
this, says Herodotus, was one of the *semeia* sent by deity
to the people of Chios before the sea battle in which they
were defeated (6.27). The collapse of the tower of Siloam,
killing eighteen people, was viewed as a judgment of God
upon their wickedness (Lk. 13.4). Had the rocks that fell
from the ceiling of a *praetorium* killed Tiberius, in fulfillment of widespread expectations of his imminent death
(Suetonius, *Tib.* 39), that would doubtless have been
referred to deity. Such attributions to deity did not
nullify explanations of other collapses in terms of
construction and age of a building. The two kinds of
explanation might stand side by side.[95] A Plutarch might
have said that the cause of the collapse was faulty
construction but that its purpose was to forewarn. However,
as with Pliny's attempts to predict earthquakes, prediction
of the precise moment of a building's collapse is an
approximate science at best and this contingent situation
is referred to deity.[96]

Herodotus provides another example of *post hoc*
argumentation in which the same event is interpreted, this
time by rival communities, both with and without reference
to the divine. A disastrous Athenian expedition is blamed
by the Athenians on divine power (τοῦ δαιμονίου, 5.87):   a
thunderstorm accompanied by an earthquake drives the

Athenians into a frenzy (ἀλλοφρονῆσαι) and they kill each
other off, all but one (5.85). Their enemies' version is
that they had already surprised the Athenians and cut off
their escape when the thunderstorm and earthquake struck
(5.86), and so it was they and not deity that had destroyed
the Athenians (5.87). Each side could have supported its
case. Thunder and earthquakes were often signs of divine
wrath or the means to execute it (Greek and Roman examples
in Luterbacher, 1904, 6-8; Krauss, 1930, 46-48). On the
other hand, not every thunderstorm or quake was necessarily
a divine warning or judgment.[97] The competing interpretations here are clearly influenced by social factors.[98]

Events in themselves considered ordinary or not
necessarily extraordinary may be referred to deity when
they are associated with great men. In Arrian's narrative,
Alexander's career is marked by such signs. A shift of
wind from south to north, making it possible for Alexander
to advance, came about "not without divine action [τοῦ
θείου], as Alexander and those about him interpreted it"
(*Anab*. 1.26.2). Thunder and lightning in the night after
he has cut the Gordian knot are *semeia* from the gods,
authenticating his act.[99] And a sudden and violent thunderstorm at just the moment when Alexander is surveying a
possible site for a temple to Zeus seems to him to be a
sign from deity (ἔδοξεν ἐκ θεοῦ σημανθῆναι) that he should
build in that spot (1.17.6). On the other hand, a severe
storm that keeps Alexander from attacking Darius is not
referred to deity (2.6.2), though the Persians for their
part might well have done so.

The flight of birds, so important to augury, also
figures in Arrian's narrative. An eagle perching on the
shore near Alexander's ship is regarded as a divine sign
(θεῖον) (1.18.6-9).[100] The behavior of a swallow, which
circles over Alexander's head during his midday nap,
strikes fear into his fellow Macedonians, and a *mantis* is
called to interpret the θεῖον (1.25.6-7). A *mantis* is
likewise called on to interpret the behavior of a bird who
drops a stone on Alexander's head (2.26.4). On the other
hand, reports of such behavior or their numinosity might be

disputed, as when Celsus' Jew questions on epistemological grounds the apparition (φάσμα) of the bird reported by Jesus' followers for his baptism (*C. Cels.* 1.41). Again, reference to deity or denial of it was contingent on prior commitments. "Miracle" was in the eye of the beholder(s). Some of these commitments and their implications for the study of conflict will be examined in subsequent chapters.

4

LANGUAGE AND MIRACLE

Demarcation of extraordinary from ordinary, explanation of
the demarcation, and conflict over it--the subjects of the
preceding chapters--are evident also in the use of specific
terms to set extraordinary off from ordinary phenomena and
in disputes over the application of these terms to specific
cases. The terms sometimes have divine reference and
designate "miracle" whereas at other times they denote the
extraordinary but with divine reference excluded, implicitly or explicitly. Several Greek and Latin terms will
serve to illustrate these demarcations and conflicts, with
"magic" providing a parade example of conflict over miracle
and the role of social and cultural factors in such
conflict.

4.1 Greek Terminology

Byzantine lexicography regarded *semeion* and *teras* as
synonyms.[1] Although its attempts to distinguish the two
terms are rendered invalid by examination of actual usage,[2]
there is a distinction in that the basic meaning of *semeion*
--identifying mark or sign--has no necessary divine
reference (see Rengstorf, 1964, 202.23ff., 205.19ff.) and
can cover a variety of situations, including extraordinary
ones (see LSJ, s.v.). It is in the latter cases that it
functions as a synonym of *teras* and can be used inter-
changeably with it or linked in the familiar hendiadys
semeia kai terata (see Rengstorf, 1969, 115-16). It is the
extraordinariness and inexplicability of the phenomenon
that gives *semeion* and other such terms their divine
reference. If the inexplicability is dispelled, the terms
lose such reference.

     An example cited in the last chapter is the

conflict between two traditions of knowledge--the divination characteristic of popular cultic piety and the study of anatomy by natural philosophy--which comes to a head in a dispute over the application of *semeion* to the phenomenon of a one-horned ram (see above, ch. 3.3.1). The terms *semeion* and *teras* figure in a similar dispute in Theophrastus' *Historia plantarum*. His remarks regarding interpretation of spontaneous change (αὐτομάτη μεταβολή) in plants set forth a rationale for denying divine reference-- and miracle terminology--to certain unusual phenomena. Instances of spontaneous change, he says, are regarded as contrary to nature (παρὰ φύσιν) by *manteis*, who designate them *semeia* or *terata*.

But the ordinary kinds of changes they do not marvel at whatever, for example, when the vine called "smoky" bears both a white cluster of grapes instead of a black and a black instead of a white. The *manteis* do not single such changes out, nor those in which the soil effects a change by nature [πέφυκεν], as was said of the pomegranate in Egypt [see 2.2.7]. But here such a thing is a marvel [θαυμαστόν] because it occurs only once or twice, and these instances are rare over the whole period of time (2.3.2).

Something that can be demonstrated to occur regularly and frequently belongs to the ordinary course of things, to "nature," and ceases to be a *semeion* or *teras* with their divine reference.

Aristotle's discussion of genetic malformations (τέρατα) in *De generatione animalium* (769b.3ff.) makes no explicit reference to the divine reference in the word *teras*, but his discussion presupposes the cultic setting of *teras* seen in Plutarch and Theophrastus and many other Greek texts, and the effect of his discussion is to dispel any mystery surrounding *terata* and any reference to the divine (in the cultic sense). Aristotle identifies various phenomena that people call *terata*, examines (and often disputes) their reasons for doing so, and then by placing these *terata* into a coherent system of reproduction governed by *physis* disputes the label *terata*.

A *teras* in the animal world, he states, is "a kind of malformation" (ἀναπηρία τιϛ, 769b.3c), an offspring unlike the parents.[3] It is called a *teras*, for example, when a human offspring not only does not resemble any of

its forebears but reaches a point where it does not seem to
be a human at all but only some sort of animal.[4] Such may
be the appearance, but the appearance is deceiving: such
phenomena are "resemblances only" (ἐοικότα μόνον, 769b.17),
because the differing gestation periods preclude the formation of one kind of animal within another kind (769b.22-25).
Another kind of *teras* is the formation, within a species,
of animals with redundant parts (769b.26ff.). Such a *teras*
is explicable as the product of superfetation, which
Aristotle then explains at length as a physiological
process occurring in certain animals under certain circumstances (769b.31ff.; see above, pp. 31-32). Thus viewed,
it is a regularity, and what occurs regularly is not a
teras, as Aristotle observes in the course of showing the
relation between *teras* and *physis*. A *teras* is contrary to
physis (understood as the majority of cases)[5] but it is not
contrary to that *physis* which functions to maintain the
economy of reproduction.[6]

Even while dispelling the mysteries surrounding
animal *terata* and denying that label to them, Aristotle
continues to use the term, thus testifying to the force of
common usage, the original and ordinary context of which is
settings like those described by Plutarch and Theophrastus.
In these, deity is the customary explanation of otherwise
inexplicable genetic formations.

The multivalence of *semeion*, *teras*, and other Greek
terms for miracle reflects the conflicts we have observed
repeatedly over what was and was not a miracle. The same
is true of Latin terms for miracle.

4.2 Latin Terminology[7]

The *Sitz im Leben* of the Latin terms is the rather stereotyped Roman procedure for dealing with extraordinary,
puzzling phenomena. The sighting of such phenomena was
followed by reporting of them to the authorities, who
investigated their authenticity, consulted the professionals
in such matters, and then decreed their expiation.[8] Livy's
account (31.12) for the year 200 B.C.E. is illustrative
both of the procedures involved and of the various kinds of

phenomena denoted by the term *prodigium*. Included are
genetic malformations of the kind observed above in the
Greek sphere as well as anomalies in inanimate nature,
celestial and terrestrial.[9] F. B. Krauss's interpretation
(1930) of many *prodigia* in the inanimate category as caused
by or associated with volcanic disturbances or other
natural phenomena is anticipated, though unsystematically,
by Roman authors. Rivers flowing with blood are explained
by Cicero as caused by discoloration from the soil and the
sweating of statues as condensation of moisture--"blood or
sweat come only from a body."[10] Pliny says "most persons"
(*plerique*), i.e., most of his authorities, attribute to the
wind--*scil*. rather than to deity--the raining of stones.[11]

Pliny (*N.H.* 7.34) makes the sociological observation that the birth of hermaphrodites, which were once
called androgynes and regarded as *prodigia* (see above.
ch. 3, n. 63), are now viewed as curiosities (*deliciae*).
Pliny offers no explanation of the malformation; he presupposes that his readers will concur with his report of
the change in attitude. That there was a change in
attitude toward prodigies, at least on the part of the
Roman ruling classes, is indicated by the discontinuance of
the annual publication and expiation of *prodigia* and by the
fact that not even the restorators of religious traditions,
such as Augustus and Claudius, attempted to revive the
custom.[12] Changes in the intellectual climate played a
role here, but for both the rulers and the populace
generally the political manipulation of *prodigia* and of
their interpretation contributed to a dispelling of the
numinousness and inexplicability that once surrounded them
(examples in Bloch, 1963, 138-42).

Cicero and Pliny both apply a canon observed above
in Aristotle--frequency and regularity--to explain away
what are taken to be *ostenta*. In reply to the Stoic view
that a snake entwined about a boy presaged fame (1.36.79)--
which proved to be true--Cicero in *De divinatione* (2.31.66)
says that in that particular locality snakes are so common
that finding one in a cradle is not wondrous ("non tam est
mirum")--"these kinds of *ostenta* have nothing marvelous

about them" ("haec ostentorum genera mirabile nihil habent"). Pliny observes that multiple human births that go beyond triplets are considered *inter ostenta*, except in Egypt where drinking the water of the Nile causes fertility (*N.H.* 7.33).[13] Divine communication need not be inferred.

Varro argues similarly with regard to foaling by mules: what is a *portentum* in one land, because infrequent, is common in another and, therefore, not a *portentum* there.[14] Another way of dissolving a *portentum* was to attack it on epistemological grounds, as when Livy suggests that certain *portenta* may have been illusions occasioned by fright (3.5.14: *vanas exterritis . . . species*).

Miraculum, though it often meant little more than something that aroused wonder,[15] was also used of wondrous events explained by reference to deity.[16] Livy dissipates the divine reference of one Roman tradition by ascribing it to benevolent manipulation: Numa invented his reported nocturnal meetings with the goddess Egeria since he knew that without some fabrication of a miracle (*sine aliquo commento miraculi*) the rites and priests he established would not be accepted (1.19.4-5). Pliny, by giving a physical explanation of how rainbows occur, places them *extra miraculum . . . et extra ostentum*;[17] in fact, they are not even reliable portents of the weather (*N.H.* 2.60. 150).[18]

In these brief observations on miracle terminology the role of social and cultural factors in different judgments of extraordinary phenomena is evident. That role is especially conspicuous in our next sample, the use of the term "magic."

4.3 "Magic" and "Miracle"

Christians in the second century employed the label "magic" to nihilate miracle claims of pagans and of other Christians, and what little direct evidence there is indicates that pagans were apt to treat Christian miracle claims in the same way. As with miracle terms, there are several Greek and Latin words that function as synonyms to designate what is covered by the English word "magic." The

phenomena thus labeled bear certain structural similarities
with those designated "miracles": they are extraordinary,
and inexplicable in terms of ordinary causation and
agency.[19] Why and on what grounds, then, are some labeled
"magic" and some "miracles"?

These questions are complicated by the long history
of the word "magic" and "magician." A. D. Nock noted three
major senses in which ancients used the word magic. One
was to designate "the profession by private individuals of
the possession of technical ability enabling them to supply
recipes or perform rites to help their clients and damage
their clients' enemies." Another referred to the use of
such recipes and rites to harm others, while still another
was to "denote the religions belonging to aliens or on any
general ground disapproved" (1933b, 171 = 1972, vol. 1,
315). The original denotation of *magos*--high caste Persian
priest--also persisted and was sometimes appealed to by
practitioners of magic (see below, pp. 68-69). "Magic" had
mainly negative connotations, however, which have carried
over into modern usage as well as into scholarly study of
ancient texts.

The difficulty of distinguishing magic from
religion or from miracle, whether in ancient texts, modern
treatments of these texts, or in anthropological studies of
peoples of the Third World,[20] is evidenced by the unending
stream of books and articles on the subject, with a variety
of criteria posited to make the distinction, though in
actual practice the distinctions are often hard to maintain
or tend to be forgotten.[21]

Part of the difficulty stems from the attempt of
one culture--the Western learned tradition--to translate
into its own system of symbols and referents elements from
other, often quite different cultures. Magic is thus
commonly measured against Western science or Western conceptions of religion or rationality variously defined.
Even where the intention is to understand rather than to
polemicize, the comparisons are generally invidious--most
materials suffer in translation, and assumptions of

cultural superiority are perhaps inevitable (the studies cited in n. 20 give examples).

With respect to the Greco-Roman world, part of the difficulty lies in the materials themselves, however. "Miracle," as we have seen, is not a univocal term. Neither is "magic." Practices that ancients label with a term associated with what they call "magic" they may in another context ascribe to divine power, i.e., regard as "miracle." The criteria put forward by moderns to distinguish magic from miracle or from religion often reveal little more than that "magic" has many "religious" elements, and vice versa, and that "your magic is my miracle, and vice versa" (R. M. Grant, 1966, 93). Even "magic" itself, and related terms, though generally pejoratively used, are in some contexts badges of honor. The demarcation of magic and miracle (or religion) involves social and cultural judgments, on the part both of ancients and moderns. This does not necessarily mean there are no "objective" criteria, i.e., canons mutually agreed upon between social groupings or at least within such groupings. It does mean that attention to the social and cultural conditioning of the terminology and the way its referents are viewed cannot be ignored, and, indeed, deserve more systematic treatment than has usually been given them. Especially is this the case where polemics are involved, whether of Christians against pagans or against certain kinds of Christians, or of pagans against Christians or against certain persons within pagan society.[22]

Our procedure in the following pages will be to examine texts in which magic is an issue or is exemplified, asking what distinctions are expressed or implied that would demarcate magic from miracle and would lead to conflict over the demarcations. These will be compared along the way with distinctions posited by moderns, with some conclusions being drawn for our investigation.

4.3.1 Second-Century Christian Usage

In the second century the use of μάγος, μαγεία, and derivative or related words is almost uniformly negative in the extant Christian sources. The terms occur in several contexts.

One concerns the tradition of *magoi* coming to worship the infant Jesus. In the Matthean version these fit the pattern of the original *magoi*: upper-caste Persian priests versed *inter alia* in astral lore, figures familiar to the Greco-Roman world through Herodotus and others.[23] Whatever the motives and assessments in the Matthew account,[24] second-century Christian writers generally viewed them negatively as "magicians" and/or interpreters of the stars whose coming to Jesus signified his greater power, which freed the *magoi* from servitude to magic and astrology and, indeed, had put an end to the power of magic and placed such knowledge of the stars in the service of Christ.[25] In these passages it is assumed that readers and hearers will know what *magoi* or *Chaldaioi* and *astrologi* are, and that these are reprehensible titles.

Another common concern is polemic and warnings against magical arts and magicians. Such warnings are included in some early Christian ethical instruction.[26] Justin numbers "magical arts" (μαγικαῖς τέχναις) among the things he considers Christians to have left behind on entering Christianity (*1 Apol.* 14.2). As part of his demon theory of pagan religion he labels some extraordinary feats "magic" worked by demons to enslave humans (*1 Apol.* 14.1, διὰ μαγικῶν στροφῶν). The demons and the angels who fathered them[27] also used "magical writings" (διὰ μαγικῶν γραφῶν) and the rites of pagan cult to enslave the human race (*2 Apol.* 5.4). The feats worked by the *magoi* at Pharaoh's court Justin explains as imitations of the divine power operative through Moses (*Dial.* 79.4).

These themes are echoed in several passages in Tertullian. *Magia*, or its author Satan,[28] is "the multiform plague of the human mind, the contriver of all error, the destroyer both of salvation and of the soul."[29] The feats worked by magicians may indeed be extraordinary, but however real in appearance they do not represent what magicians claim they represent. They are merely phantoms[30] produced by trickery and deceit[31] and through the agency of demons.[32] Christians, thanks to their knowledge of this demonic agency and through the power available to them (*De anim.* 57.2), are able to expose and exorcise the demons who masquerade as gods (*Apol.* 23.4-5, 8; *De anim.* 57.2) or as the souls of dead persons (*De anim.* 57.2ff.), forcing them to reveal their true identity.

In Christian polemic the supreme example of the *magos* is Simon, with those regarded as his followers a close second. In the *Acts of Peter*[33] the apostles' superior power and authentic miracles prove Simon to be a magician and a deceiver,[34] his wonders illusory,[35] and his activity harmful.[36] Justin labels the *dunameis* of Simon μαγικάς (*1 Apol.* 26.2) and explains them (and those of Menander) as worked by the magical art of demons.[37] Similarly Irenaeus: Simon, Carpocrates, and Marcus, and their followers may perform impressive feats that lead some away from the truth, but the means they employ are magical, worked in cooperation with demons, and the results are illusory and transitory (*Adv. h.* 1.13 [Harvey ed., 1.7]; 2.31.2-3 [2.48.2-3]; 2.32 [2.49]).

Another context in which second-century Christian texts use the term "magic" and related works is in refuting the charge that Christian miracles are worked by magic. In non-canonical acts literature the apostles' miracles provoke the charge from their pagan opponents, thus providing the dramatic backdrop for the divine authentication of the apostles and the eventual discomfiture or conversion of the opponents.[38] That such charges were not invented solely for dramatic effect but have some foundation in fact is shown by Celsus' characterization of Jesus as a γόης (*C. Cels.* 1.71) who worked wonders (1.6, παράδοξα; 1.28, δυνάμεις), by magical art (1.6, γοητεία, μαθήματα). In two important second-century apologies, by Justin and Tertullian, much time is spent refuting the charge, by Jews or pagans, that Jesus was a magician and that his or Christians' miracles were to be attributed to magic.[39]

Common to these passages is the conviction that magic is reprehensible and that Christians have--or should have--nothing to do with it. Its function as a term of

abuse is indicated already by the fact that Christians
hardly find it necessary to justify its pejorative use,[40]
whether they are addressing pagans or fellow Christians.
Magic was a convenient label that served to discredit extraordinary phenomena. But on what grounds was the label
applied?

4.3.2 Demarcating Magic from Miracle
4.3.2.1 Manipulations

One distinguishing mark of magic is commonly said
to be the presence of manipulations.[41] Incantations,
recipes for potions and directions for obtaining and use of
other *materia magica*, instructions on bodily movements and
gestures, and the like fill the papyri labeled "magical" by
moderns and appear in literary descriptions of persons
called magicians or sorcerers by ancients. In the dispute
between Celsus and Origen over the wonders attributed to
Jesus or claimed by Christians there seems to be agreement
that what Celsus is talking about is to be called "magic"
and that one of the elements in magic is the presence of
such manipulations.[42] Celsus says Christians seem to exercise a power derived "from the names of certain demons and
from invocations" (*C. Cels.* 1.6). The importance of names
in magic and exorcism is well known, and Origen interprets
the word Celsus used to denote the invocation of daemons--
κατακλήσειϛ--as equivalent to κατεπᾴδειν, a common term for
casting of spells (see LSJ, s.v., 1). Celsus calls Jesus
a γόηϛ (1.71) who accomplished his δυνάμειϛ (1.28) through
γοητεία (1.6). *Goēteia* involves use of formulas or recipes
(μαθήματα, 1.6) that can be learned by others to produce
the same effects (1.6). Celsus gives some examples of the
wonders claimed by *goētes*, whom Celsus links with persons
who studied with Egyptians (1.68), even as he gives Egypt
as the source of Jesus' *goēteia* (1.28): such persons show
up in the marketplace and for a fee reveal their venerable
formulas, "blow away" diseases, summon the souls of heroes,
display tables with non-existent foods, and make things
appear to move as though alive (1.68). The reference to
mathēmata is the only explicit mention of manipulations

used by these marketplace sorcerers, but the previous
explanations of Jesus' wonders as performed through use of
mathēmata (1.6) and the reference to sorcerers' being
taught by Egyptians (1.68) suggest that Celsus sees manipulations as involved in the production of these wonders,
though to explain their extraordinariness Celsus has
recourse to demonic agency (1.68, κακοδαιμόνων). Origen,
who in another passage reveals that he has knowledge of
magical writings,[43] recognizes Celsus' characterization as
a description of μαγεία, μάγοι, and γόητεʃ (1.38; 1.68).
Elsewhere Origen contrasts wonders worked by *goētes* through
demonic agency and the use of spells, on the one hand, with
wonders worked by divine power, on the other (2.34; 2.50-
51). For both Celsus and Origen the basic issue is: Are
the wonders worked by divine agency or not?[44] If they are
not, they may be wondrous but they are not genuine and
represent no claim to serious attention, i.e., they are not
miracles. By associating with magic and sorcery Christian
claims that Jesus healed and resurrected people and fed
many with a few loaves (1.68) Celsus seeks to rob them of
their divine reference and Jesus of the divine claims made
for him. Manipulations are here one mark of magic.

In responding to the charges about Jesus Origen
does not take up the question of how Jesus worked his
miracles, whether by manipulations or in some other way.
Instead he focuses on the ends to which Jesus put his
extraordinary power, contrasting these with those of *goētes*
(1.68).[45] In answering the charge of magic other post-
second century Christians also conveniently overlook the
manipulations mentioned in the gospel miracle accounts (cf.
Arnobius, *Adv. nat.* 1.43-44, 48) or explicitly state that
the cures attributed to Jesus or his followers are accomplished without magical materials.[46]

In the first century the absence from the Gospel of
Matthew of many of the thaumaturgical details found in Mark
and Luke is commonly interpreted as deliberate omission on
the part of the evangelist, but whether his motives have to
do with avoiding charges of magic is difficult to say.[47] A
few second-century texts do state that Jesus worked his

wonders by a mere word, but if a contrast with magic manipulations is intended it is not very explicit. A passage
in Book 8 of the Sibylline Oracles predicts the coming of
one who will do everything with a word, healing every
disease, and with a word stilling the winds and calming the
seas (8.272-73). This is part of a theology in which the
logos is credited with creation and with healings and
resurrections (8.267, 285-86). No indication is given that
magic manipulations are the foil, nor is there any in *Adv.
h.* 3.11.5 (Harvey ed., 3.11.9), where Irenaeus' statement
that the logos made water from wine, though he had the
power to do so apart from any created materials, is
directed against those who deprecate the material as such.
Similarly in 5.15.2: Jesus healed some by a word but with
others he utilized an external act and materials such as
clay and spit, making the blind man's eyes as God did for
the first human. When Marcion asserts that Jesus, in
contrast to Elisha who employed "water and seven times,"
healed through his word alone (*verbo solo*),[48] he is
opposing miracles connected with the just God who created
matter (see below, ch. 8.3.3). Insofar as magic used
materia, it would fall under the same condemnation. But
that is not Marcion's first concern.

The contrast between "word" and "magic" is clearest
in Justin, *Dial.* 69.6-7, where, after asserting that Jesus
did his wonders by his word (τῷ λόγῳ αὐτοῦ), Justin says
that his contemporaries called him a μάγοϛ and a λαοπλάνοϛ
and said it was all magical illusion (φαντασίαν μαγικήν).[49]
In what seems to be a similar passage in Tertullian, however, the ability to work wonders by a mere word is taken
as the basis of the Jewish accusation that Jesus was a
magician (*Apol.* 21.17). Words themselves could be
construed as magic manipulations, as Origen states explicitly (*C. Cels.* 1.24-25; 5.45) and as is clear from the
magical papyri, amulets, cursing tablets, and literary
texts concerning magic, with their abundant formulas for
incantations and their special words or syllables for
apotropaic and other uses. To assert, as do some
scholars,[50] that wonders worked by a word are "miracles"

(and Christian) and those involving formulas or manipulations are "magic" (and pagan) is to overlook the two-edged
nature of this distinction--magicians sometimes employed
only words, so that Tertullian, e.g., goes on to distinguish Jesus' word from the magical word by identifying him
as the word of God, the primordial logos who was making and
had made all things.[51]

To say that the Jesus of the Synoptics worked his
wonders simply by a word is erroneous.[52] Many of them
simply happen, and in others he employs manipulations and
material objects.[53] These manipulations and *materia* can be
paralleled from the magical papyri and from texts
describing magicians, suggesting that if pagans had chosen
to attack Christian miracles on these grounds, as Celsus in
fact did, they could have supported their case well and
that for Christians to argue to the contrary would have put
them on shaky ground. These parallels have been demonstrated in detail by a number of scholars and need not be
rehearsed again here.[54] That pagans other than Celsus were
aware of miracle traditions concerning Jesus, and reacted
negatively to them, is suggested by the fact that Christians felt it necessary to defend him against charges of
magic (above, p. 56). But certain communal activities of
Christians, to which moderns apply the label "liturgical,"
were also such as to suggest "magic" to outsiders. The
fact that these took place in small groups (themselves
suspect),[55] away from the public gaze, and sometimes
deliberately concealed would heighten suspicion, since
magic was clandestine either by nature (see Hopfner, 1928,
371-73) or because of legal interdiction (see below, p. 69)
or both. The cross, in word and sign, so prominent in
Christian preaching, teaching, eucharist, baptism, blessing,
exorcism, and healing, not to mention apologetics addressed
to outsiders,[56] could easily be associated by pagans with
the *ousia*--parts of corpses, or objects associated with
persons who had suffered violent deaths--that were commonly
employed in the practice of magic (details in Hopfner,
1928, 205-05, 330ff.). The rationale underlying their use
was that souls thus forced to depart their bodies before

their time lingered on and were accessible with their
special powers to those who possessed *ousia*.

This belief is an old one in Greek religion (Hopfner, 1928, 306). That it was not limited to those practicing magic but was common knowledge in the Greco-Roman
world is shown by a number of texts. In the first century
B.C.E. Horace describes the ritual murder of a boy in order
to obtain his liver to work a love charm (*Epod.* 5). In the
next century, in Lucan's *Pharsalia*, a Thessalian *vates*
revives the corpse of a man just killed in battle in order
to obtain knowledge of the future from him (*Phars.*
6.619ff.). Early in the third century Tertullian discusses
at length this practice of summoning for purposes of necromancy the souls of those who had died untimely (*ahori*) or
violent deaths (*biaeothanati*).[57] In the second century
Apuleius has more than one tale of the obtaining of *ousia*
(*Met.* 1.12-13; 2.21ff.; 3.17) and mentions specifically the
noses and fingers of crucified persons and nails fresh from
crucifixions.[58] Crucifixion is listed by Lucian as one of
the deaths which cause the souls of the dead to manifest
themselves to the living.[59] The potency of a ring made
from iron (nails) from crosses and used with an incantation
is assumed by the characters in the same satire.[60]

Christians who ate the flesh of a crucified man and
employed the cross in various ways might well be suspected
of magic. Some Christians for their part stressed the
potency of the cross, the eucharistic bread, and other
ritual elements in a way that pagans might consider magical.
Thus in the *Acts of Thomas* when a murderer begins to eat
eucharistic bread that has been marked with a cross, his
hands wither; after his confession of his guilt, they are
restored by water over which an invocation has been pronounced (*Act. Thom.* 50-52). A baptism begins with an
invocation to the oil, "hidden mystery in which the cross
was shown to us" (*Act. Thom.* 121: μυστήριον κρυφιμαῖον ἐν
ᾧ ὁ σταυρὸς ἡμῖν ἐδείχθη). Oil, water, and bread are all
employed in the baptism, which is followed by a voice from
heaven, resulting in a conversion.[61] It is not surprising
that the apostle is accused by the pagan king of being a

magician who "bewitches [μαγεύει] people with oil and water
and bread" (*Act. Thom.* 152). As long as Thomas has not
given a person these elements, he has no power over him or
her (ibid.). Baptism and chrism with oil are desired by
converts as the seal that will bring them revelations,
render them invulnerable to the perils that beset them, and
assure them eternal life (27; 49; 118; 120-21; 131-33; 152;
157). In other non-canonical Acts literature the potency
of the cross is also stressed.[62] In baptismal rites
generally the sign of the cross and the apotropaisms might
well be regarded as magical.[63]

   In these examples it is evident that manipulations
as such do not really demarcate "miracle" from "magic,"
except for persons determined beforehand to make the demarcation. Such determination roots in social and cultural
settings, which are more important in understanding such
conflicts than are the manipulations, which are found both
in "magic" and in "miracle."

4.3.2.2   Compulsion, for Base or Mundane Purposes

   Another way moderns commonly distinguish between
magic and religion is to say that the former compels the
superhuman agents and employs them for its own base or
mundane purposes while the latter petitions deity and sub-
mits its requests to the divine will. Such a distinction
would bear on the relation between magic and miracle insofar as the latter is placed in the category of religion and
its approach to deity contrasted with that of magic. Is
this kind of distinction discernible in the extant sources?
Are pagans and Christians conscious of such a distinction
with respect either to their own or to the others' extraordinary phenomena?

   In general one may say that the closer students of
antiquity scrutinize the sources the more it is necessary
to qualify this distinction or to interpret it differently.
A. J. Festugière (1932, 281-328), to be sure, maintains
the traditional view, with well-taken strictures against
parallelomania (to borrow Sandmel's convenient term). His
documentation of the "magical" side is impressive, but

things are not quite as neat as his reading of the papyri
would suggest. Nilsson regarded Festugière's distinction
between religion as submission to deity and magic as
compelling of deity as correct in theory but hard to maintain in practice.[64] More specifically, Nock, in discussing
the religious element in the magical papyri, noted the
supplicative nature of some of the passages[65] and in
another study concluded, "There is not, then, as with us,
a sphere of magic in contrast to the sphere of religion.
Further, the words used to designate magical acts do not
for the most part possess a precise and technical
meaning."[66]

On the other side, the "religion" that Festugière
presupposes as a foil to "magic" is a particular kind of
religion, a highly "spiritual" version with deity and the
service and glorification of deity as its goal.[67] Such a
definition of religion would ostracize into the camp of
magic many beliefs and practices of many religions.
E. R. Goodenough observed (1953, esp. 159-60) how exponents
of a more mystical or spiritual variety of religion
frequently mark themselves and their beliefs off from
religion directed to material ends obtained with material
means and entertaining greater expectations of direct
divine response by labeling such religion "magic." In
another terminology, one may say that Goodenough was
pointing to the social and cultural conditioning of assessments of magic and religion.[68] Like many anthropologists
(see above, n. 21) Goodenough places religion and magic on
a spectrum, with close structural similarities. If "magic"
includes the idea of supernatural power residing in persons
or objects, then how does one classify priests and the holy
objects of religion?[69] If magic has immediate, concrete,
and selfish ends,[70] how are these to be distinguished from
the objectives of "physical security, prosperity, and
health, [that] are the concern of people of every religious
faith"[71] and, one may add, that are the goal and result of
many miracle narratives?[72] As to compulsion, sacraments
construed as working *ex opere operato* and effective regard-
less of the performer imply some sort of compulsion.[73]

These rather general remarks can be specified from ancient sources by reference to two groups of words, one generally associated with religion and miracle, the other with magic. These are the Greek and Latin words for "prayer" and "spell" (commonly, εὐχή and ἐπῳδή or ἐπαοιδή; *prex* or *supplicatio* and *carmen* or *incantamentum*). In his study of prayer and miracle O. Weinreich noted the difficulty of distinguishing sharply between prayer and spell.[74] F. Pfister, who devoted considerable attention to these terms (1922, 2107ff., passim; 1924b) drew conclusions not dissimilar.[75] From his collection of data several observations may be made.

One is that *epodē*, though it acquired pejorative connotations, in many contexts was employed in a neutral or an honorable sense. In early texts, for example, we hear of *epodai* used in healing,[76] in midwifery,[77] and (without obloquy) in cult (Plato, *Symp.* 202E). The word is also used to designate song or poetry (Pindar, *Nem.* 8.49; Plato, *Laws* 2.659E).

Second, it is in situations of social and cultural conflict that *epodē* acquires its negative overtones, as when a representative of Hippocratic medicine characterizes the use of καθαρμοί and ἐπαοιδαί (*Sacred Disease* 2.12-13) in treating epilepsy as a counsel of despair conceived by persons, ignorant of its true causes, whom the author likens to the magicians, purifiers, begging priests, and charlatans of his own day.[78] Here two traditions of healing are in conflict (cf. above, ch. 3.2.3). However, the author argues not only on medical grounds but also from a different view of religion. Those who recite the spells expect them to overpower the deities whose indwelling is viewed as the cause of the "sacred" disease.[79] But gods who can be overpowered and enslaved by human will,[80] using magic and sacrifices,[81] rites and ken and practice,[82] cannot be divine, says the author, and persons who think they can are impious and do not believe the gods exist or that they are powerful (*Sacred Disease* 4.8-9). If a deity is responsible for the disease, and if the sufferers are indeed polluted, as the use of purifications implies, then they should be brought to the temples, with sacrificing and prayer (θύειν τε καὶ εὔχεσθαι) and supplication of the gods (ἱκετεύειν τοὺς θεούς) (4.36ff.). Here prayer and supplication are distinguished from spells and compulsion, but the criteria for so doing are not "objective": it is rather the adherents of one culture pitted against those of another, with antithetical premises and values. They share the belief in pollution that was common in their day,[83] but they identify the dangers to society differently and so "pollute" different things:[84] the *kathartai* regard the sufferers from the disease as polluted, viewing the disease as a mark of divine disfavor placing them outside ordinary society, whereas the Hippocratic treatise views the sufferers as patients, to be treated as other patients, and instead stigmatizes the *kathartai* as threats to religion, health, and the practice of medicine and gives a pejorative cast to their means of purification and the terminology that designates it.

Several passages in Plato also attest a conflict, perhaps related to the preceding, that conditions the assessment of certain personnel and rites and the words designating them, including "spell" and "prayer." *Manteis* and their rituals occupied a prominent and respected place in the cult of the Greek *polis* of the classical period (see Nilsson, 1967, 791-95). However, alongside this more or less official piety functioned another one, more accessible and more responsive to daily private needs (ibid., 796) but also displaying characteristics which many Greeks came to describe as *deisidaimonia*, "superstition."[85] In his attack on the enemies of religion the elderly Plato includes some of the personnel and practices of this other system. He recommends severe punishment of those *manteis* who, for a fee, promise to prevail upon the gods by charming them with sacrifices, prayers, and spells, to the ruin of individuals, households, and cities.[86] It is not as clear in this text as it is in the Hippocratic one that the sacrifices, prayers, and spells are thought to compel deity; Plato focuses instead on the ends to which they are put. What is clear is that words and referents honorable in other

contexts are here used pejoratively and that both the word
for "prayer" (εὐχή) and the word for "spell" (ἐπῳδή) suffer
this fate. If *epodē* belongs to "magic" and the compelling
of deity, so does *euchē*. However, neither word necessarily
belongs to "magic"--or to "religion." It was through
euchai offered to the gods by Orpheus that a storm wind
ceased, leading to the inference that deity was responsible
for the deliverance, i.e., a miracle had taken place.[87] In
the Paris magical papyrus, on the other hand, the gathering
of plants by the operator is to proceed μετ' εὐχῶν (*PGM*
4.2973) followed by entreaty (παρακαλῶν, 4.2975) for their
effectiveness and a long *epiclesis* reciting the aetiology
of the plant.[88]

  Turning to Christian texts one finds some effort to
distinguish Christian from pagan thaumaturgy by characterizing the latter as worked by spells and the former
through prayers.[89] On a pagan, however, the distinction
might well be lost, especially in view of the technique
employed. What was to distinguish the invoking of the name
of Jesus, mentioned by Irenaeus and other Christian
writers,[90] from the invoking of other deities by magicians,
especially when the Christian practice was coupled with
recital of a Christian credo,[91] which might well recall
aretalogical and aetiological recitals by magicians to
empower their *praxis* (see Hopfner, 1928, 343). The
rationale of such invocation, also for Christians (see
Heitmüller, 1903, esp. 54ff.), was that the name of a
stronger deity overpowered that of a weaker deity; this too
is attested in the magical papyri (see Pfister, 1924b, 331-
32). The confidence in their deity that many Christians
regarded as a virtue in prayer (Jas. 1.6-7; Hermas, *Shepherd*, *Mand*. 9.1, 11-12) or thaumaturgy[92] could be likened
by outsiders to the claims of magicians to perform the
impossible by compelling deity. Moreover, wonders performed
by the followers of a new religion might be explained as
effected through spells and sorcery, if earlier instances
provide any precedent.[93]

  In sum, one may say that there is some agreement
between representatives of opposing cultural and social

groups that "magic" involves compulsion;[94] that is, the
distinction might function as an "objective" criterion.
The same could be said of use of manipulations and *materia*.
But at best the canons were not tight, and the texts we
have examined suggest that judgments were not made by
impartial testing but on other grounds, to the detriment
of "their" rites and wonders and to the advantage of
"ours."

4.3.2.3 Group Consciousness

This consciousness of "we" and "they" in the demarcation of magic from miracle is evident in a number of
second-century Christian texts.

In discussing necromancy Tertullian cites some of
the persons traditionally associated with magic[95] and says
there is general agreement that magic is a deception, but
only Christians know the reason.[96] There follows a long
description of how Christians, through their knowledge of
the demonic basis of magic, are able to expose it. The
counterfeit nature of the wonders produced by magic is
shown, for example, by the fact that "the truth of Moses
devoured the lie" of Pharaoh's magicians[97] and by the
reality of the blindness wrought by the apostle on the
magus Elymas who, like Simon, opposed the apostles.[98] In
the *Apology* what Tertullian labels "magic" turns out to be
extraordinary phenomena which pagans refer to the divine,
i.e., pagan miracles. Thus pagan healings are ascribed to
venefici[99] and are not really genuine.[100] Other well-known
pagan *miracula* are also placed in the framework of magic.[101]
Revealing of knowledge ordinarily hidden to humans, whether
by oracles or through necromancy, is ascribed to magic or
to its authors, the demons.[102] It is Christians who are in
a position to sort out the true and authentic--"miracle"--
from the false and unreal, "magic."[103]

A strong consciousness of "we" versus "them" is
found also in Justin, as an examination of the passages
cited earlier will show.[104] Likewise the contests in the
Acts literature are narrated in the consciousness of the
superiority of one group and its champion over another.

Origen tells his pagan opponent that in "*my* scriptures" are found instances of miraculous releases from prison which Celsus, however, would probably ascribe to sorcery (*C. Cels.* 2.34). We Christians, he says, avoid pagan cult because we know that it is demon worship (Ps. 95.5 is cited)[105] connected with various forms of magic (*C. Cels.* 7.69).

Irenaeus describes as magical deceptions[106] the manipulations of Marcus "the magician" (*Adv. h.* 1.13.2, 4, 5 [Harvey ed., 1.7.2-4]). The liquid[107] that changes color and the small cup whose contents overflow a larger cup are acts familiar from magical literature.[108] But even as presented by Irenaeus,[109] with the communal participation, the prayer of consecration, and theological undergirding, these constitute what today are called liturgical acts, "religion," not "magic." We have seen how Christian liturgical acts generally, with their *materia*, sign of the cross, and invocations, could be construed by pagans as magic. Here Irenaeus applies the label to Christian opponents.

What might the Marcosians have said in their defense? That they were not practicing magic?[110] Or that they were but it was an honorable craft? Would they have defended their combination of manipulations and theology the way Iamblichus expounds theurgy in terms of philo-sophical theology (e.g., *De myst.* 4.2)? If many Christians were conscious of themselves and their wonders as distinct from magic, pagan and Christian, there are also pagan texts which give an indication of how persons who practiced magic or were accused of doing so viewed the art and the words that designated it.

Like the word *epodē* (see above, p. 64) the words *magos* and *mageia* have a neutral or honorable sense in some texts and settings. Practitioners of *mageia* could refer to their art as "divine" or "holy"[111] and themselves as divinely possessed or as divine (references in Abt, 1908, 109-10). In Egypt the invention of magic and the use of spells were attributed to deity (cf. Nock, 1929, 228 = Nock, 1972, vol. 1, 188), and the same ascription is found in magical papyri.[112] In two letters which, if not

authentic, are yet probably a genuine reflection of his
views, Apollonius of Tyana,[113] who was widely regarded as a
magos,[114] defends himself by defining *magoi* as persons who
are θεοί τε καὶ δίκαιοι (*Ep.* 16) and attributes this understanding to the Persians.[115] Apuleius, on trial for practicing magic, as part of his defense also points to the
honorable origins of the term *magus* in Persia, where it
means "priest,"[116] and goes on to cite Plato[117] as saying
that the education of the heir to the Persian throne
includes "the *mageia* of Zoroaster, son of Oromazos"
(μαγείαν . . . τὴν Ζωροάστρου τοῦ Ὠρομάζου), which is
explained as being worship of the gods (θεῶν θεραπεία).
Apuleius also knows, however, that there is a more common
definition of magician, namely, as one who "through
communion in speech with the immortal gods is able to do
all the incredible things he wishes, through some power of
spells."[118] Magic, in this view, is inimical and worthy
of prosecution. It thus parallels pagan tradition
regarding the Persian *magoi*, which is more ambiguous than
Apuleius allows. The *magoi* are, it is true, esteemed as
upper-caste priests possessed of an ancient and esoteric
lore, but they are also viewed as immoral and as practitioners of rites that seemed to the Greeks like practices
in their own culture that they associated with persons who
employed spells, herbs, and special rites to produce extraordinary effects often harmful to others.[119] Nock's
suggestion that Greek hostility, ethnocentricity, and
ignorance of Persian religion contributed to this understanding (or misunderstanding) of the *magoi* is plausible
and finds support in various sources.[120] Similar factors
figure significantly also in the trial of Apuleius and
deserve examination for the light they shed on pagan-
Christian recriminations of "magic."

  That Apuleius' *Apology* is not merely a rhetorical
exercise but rather an expanded version of an actual
defense has been argued cogently by A. Abt (1908, 77-82).
By the time of Apuleius the practice of magic was a capital
offense also in the Roman provinces.[121] Apuleius is
accused specifically of love magic,[122] employing *carmina*[123]

and *venena*,[124] and of forbidden rites.[125] Legal prohibi-
tions have a two-fold social aspect. They show that a
number of people find what is prohibited offensive, enough
so to require action by those in authority. They also
reveal that a number of people also found the offensive
attractive, enough so to necessitate a formal prohibition.
The continuing prosecution of cases under the law or laws
attests the continuance of the same or similar conditions.
Some such conditions are presupposed in Roman law forbidding
magic, from the time of the Twelve Tables onward.[126] They
are presupposed in the *Apology* also.

But why is Apuleius singled out and charged with
the practice of magic? Several social and cultural factors
figure in the bringing of the charges against him.

First, Apuleius is a foreigner, a common element in
the applying of the label "magic" (see n. 93 of this
chapter). His accuser makes a point of the fact that
Apuleius is not a native son (*Apol.* 24).

Second, Apuleius, by marrying a widow of the town
where he stops for a recuperation that lengthens into an
extended stay, causes some rents in the social fabric of
the town. The relatives of the disappointed suitor charge
that sorcery explains how Apuleius has been able to win
over the wealthy widow, a free woman considerably his
senior and already betrothed.

Third, Apuleius engages in activities that his
accusers construe as "magic" but which, in the trial, he
explains either as legitimate worship or as connected with
scientific research. As to the first, Apuleius' identification of the deity in question as Mercury is not a
compelling argument in view of the association of Hermes-
Thoth with "magic." The accusation and reply illustrate
again the difficulty of distinguishing "magic" from "religion" in ancient texts.[127] What is clear is that for
Apuleius' accuser *occulta pieta* is apt to be magic.
Regarding the second, we may note the antithesis between
philosophers and others (see below, ch. 5.1), with the
former often regarded as thaumaturgists. Even taking at
face value Apuleius' explanations of his purchase and use

of certain species of fish as intended for scientific
research, or his attention to two epileptics as legitimate
medical care, to a person standing outside this culture
these might easily be construed as magic, especially since
such materials are attested in the practice of magic (see
Abt's commentary, 1908, 135ff., on *Apol*. 29ff.) and
sudden seizures might be construed as the effect of magic.[128]
Apuleius' accuser may not have been as rustic and unlearned
as Apuleius suggested, but there was a definite cultural
and social gap between the two men,[129] resulting in misunderstanding and antagonism which Apuleius' parade of
learning and air of superiority could only have exacer-
bated.[130]

Against this background pagans' and Christians'
labeling each others' miracles as "magic" is intelligible
as one facet of rivalry between pagan society and culture,
on the one hand, and, on the other, Christianity as an
alien social group, barely legal or considered illegal, and
nurturing a counterculture with many practices little
known or little understood by outsiders. Both of these
factors--Christianity's often aggressive criticism of pagan
culture and society and its actual disruption of the social
fabric on many occasions--as well as paganism's ignorance
of Christianity, combined to provoke the charges that
circulated against Christians. They also play into the
magic-versus-miracle conflict. Some of the Christian
claims for the thaumaturgical powers of their deity Jesus
and for their own thaumaturgy were in their impossibility--
notably resurrections--not unlike the claims made by
magicians. The manipulations, where they were known, were
similar to those used by magicians, and where they were not
known smacked of the secretive and the occult associated
with magic. The Christians' marginal place in society and
the countercultural nature of Christian teaching and mores
would confirm such judgments. Christians, in turn, saw the
self-consciousness they cultivated among themselves
regarding Jesus' miracles and pagan "magic" vindicated by
the success they observed in the miracles worked in their
own communities. Viewed sociologically, the charge of

"magic" which pagans and Christians leveled at each other
served as a kind of social classifier that helped "to
distinguish between various groups of people from the perspective of the speaker but does not necessarily imply any
essential difference in the actions of the participants"
(Segal, 1981, 367). That those persons regarded as magicians in the Greco-Roman world went against the grain of
much in their society is evident from the laws against them.
However, by operating individualistically and in secret,
they evaded overt conflict with the socially recognized
thaumaturgy and its social matrices. By contrast, Christianity's miracle claims--which were part of a new social
consciousness, visible in practice and often vigorously
defended--involved it ineluctably in covert as well as open
conflict with both the clandestine and the public thaumaturgy of paganism.[131]

MIRACLE AND ITS SOCIAL AND CULTURAL MATRICES

The sources considered in the preceding chapters have made
evident how relative were the judgments from case to case
of what was and was not to be considered a miracle. Canons
of the ordinary ranged from loose to tight and were applied
with varying degrees of consistency. Modes of explanation
were quite diverse, with a number of options available for
explaining puzzling phenomena other than by reference to
the divine. In its relativity "miracle" offered fertile
ground for conflict.

Important in understanding such conflict are the
social and cultural elements in the perception and assessment of extraordinary phenomena. These elements were
observed at a number of points in the preceding chapters.
The present chapter will draw some of these together along
cultural and social lines and note the implications for the
study of pagan-Christian conflict over miracle.

In the discussion that follows I use "culture" in
an inclusive, non-elitist sense to refer to the environment
--material or intellectual and spiritual--that humans
produce and bequeath to subsequent generations.[1] For
example, the liver models employed in hepatoscopy to
facilitate ascertainment of the divine represent culture in
a material sense while the traditions of language,
technique, and interpretation associated with the models
are part of the intellectual and spiritual heritage transmitted from one generation of diviners to the next.[2]

"Society" I regard as an aspect of culture, inasmuch as it is a human product, but also as the matrix
within which culture is inculcated and transmitted.[3] More
than one culture may be operative in a society at a given
time. Such pluralism is characteristic of Greco-Roman

societies. A society may originate in a certain geographical location and is always located somewhere, but social structures are also portable, though generally at the price of modification through contact with other cultures and societies. The Greek *polis* in the Hellenistic era is an example, as are the Jewish and other ethnic communities in the Hellenistic and Roman periods. There are also other lines of social demarcation. The diviners just mentioned, for example, represent a subgroup, defined along vocational and professional lines within which specific aspects of culture were fostered.

Certain fundamental human needs were answered in the Greco-Roman world by some of the cultural traditions observed in the preceding chapters: agriculture, architecture and building, medicine, philosophy, divination, astronomy, historiography, biology, zoology, paradoxography. These varied from one culture and society to another, but many elements are found to recur from one of these to another, whether through diffusion or because of common function or both, so that one may speak of shared cultures or commonality of cultures as well as of discrete cultures.[4]

Within these various cultural traditions there was discernible a traditional, generally dominant culture that I shall call mainstream or popular cultic piety. It is popular in the sense that it has statistically numerous representation; it is not necessarily *volkstümlich*, since educated and upper-class persons may also share in it. "Mainstream" refers to this statistical datum as well as to the primacy and persistence of this tradition in Greco-Roman societies. It is cultic in the sense that it has to do with the deities and worships of the period. It possesses canons of the ordinary, but these tend to be unexamined, loose, and inconsistently applied. It cherishes the expectation that extraordinary phenomena could and would be worked by deities or their agents, and it is apt to ascribe to them puzzling, otherwise inexplicable phenomena. It is cross-cultural, found in a variety of pagan, Christian, Jewish, and other social groups and cultures of the Greco-Roman era (and since).

In our analysis we have also observed demarcations
and explanations of extraordinary phenomena that differed,
often markedly and consciously, from those of the mainstream. These were seen to be associated with certain
cultural currents such as philosophy, medicine, biology,
and other self-conscious traditions of knowledge. Sometimes these currents reach such a degree of divergence that
they may be designated countercultural. When these traditions are nurtured and transmitted within a distinct social
group, one may properly speak of a counterculture. The
most prominent such group in Western antiquity is the
philosophers. Another emerged in the first and second
centuries: Christianity.

5.1 Philosophy as Counterculture

Despite their divergences, philosophers in the Greco-Roman
world constituted a distinct social type, marked by
distinctive garb, self-conscious acquisition, possession,
and transmission of a body of knowledge, and a distinctive
life-style.[5] The countercultural nature of philosophy is
indicated by the intensive resocialization--what Nock
(1933a, ch. 11) has called a conversion--which was required
of persons seriously aspiring to philosophy and which
philosophers were constantly cultivating in and among themselves and to which they sought to bring others.[6] It is
seen also in the persecutions and ostracisms to which
philosophers were subjected from time to time.[7]
The various schools of philosophy, which by the
second century C.E. were syncretistic in varying degrees as
a result of centuries of debate and interaction, were yet
distinctive enough to constitute discrete matrices of
thought and action, recognizable to themselves and to
others as "Stoic," "Platonic," and so forth.[8] Their
attitudes toward extraordinary phenomena, though varied,
are yet distinct from popular cultic piety thanks to a long
tradition of reflection on cosmogony and cosmology, which
enjoyed a greater number of options for assessing such
phenomena than did cultic piety. This tradition was able
to explain cosmic origins and cosmic order without literal

reference to the deities worshiped in the cults and cele-
brated in the stories about the gods.[9] The effect was to
remove cosmic origins and order from the sphere of the
arbitrary, from something as capricious as the will and whim
of an unpredictable deity.[10] Through philosophical reflection the conception of the divine and of the cosmos and the
relation between them changed. Whether deity was identified with the cosmos, or viewed as permeating it, or placed
at a far remove from the world humans inhabited, deity did
not act arbitrarily. For those philosophies that postulated
something more than a null relation between deity and the
cosmos, the divine was responsible for the order in the
cosmos. And if that order was as perfect as deity could
make it, why should there be departures from it, that is,
extraordinary happenings inexplicable without reference to
that order?

Persons with philosophical training did not necessarily reject a priori the possibility of such happenings.
They had been reared in social contexts in which the gods
were honored with cult, their schooling included heavy
doses of Homer and the other Greek poets, and they often
continued to participate in local cults and to support
these or their traditions. There is a persisting religious,
often mystical strain in philosophy, associated with names
like Pythagoras, Empedocles, Socrates, Plato and, under the
Empire, Philo, Apuleius, and the Neo-Platonists. In the
Greco-Roman period, as Nock has noted, "The philosopher was
in popular imagination superhuman and liable to be
thaumaturgic."[11] The tension between the popular view of
the philosopher, based in cultic piety, and the philosophical ideal governed by the Socratic paradigm (cf. Tiede,
1972) and by the philosophical tradition of knowledge we
have sought to delineate is another indication of the
countercultural nature of philosophy. It was a tension
that existed not only between and within social groups but
also between and within individuals. In the second century
a shift in the attitude of many philosophers toward cultic
piety and the miraculous gradually becomes evident. Philostratus' life of Apollonius, an early third-century

"philosophization" of a late first-century philosopher-
thaumaturge, illustrates this greater cordiality and
interest (see below, p. 104). However, the tradition of
explaining phenomena in terms of orderly, familiar causation, with close attention to epistemological questions and
with symbolic constructs like *physis* often providing theoretical instruments, constituted a continuing legacy which
was still operative in the second century and beyond. To
employ a terminology introduced earlier (above, p. 18)
common to persons with philosophical training was an ethics
of belief, whatever their philosophy, their personal pre-
dilections, or their attitude toward cultic piety or other
forms of religion.

Perhaps the chief characteristic of this ethic is
the intention to look for orderly (often "natural") causation both of ordinary and extraordinary phenomena.[12] Such
an ethic stands in contrast with mainstream piety's perception of extraordinary phenomena as directly caused by
deity, as unpredictable as personal whim and representing a
threat to human life and society that was met by referring
these phenomena to persons and institutions designated to
explain them and, if necessary, to get things right with
the gods. That it is not unjustly construed as an ethic
is indicated by conception of it as a goal to be pursued
(above, ch. 2, n. 86: Seneca and Galen), by the judgments
of value associated with it,[13] and by the commitment it was
expected to entail.[14] Some pursue the goal rigorously
(e.g., Cicero and Lucian, above, pp. 35-36), others with
less persistence (e.g., Pliny, above, p. 18). Some pursue
it as far as they are able and then resort to the divine as
explanation (Pliny, above, p. 44). Some deliberately seek
to combine explanations from philosophy and cultic piety,
the "both-and" mentality noted above (above, ch. 3.3.1).

This last illustrates again the tension between
philosophy and the mainstream culture regarding extraordinary phenomena. Persons like Plutarch, firmly rooted
in the mainstream culture by reason of predilection[15] and
of his social role as a priest of Delphi, yet thoroughly
versed in philosophy, sought to "save the phenomena" (above,

ch. 3.2), the wondrous divine manifestations endemic to
cultic piety. Through resort to allegory the Stoics, a Jew
like Philo, a Christian like Origen, as well as Plutarch,
sought to save many of the phenomena of their respective
traditions. However, a person of Cicero's temperament,
though also versed in philosophy and occupying the role of
augur, was determined to reject those phenomena.

   An important motivation of this ethic is the pursuit of the ἀπάθεια or ἀταραξία familiar from philosophical
ethics generally.[16] We observed this motivation earlier in
Cicero's statement that a result--and a goal--of providing
natural explanations of prodigies was the dispelling of any
terror these might have aroused (above, pp. 35-36). Lucian
extols Epicurus for liberation from the two tyrants, hope
and fear, which drive people to Alexander of Abonoteichos
with his promises of miracles and revelations of the future
(Alex. 8); Lucian credits Epicurus' Kyriai Doxai with
bringing peace, tranquility, and freedom (εἰρήνην καὶ
ἀταραξίαν καὶ ἐλευθερίαν) by liberating from terrors,
apparitions, and portents (δειμάτων μὲν καὶ φασμάτων καὶ
τεράτων ἀπαλλάττον) (Alex. 47). Epicurus' Roman disciple,
Lucretius, after providing physical explanations of phenomena ascribed to deity by mainstream piety, states that
these produce the tranquil spirit in which one can properly
worship the gods (De rer. nat. 6.48-78; 6.78: animi
tranquilla pace). Earthquakes are not caused by the gods,
says the Stoic Seneca, and the person who understands this
and the true causes of earthquakes or of other extraordinary phenomena will be assisted in losing his fear of
them, since fear is caused by ignorance.[17]

   There is a significant cultural difference here
between mainstream cultic piety and philosophy. The former
relied on diviners and expiations to still any fear and
terror aroused by extraordinary phenomena. The latter's
explanations of such phenomena served to render diviners
and expiations superfluous, as we have seen repeatedly.
The two are in implicit conflict, which on occasion becomes
explicit.

   Yet for all their differences with the mainstream,

persons standing in the philosophical tradition generally
affirmed the former in some way as a legitimate culture.
That was evident in the "both-and" mentality. But even
persons who prided themselves on their consistent adherence
to the philosophical ethic of belief with regard to extraordinary phenomena were generally able to find a niche for
mainstream piety, its rites and sometimes its miracles, if
not for themselves then for others.[18] In this it contrasted
with another counterculture, Christianity.

5.2 Christianity as Counterculture

Both popular cultic piety and philosophical culture are
found in second-century Christianity. In relation to pagan
culture generally, however, second-century Christianity
constitutes a counterculture with certain structural
elements akin to those of philosophy.

As in philosophy there are various "schools," i.e.,
varieties of Christianity, distinctive enough to be recognized as such by other Christians, though the discreteness
might be lost on outsiders. However, there are also
certain common symbols ("Jesus," "savior") and rites
("sacraments") and some shared knowledge having to do in
some way with the Christian deity, the story of Jesus and
events preceding and following it. There is a body of
writings, ancient and contemporary, the demarcation of
which varied from group to group but for all its variety
was generally sufficiently distinctive to be recognized as
non-pagan. There is a distinctive life-style, with "a
permanent object of desire" (Nock, 1933a, 185). Moreover,
Christians constituted self-conscious social groupings,
locally in the first instance but with a network of ties
connecting local communities. Entry required resocialization of varying intensity. Within these social matrices a
culture was fostered, with concerted efforts being made to
win others to it. These factors and the suspicions Christians frequently aroused as well as the ostracisms and
persecutions to which they were occasionally subjected
point to the countercultural nature of Christianity.

Some of the canons of belief and explanation which

popular cultic piety in Christianity shared with its pagan counterparts have been indicated at various points in preceding chapters. The cultural and social aspects of this piety as it relates to miracle will be considered further in Part Two. Here it may be observed that even as philosophically versed pagans were set apart from other pagans by the wider variety of options they possessed for assessing miracle claims, so, too, Christians acquainted with philosophy were set off, in varying degrees, from the larger body of Christians. Whether the cultural elements these philosophically minded Christians shared with their pagan counterparts led to conflict over miracle, or rather to rapprochement, will be explored in Part Two.

5.3 Conflict: Social and Cultural Dimensions

It should now be evident that any attempt to understand conflict over miracle in the second century must take account of the social and cultural components in the demarcation, explanation, and assessment of the extraordinary. Celsus' efforts to dispel Christian miracles, for example, root in an anxiety over the future of pagan culture and society whose foundations he sees as being undermined by this *nouveau* religion, with its miracle claims among the chief offenses. It was a well-founded anxiety in view of Christianity's increasing social weight as it grew in numbers and intellectual prowess and drew admiration for its morality. In his attack Celsus capitalizes on Christianity's largely lower-class constituency, attaching this opprobrium to its founder, its Jewish antecedents, and its thaumaturgists (see below, ch. 8). On the other hand, Christianity's thaumaturgy, its miracle stories, its appeal to antiquity, and its nihilations of other miracle claims functioned as a way to win converts and as a means of social legitimation within the larger pagan society. Within Christianity itself conflicts over miracle also had significant social dimensions, as is clear in the Montanist controversy (see below, ch. 10.7).

Several kinds of possible pagan-Christian conflict over miracle may now be envisaged.

Pagans acculturated in mainstream cultic piety
would be able to recognize Christian thaumaturgy and
miracle claims as akin to their own: extraordinary events
or phenomena occurring or worked through more-than-human-
or-ordinary causation or agency. However, in view of the
countercultural nature of Christianity, they might be
inclined to suspicion of Christianity and of its miracle
claims and to attack the authenticity of the claims or, if
they recognized them as authentic, the power responsible
for such departures from the ordinary. On the other side,
Christians in the cultic piety tradition might attack pagan
thaumaturgy and miracle claims as inauthentic or worked
demonically or by means of magic, with a corollary assertion of the exclusivity of the Christian deity and the
miracles worked by him. Because of the close association
of pagan cult with the rest of pagan culture and society,
such a Christian interpretation would be apt to be viewed
by pagans as an attack on the latter as well. Some of
these factors will be seen to be operative in the conflicts
examined in chapters seven and ten.

Pagans initiated into the philosophical tradition
might bring to Christian thaumaturgy and miracle claims
canons of judgment similar to those they applied to pagan
cultic piety, resulting in a similar kind of conflict.
Both of these kinds of conflict are seen in Celsus' attack
on Christianity, which will be treated in chapter eight.
Christians versed in philosophy would, in turn, have more
options for assessing and attacking pagan miracle claims
and the conceptions of deity related to them. Joined with
this might be an alienation from pagan culture in general
and from its philosophies in particular.

Philosophically trained pagans might also recognize
Christian philosophers as kindred spirits, yet feel
estranged from them because of their affirmation of Christian miracles, their use of philosophy in defense of this
affirmation, and their adherence to a culture opposed not
only to pagan culture generally but often to philosophy as
well, whether explicitly or implicitly. Some philosophically trained pagans, on the other hand, might find

Christianity attractive, in part because of its thaumaturgy
and miracle claims and other claims and promises associated
with these. Justin Martyr is an example who will be discussed in chapter nine.

Conflicts, as was noted in the Preface, might be
both implicit and explicit. The only really certain
example of explicit conflict in the second century is
Celsus' polemic. The precise identity of his opponent(s)
is a disputed issue, but he makes clear at a number of
points when he is attacking Christians and Christian
teachings. When Christians defend Christian thaumaturgy
and miracle claims, it is often very difficult to determine
whether they have a Christian or a pagan opponent in view,
and if the latter, which one. However, the positions taken
can often be seen to be in implicit conflict with pagan
positions.

If one were to propose to all humans that they
choose the best customs (νόμοι) out of all the customs
there are, says Herodotus, each, after examination, would
choose its own, so convinced are they that these are the
best.[19] The next chapter will suggest how insights from
the sociology of knowledge can assist to an understanding
of such choices and of the conflicts that ensue from them.

MIRACLE AND SOCIOLOGY OF KNOWLEDGE

6.1 Sociology of Knowledge
The sociology of knowledge investigates the relation of
thought to its social settings. The theoretical foundations of the discipline were laid in the 1920s by Max
Scheler (1960). He and Karl Mannheim, another of the
earliest and most noted of the theoreticians, focused on
the history of ideas as these were formulated by the
thinkers in a society.[1] Some recent sociologists of knowledge have defined "knowledge" more broadly to include
also the presuppositions and maxims of the day-to-day,
"what people 'know' as 'reality' in their everyday, non-
or pre-theoretical lives. In other words, commonsense
'knowledge' rather than ideas. . . . It is precisely this
'knowledge' that constitutes the fabric of meanings without
which no society could exist" (Berger and Luckmann, 1967,
15).

This broader conception of the sociology of knowledge is appropriate to first- and second-century Christianity, where the socially and intellectually elite were a
small (though important) minority[2] and much of the literature produced was popular.[3] It is also appropriate to the
popular cultic piety that we saw to be important in the
demarcation of miracle (Part One of this study; cf. also
M. Smith, 1971, 179-81). At the same time it does not
preclude taking account of the thinkers in second-century
society, as represented by the philosophical schools and
those--whether pagans or Christians--who were influenced by
them.

Sociology of knowledge observes that what passes
for knowledge in a society is conditioned by the various
social structures in a society, beginning with the primary

socialization of infancy and childhood and continuing on
into the secondary socialization of later childhood and
adulthood. These social settings give credence to the
knowledge thus acquired, and societies possess various
means of maintaining and reinforcing it.

Conversion, one of the phenomena discussed by
Berger and Luckmann (1967, 156-63), illustrates some of the
generalizations and terminology of the sociology of knowledge and how they may be applied to early Christian data.
It figures importantly in the story of Justin, which will
be considered in chapter nine.

A. D. Nock saw conversion (in contrast to adhesion)
as characteristic of the way in which persons entered
early Christianity.[4] The social processes involved, which
he did not attempt to spell out, may be outlined briefly.
One begins with the convert before conversion. To the
child, social mores, values, and institutions present themselves, and are presented, as the only ones possible, that
is, as objective reality. Primary socialization takes
place in an emotionally charged atmosphere in which this
"objective reality" is internalized (Berger and Luckmann,
1967, 60-61). Secondary socialization presupposes the
primary and builds upon it but is generally not as intense
and emotionally charged (ibid., 138-47).

Viewed in these terms, conversion is an intensive
resocialization that resembles primary socialization. This
is a necessary resemblance because converts are urged to
abandon or reinterpret many of the basic maxims and more of
their primary socialization, and these are generally not
surrendered without a struggle. Many of the basic structural elements of primary socialization are requisite,
therefore, especially a social setting in which the convert
sees how the new premises and values are embodied and acted
upon. Important to the setting are "significant others"
(ibid., 138-40, 145), that is, persons with whom the
convert identifies and whom he imitates, thus replicating
in some way and to some degree the emotional element of
childhood rearing. Berger and Luckman call this kind of
social setting a "plausibility structure," a "laboratory"

within which the convert internalizes the new reality,
acquiring a new "symbolic universe" (ibid., 144, 89-95).

Many of the elements in this description can be
found, without distortion, in early Christianity. There
are the significant others, authority figures with whom the
convert identifies and whom he imitates and obeys. In
addressing his converts Paul employs language from the context of primary socialization: they are children and he is
their father[5] who expects them to imitate or obey him or
Christ.[6] It is a form of reality maintenance when Paul
tells the Corinthians he has sent Timothy to remind them of
his "ways in Christ, even as I teach everywhere in every
church" (1 Cor. 4.17). If they fail to heed Timothy, Paul
himself will come and demonstrate the divine power (1 Cor.
4.18-19). Even at a distance, however, Paul is able to
enforce the new reality, through the presence of his *pneuma*
in the assembled community:

. . . for though absent in the body, I am present in the spirit, and as
though present I have already pronounced judgment in the name of the
Lord Jesus on the person who has done this thing; when you have
assembled and my spirit is present with the power of our Lord Jesus,
deliver such a person to Satan for the destruction of the flesh in
order that his spirit may be saved in the day of the Lord Jesus (1 Cor.
5.3-5).

The importance of the community in giving credence to a new
reality is evident here and will be observed also in other
contexts (see below, Part Two). In this instance--a crisis
in the community caused by a flagrant violation of the
morality Paul is seeking to inculcate--the reality maintenance requires the pain of expulsion from the community,
with the purpose of fitting the offender for the ultimate
telos of the community, its final deliverance by its savior.
Such a situation is an example of "therapy" (Berger and
Luckmann, 1967, 112-15), a heightened form of reality maintenance in the time of crisis for the purpose of retaining
the integrity of the community and of its members.

Observance of the social context of knowledge is
important also in other areas of early Christianity. The
community at worship, for example, is a powerful

plausibility structure in which the new reality is
embodied.[7] Ethical statements function not only logically
--"love one another as Christ loved you"--but also socie-
tally. ". . . 'Christ loved you' is a shorthand way of
referring to a whole pattern of discourse and memory, of
symbol and story, of experience and reflection belonging to
the lore of the community" (Meeks, 1973, 99). Turning to
beliefs about miracle, the assertion that "With God all
things are possible" is prominent in early Christianity.[8]
But like the love command it too is "a shorthand way" of
referring to symbolic universes of various Christian
communities. To distinguish such a statement from very
similar assertions by pagans[9] requires reference to their
communal settings. Pagan-Christian conflicts over miracle
are not simply clashes of ideas but also reflections of
rivalry between communities with competing symbolic
universes, social structures, personnel, and worships.

6.2 Precursors

The history of modern historiography may be viewed from one
perspective as a sharpening of tools (as has happened, e.g.,
in textual criticism and linguistic study), a borrowing of
tools (the use of astronomy, e.g., in the study of the
story of the Magi in Matthew 2 or the dating of the crucifixion), and an acquiring of new tools in order to understand the data better and the relation of the historian to
the latter, with the result that historiography may justly
be characterized as "a field encompassing field" (Harvey,
1966, 54ff.). One of the concerns of modern historiography
has been "to investigate as painstakingly as possible the
concrete relationships between thought and its historical
situation" (Berger and Luckmann, 1967, 5). Though sociology of knowledge is a relatively recent discipline, its
basic purpose is thus not alien to historiography. Rather,
as Berger and Luckmann point out, it "takes up a problem
originally posited by historical scholarship--in a narrower
focus, to be sure, but with an interest in essentially the
same questions."[10] Its use in historical study is another

example of the acquiring of a new tool that illuminates the
sources in a way that those in use hitherto have not.

A review of previous study of accounts of extraordinary phenomena in pagan and early Christian sources
reveals a number of thinkers and researchers who discerned
various social aspects of such accounts or made observations that may justly be termed "sociological." A methodological caveat is in order, however. It is common for
proponents of a new approach to find earlier practitioners
of it on every hand. As Albert Schweitzer once asked, "Who-
ever discovered a true principle without pressing its
application too far?" (1910, 85). Some distinctions put
forward by Robert Merton are useful therefore. Reviewing
the history of theory in various academic disciplines,
Merton (1967, 9ff.) distinguishes between prediscoveries,
anticipations, and adumbrations. A prediscovery is one
that was forgotten and substantially rediscovered later.
An anticipation is an insight or a finding which in its
formulation overlaps later ones but is not pursued further
nor are the implications developed or applied in a systematic and significant way. An adumbration vaguely approxi-
mates later findings, with practically none of the implications being developed.

These distinctions help to guard the proponent of a
new insight or methodology from claiming too much in the
way of antecedents by offering a way of weighting them and
their continuity or discontinuity with one's own findings.
One can be grateful to these predecessors for sharpening
one's perception of the data and for indicating that one is
not simply engaged in eisegesis: in an earlier time they
made similar findings from the extant data. It will be
incumbent upon the investigator in the present day, however,
to pursue his or her research more systematically than they,
to order findings in a coherent way, and to provide a
theoretical justification for the manner in which he or she
does so.

Some examples for the study of miracle are now in
order.

Falling in the category of adumbration is the awareness by a number of writers in the Western Catholic tradition that education and culture affect one's judgment of extraordinary phenomena. Educated pagans were generally distinguished from those of little or no schooling by their knowledge of the causes of eclipses (see ch. 1 above, pp. 4ff.). Augustine, in a conflict situation, makes this awareness explicit in order to debunk the belief that Romulus, by his divine power, caused an eclipse of the sun: "the ignorant multitude [*imperita . . . multitudo*] . . . did not know that it was brought about by the fixed law of the sun's course."[11] Aquinas, in seeking to define *miraculum* according to its cause, must deal with the problem of variance of judgment from one person to another in regard to causes. An untutored person (*rusticus*), he observes, will marvel at a solar eclipse whereas an astronomer will not.[12] Neither Augustine nor Aquinas has any interest in developing these insights, which both men employ incidentally in defense and exposition of Christian thought. Similarly Karl Rahner and other modern Roman Catholic thinkers argue for certain of the Gospel miracles by singling out their cultural contexts as figuring decisively in their acceptance or rejection.[13] By contrast, thinkers in the Enlightenment tradition sometimes point to the social conditioning of miracle claims in order to discredit them or reduce their number: the more barbarous and uncultured a people or social group, the greater the number of miracle accounts.[14] Much of Hume's polemic against uncritical acceptance of extraordinary phenomena consists of keen observations on the effect of education and culture on perception of such phenomena. His distinctions between various societies, or between urban and rural peoples, or between ancient and "enlightened" times, and his observations of the effect of geography or religion on perceptions are suggestive of later historical and sociological study (Hume, 1894, 113-29).

Also falling in the category of adumbration is the observation by J. B. Mozley (1865, 2) and W. Hermann (1908, 43-48) that it is not only persons trained in natural or

historical science who find belief in miracles difficult;
others do, too, inasmuch as miracles go counter to everyday
experience. We saw this to be true when examining canons
of the ordinary in the Greco-Roman world. In his discussion of "present knowledge" Van Harvey (1966) has explored
the methodological implications of insights like those of
Mozley and Hermann.

Related to education and culture are social status,
power, and group loyalties, which played a role in ancient
assessments of extraordinary phenomena. Hume (1894, 125)
drew attention to the biasing effect of political loyalties
while Kant noted how class and power operated to allow for
the possibility of miracles in the past but not in the
present for fear of upsetting the status quo.[15] Neither
made much of these insights, however, and these factors
have generally been neglected in discussions of miracle.

One of the distinctions most commonly drawn by
historians, including students of miracle, is between
ancient and modern presuppositions. After the natural
sciences in the modern period began to offer comprehensive
explanations of ordinary and extraordinary phenomena, such
explanations were commonly put forward as warrants for
dissolutions of ancient miracles. In the first flush of
Newtonian physics, "the laws of nature" were invoked as
sanctions of such dissolutions, a practice that has
persisted down to the present (cf. above, ch. 2, p. 20,
and n. 98). Either polemically or matter-of-factly, the
ignorance of past ages has been contrasted with present
knowledge, which could be utilized to provide explanations
of ancient miracles that denied their divine reference or
called it in question.[16] Twentieth-century discussion
conversant with the natural sciences and aware of the
nature of scientific claims has been less categorical about
the causation and demarcation of extraordinary phenomena.[17]
The upshot of such discussion has been a recognition of the
role of a priori commitments in demarcation of certain
extraordinary phenomena as "miracles," the same phenomena
being adjudged miraculous or non-miraculous according to
whether or not one approaches them with belief in divine

agency and causation of a kind that manifests itself in
miracle.[18] Though these observations are not characterized
by their authors as "sociological," they may not unjustly
be assessed as adumbrating a sociological approach to
miracle: judgments of extraordinary phenomena are relative,
differing from age to age as well as within a particular
age, depending on such factors as social status, education,
power, and group loyalties, and are nurtured and transmitted within specific social matrices.

It is on this point--socialization--that some rare
observations were made by H. S. Reimarus and D. F. Strauss
that anticipate certain insights of the sociology of knowledge. Reimarus spells out at length how primary socialization affects religious belief, including belief in miracle.
Against those who maintain that non-Christians may be led
to Christianity through reasoned demonstration, Reimarus
argues that both Christians and non-Christians are strongly
inclined to persist in the religion of their first
nurturing.[19] Christians (in Germany) sometimes decide
already before marriage, through contracts, in which Christian confession their children will be reared; that is, the
upbringing is consciously socially determined (Reimarus,
1897a, 325). For the children this species of religion is
the only religion they know; in Berger and Luckmann's
terminology, it is "reality."[20] Were children not taught
from early on to accept the historical veracity of the
Bible, on reaching adulthood they would read it as a novel,
a collection of ancient fables (1897a, 353). Accordingly,
Reimarus elsewhere asserts that a people accustomed to a
general belief in miracles will incline to belief in specific miracles or in the possibility of miracles (1897b, 315-
16; E. T., 1970, 251-52). Indeed, belief in miracle may
actually make extraordinary phenomena possible.[21] When
such general belief was lacking, even Jesus could work no
miracles.[22] Conflicts between peoples with differing
miracle beliefs are inevitable, and unresolvable by appeal
to objective criteria, i.e., criteria mutually agreed on by
those peoples (1897a, 320-21).

As a professor of oriental languages, Reimarus had

some acquaintance with the sacred books of other religions (cf. 1897a, 353, and above, n. 19 of this chapter). He notes that Europeans had been in contact with non-European peoples for two to three centuries (1897a, 335). Yet this had not resulted in a general consciousness of the relativity of religious commitments and their social and cultural conditioning: Reimarus felt constrained to confide his thoughts on this subject only to private manuscripts. In retrospect they may be seen as anticipating the sociology of knowledge at a number of points, though at times his judgments are too crude.[23]

David Friedrich Strauss's observations on how the presuppositions of different eras and of different peoples within them affect assessment of extraordinary phenomena mark him off as a competent and pioneering historian (Harvey, 1961); they also belong to the genuine anticipations of the sociology of knowledge. Against writers on the New Testament who credited first-century Jews with holding modern explanations of psychic disorders, Strauss asks for the evidence, maintaining that such judgments are anachronistic and that persons from one era transported to another would still assess such disorders from the standpoint of their own era.[24] Strauss faults his contemporaries with failing to perceive the effect of present knowledge on their judgments of ancient phenomena.[25] Translated into the language of sociology, Strauss is here drawing attention to the effects of socialization and social contexts on knowledge.

Strauss is generally keenly aware of the relativity of thought and its social conditioning. He observes that "what is ordinary and regular in our estimation" may differ from "what was so in the ideas of the author whose writings are to be explained," something the rationalists of his day did not perceive.[26] Myths, that is, narratives originating in and embodying ideas rather than historical fact (Strauss, 1972, para. 15, p. 86), Strauss regards not as the inventions of individuals seeking to hoodwink their contemporaries, but rather as expressions of the maxims and beliefs of groups, within which "the one who invents the mythus is

only obeying the impulse which acts also upon the minds of
his hearers, he is but the mouth through which all speak,
the skilful interpreter who has the address first to give
form and expression to the thoughts of all" (para. 14,
p. 81). The social contexts of thought, Strauss notes, were
not uniform within the Roman Empire but varied from people
to people; Reimarus and Hume had already observed this, as
we have seen, and Strauss carries these reflections further
(para. 13, pp. 74-75). Thus one sees scattered in Strauss
a variety of insights anticipating sociology of knowledge
and brought to bear on the interpretation of miracles in a
more systematic way than heretofore, and, often, subsequently.

In the twentieth century, form criticism, with its
search for the typical social settings of ancient texts,
was explicitly formulated in the New Testament area as a
sociological method (see Bultmann, 1957, 4-5; Dibelius,
1966, 57). Dibelius especially offered significant leads
for placing Christian miracle accounts in typical life-
situations in Christian communities. However, this remains
to be pursued in a more systematic way for early non-
canonical and pagan miracle stories. And as Oscar Cullmann
noted long ago (1925, 573), the speculative impression
conveyed by much of New Testament form-critical work
derives from its failure to offer adequate sociological
parallels to New Testament data. A number of suggestive
parallels are to be found in current anthropological and
sociological literature. These offer concrete illustrations of how group settings can function as plausibility
structures of extraordinary phenomena.

W. B. Cannon, for example, in seeking to explain
the physiological mechanisms that produce death in a person
who has been cursed had recourse to the social setting of
such a scenario. When the curser, the one cursed, and the
community to which they belong all believe in the efficacy
of cursing, the victim is treated as a dead man, a social
reality with which his sympathico-adrenal system is unable
to cope, producing low blood pressure and irreparably

damaging vital organs, which together with his rejecting of
food and water results in death.[27]

Even where a healer is himself skeptical or dubious
of the possibility of unusual healings, he may still be
able to perform such healings when his community believes
in them and in him. Lévi-Strauss cites the example of a
certain shaman of the Kwakiutl Indians in British Columbia
who was skeptical of shamans' cures and undertook to expose
them. However, the close association with shamans that this
necessitated led to his being identified as one himself,
with persons coming to him for healing. Even after he has
acquired a formidable reputation, he remains unconvinced of
shamans' powers generally and ambivalent about his own,
though he is proud of his achievements and defends his
techniques. Lévi-Strauss sums up the relation between the
shaman and his social group by saying that "he did not
become a great shaman because he cured his patients; he
cured his patients because he had become a great shaman."[28]
The healings were performed in a social and cultural
setting in which shamans were expected to heal, and the
shaman, however skeptical personally, conformed to and fulfilled those expectations in performing his healing
rituals (further examples in Kiev, 1964, 8-11, 15, 26,
etc.).

Against such a background, the report of Jesus'
inability to perform mighty works in a hostile setting
appears sociologically well-founded,[29] as do, contrariwise,
the Gospel accounts of healings in which the communal
setting is reported as congenial.[30] The second century
offers a number of examples, pagan and Christian, in which
social groups function for their members as plausibility
structures of extraordinary happenings. Some of these will
be considered further on.

The anticipations adduced in this chapter of an
approach to miracle via the sociology of knowledge confirm
what we have already seen to be true, that assessments of
extraordinary phenomena are socially and culturally
influenced and that such influence must be taken into

account in analyzing conflicts over miracle. This we have sought to do in Part Two, in which insights from the sociology of knowledge enhance the understanding of such conflicts gained from more tradtional historical study.

PART TWO

ASCLEPIUS PIETY:
CASE STUDIES IN CONFLICT

MAINSTREAM PIETY, ASCLEPIUS, AND JESUS:
AELIUS ARISTIDES

7.1 Asclepius Piety and Jesus Piety

The interface between Asclepius piety and Jesus piety has
been investigated more than once by scholars, who have
called attention to the antithesis between these two
healing deities. With respect to some of the earlier
sources, conflict between the two pieties has been inferred
where antitheses to characteristic marks of Asclepius cult
occur (Rengstorff, 1953). In later sources, instances of
explicit conflict can be cited from both the pagan and the
Christian side.[1] Instances of Asclepius piety in implicit
conflict with Jesus piety can also be discerned in these
sources. In two important instances of conflict, Aelius
Aristides and Alexander of Abonoteichos (ch. 10 below), the
social settings of Asclepius cult are discernible in the
data and suggest reasons why pagans standing in the tradition of mainstream piety might resist Christians' miracle
claims for their savior Jesus. Celsus offers an example of
explicit pagan affirmation of Asclepius piety, with its
wondrous manifestation of the deity and of his power, over
against Christian claims on behalf of Jesus. Why Celsus,
standing in the philosophical tradition, which, as we have
seen, is frequently at odds with mainstream piety in
assessing extraordinary phenomena, should defend Asclepius
piety so vigorously is a question illuminated by consideration of Celsus' social and cultural setting vis-à-vis the
new religion, Christianity, and such of its representatives
as Justin and Christian gnostics (these issues will be
examined in chs. 8 and 9).

7.2 Aelius Aristides and the Savior Asclepius

The primary sources for the study of Aristides are his
treatises and orations and the *Hieroi Logoi*, his narrative
account of his illnesses and of his dreams.[2] These and
other sources enable one to construct a picture of Aristides
and his social world.[3]

Although educated in both rhetoric and philosophy,
having studied with prominent representatives of each,[4]
Aristides chose the former as his profession, to which he
developed a passionate attachment. Some of his writings
are reflections on rhetoric and defenses of it, especially
against philosophical detractors.[5] When illness threatened
his career, he turned for help, not to the resources of
philosophy, but to Greek and Egyptian dieties, i.e., to
mainstream cultic piety.[6] When a choice was to be made
between medicine as practiced by physicians and the prescriptions of Asclepius, Aristides chose the latter and
consulted those physicians who were willing to cooperate
with the deity in prescribing treatment for his devotee.[7]
It is in the context of such piety that Aristides had his
origins (he came from a priestly family; see Behr, 1968,
4 and n. 6) and found relief from his afflictions, thus
making it possible for him to resume his career. His
belief in Asclepius' power to work wonders of healing has
often been assessed as credulous, but, however idiosyncratic, it was hardly unique, as the long tradition of
Asclepius piety shows, from the Epidaurus inscriptions of
pre-Christian times (in Edelstein, *Asclepius* 1, T. 423-24)
down to Aristides' circle of sophisticated friends at the
Asclepius temple in Pergamum about the middle of the second
century C.E.

Aristides' theology included the familiar Greek
gods as well as the popular Egyptian deities Sarapis and
Isis (see Behr, 1968, 22-22, 25-26, and especially ch. 6).
He turned to Sarapis, and then later to Asclepius,[8] for the
same reason many other persons did: human physicians were
unable to provide healing.[9] It is Aristides' two years as
an incumbent at the Asclepius temple in Pergamum that

illustrate in some detail the social setting of Aristides'
piety as well as the representative nature of that piety.

The temple community fits well Berger and Luckmann's
designation "plausibility structure." The temple complex
itself was an imposing assemblage of monuments.[10] It
impressed itself on Aristides' subconscious and appears
repeatedly in his dreams (*Hieroi Logoi* 1.10-12, 30-32, 35;
Keil ed., pp. 378-79, 383-84). The temple personnel, who
also figure in his dreams, included a hereditary priesthood,
temple wardens, various attendants, and a chorus of singers
(see Behr, 1968, 30-31). The paeans of the latter appear
in his dreams (*Heiroi Logoi* 1.30, Keil ed., p. 383; 4.39,
Keil ed., p. 435) and were employed by one of his physicians to alleviate some of his symptoms (4.38, Keil ed.,
p. 435).

The temple ritual included daily rites with
lighting of the sacred lamps; purifications involving water
from the sacred well and the wearing of white robes;
speeches in the theater, in honor of Asclepius; ceremonies
with branches and torches; sacrifices; the incubations; and
festivals with games, poetry contests, and nocturnal vigils
(evidence in Behr, 1968, 32-35). These were significant
communal events, in which Aristides took an active part and
which appear in his dreams and figure in his therapy.

In addition, Aristides came to belong to a small
circle of cultivated men of considerable social status who
were connected with the temple or were incumbents there.
They discussed literary and intellectual issues as well as
their ailments and their dreams (see Behr, 1968, 42, 47-49,
190). This community within the Pergamum Asclepius
community gave further credibility to the therapy Asclepius
prescribed for Aristides. These companions urged him to
follow the god's leading and to return to the study and
practice of oratory. By reason of their rank or renown[11]
and their own belief in Asclepius' powers,[12] they constituted "significant others" for Aristides. In Behr's words
(1968, 47):

If at first, the God's enjoinders and approval seemed little more than
emanations from a world without substance, [their] . . . vigorous

support and encouragement . . . provided a real confirmation of what
was taking place, until faith in the God grew robust enough to stand
alone and Asclepius invaded the world of reality.

Within this setting Aristides experienced the
healings which were beyond the art of human physicians and
which he designates with various miracle terms.[13] He
continued to worship deities besides Asclepius, and in his
oration to Zeus he theorizes that Asclepius healed through
delegation of power from the supreme god, Zeus (*Or.* 43,
Keil ed.; cf. Behr, 1968, 72-73). In time of need or in
obedience to divine behest, Aristides wrote orations in
praise of various deities, or turned to such for help,
whether Zeus, Asclepius, Apollo,[14] Sarapis or Isis,[15]
Heracles,[16] Athena,[17] or Telesphorus.[18]

7.3 Aelius Aristides and the Savior Jesus

Is there any indication in Aristides' writings that he was
aware of the healing deity Jesus, called ὁ σωτήρ by many of
his followers even as Asclepius was by his, especially by
Aristides?[19] Had he been thus aware, what might have been
his assessment of Christian accounts of this Christ's
healings, past or present?

Like other educated persons of his time, such as
Galen, who was practicing in Pergamum around the year 160,[20]
and Celsus, who opposes Asclepius to Christ, Aristides was
probably cognizant of Christianity. It is attested for
Smyrna (his home city) and for Pergamum in the letters of
the book of Revelation, and for Smyrna also in the Ignatian
correspondence (references in BAG, s.v. Σμύρνα) at the
beginning of the second century as well as in the *Martyrdom
of Polycarp* around the middle of the century. One passage
in Aristides' oration *To Plato: In Defense of the Four*[21]
has sometimes been interpreted as an attack on Christians
and/or Jews.[22] Aristides does not name those he is
attacking, and this, together with ambiguities in his syntax[23] and in his invective, makes their identification
uncertain, a state of affairs reflected in the division of
scholars on this point. For our purposes this is not a
difficulty. The traits Aristides views as reprehensible in

the objects of his polemic--whether these are Christians,
Jews, pagan philosophers, or any confusion or combination
of these three--were accusations commonly leveled at each
of these groups. Whether or not he is attacking Christians, his polemic suggests what he finds--or would find--
objectionable in the Christian movement.

What Aristides attacks is the offense offered by
these persons to Greek society and tradition, seen in their
wilfullness,[24] shamelessness,[25] and disrespect, both in
attitude[26] and in speech;[27] their neglect of the common
weal[28] and their shirking of civic rites and duties,[29]
indeed their undermining of institutions like the household,[30] and their aloofness[31] and secretiveness.[32] Persons
guilty of such offenses were enemies of the present order,
of which Aristides was an honored member.[33] With respect
to the cultic aspect of that order, he, like Plutarch, came
from a priestly family, in this case of Olympian Zeus
(see Behr, 1968, 4). That is, his primary socialization
was in this cult, and his orations show that he remained
true to it, even as he remained devoted to the other
deities with which every Greek schoolboy grew up. His two
years in the Pergamum Asclepius community, which amounted
to an intensive process of socialization, won him over to
that Greek deity.

All this suggests that Aristides would not have
been receptive to Christianity. It had a reputation as an
enemy of the pagan order. Furthermore, the testimony of a
number of Christians indicates that part of the price of
entry to or acceptance in many Christian groups was a
nihilation of Asclepius in favor of Christ (see the works
cited in n. 1 of this chapter). A high price to pay, for a
person of Aristides' background in pagan cult and his
experience of Asclepius' wondrous power and beneficence.
Moreover, Asclepius' healings were untainted by some of the
offensive traits of the Christian *sōtēr*. Insofar as the
aura of secretiveness attaching to Christian rites also
attached to the wonders they claimed to perform (cf. above,
p. 60), these would fall in the same category as the
θαυμαστά Aristides condemns in the passage discussed above

(see n. 32 of this chapter). Aristides' visions of
Asclepius stand in a long tradition of such visions and (he
might argue) in favorable contrast to esoteric visions of a
nouveau deity[34]--a crucified man at that--of lowly and
shameful origins, as Celsus pointed out.[35] To Christian
apologists who appealed to Plato (*Rep.* 408b-c) and Pindar
(*Pythia* 3.54-58) in charging that Asclepius practiced
healing out of avarice and was powerless against Zeus's
thunderbolt,[36] Aristides might have replied that a god
would not be subject to degradation, as Christ was, and
that Christ, too, was powerless in the face of death.[37]
Against the traditions of Christ's exaltation Aristides
might have opposed the traditions of Asclepius' exaltation
(sources in Edelstein, *Asclepius* 1, T. 236-56), something
Aristides accepted, in any case (see n. 6 of this chapter).

    In Aristides one can see antithesis, implicit at
least, to Christianity and its miracle claims, and the
cultural and social context of such antithesis. Though
the manner and degree of Aristides' devotion to the healing
god Asclepius may be eccentric, that piety as such is not
atypical.[38] Aristides' elitist circle at Pergamum shared
in it as did the many other suppliants at the Asclepius
sanctuaries in Pergamum and a variety of other cities under
the Empire.[39] The popularity of the Asclepius cult in the
second century, among persons of many social and educational
strata,[40] at a time when many traditional worships were in
decline (cf. Edelstein, *Asclepius* 2, 115-16), may be
accounted for in various ways (ibid., 101-108, 111-25). It
would be inexplicable in a society which did not prize life
and health and in which illness did not have grave social
consequences (on these matters see ibid., 122-24, 174-75,
177-78). The looseness of warrants surrounding healings,
which we observed earlier (above, p. 15 and ch. 3.2.3),
made wondrous healings seem possible to many, while the
social settings of Asclepius healings which we observe with
Aristides (temple, rites, personnel, fellow incumbents) but
were not peculiar to his case (cf. Edelstein, *Asclepius* 2,
ch. 4), constituted plausibility structures for such
healings. The continued relation between the practice of

medicine and the healings of Asclepius, the patron of medicine, also contributed to belief in the god's powers.[41]
Another social dimension of the popularity of Asclepius
cult was the accessibility of the deity to the individual
and his or her concerns,[42] as is very evident in the case
of Aristides, who attributed the recovery of his health and
the salvaging of his career to Asclepius.[43]   Although
Aristides never mentions the Christian *sōtēr* as another
possible healing deity, it is clear that Jesus was unnecessary to him as a *sōtēr*, stood outside his social and
cultural world, and was repugnant to much in that world.
From another social and cultural matrix Celsus expresses
such repugnance sharply--the subject of the next chapter.

PHILOSOPHY, ASCLEPIUS, AND JESUS: CELSUS

The factors enumerated at the end of the preceding chapter
help to account for the presence of philosophers at the
Asclepius temple in Pergamum.[1] However, the canvas is
broader, as may be recalled from chapter five. There we
saw that philosophers constituted a counterculture critical
of the disorder entailed by divine interventions in the
cosmos. At the same time, however, having been reared in
the mainstream culture and continuing to live in it, they
generally affirmed it in some way as legitimate and necessary and found a niche for its rites and sometimes its
miracles (see above, ch. 5.1). Philosophers embodied a
tension between popular and critical thought in regard to
the extraordinary, with some inclined to be more critical,
some less so.

In the second century C.E. there is a fair amount
of evidence to support the thesis that philosophers were
generally inclined to be less critical in assessing extraordinary phenomena than in the centuries immediately preceding and more cordial toward religion generally and mainstream piety and its wonders specifically.[2] The shift
within the Academy from the critical questioning of
Arcesilas and Carneades to the more affirmative epistemology of Philo of Larissa and Antiochus of Ascalon in the
first century B.C.E. (see Pohlenz, 1970, vol. 1. 248-53),
eventuating in the Middle Platonism of the second century
C.E., with its religious concerns,[3] is an important element
in this change. The legacy of critical philosophical
thought is represented at full strength in persons like
Lucian of Samosata, the Celsus to whom he addresses his
portrait of Alexander of Abonoteichos (*Alex*. 1, 17, 21, 61),
and Sextus Empiricus (selections in de Vogel, 1964, 226-30),

while the tension between critical epistemology and mainstream piety and its wonders also persists and is evident
in Middle Platonists like Plutarch, Apuleius, Maximus of
Tyre, Celsus, and Justin.[4]

In analyzing the arguments between pagan and Christian apologists, Geffcken, noting how the antagonists often
employed the same weapons but only against the other side
and/or in defense of their own stance, characterized such
exchanges as "ein wahres Chaos der Polemik,"[5] classic
instances, one might say, of opponents "talking past" each
other. This is an apt description of Celsus' championing of
Asclepius cult as a foil to certain Christian miracle
claims. Epistemological arguments that Celsus mounts
against them would apply as well to the healings and divine
manifestations and communications in the Asclepius cult,
but Celsus does not make the application, thus suggesting
that the true warrants of his argument are not the ostensible ones but are to be sought rather in the social and
cultural setting of Celsus' polemic. Carl Andresen's
detailed exposition (1955) of this setting and of Celsus'
concern for its health and survival in the face of an
aggressive, burgeoning Christianity helps make intelligible
his inconsistency in argumentation. In terms of the sociology of knowledge, one can observe how such factors as
group loyalty, socialization, social status, and cultural
traditions motivate his argument and illuminate his quarrel
with Christianity.

8.1 Consistent Inconsistencies and their Social and Cultural Matrices

In reviewing the Asclepius traditions one observes that the
chief elements are much like many in the Jesus traditions.
A man renowned for healing and even for raising the dead is
yet powerless in the face of his own death, but after his
death is exalted and worshiped as a deity (cf. Edelstein,
Asclepius 2, 133-34). In the cult that grew up around
each, Asclepius and Jesus manifest themselves to their
worshipers, heal them, and reveal the future to them. Why,

despite the similarities between Jesus and Asclepius, does
Celsus reject the one and defend the other?

Asclepius, according to Celsus, is a deity elevated
to divine from human status, a benefactor of humankind in
his many deeds on their behalf, namely, his healings and
his predictions of the future. One sees here the typical
portrait of the hero: a being exalted to deity because of
more than human deeds or faculties and still beneficent
after his death (see ch. 2.2.1 above). Celsus mentions
other such heroes, both Greek and non-Greek (3.34; 7.35),
but does not place Jesus in this category even though he,
too, was credited with beneficent wonders--healings,
wondrous feedings, and resurrections--as Celsus is well
aware (1.68; 2.48). Such accounts he attributes to the
disciples' spinning of yarns.[6] He discredits the accounts
by questioning the authenticity of what they report[7] and
the motivation of those who claim such wonders.[8] On the
other hand, Celsus passes over without mention the traditions of Asclepius' raising of the dead (in Edelstein,
Asclepius 1, T. 66ff.), which were current in mainstream
piety[9] but were often disputed by philosophers and other
educated persons.[10] For Celsus to have acknowledged such
traditions would have conflicted with his Platonism, which
looked with disdain on the resurrection of the body (5.14;
see further, below, p. 108). The tension between mainstream
piety and the philosophical tradition is evident here, and
the inconsistency of Celsus' argumentation is seen again:
what he vehemently rejects in Jesus he conveniently ignores
in Asclepius.

Asclepius' helplessness before Zeus's thunderbolt
(see Edelstein, *Asclepius* 1, T. 232ff.) is likewise ignored
by Celsus when he takes signs of Jesus' helplessness--the
flight into Egypt (1.66) and the death on the cross (2.68)
--as disproof of divine favor, of Jesus' deity, and of his
ability to work miracles such as vanishing from the cross.
Celsus' Jew argues that if Jesus were indeed God, he could
not have run away nor have been bound and led away (2.9).
Jesus, a man dishonored, led away under arrest, and crucified, is not the pure and holy Logos that Christians should
offer as evidence that Jesus is the Son of God (2.31).

Other inconsistencies in Celsus' argumentation are seen in his application of epistemological criteria to Asclepius and Jesus traditions. Sense perceptions are to be carefully scrutinized to distinguish what *is* from what only *seems* to be, and multiple, public attestation of extraordinary phenomena is to be preferred to solitary experience of such phenomena by those already inclined to belief in them.

The first of these criteria was observed above in Celsus' questioning of the authenticity of marketplace marvels. By adducing these (1.68) Celsus both relativizes Christian claims to healings, resurrection, and the multiplication of loaves and seeks to show that errors in perception underlie the Christian claims as well as the wonders worked by non-Christian *goētes*. For Asclepius himself Celsus claims actual appearances, not visual illusions (3.24, οὐ φάσμα αὐτὸ τοῦτο). He claims the same for other pagan heroes.[11] Many persons, both Greeks and barbarians, saw, and still see, Asclepius healing the sick and foretelling the future (3.24). Other Greek heroes also manifest themselves regularly (ἀεί)--not once and stealthily (οὐχ ἅπαξ παραρρύενταʃ)--to those who so desire (7.35).

Standing in contrast is what Celsus observes among Christians. They impiously reject pagan theophanies as mere phantoms (*eidōla*)[12] while at the same time worshiping a man who is worse than a real phantom and, indeed, is no longer a phantom but is now dead (7.36; similarly, 7.68). Who saw Jesus risen from the dead, and how often did he appear? Only once, and stealthily (7.35), to a frenzied woman, and perhaps to another person under the same spell (a reference to Peter?); her mental state disposed her to dreaming, and wanting to see Jesus risen, she imagined, through an error in perception (a common experience), that she did see him--or else she wanted to astound others with this marvel and thus to pave the way for other begging prophets.[13] Why did the risen Jesus not make public appearances, specifically to his enemies (2.63), instead of only to persons who were already his followers (2.70)?[14] Similarly, with the baptism of Jesus: Who besides Jesus heard the voice or saw the bird (1.41; the bird was a *phasma*)?

Celsus' inconsistency in argumentation here is seen in his treatment of the story of Aristeas of Proconnesus, the man who wondrously (δαιμονίωſ) disappeared from among humans and then reappeared visible (ἐναργῶſ) and later visited many parts of the world and recounted many marvels (θαυμαστά) (3.26). Celsus evidently cites this story in order to relativize accounts of Jesus' resurrection: just because someone is reported as wondrously disappearing and then reappearing does not vouch for his divinity. Whether or not Celsus personally credits the Aristeas story,[15] for the purposes of his argument he treats it as true, without troubling himself about the epistemological canons of multiple attestation and careful scrutiny of sense perception by which he measures Christian claims of resurrection appearances.[16]

This is not to say that Celsus is uncritical of pagan resurrection accounts. He characterizes such traditions (and, therefore, Christian resurrection claims as well) as put forward to beguile the simple (2.55); and he expresses skepticism--common enough, as we have seen (above, ch. 2.1 and pp. 37-38)--regarding resuscitation of the dead, though his phrasing of this in terms of resurrection of the body (2.55) is doubtless informed by his Platonism (see above, p. 106). But when confronted with Christian resurrection claims, this tension between affirmation and disapprobation of pagan accounts is resolved in favor of affirmation. Nihilation of Christian claims takes precedence over logical consistency.[17]

Origen more than once (2.33; 7.45) notes the inconsistency in Celsus' argumentation. In the modern period Harnack called it a "puzzle" (*Rätsel*) that Celsus (and Origen) should so mingle "schlimmster Aberglaube" and "verständiger Kritik" in defending (respectively) Asclepius (and Christ).[18] Prescinding from the judgments implied by Harnack's terminology, it may be observed that the phenomenon to which it points is less puzzling when one keeps in view the social and cultural context in which Celsus stands

and which he sees himself as called to defend over against
the Christians. In his defense of oracular revelations by
Asclepius and other heroes this context emerges more
clearly than in the passages considered in the preceding
paragraphs. We have seen that Celsus credited such revelations (3.24; 7.35), even though, as Origen notes (8.45),
some philosophical schools did not do so.[19] Some did,
however,[20] so that there was a tension in this respect not
only between philosophical and mainstream cultures, but
within philosophy as well.[21] Celsus falls in the camp of
those philosophers who affirm revelation through oracles.[22]
That this is an article of belief for him is indicated both
by his impassioned recital of the significant role played
by oracles in pagan society and culture in the past (7.45)
and by his neglecting to employ here the epistemological
criteria he applies to Christian wonders, either as a test
or as a defense of the report of oracular revelations in
the pagan sphere. Origen, therefore, quite rightly asks
why Celsus affirms such revelations in the pagan sphere as
clearly perceptible[23] but regards as *mythoi* wonders attributed in "our" writings to Jews or to Jesus and his
followers (7.45).

Again, this is not to say that Celsus is uncritical
of pagan myths. In one passage he explicitly states his
disbelief in the old *mythoi* (1.67), and in others his
attitude is critical (see Andresen, 1955, 51-53), a stance
deriving from the philosophical tradition generally and
more specifically from his (Middle) Platonism, with its
transcendent deity.[24] Over against Christianity, however,
Celsus is willing to affirm the myths, saying, for example,
that they evidence the beneficence of their protagonists,
so that the myths "do not seem incredible; but you, [scil.
Jesus,] what have you done, in deed or in word, that is
good or admirable?" (1.67).

In Celsus' eyes Christianity represents a departure
from that ancient culture which Greeks and non-Greeks, past
and present, have shared,[25] held in esteem, and sought to
inculcate in their children as a continuing heritage. His
loyalty to this culture and its social matrices, despite

reservations he shared with philosophers and educated
persons generally about many aspects of it, motivates his
often logically inconsistent attacks on the Christian movement. This view of ancient culture as the foil to Christianity and the canon by which it is to be measured is a
recurring element in Celsus' treatise, if indeed it is not
the theme of the entire work (thus Wifstrand, 1942,
followed by Andresen, 1955, 32). "There is an ancient,
primal doctrine [ἀρχαῖος ἄνωθεν λόγος] that has always been
a concern of the wisest peoples and of cities and of wise
men" (1.14c). Celsus then lists (1.16b) various bearers,
both Greek and non-Greek, of the ancient doctrine (*logos*)
that he is defending against Christian corruptions of it,
and in 1.14c and 1.16a gives a catalog of ancient and wise
peoples, both Greek and non-Greek, who adhere to that
ancient custom (*nomos*) that he sees Christianity as intent
on destroying. These two motifs are then pursued in the
various parts[26] of Celsus' treatise. Celsus' defense of
the Asclepius cult and of much of popular pagan piety, as
well as his attack on Christian miracle claims, are but
aspects of his defense of ancient culture generally.

This culture is threatened, if not by the growth
and size of the Christian movement,[27] then certainly by its
character, which undermines culture and society as perceived by Celsus. Unlike adherents of pagan religions,
Christians deliberately shut themselves off from other
people.[28] They shirk military service (8.73) and exercise
of public office which sustains laws and piety.[29] They
constitute secret societies, contrary to the laws,[30] and
practice and teach their doctrines in secret.[31] Their
aniconism is symptomatic of secret societies[32] and accords
with their general rejection of and contempt for pagan cult
evident in their intolerance of temples, altars, and
images,[33] their actual ridicule of pagan cult and cult
narratives,[34] of deities,[35] and of images,[36] and their
designation of the latter as phantoms or idols.[37] Their
incomprehension of, and alienation from, pagan culture is
shown by their euhemerizing (3.22) and demonizing (7.62)
interpretations of pagan deities.

While familiar to educated pagans, such theories
were not necessarily employed by them, as they were by many
Christians, to nihilate pagan cult.[38] For Celsus such
attitudes on the part of Christians are pathognomic symptoms
of Christian rejection of that ancient *nomos* that he sees
as vital to life in the ancient world.[39] This rejection is
not surprising, however, in view of the origin of Christians (and of Jews) in a revolt.[40] However, Jews, along
with other peoples, at least have their own *nomos*,[41]
whereas Christians do not. The latter are nouveaux, unable
or unwilling to reveal their origins or the originator of
their hereditary laws.[42] In point of fact, their origins
lie with the Jews (5.33). Yet since they have rebelled
against the Jews (5.33), what ancient *nomoi* can they
possibly have? Rebellion against society brings novelty.[43]

In a passage that is revealing of his view of a
necessary relation between religion and society, Celsus
argues that since Christians choose to participate in the
institutions of society such as marriage and family, then
they should offer homage to the deities or daimons[44] placed
over these institutions (8.55). "For it is unjust for
those who share in what one knows is their [scil. the
daimons'] possession not to offer something to them" (8.55).
But, as we have seen, Christians do not do so, and indeed
do quite the opposite, and therefore constitute a threat
to existing social institutions. Celsus' concern for pagan
culture and society over against this threat is the consistent warrant of his often logically inconsistent arguments
against Christian miracle claims and on behalf of pagan
ones such as those in the Asclepius cult.

Similarly, with the ancient doctrine (*logos*) taught
by the wise men of various peoples (above, p. 110) and
vital to ancient culture. As an instance Celsus cites the
relation of humans to deity. There is in humans that which
is superior to their earthly part and akin to deity
(συγγενὲς θεοῦ) and which, when it is healthy, yearns for
its kin and longs to hear and be reminded of it
(ἀναμιμνήσκεσθαι).[45] However, unless one follows the *logos*
(i.e., the ancient doctrine) and those versed in it,[46] one

is sure to be deceived and end up like begging priests of
Cybele, diviners, followers of Mithras or Sabazios or
apparitions (φάσματα) of Hecate, or others whose ignorance
and gullibility are exploited by rapscallions.[47] Christians are to be included among those whose belief is
uninformed by *logos*,[48] as is evident (a) from their rejection of questioning and of providing of warrants for their
beliefs in favor of implicit belief[49] and (b) from their
deliberate appeal to the immature, the ignorant, and those
unschooled in Greek thought.[50] Their making a virtue of
foolishness (1.9) and of ignorance (3.44) sets them apart
from a person of Celsus' background and from the ideals of
Greek *paideia*. "Why is it bad to have been educated and to
have studied the best doctrines[51] and to be and to seem
intelligent?"[52]

In the terminology of the sociology of knowledge,
by rejecting pagan education, specifically Greek *paideia*,
Christians exclude an essential element in the process of
socialization through which the ancient *nomos* and *logos* are
transmitted from one generation to the next. In one
passage (3.55) Celsus gives a glimpse of how he sees this
occurring, to the undermining of pagan culture and its
social matrices. Christians, likened by Celsus to disrepu-
table persons seen in the marketplaces, are not found in
the company of intelligent men (φρονίμων ἀνδρῶν) but rather
with adolescent boys and slaves[53] and stupid people (3.50);
they prey upon vulnerable sorts--women and children--when
they are alone with them in private houses. There they
urge disobedience to fathers and to teachers but obedience
to themselves, who alone are able to tell their victims how
to live and arrive at perfection (τὸ τέλειον) and how to
achieve well-being in their homes. They vilify fathers and
teachers as foolish and senseless, occupied with empty talk,
and capable of nothing good. But when actually confronted
by a father or teacher or any intelligent person, they
either scatter in all directions or whisper to the children
that in the presence of such empty-headed and corrupt
persons (who punish children!) they are unwilling and
unable to give any instruction. In this vignette one sees

two cultures and their social matrices in conflict, each
contending for the loyalty of the next generation. It also
offers an example of Celsus' view of the subversive nature
of the Christian movement, in accord with its origins in a
revolt (above, p. 111). Celsus' description of Christian
attempts to win followers fits Nock's delineation of conversion in the Greco-Roman world: the candidates turn
their backs on their present way of life and embrace
another which presents "a permanent object of desire."

The elitist social consciousness out of which
Celsus speaks is indicated by these and other passages in
which Christianity is presented as a religion of the lower
strata of society.[54] The Christians represented in 3.55 as
leading women and children astray are, by occupation, wood-
workers, shoemakers or workers in leather (σκυτοτόμουϛ),
and bleachers or fullers (κναφειϛ). How preposterous that
persons of such lowly occupation and education,[55] from whom
one would properly expect only silence in the presence of
their elders and owners,[56] should undertake to instruct the
young. And how incongruous that when this furtive Christian instruction in private houses encounters difficulties
with the persons entrusted with this responsibility it
should adjourn to the shops where these menial slaves
pursue their occupations[57] and that there the children, and
the women who accompany them, will attain perfection (τὸ
τέλειον), a term associated in Greek tradition with high
and holy things such as deity and the mystery religions![58]
With this passage may be compared others in which Celsus
says that Christians, in contrast to Socrates who claimed
only human wisdom (6.12, citing Plato, Apol. 20D), claim to
impart divine wisdom--and to whom? To the most uneducated
and most ignorant persons and to slaves.[59] In one of his
most acerbic passages (4.23) Celsus ridicules the assemblies
of Jews (συνεδρεύουσιν) and Christians (ἐκκλησιάζουσι)--
exalted gatherings in their own eyes--by likening them to
argumentative and narcissistic councils of bats, ants,
frogs, and worms. Andresen (1955, 227) points to Celsus'
view of Christians (and Jews) as nobodies, their theology
reflecting their social circumstances: "Synhedrion und

Ekklesia galten ihm [Kelsos] als Winkelstätten, als
Schlupflöcher der kleinen Leute. . . . Kelsianisch ist vor
allem die Art, wie die Theologie der Gegner als Reflex
ihrer sozialen Verhältnisse verstanden wird. . . . Eine
kleinbürgerliche Theologie der kleinen Leute!" Christians
are in fact ignorant of the true way to God (7.36; cf. also
above, n. 49 of this chapter), and their teaching is such
as appeals only to the ignorant, that is, persons of the
lower social levels with whom Christians are seen in public
and whom they seek to win over (above, p. 112). By contrast
cultivated men (χαριεστέρουϛ) are not prepared to be
deceived (6.14) and, if they are like Celsus, follow Plato
who provides a foil to the Christians' mode of teaching in
that, unlike Christians (above, p. 112), he does not fail
to supply warrants (λογισμόν)--even when speaking of the
ineffable (6.10a)--and discloses the source of his teaching
(6.10b), and, unlike Jesus, does not claim to have come
down from heaven (6.10b).

These data accord with Christianity's humble
origins. The founder came from a Jewish village, the
illegitimate offspring of a poor country woman whose means
of livelihood was spinning; married to a carpenter, she was
sent packing by him after her adultery and while wandering
ignominiously about secretly gave birth to Jesus; he,
because of his poverty, hired out as a worker in Egypt
where he learned the extraordinary powers on which he based
his claim to deity (1.28). Though Celsus' vignette doubtless draws on anti-Christian, probably Jewish polemic (see
Lods, 1941), his own elitist sympathies are clear from the
detail with which he repeats this tale of sordid happenings
among the simple inhabitants of a rustic village and from
the tacit assumption that such a tale constitutes prima
facie evidence against Jesus.[60]

Similarly with Celsus' ridicule (6.34) of the
references by Christians "everywhere" (πανταχοῦ) to "the
tree of life or resurrection of the flesh through the tree":
these presumably derive from the occupation of the Christians' teacher and his manner of death, and had he met a
different death or pursued a different occupation, the

Christians' vocabulary and conception of salvation would
have differed accordingly (see 6.34 for the details and the
sarcastic tone). A final elitist touch is the conclusion
that even an old woman who sings children to sleep with a
story would be ashamed to whisper such things to them.[61]

Going behind Jesus and the Christians to the Jews,
Celsus points to their origins in the tending of flocks and
in slavery. They were goatherds and shepherds who were
deceived by Moses into thinking, without cause (ἀλόγωſ),
that there is only one God. With obvious sarcasm Celsus
speaks of the Jews as that "illustrious and extraordinary
race" (λαμπρὸν καὶ θεσπέσιον Ἰουδαίων γένοſ) who were
commanded by their leader to dwell and pasture their flocks
on worthless lands[62] somewhere outside of Egypt (4.47).
Their escape from Egypt was a flight of runaway slaves
(δραπέταſ) who never did anything worth mentioning and have
never been held in regard or esteem,[63] as is evident from
Greek silence on their history (4.31). The details in the
biblical traditions are cleverly employed by Celsus, as
Andresen observes, "um das soziale Milieu der Juden
möglichst abträglich zu schildern."[64] In designating
Christians or those to whom they appeal as ἄγροικοι (3.55;
3.75b; 6.14; 8.49), literally "rural," Celsus may be
alluding to these Jewish roots of Christianity;[65] or he may
simply be characterizing them, according to common usage
(see Andresen, 1955, 177, n. 15), as boorish,[66] even as he
elsewhere refers to them as ἰδιῶται (1.27) and their
teaching as ἰδιωτικόſ (1.27; 3.68), i.e., as "simple," in
the senses "untutored," "uncomplicated," and "obtuse";[67] or
he may be doing both. When Celsus wishes to compare Christians with contemporary religious groups he singles out
non-Greek mysteries, which are also characterized by a
mindless (ἀλόγωſ) piety associated with lack of schooling
(τῇ ἰδιωτείᾳ) (1.9).

Thus the Christians' origins, their occupations
(and, implicitly, their income), the slave status of some,
their education, the places they frequent, the company they
keep and are allowed to keep, and their social and cultural
affinities with other groups in the Greco-Roman world all

serve to locate them among the lower social strata. Whatever his actual social status, Celsus' polemic against
Christians, and against persons and groups he regards as
their social peers, demonstrates that he does not view himself as belonging to the lower social strata, as do the
Christians.

Celsus' view of Christians as credulous with regard
to extraordinary phenomena, noted earlier (above, pp. 106,
107), comports with his view of Christians' low social
status and poor education. Unwarranted belief is what one
may expect of such persons (above, p. 112). In the terminology employed in this study, Celsus' conflict with Christians over their miracle claims is in part a conflict with
Christian popular cultic piety. His class consciousness,
his level of education generally, and his philosophical
training specifically, distance him from such piety and
provide him with criteria by which to assess its extraordinary phenomena and with options to interpret them in
other than the popular way. That his attack on popular
cultic piety is selective, rejecting the Christian expression wholeheartedly and sometimes pagan manifestations of
such piety and yet affirming much in the latter, illustrates
the tension between philosophy and popular piety generally
but may now be seen also as motivated by his perception of
Christians as alien to and subversive of ancient culture
and its social matrices. Whatever its credulity and
philosophical naivete, pagan popular piety, of which
Asclepius piety is an instance, was still a part of his
social world and Celsus was able to affirm many of its
extraordinary phenomena that his philosophical training
might have led him to disavow.

8.2 Celsus and Christian Allegorists

Had Celsus been aware of Christians with a philosophical
sophistication like his own or greater than he credits
Christians with generally, would he have given them a more
cordial hearing? That he was acquainted, directly or
indirectly, with such Christians, who differed from those
described in the passages just discussed, is indicated by a

number of passages which show that his view of Christianity
as fissiparated (3.10, 12; 5.61-64) is not merely his
polemical invention but is based on knowledge of a variety
of Christian groups and/or sources.[68] In 1.9, for example,
the fact that he qualifies with "some" (τινας) his description of Christians as refusing reasoned discourse points
to an awareness that not all Christians do so. This is
borne out by 1.27, where Celsus speaks of "some" (τινας)
Christians who are "moderate, reasonable, and intelligent,
and prepared to allegorize,"[69] and by 1.17 and 4.38, 48-50,
where "the more reasonable" (οἱ ἐπιεικέστεροι) of the Jews
and Christians are said to be ashamed of the Jewish
creation and other stories and take refuge in allegory.
Celsus' assertion that "some" (τινας) Christians misunderstand Plato (6.19a) presupposes study of Plato on the part
of at least some Christians. The whole section 6.1-7.58,
in which Celsus seeks to demonstrate Christianity's
dependence on (but misunderstanding of) pagan culture,[70]
presupposes acquaintance on the part of some Christians
with Plato, whom Celsus refers to or quotes passim.[71]
Immediately preceding this section Celsus speaks of Christians possessed of some learning who claim to know more
than Jews do.[72]

These Christians, too, Celsus rejects, manifesting
an inconsistency that again points to social and cultural
factors as the real warrants of his argumentation. Thus,
though he himself allegorizes Homer and the cult narratives
of certain mysteries (6.42), in accord with long-standing
philosophical tradition, he characterizes Jewish stories
that "the more reasonable Jews and Christians attempt to
allegorize somehow" as "manifestly fables of the worst
sort" and "not susceptible of allegorical interpretation,"[73]
while their attempts at allegorization are "much more
shameful and more absurd than the fables" themselves.[74]
Celsus' reasoning here is instructive:

8.2.1 He offers no hermeneutical principle about when
an offensive story may be allegorized and when not. But
his concern is evident: to demonstrate that stories in the

Jewish and Christian tradition which are absurd or offensive to persons standing outside that tradition are
irredeemable through allegorization, a common device for
"saving the phenomena" (cf. above, ch. 3.3). Celsus thus
again justifies his rejection of Christianity, even as
interpreted by the "more reasonable" Christians acquainted
with Plato and capable of allegorization. His special
pleading, permitting allegorization of Greek traditions but
not of Jewish traditions, indicates that his polemic does
not proceed according to canons of formal logic. The
warrant that makes his argument intelligible is that Christianity is an alien culture that does not share in the
ancient *logos*. His conflict with Christian allegorists is
a communal conflict in which Greek religious traditions as
interpreted by philosophical thinkers are pitted against
Jewish religious traditions as interpreted by Jews and
Christians acquainted with allegorical interpretation. The
Jewish "fables" to which Celsus refers in the passages
cited above are various of the Genesis accounts--creation
(4.36) and fall (4.36, 39-40),[75] flood (4.41), procreation
beyond the age for procreation (4.43; "most absurd"
[ἀτοπωτάτην], says Celsus), the worse-than-"Thyestian"
story of Lot and his daughters (4.45), the Joseph cycle
(4.47). These accounts are not intrinsically more shameful
or unlikely than some of the actions ascribed to pagan
deities, the immorality and improbability of which Christian apologists were quick to point out,[76] for which they
had ample precedent in the philosophical tradition itself.[77]
As noted earlier (above, p. 115), however, for Celsus the
Jews are an insignificant people lacking in the wise men
who transmitted the ancient *logos* and whose traditions
stand apart from that *logos*. Their extraordinary tales are,
therefore, a priori not susceptible or worthy of the
allegorization that was the customary method of harmonizing
such troublesome phenomena with philosophical teaching. By
giving the Genesis accounts a literal reading, Celsus
readily justifies his rejection of them as "fables" (μῦθοι),
even as Marcion and Apelles, rejecting Christian

allegorizations of narratives in the Jewish scriptures,
reject the deity who figures in them (see below, pp. 131-
34).

8.2.2 Celsus views Jewish and Christian allegorical
interpretations as incongruous with what they are intended
to allegorize. The allegories that are "much more shameful
and more absurd than the fables" themselves, says Celsus,
"join together things utterly impossible to reconcile with
some bizarre and wholly senseless foolishness."[78] Celsus
does not specify the "foolishness" further, whether he has
in mind the materials being allegorized or that with which
they are linked. Origen interjects that the allegorists
Celsus may have in mind are Philo and "Aristobulus."[79]
Celsus himself, however, gives as an example the now lost
Dispute of Papiscus and Jason.[80] Unfortunately he dismisses
it with a few words of contempt and says nothing about its
allegorizing.[81] Although it is doubtful that Celsus bases
his opinion of Christian allegorization solely on the
Dispute (see below, ch. 9.4), which Origen himself characterizes as undeserving of the attention of "the more
intelligent persons" (τοὺς συνετωτέρους), it accords with
his general disapproval of Christians on cultural grounds
that as a foil[82] to the *Dispute*, and evidently to Jewish
and Christian allegorizing generally, he posits some
typically Platonic teaching: that the soul is immortal,
made by God, whereas the body is secondary, the work of
immortal beings,[83] there being no difference between body
of human, beast, or insect since all are equally subject to
corruption.[84] For Celsus, Christian writings stand outside
the pale of philosophy, one of the most important elements
of the ancient *logos*. If in their allegorizing Christians
(and Jews) employ Plato, who for Celsus is the sum of
ancient wisdom and the shaping force of the ancient *logos*
(see Andresen, 1955, 70, 126ff.), they earn no plaudits
from Celsus for doing so.[85]

8.3 Celsus and Christian Gnostics
Some Christians toward whom Celsus might have been expected

to show sympathy in view of their docetic and/or non-
literal interpretation of extraordinary phenomena in the
Christian tradition are those called "gnostics" by themselves or others (see App. D, "On the Definition of
'Gnostic'"). Over half a century ago W. Völker (1926)
called attention to affinities between certain of Celsus'
critiques of Jesus traditions and gnostic "corrections" of
the same. Is it possible to discern how Celsus viewed, or
might have viewed, some of the gnostic interpretations of
extraordinary phenomena?

Whether in referring to self-professed "gnostics"
Celsus has in mind a specific group or is employing a
general term is difficult to say (5.61c; cf. App. D below).
However, in the fragments preserved by Origen, Celsus seems
to refer to several different groups which others have
classified as gnostic. The diagram described by Celsus
(6.24, 25, 30, 33, 34, 38), the significant role assigned
to the serpent of the narrative of the fall (6.28), and the
negative view of the God of the Jews (6.27) accords
generally with what other sources report concerning the
Ophites.[86] The "Simonians" or "Helenians" also receive
passing mention (5.62a), as do Marcellians, "Harpocratians,"
and followers of Mariamne and Martha (5.62b).[87] Celsus
also speaks of Christians who "call some psychics and
others pneumatics,"[88] leading Origen to suggest that Celsus
may be referring to Valentinians.[89] Celsus mentions
Marcion and Marcionites explicitly (5.62c), at several
points describes teachings like those ascribed to Marcion
by his Christian opponents,[90] and is familiar with the
conflicts between Marcion(ites) and other Christians.[91]
Whether Marcion and Marcionites are to be classed as
"gnostic" has been a matter of dispute among scholars,
though the pendulum has gradually swung in that direction,
or at least away from Harnack's view of Marcion as a
"biblical theologian."[92] Whatever the label employed, at
certain points Marcion and his followers show affinities
with some of the concerns of Celsus and gnostics and may
therefore profitably be discussed here. The differences
between Marcionite teaching on extraordinary phenomena and

common gnostic interpretation of them are also illuminating
in this context.

In citing these various groups Celsus writes as a
polemicist, not a historian of religion (cf. n. 18 of this
chapter), and his piece shows little concern for sharp or
accurate differentiation of one gnostic group from another,
even were that possible in view of the fluid boundaries
between them.[93] Nor does he make anything of the interpretation of some of the extraordinary phenomena of Christian
tradition by various gnostic groups. If he knew such
interpretations, it does not come to light in the extant
fragments of his work. Yet these interpretations show
close affinities with some of the premises of his own
objections to Christian claims of extraordinary phenomena.
Given these premises, Celsus might have accorded some of
these interpretations recognition as attempts to reconcile
Christian traditions with pagan culture. But given his
view of Christians as persons subversive of pagan culture
and society, such recognition is unlikely, even had he been
acquainted with such interpretations, any more than Aelius
Aristides would have transferred his loyalties from the
savior Asclepius to the savior Jesus.

8.3.1 Deity in Humanity: Gnostic Christologies

Some of Celsus' sharpest disagreements with Christians
come at the points where he sees their traditions violating
the premise that deity is distinct from matter and remote
from it. Over against Christian claims to divine incarnation, for example, Celsus objects that deity is not
constituted to love a corruptible body (οὐ πεφυκὼς ἐρᾶν
φθαρτοῦ σώματος) and, moreover, would hardly have become
enamored of a woman of such lowly social status as Jesus'
mother (1.39; on her social status cf. above, p. 114). Had
God wished to send down a spirit, he was capable of forming
a body without having to breathe into the womb of a woman
and involving his spirit in such pollution (μίασμα) (6.73).
Deity would certainly not have had a body like that of
Jesus (1.69a), born as he was (1.69b), eating as he did
(1.70a), and speaking with a human voice (1.70b).

Christians are deluded in thinking themselves religious
when they accord deity to Jesus--who was formed of a mortal
body (3.41) and had flesh more corruptible than the gold,
silver, and stone (3.42a) from which images are fashioned.

With these statements one may compare tendencies of
gnostic groups toward (as Nock put it) "restrictions upon
direct intercourse between the divine and the human" and "a
repugnance to the idea of full incarnation" (Nock, 1948,
258; in 1972, vol. 2, 679). In the christology associated
with the name of Ptolemaeus,[94] the second-century Valentinian, the Savior "puts on" a psychic Christ[95] so devoid
of the material that he is invisible.[96] In order that he
may be perceptible to the senses he receives a body--the
body of Jesus[97]--divinely fashioned[98] in a virgin[99] by
ineffable art[100] from invisible, psychic substance.[101] The
Savior, the Christ, and Jesus are thus distanced from the
materiality and pollution that Celsus takes to be
inevitably associated with human birth. Other Jesus traditions are interpreted by this christology along similar
lines. The "I am" sayings spoken by Jesus (in the
Johannine tradition) show that Jesus was actually "other"
than those elements he assumed (*Exc. Theod.* 61.1), while
the fact that (in the Synoptic tradition) he speaks of his
suffering and death in the third person demonstrates his
impassibility (61.4). The Spirit which descended on him at
the Jordan left him, so that death might work its effect on
his body (61.6); but the Savior, repulsing the ray of power
that had come upon Jesus (ἀναστείλας τὴν ἐπελθοῦσαν ἀκτίνα
τῆς δυνάμεως), destroyed death and raised his mortal body,
but after first banishing passions from it (6.17). That
is, even as Jesus' body was quite out of the ordinary to
begin with, the body thus raised is also other than
ordinary.

Other gnostic christologies are similar in adhering
to common Jesus traditions while interpreting them doceti-
cally.

The Ophites mentioned above, for example, view
Jesus (according to Irenaeus) as a man fathered from a
virgin by a divine emanation in order that he might be a

pure vessel (*vas mundum*) for the Christ and Sophia (from
above), their descent on him resulting in Jesus Christ.[102]
Before the crucifixion the Christ and Sophia leave Jesus
(*Adv. h.* 1.30.13; Harvey ed., 1.28.7), thus preserving
their impassibility. The miracles that had commenced with
their descent cease with their ascent (ibid.). As in the
Ptolemaic christology outlined above, the Christ revives
Jesus' crucified body, constituted now not of flesh and
blood but a *corpus animale et spiritale*, with everything
worldly returned to the world.[103]

        Turning to an early second-century gnostic,
Basilides, one observes a christology which, though
probably not as docetic as Irenaeus portrays it,[104] yet
emphatically distances deity from the world. Basilides
employs a series of negatives in order to stress deity's
transcendence,[105] and his Jesus is an abstract figure whose
ministry, to be sure, is said to have taken place in a
similar way (ὁμοίωϛ) to what is written in "the gospels"
(Hippolytus, *Ref.* 7.27.8) but whose mission is to effect
differentiation of the undifferentiated cosmos[106] and to
free the "third sonship" (7.26.10; 7.27.11-12). With
Celsus' emphatic assertion--over against Christian incarnation claims--that deity does not come down (*C. Cels.* 4.2-4,
11, 14; 5.2), one may compare Basilides' interpretation of
the relation between deity and world in common Christian
traditions. The gospel "truly came" into the world, and
yet "nothing came down from above, and the blessed sonship
did not become separated from that incomprehensible and
blessed non-existent God."[107] The movement, is, rather,
from below upwards, thus safeguarding divine transcendence,
as is clear from the simile employed by Basilides here: as
Indian naphtha is ignited by a mere glance falling upon it
from afar,[108] so also "from below, from the formlessness of
the heap, the powers reach as far up as the sonship,"[109]
that is, up to "the blessed sonship beyond the boundary"[110]
between the cosmos and what is above the cosmos.[111] When
light descends on Jesus, it is light from the Hebdomad (*Ref.*
7.26.8), i.e., from the planetary region below the Ogdoad,
which light, in turn, has descended from the Ogdoad (7.26.8)

and is removed from the non-existent deity.[112] In the
resurrection of Jesus that which rises is not flesh but,
rather, the psychic part (ψυχικὸν αὐτοῦ μέροʃ), which came
from the Hebdomad and here returns to it (7.27.10). In
support of these various statements Basilides cites scriptures from the Christian tradition (e.g., 7.22.3-4; 7.25.1-
4; 7.26.2-4; etc.).

In these gnostic christologies Celsus' principal
objections would seem to be met: deity's transcendence is
safeguarded and Jesus is distanced from the material both
in his incarnation and resurrection. That deity is capable
of fashioning a body, as Celsus says, is here stated as
indeed having happened in the case of Jesus; possessing
such a body he would not have been guilty of the material
eating and speaking that Celsus finds offensive in Jesus.
Given such a Jesus, how might Celsus have responded to him?
In the continuation of the passage outlined above on
p. 122, Celsus gives an answer. Even were the offense of
Jesus' body removed by his putting off bodily traits[113]--
or through docetic interpretations by gnostics--it is clear
what choice Celsus would make: "But having put off these
[bodily traits], will he then be a god? Why not rather
Asclepius, Dionysus, and Heracles?"[114]

True to his consistent inconsistency noted earlier
regarding popular cultic piety--pagan and Christian--Celsus
again chooses the former over the latter. Jesus, Asclepius,
Dionysus, and Heracles, through their divine and human
parentage, all participate in the pollution of materiality,
but Jesus is not part of pagan culture whereas Asclepius,
Dionysus, and Heracles are. Celsus cites pagan traditions
of liaisons of the divine with the human (1.37) in order to
relativize Christian claims of Jesus' virgin birth but
ignores the fact that his critique of such claims (1.28,
39) would also apply to the pagan stories. This critique,
and those noted above of divine incarnation in Jesus, root
in the typically Middle Platonic doctrine of transcendent
deity (see p. 109 above). Justin reconciles this doctrine
with Christian traditions of incarnation (see below, ch.
9.4). Celsus turns it against such traditions. Whatever

their affinities with Celsus at this point, the Ptolemaic
Valentinians, for their part, choose Jesus, interpreting
extraordinary phenomena in the Jesus traditions to make
them less offensive, often drawing on the scriptures in
their Christian culture in order to do so (cf. above,
p. 122, and, further, *Exc. Theod.* 61.5), even as they might
have interpreted Asclepius traditions in the same way had
they looked on Asclepius as their savior. Unlike Aelius
Aristides, Celsus does not regard Asclepius as his savior,
but he does view Asclepius--an important figure in pagan
culture and society--as a savior of some people, as we
noted earlier. He is therefore prepared to overlook in
Asclepius and similar figures that which is, in fact,
offensive to his philosophical presuppositions. He is not
willing to do the same with the Christians' savior. Whatever the affinities between these gnostic christologies and
Celsus' objections to popular Christian views of incarnation, and whatever the gnostics' social standing,[115] to
which much of Celsus' elitist ridicule noted earlier would
not apply, their loyalty to Christian tradition would, in
his eyes, count as prima facie evidence against them and
their interpretation of Christian miracle claims.

Similarly with Celsus and Marcion(ites). Earlier
we observed the difficulty of determining whether Celsus'
knowledge of Marcion(ites) was based on first-hand knowledge of persons and/or sources or, rather, upon anti-
Marcionite polemic by other Christians.[116] The extant
fragments of the *Alethes Logos* do not, in any case, take
notice of Marcionite views on Jesus' incarnation which in
some respects show affinities with Celsus' own view of the
relation between deity and humankind. Thus Marcionite
aversion to matter and its creator,[117] as seen with respect
to the incarnation in Marcion's excision of the genealogy[118]
and birth narrative[119] from the Gospel of Luke and Pauline
letters and in his portrayal of the Christ of the good God
as a phantasm who in the fifteenth year of Tiberius
descended from the supreme heaven[120] in the form of a
man[121] (like the angels in the Abraham and Lot story)[122]
and performed miracles by his word alone without recourse

to matter,[123] may be compared with Celsus' view of deity as remote from matter, capable of manifesting its presence among humans without recourse to the polluting process of human reproduction, through a body that would assuredly be different from ordinary human bodies (on these Celsian views see above, p. 121). To one reared in the tradition of pagan polytheism the fact that Marcionite theology had multiple deities (i.e., the just God and the good God and their respective Christs) might be interesting but ultimately no less offensive than other Christian theology because the deities originated outside pagan religion and stood apart from it, the Marcionites in their devotion to the good God and his Christ being at least as exclusivistic as other Christians.[124] The Marcionite Christ, too, though passing some of Celsus' tests of a respectable deity, would nonetheless prove unacceptable, for, despite Marcion's interpretation of Jesus' incarnation in the direction of such tests, he yet retains certain common traditions that would place his Christ outside Celsus' pale. Included here are many of the miracle stories. As will be seen in the next section, Marcion is no allegorizer, and his literal acceptance of the stories would be vulnerable to Celsus' relativizing and ridicule of them. Moreover, though not possessing human flesh, Marcion's Christ is crucified,[125] which would fall under Celsus' stricture[126] that a man thus punished cannot be shown to be a son of God.[127]

These comparisons of Celsus' polemic against Christian claims of extraordinary divine involvement in the world of humans with interpretations of those claims by certain Christian groups in the direction of some of his concerns indicate that however much saviors like Asclepius and Jesus might resemble each other in their earthly manifestations Celsus would still choose Asclepius and the other deities of pagan cult. Amidst his logical inconsistencies, the consistent warrant of Celsus' polemic is the sanctity of pagan culture and its social matrices. For their part, the Christians considered above stand within Christian communities and traditions, to which they remain loyal even while reinterpreting many of the traditions in ways that involve them in conflict with other Christian groups.

8.3.2 Gnostic Allegorization of Miracle Accounts

Although Celsus does not characterize the gnostics he cites as among the Christian allegorizers he mentions (see above, p. 117), allegorical interpretation was common among them.[128] Examples are extant of allegorical or non-literal interpretation of extraordinary phenomena by Christian gnostics, including members of those groups of whom Celsus evidently had some knowledge (see above, p. 120), and one may ask whether such interpretation might have redeemed the interpreters and the phenomena in Celsus' eyes. The answer, again, would seem to be that though these interpreters share certain basic premises with Celsus, such as transcendence of deity, aversion to matter, and reserve or aloofness toward popular cultic piety's literal interpretation of extraordinary phenomena, the phenomena thus interpreted he would find repulsive, with no antecedent history in pagan culture to commend them, while the interpreters' loyalty to fellow Christians (gnostic or otherwise) and to certain crucial (but to Celsus despicable) Christian traditions would constitute evidence sufficient to lump them with Christians generally as persons subversive of pagan society and its culture.

We have already noted (pp. 122-24) the non-literal interpretation of Jesus' resurrection by Ophites and by Basilides. Another group mentioned by Celsus, the Simonians,[129] is reported by Irenaeus to deny the possibility of bodily resurrection in favor of resurrection interpreted as knowledge of the truth they teach.[130] Some Valentinian treatises from Nag Hammadi, dated to the second century, also conceive of resurrection in a non-literal way.[131] We have suggested above what might have been Celsus' reaction to such interpretation.

Valentinians are another group of gnostics of whom Celsus seems to be aware (see above, p. 120). Their Christian adversaries have preserved examples of elaborate allegorizing by Valentinians, including allegorizing of

miracle accounts. In Ptolemaic Valentinian exegesis,
according to Irenaeus, the twelve-year-old daughter of the
synagogue official (Mk. 5.21-43 par.) is interpreted as a
type or symbol (τύποϳ) of Achamoth, Sophia's purpose or
desire (ἐνθύμησιϳ), who becomes separated from her and the
pleroma[132] but is helped to return by the savior Jesus.[133]
His raising of the girl is taken to mean that he led
Achamoth to a perception of the light that had once
illumined her but had now forsaken her.[134] This separation
and return of Achamoth is found again in the healing of the
hemorrhaging woman in the same gospel pericope: ill for
twelve years, her healing symbolizes the suffering of the
twelfth aeon, Sophia,[135] and in saying "Who touched me?"
the savior was teaching his disciples the mystery that was
then taking place among the aeons.[136]

Heracleon, a contemporary of Celsus and "the most
eminent of the Valentinian school,"[137] uses the healing of
the official's son (Jn. 4.46-53) as a vehicle for expounding
the process of conversion of psychics.[138] The details are
interpreted allegorically to accord with Valentinian
thought: the official is the demiurge, the son's sickness
denotes his state of ignorance and thought there in Caper-
naum "near the sea," i.e., "adjoined to matter" (τῷ
συνημμένῳ τῇ ὕλῃ), his healing symbolizes the forgiveness
that makes him alive, and so forth. The turning of water
into wine (Jn. 2.1-11) symbolizes the transforming of the
human into the divine in the marriage of the elect with
Christ.[139] The miracles in the Jesus traditions are no
more to be taken literally than are the other events
reported there. It is psychics who need signs and wonders
(Jn. 4.48) since their nature is such that they are
persuaded through sense perception and do not believe the
word.[140]

Though Celsus and these gnostic allegorizers share
certain basic premises, such as transcendence of deity,
aversion to matter, and reserve or aloofness toward popular
cultic piety's literal interpretation of extraordinary
phenomena, the phenomena thus allegorized he would find no
less repulsive than those other subjects of Christian

allegorization, the Jewish stories which Celsus scorns as "fables"[141] with no rooting in pagan culture to commend them, while the allegorizers' loyalty to fellow Christians (gnostic or otherwise) as well as to the Christian savior and to common traditions about him would constitute evidence sufficient to lump these gnostics with Christians generally as persons subversive of pagan society and its culture.

No less subversive would be gnostic allegorizing that appropriated pagan culture for its own purposes. For Celsus, such interpretation would constitute a perversion, rooting in misunderstanding of that culture (see above, p. 117). The Naasene gnostics, for example, intertwine pagan, Jewish, and Christian texts in allegorizations offered in explanation and support of their particular tenets (Hippolytus, *Ref*. 5.7.9-15, 20-24, 30-32, etc.). The late second-century Valentinian writing, *The Exegesis of the Soul*, from Nag Hammadi, cites Odysseus, deceived by Calypso, and Helen of Troy, deceived by Aphrodite, as symbolic of the soul's plight.[142]

At other times gnostic subversion of pagan culture would take the form of polemic against various aspects of that culture. Thus Heracleon quotes the admonition in *Kerygma Petrou* not to worship as Greeks do, accepting the things of matter and serving wood and stone.[143] Though Heracleon gives a symbolic interpretation to "Greeks,"[144] for Celsus his citation of the passage would doubtless have constituted another instance of Christians' incomprehension of pagan cult which he asserts is misunderstood if its images are understood crassly as gods rather than as votive offerings and images of gods (*C. Cels*. 7.62).

Nor would occasional thrusts against pagan philosophy by the allegorizers or other gnostics endear them to Celsus. For example, to the philosophical belief in immortality of the soul Heracleon opposes the Christian traditions that soul and body are destroyed in gehenna (Mt. 10.28 par.) and that the mortal puts on immortality when death is swallowed up in victory (1 Cor. 15.53-43) (Fr. 40). In a gnostic document dated to the late second or early

third century,[145] the *Sophia Jesu Christi*,[146] and in its
cognate writing the *Letter of Eugnostus*,[147] three solutions
proposed by "all philosophers" to the question of the
ordering of the world are rejected.[148]

8.3.3 Miracles Literally Interpreted

The fact that allegorical exegesis is not the only mode
of gnostic interpretation (see the examples in Barth, 1911,
102ff.), also with respect to extraordinary phenomena, so
that these phenomena are sometimes taken literally, would
sharpen the points of conflict noted above between gnostics
and Celsus and reinforce the negative judgments of gnostics
suggested to a person like Celsus by those conflicts. The
Ophites, who, as we have seen, interpreted Jesus' resurrection as something other than raising of flesh and blood
(above, p. 123), evidently saw no need for non-literal
interpretation of miracles ascribed to Jesus. Indeed,
according to Irenaeus they appealed to such miracles as
evidence that the Christ and Sophia, who had descended on
Jesus, ascended before his crucifixion, when the miracles
that began with their descent cease.[149] *The Treatise on
the Resurrection* mentioned above insists on resurrection in
the flesh,[150] though it also puts forward the familiar
gnostic themes of present resurrection (49.13; E. T. in
Foerster, *Gnosis* 2, 75) and future spiritual resurrection
(45.30ff.; E. T., ibid. 2, 73). Similarly the *Gospel of
Philip* asserts the necessity of present resurrection
(Sayings 21, 90) and denigrates the body (22) and the
desire to rise in the flesh (23; cf. 108 and 123) but also
attacks those who deny resurrection in the flesh and states
that resurrection apart from flesh is impossible.[151]

Of the persons, groups, and writings being
considered in this section Marcion and the Marcionites are,
with certain significant exceptions, the most literalistic
in their interpretation of miracle accounts. One of the
exceptions is Christian incarnation claims where, as we
have seen, Marcionite insistence on the transcendence of
the good God results in a Christ who would meet some of
Celsus' tests of a divine messenger (above, pp. 125-26).

Another exception is resurrection where Marcion, like
Celsus (*C. Cels.* 5.14), rejects resurrection in favor of
deliverance of the soul alone.[152] Otherwise, however,
miracles in the Jewish and Christian traditions are taken
literally by Marcionites, who either accept them as having
happened or, in the case of Apelles, attack some as
incredible. How does this literalism compare with Celsus'
views of the same phenomena?

Celsus shares with Marcion the opinion that extraordinary phenomena reported in the Jewish scriptures should
not be allegorized. His reasons are different, however.
Celsus associates allegorizing with reason and intelligence, and in his view those phenomena are so shameful and
unworthy of deity that they should not be dignified by
allegorization (above, p. 117). They are, moreover,
incredible--"fables" not deserving credence (above, p. 117).
On these grounds Celsus turns them against the Jewish God
and his followers, Jewish or Christian. Marcion shares
this hostility to the Jewish God and to the anthropomor-
phisms and the anthropopathisms that Celsus ridicules[153]
and that troubled a number of Marcion's Christian contemporaries.[154] Operating on the principle that the interpreter should read texts literally unless the texts themselves indicate otherwise (see the texts cited in Harnack,
1924a, 259*-60*, and Harnack's comments, pp. 66-67),
Marcion rejects the allegorizing employed by his Christian
contemporaries to mitigate those troublesome traits of the
Jewish God and the typological foreshadowings and proofs
from prophecy that those Christians found in the Jewish
scriptures.[155] Here again Celsus should have had no
quarrel with Marcion, except as the latter uses the Jewish
God as a foil to enhance the character of the Christ of the
good God.

Unlike Celsus, however, Marcion does not scorn as
"fables" the extraordinary happenings recorded in the
Jewish scriptures. These, too, he takes as they stand.
What interests him is not their extraordinariness, which he
does not dispute, but their mode and their motivation. The
wonders worked by the just God are inferior to the wonders and

teachings of the Christ of the good God because they employ
matter or are injurious, whereas Christ is capable of
healing with a mere word, forbids hurt, and works beneficent wonders,[156] sometimes breaking the rules of the just
God in order to do so.[157]

   In Marcionite editing of the miracle accounts in
the Gospel of Luke the concerns are similar.[158] Passages
that would suggest recognition of the just God by Marcion's
Christ are excised or modified. Thus, Christ heals in
violation of Jewish Law (see n. 157 of this chapter). On
the other hand, in his goodness he tells the leper he has
healed to go to the priest (Lk. 5.12-14), as required by
the law, because that was expected of a cured leper;[159] and
patient of the blind man's mistaken notion that the Christ
is the son of David, he heals him (Lk. 18.35-43), in
contrast to David's treatment of the blind.[160] The divine
voice at the miracle of the transfiguration (Lk. 9.28-36)
puts the stamp of approval on Marcion's Christ: hear *him*,
and not Moses and Elijah, the representatives of the creator
God (Tertullian, *Adv. Marc.* 4.22, especially 4.22.1).
Though not all the Lukan miracle accounts are attested for
Marcion's gospel,[161] there is no indication that he
rejected any as incredible.[162]

   Noteworthy here is the function of miracles in
Marcionite christology. Having rejected proofs from Jewish
prophecy as well as typological interpretation of Jewish
scriptures as ways to establish Christ's divine sending,
Marcion was left with a Christ devoid of divine antecedents
and authentication.[163] Yet Marcion postulates a Christ
divine in origin and nature, to the point of docetism (see
n. 125 of this chapter). Extraordinary phenomena, as we
have seen, were commonly regarded as proof of deity and of
divine sending, and the miracle accounts in the gospel so
function for Marcion's Christ. Marcion, in Tertullian's
telling, states the issue succinctly: there was no need
for preparatory antecedents of Christ "since through the
data of miracles, he would immediately demonstrate himself
to be in actual fact the son and emissary and Christ of
God."[164]

With respect to his christology Marcion's situation was similar to that of the followers of Sarapis. As a synthetic deity whose cult combined Egyptian and Greek elements,[165] Sarapis had no genealogy and no narrative of origins. In their place, therefore, the *aretai* that mani- fested his deity were narrated (see Weinreich, 1919, 11-12; in 1969, 418-19). So also Marcion's Christ, loosed from all moorings in antecedent Judaism and, like Sarapis, with- out genealogy or birth narrative, required miracle accounts to establish his deity.

That Celsus would reject Marcion's literal miracles is evident from his epistemological critique of Christian miracle accounts. All the more so in Marcion's case in view of the conflict between deities and divine emissaries which is basic to Marcion's interpretation of Jewish and Christian miracle accounts but which Celsus, evidently with reference to Marcionites, looks on as absurd squabbling (*C. Cels.* 6.74). That Celsus could, on the other hand, accommodate himself to miracles, literally understood, in pagan culture (examples on p. 108 above), and in criticizing conflicts between deities in Christianity could ignore the well-known disputes between pagan deities, are further indication that what matters for him is the defense of pagan culture at all costs, rather than even-handed or even consistent weighing of the merits or demerits of phenomena that are in many respects similar in nature.

By way of comparison, Apelles, one of Marcion's less than faithful followers,[166] rather than turning the creator God's miracles, literally understood, against him, as did Marcion, turns their incredibility against him. How could an ark with space insufficient to accommodate even four elephants hold all the animals that reportedly entered it plus their food for an entire year?[167] For Apelles, as for Celsus, such tales are false and prove that the writing containing them is not from God.[168] Though Celsus might have found Apelles' thought congenial on other grounds as well, the latter's loyalty to crucial Christian traditions such as the crucifixion and Jesus' resurrection in the flesh[169] would hardly have earned him a sympathetic hearing from Celsus.

Celsus would also have been unimpressed by the report that Apelles credited the revelations of a Christian prophetess, Philoumene,[170] and by the claim that she worked wonders.[171] Similarly with groups such as the Simonians, the Carpocratians, and the Marcosians, who are reported as performing extraordinary feats or as ascribing them to their leaders. Such thaumaturgy is a consistent strand in the traditions about Simonian gnostics. Persons venerated by them as their founder (Simon) or as their subsequent leaders (Dositheus, Menander, and others) are credited with divinity or with performance of extraordinary feats.[172] In reports of Simonian teaching Simon and Menander are connected with gnostic systems of descent and ascent[173] and are said to offer their followers deliverance from malevolent powers through "knowledge"[174] or "magical knowledge" or through ritual acts.[175] The Carpocratians similarly are reported as employing manipulations and incantations and claiming power to rule over the archons and makers of this world and over all the works within it.[176] Earlier (above, p. 123) we noted the Marcosians' use, in their cult, of manipulations with extraordinary effects. In these examples one observes that thaumaturgy is not only practiced by some gnostics or claimed for their leaders but that it is sometimes connected with the common gnostic goal of deliverance from evil powers.

Recalling Celsus' characterization of Jesus as a *goēs* who practices magic and his scorn of such practitioners (above, p. 57), and noting his polemic against wandering Syrian and Palestinian prophets who claim divinity for themselves[177] as well as Christian labeling of Simon, Simonians, Carpocratians, and Marcosians as "magicians" (above, pp. 56, 68 and nn. 172, 175 of this chapter), one may surmise that Celsus' opinion of the practice of thaumaturgy by these gnostic groups would be little different.

That this implicit conflict between Celsus and

Christian gnostics practicing thaumaturgy would have become explicit had he actually confronted such persons is suggested by the reaction of another, later Platonist--Plotinus--to gnostics engaged in such practices. Even as Platonic philosophy is the context that informs Plotinus' attack on gnostic "magic," so Greek culture is the context of that philosophy, and Plotinus, like Celsus, is a self-conscious representative of both. As well as suggesting what Celsus' response might have been to those gnostics in his day who are reported as practicing thaumaturgy, Plotinus' treatise also underscores the social and cultural dimensions of such conflict. Whatever the affinities in thought between at least some gnostics, on the one hand, and Celsus and Plotinus, on the other, the antitheses between their social and cultural worlds inhibit, if not preclude, mutual understanding.[178]

Such antitheses underlie the mutual denial of "miracles" noted at various places in this study. In the terminology of the sociology of knowledge, only a resocialization is apt to affect such denials: a person comes to accept what he formerly rejected. He adopts new social and cultural worlds, often at the price of nihilating his former worlds and/or rearranging their furniture to harmonize with the decor of the new worlds. He is "converted" (see above, ch. 6.1).

These observations are illustrated by our next example of conflict over Asclepius piety, Justin Martyr. Like Celsus a Platonist, he is converted from paganism to Christianity, whereupon he accommodates his Platonism and his pagan past generally to his Christianity, sometimes nihilating them, sometimes reorienting them. His is an important and instructive example, not only because of the quantity and quality of his literary legacy, but also because of the antithetical yet consanguineous relation between him and Celsus.

9

CELSUS VS. JUSTIN:

SOCIAL AND CULTURAL WORLDS IN CONFLICT

In examining the attitudes of Celsus and Justin to Asclepius
and to Jesus one is struck by the fact that two persons of
somewhat similar backgrounds assess the two saviors and
their wondrous deeds so differently. Celsus defends
Asclepius and nihilates Jesus. Justin, an erstwhile pagan
and, like Celsus, standing in the Middle Platonic tradition,
accepts Jesus as savior and nihilates Asclepius or presses
Asclepius traditions into the service of the Christian
savior. In this chapter we will examine this conflict over
miracle, again with an eye to social and cultural factors.[1]

Celsus, as we have seen, sometimes compares extraordinary Christian phenomena with pagan ones in order to
relativize them and thus diminish Christian claims to the
uniqueness or authenticity (i.e., miraculousness) of those
phenomena; at other times he subjects the Christian phenomena to direct attack, using weapons that might equally
well have been leveled at similar pagan phenomena. Standing
in the philosophical tradition, his attitude toward such
phenomena is ambivalent, though toward Asclepius cult and
some of its wonders his attitude is quite positive. This
ambivalence in Celsus' polemic, and the logical inconsistencies, we explained as rooting in his defense of pagan
culture and its social matrices, which is the fundamental
and unswerving warrant of his argument.

In what Justin has to say about the wondrous deeds
of Asclepius, about other extraordinary phenomena in pagan
culture, and about pagan culture generally there is also
inconsistency and ambivalence. On the one hand, Justin
cites these phenomena as parallels to Christian miracle
accounts, thus showing that the latter are not unique. On

the other hand, he argues that the Christian accounts are
indeed unique and the pagan varieties derivative from them.
It has been observed that such ambivalence is common to the
early Christian apologists: "Before Christianity could be
shown to be unique and without parallel, the apologists had
to show what it was like, and, by implication, what it was
unlike."[2] Another example is the attitude of Christian
apologists to Greek philosophy: on the one hand, they sometimes seem to fall under its spell, affirming its (partial)
truth; on the other hand, they view it as derivative from
Christianity's antecedents and/or turn its weapons against
pagan culture.[3] In the conceptuality of the sociology of
knowledge, the apologists reorient their pagan social and
cultural worlds to fit their corresponding Christian worlds.
Justin's defense of Christian miracle claims illustrates
these general statements.

9.1 Justin's Defense of Christian Miracle Claims
In order to show that the extraordinary phenomena claimed
by Christians should not be regarded by pagans as something
novel (καινόν τι) Justin cites similar phenomena reported
of Zeus's offspring, including Asclepius, who performs
healings and ascends to heaven.[4] The examples Justin cites
shows that he shares with pagans the human being as a canon
of the ordinary, and that he wishes them to know that he
and they share this canon: it is ordinary human reproduction, stature, strength, and prowess from which these
stories of Zeus's offspring, as well as the Christian
accounts, represent departures.[5] If according to this
canon one assesses (negatively) the reports of Jesus'
unusual birth and prowess and his resuscitation and ascension, then according to this same canon one should assess
(also negatively) the similar phenomena reported of Zeus's
progeny. Contrariwise, for Justin to dispute the pagan
phenomena according to this canon would be to impugn the
similar Christian phenomena. Instead, he (1) seeks to discredit these stories by pointing to their shamefulness, (2)
insists that the Christian stories are alone true, and (3)
explains the pagan accounts as inspired by demons in

imitation of the older, Christian accounts. He thereby
sets these accounts off from the pagan ones and sets himself and other Christians apart from pagans.

(1) Justin's recital of shameful details in some of
the stories of pagan deities--parricide, sodomy, adultery
(references, ch. 8, n. 76)--stands in the hoary tradition
of pagan critique of such deeds on the part of the gods
(see ch. 8, n. 77). Justin points to the familiar place of
these stories in pagan socialization and the deleterious
consequences: such stories are recounted for the (supposed)
benefit of persons being educated, since imitation of the
gods is considered a worthy aim and a useful pedagogical
device.[6] The imitation ethic is one that Christians shared
with pagans,[7] and Justin does not question it. Rather, in
implying that the deeds recounted in the pagan stories are
unworthy of imitation Justin also implies that the Christian
stories he mentions are free of such shameful details.
Later he makes this explicit.[8] Here, too, Justin stands in
a tradition, that of dispelling the wondrous by discrediting
the morality of those associated with it (cf. above, p. 41,
and below, ch. 10, passim).

(2) For Justin it is axiomatic that extraordinary
Christian phenomena, and they alone, are authentic, despite
their similarity to pagan phenomena: ". . . the things we
say we have learned from Christ and the prophets who
preceded him are alone true [μόνα ἀληθῆ] . . . it is not
because we say the same things as they [i.e., the pagan
authors] that we think we will be acknowledged to be
correct but because we speak what is true" (*1 Apol*. 23.1).
Thus it is Jesus alone who was fathered by God in an
unusual way;[9] he alone is God's logos, his firstborn, and
his power (*1 Apol*. 23.2). What is true of his parentage
and status is true, by implication, of his resurrection and
ascension as well: he alone rose and ascended.[10]

(3) Central to Justin's assertion of the exclusive
truth of Christianity's miracle claims is his assertion
that the prophecies predicting them are "older than all the
writers who have ever existed."[11] It was from Moses, who
antedates all Greek writers (*1 Apol*. 44.8; similarly, 54.5),

that Plato took what he had to say about moral responsibility (44.8) and about the ordering of primal matter.[12]
When Greek philosophers and poets spoke of immortality of
the soul, retribution after death, contemplation of
heavenly things, and the like, they took their cues from
the Hebrew prophets (*1 Apol.* 44.9). Justin thus turns to
Christian advantage some of the bulwarks of that culture
which we see Celsus defending so vigorously. Justin relativizes and reorders paganism's social and cultural worlds
further by construing its worships and its extraordinary
phenomena as proleptic imitations, demonically inspired, of
the genuine, Christian articles. Thus, before Jesus ever
became a human among humans, some pagans, incited by the
evil demons, were speaking as though the poets' accounts
of extraordinary phenomena actually took place (γενόμενα)
when in fact they had fabricated them (μυθοποιήσαντεϛ).[13]
These fabrications of the poets (τὰ μυθοποιηθέντα τῶν
ποιητῶν)--the stories of Zeus's alleged offspring--were put
forward by the demons whenever they learned that people
were beginning to believe the things predicted of Christ by
the prophets (*1 Apol.* 54.1-3). Their intent was to bring
it about that people would view the things predicted of the
Christ by the prophets as, on the one hand, similar to what
the poets had said (and therefore as not unique) and, on
the other hand, as mere telling of tall tales
(τερατολογίαν).[14] As specific imitations of extraordinary
Christian phenomena predicted by the prophets Justin cites
Asclepius' healings and resurrections (*1 Apol.* 54.10; *Dial.*
69.3), as well as other pagan traditions of the extraordinary.[15] The context of these traditions, namely,
popular cultic piety, also has demonically-inspired
features imitative of Christian or Jewish tradition--
sprinklings, ablutions, removal of shoes (*1 Apol.* 62), and
rites in the cults of Mithras (*Dial.* 70) and of Dionysus
(*1 Apol.* 54.6; *Dial.* 69.2)

In associating pagan piety with demons Justin
stands in a long tradition,[16] one that he develops to serve
his reorienting of extraordinary pagan phenomena and pagan
cultic piety to make them subserve his own Christian social

and cultural worlds. That these resist the reorientation
is indicated by Justin's statement that Plato misunderstood
Moses (*1 Apol.* 60), or that pagans misunderstand the truth
(44.10), or that some of the demonically-inspired imitations
of Jewish prophecies are blundered interpretations of those
prophecies (54.4, 7). For Justin, however, these very mis-
interpretations and blunderings support his knowledge of
Christianity's scriptures and his trust in them.[17] Indeed,
every kind of evidence--favorable or seemingly unfavorable
--counts for Christianity and against paganism. Thus
Justin claims for Christianity those Greeks or barbarians
who, though they lived before Christ and were considered
godless (ἄθεοι), yet lived in accord with logos (μετὰ
λόγου), for Christ, as God's first born (πρωτότοκον), is
the logos in which every people shared.[18] Seeds of truth
(σπέρματα ἀληθείας) are found among all peoples, though the
truth has not always been correctly perceived by them
(*1 Apol.* 44.10). Those, on the other hand, who prior to
Christ lived devoid of logos (ἄνευ λόγου) were enemies of
Christ and of those (implicit) Christians who lived
according to logos (46.4). As to those things in Christianity considered reprehensible by pagans--notably Christ's
crucifixion--they, too, are turned to Christian account by
Justin. Suffering and death are not peculiar to Christ;
they are attested also for the sons ascribed to Zeus by
pagans (22.3-4). The appearance of the cross in many
facets of daily life[19] and even in state or civic ritual[20]
shows that the crucifixion is the greatest symbol of God's
strength and dominion.[21] The cross appears also in Plato's
account of cosmogony in the *Timaeus*, but in a mistaken
fashion since Plato did not understand clearly (μὴ ἀκριβῶν
ἐπιστάμενος) Moses' account of the serpent in the wilder-
ness, with the result that he interpreted the τύπον in that
account as a chiastic structure of the universe rather than
referring it to the cross.[22]

In these assertions of the central place of the
cross, one observes how Justin adds a cosmic dimension to
the cross by appropriating and reinterpreting certain
elements in Middle Platonism. In Middle Platonic

speculations the σχήματα are the structural forms used by
deity in shaping boundless and unstructured matter (see
Andresen, 1952-53, 193). For Justin the σχῆμα by which the
world is constituted is the cross.[23] It is the structural
element that makes possible sailing, plowing, and occupations that employ tools having this form (1 Apol. 55.3,
where σχῆμα is the governing term). The σχῆμα of the cross
sets the human figure (σχῆμα) off from that of the irrational animals (τῶν ἀλόγων ζώων).[24] Without that σχῆμα
nothing in the world could be governed or held in harmony,[25]
a theme that has affinities in thought and terminology with
those of certain Middle Platonists (see Andresen, 1952-53,
193, citing Albinos and Plutarch). However, whereas they
ascribe this governance and harmony to the world soul,
which they identify with the world logos, Justin ascribes
it to God's strength and dominion, of which the cross is
the greatest symbol (1 Apol. 55.2). If that is the case,
why did the pagans and their sons of Zeus not come forward
with imitations of the crucifixion, as they did with other
elements in Christian proclamation and practice? Because,
says Justin, the demons, who were the instigators of such
imitations, did not understand the prophecies of the crucifixion since these were uttered in symbolic language
(συμβολικῶς) (1 Apol. 55.1; cf. 1 Cor. 2.8; Ignatius, Eph.
19).

9.2 The Axiomatic Truth of Christianity's Claims
Justin's reorientations of paganism's miracle accounts and
of its rites, symbols, and spokesmen are axiomatic in
nature. Pagans, says Justin, adduce no proofs when they
present the poets' fabrications about Zeus's extraordinary
offspring to their youth, who proceed to commit them to
memory.[26] Justin, by contrast, devotes considerable space
to demonstrating, from fulfilled prophecy, the truth of the
words and deeds of Christ (1 Apol. 31-53) and to establishing his thesis that the poets' fabrications are demonic
imitations of such prophecies (54ff.). Justin's argument
from fulfilled prophecy is, of course, inherited. For a
number of Justin's contemporaries, both pagan and Christian

(e.g., Marcion; see above, p. 131), such "proofs" did not
necessarily constitute proofs. By Justin's account, acceptance of the truth of Jewish prophecy was part of his
conversion, a radical resocialization in which Christian
social and cultural worlds came to impinge on their counterparts from his pagan socialization, reshaping and reorienting them. The old man who instructs him on that occasion
explains that the prophets alone saw and announced what was
true. Their method, however, was not demonstration (οὐ
μετὰ ἀποδείξεωʃ) of the kind familiar in the philosophical
schools; rather they were witnesses, deserving of belief
(ἀξιόπιστοι), to the truth above all demonstration (ἀνωτέρω
πάσηʃ ἀποδείξεωʃ) (*Dial.* 7.2). In the words of the old man,
"the truth is as it is" (τὸ γὰρ ἀληθὲʃ οὕτωʃ ἔχει) and is
to be accepted as such: if it has been uttered by a
renowned pagan sage such as Plato or Pythagoras, that does
not add to or enhance its truth (6.1). What Galen, a contemporary of Justin, regarded as a defect in Christian (and
Jewish) argumentation, namely, the lack of demonstration
according to commonly accepted canons of logic,[27] is here
asserted as axiomatic and as a virtue by the old man in
view of the nature of the truth involved. In the case of
the prophets the old man does offer some warrants, but they
are different from those accepted in most philosophical
schools of the day; they belong to what I have termed
(above, ch. 5) popular cultic piety: the prophets' predictions came (and are coming) true, and the prophets performed
miracles (*Dial.* 7.2-3). Once accepted, such warrants are
employed in argumentation by Justin and other Christians.
But they count as warrants only for some, namely, followers
of Christ or those sympathetic to them, as Justin implicitly
acknowledges in several places. For example, he concludes
one lengthy argument from prophecy with the assertion that
perceptive hearers (τοῖʃ τὰ ἀκούστικα καὶ νοερὰ ὦτα ἔχουσιν)
will be able to understand that such argumentation differs
from that of those who make up fabrications (μυθοποιηθεῖσι)
about alleged sons of Zeus (*1 Apol.* 53.1). The axiomatic
nature of Justin's arguments is evident also in another
passage where, after reciting a creed of specifically

Christian beliefs, Justin states that the *perceptive* person
will be able to understand what is here asserted (*1 Apol*.
46.5: ὁ νουνεχῆς καταλαβεῖν δυνήσεται). Those who disagree
with Justin on the moral responsibility of persons who
lived before Christ are labeled "unreasonable"
(ἀλογισταίνοντες).[28]

Axiomatic statements are those for which one offers
no proof except (if pressed) the widespread, common assent
to their truth. In the terminology of the sociology of
knowledge, such statements belong to the "givens" of a
social group--what passes for knowledge in that group and
is presented as "objective reality" to its young (see above,
p. 84). Justin faults pagans for offering their youths no
proofs of the extraordinary phenomena in pagan culture
(above, p. 141). But that is just the way the traditions
(including the religious traditions) of a group are inculcated during primary socialization. As Reimarus observed,
religion is presented to the young as the only, true
religion, and most adherents of a religion, therefore, find
it to be true, not because it has been "proved" to them
but, rather, because it is part of the social and cultural
worlds acquired by them during primary socialization and
made plausible within the social matrices of those worlds
(see above, p. 90). Now, in several passages in the
Dialogue Justin argues that it is (in Chadwick's words)
"the blinding effect of custom and conservatism" that keeps
most Jews from accepting Jesus as the Christ so clearly
prophesied in their scriptures.[29] That is, Justin perceives
the hold that inherited social and cultural worlds have on
a person. He does not draw the conclusion, however, that
his elaborate (and what he considers convincing) proofs
from prophecy are apt to carry conviction only with insiders
(to whom they will be axiomatic) and to persons (like himself at one time) on the way to becoming insiders.

Similarly with his statements about the extraordinary phenomena of Christianity. Outsiders who reject
those phenomena or Justin's reorientation of pagan social
and cultural worlds are, in Justin's view, unreasonable or
uncomprehending. Conflict over miracle between Justin and

a person like Celsus may thus be viewed as one facet of the
conflict between their respective communities with their
social and cultural worlds. Standing in the Middle Platonic
tradition with its stress on the transcendence of deity
(see above, p. 109), Celsus, as we have seen, is concerned
to preserve deity's remoteness from matter and therefore
scoffs at Christian claims of divine incarnation in Jesus
(above, p. 121), which would involve deity in change, such
change necessarily being from good to bad.[30] Justin, won
over to Christianity, affirms its claim that God fathered
Jesus by a mortal (*1 Apol.* 21-22, 33; *Dial.* 66.3; cf. above,
p. 138). In the world and in matter resides evil, says the
Middle Platonist Celsus.[31] It is the hope of worms
(σκωλήκων ἡ ἐλπίς), therefore, to look to a resurrection in
the flesh (σαρξίν).[32] What sort of human soul would yearn
for a body that has decayed (σῶμα σεσηπός; *C. Cels.* 5.14)?
It is a doctrine at once repulsive, detestable, and impossible (τὸ σφόδρα μιαρὸν . . . καὶ ἀπόπτυστον ἅμα καὶ
ἀδύνατον) but defended by Christians on the grounds that
"Everything is possible with God" (πᾶν δύνατον τῷ θεῷ).[33]
One of those Christians is Justin, who asserts that Christians expect to receive back their bodies, for "nothing is
impossible with God" (ἀδύνατον μηδὲν εἶναι θεῷ).[34]

9.3 Justin's Conversions

In reflecting on these conflicts in the views of Celsus and
Justin concerning miracle, one asks how Justin came to
positions so uncharacteristic of Middle Platonism when his
general philosophical position is probably most accurately
characterized as Middle Platonic,[35] a philosophy with which
he became acquainted before his conversion.[36] Also
uncharacteristic of Middle Platonism, as Andresen has
demonstrated (1955), is Justin's interest in history and
his appeal to the past.[37] The past--viewed as *praeparatio
evangelica*--legitimates Christian miracles such as resurrection and those in the story of Jesus (they are fulfill-
ments of the prophets' predictions) as well as Justin's
claim, observed above, that Christian teaching is superior
to pagan teaching (Greek writers learned from Moses and the

Hebrew prophets). Also at issue between Celsus and Justin,
as we have seen, is Justin's nihilation of Asclepius cult
and of the miracles claimed for him and other pagan deities
and Justin's affirmation of Christian miracle claims (above,
pp. 138-39).

Justin himself portrays what we have called his
social and cultural worlds as resulting from a philosophical
and religious odyssey, climaxing in the conversation with
the old man who rectifies Justin's thought regarding the
soul and epistemology and introduces him to the argument
from prophecy (*Dial*. 3-8). The stereotypical nature of
Justin's story of his odyssey (see Nock, 1933a, 107ff.;
256ff.; Skarsaune, 1976, 66-67), along with other factors,
has led to divided scholarly assessment of the authenticity
of the account as a description of an actual series of
events in the life of Justin.[38] Such objections, however,
do not impugn the veracity of the story as a dramatized
account of certain factors that Justin, after the fact,
considered important in his passage from paganism to Christianity.[39] Merrill Young has presented a closely reasoned
defense of this thesis. Although he finds Justin's account
true in this sense (1971, 206), he finds it "passes
credibility" to suppose that Justin would abandon Platonism
for Christianity as the result of "a brief interview with a
stranger who mentions the name of Christ precisely twice
and offers no account of Christian beliefs (33). By his
own admission, however, Young (along with others) has
neglected the affective elements in Justin's conversion
(see 1971, 207). The importance of such elements in conversion is recognized by sociologists of knowledge, as we
observed earlier (above, p. 84). If Young's analysis of
the structure, content, and philosophical roots and
affinities of the opening chapters of the *Dialogue* bears
out the philosophical veracity of Justin's account of his
passage from Platonism to Christianity, analysis of the
account in comparison with other conversion accounts, from
a sociological perspective, brings out its psychological
and sociological authenticity. Such analysis does not
establish that a single conversation turned Justin from

Platonism to Christianity, but it shows that a single
event, even as brief as a dialogue with an old man--or a
reading of Luther's preface to Romans--can be crucial in
striking the key log that releases a congestion of thought
and feeling accumulated prior to that event (see below,
n. 52 of this chapter). It also points to the important
role played by representatives of the faith embraced by the
convert. The role of Christians in Justin's personal
praeparatio evangelica has been noted by various scholars
(among whom Young provides the most extensive and convincing
demonstration of that role). The old man in Justin's
account, though probably a fictitious persona, modeled
after Socrates,[40] may well represent a Christian or Christians with whom Justin carried on dialogues before his
conversion, or, equally likely, he may represent Justin
himself after his conversion, engaging as a Christian
teacher in debates with Platonists.[41] The portrayal of
Justin in the dialogue with the old man as a zealous young
Platonist may, on the other hand, reflect Justin's persona
prior to his conversion and/or that of Platonists whom he
encountered in the course of his work as a Christian
teacher. Explication and substantiation of these summary
observations is now in order.

A common element in conversion accounts, ancient or
modern, is what Lofland and Stark have termed "seekership,"[42] based on their observation of converts to a small
millenarian cult on the West Coast of the United States.
Seekership is evident in a number of Greco-Roman texts
adduced by Nock.[43] In Justin's case his seeking brings
involvement of varying lengths and intensities with the
four major philosophical schools of his day (*Dial*. 2.3-6),
a path commonly traveled in the Greco-Roman period.[44] In
Justin's account the unease and discontent characteristic
of seekership are evident in his successive encounters with
representatives of the four schools. The Stoic, though
offering Justin some satisfaction for a while ("I spent
some time with him"), finally fails him because his knowledge of God proves to be inadequate (*Dial*. 2.3). By
asking for tuition money the Peripatetic offends Justin's

expectations of behavior commensurate with the profession
of philosophy.[45] The Pythagorean is unable to aid Justin
in his search because his expectations for a student of
philosophy are beyond Justin's grasp.[46] By the time Justin
comes to the Platonist teacher he describes himself as at a
loss where to turn (ἐν ἀμηχανίᾳ) (Dial. 2.6). In Lofland
and Stark's terminology, Justin the seeker has reached a
"turning point."[47]

   Judging from Justin's language, what follows is a
conversion to philosophy (cf. Nock, 1933a), in this case
Platonism: the perception of incorporeal things (ἡ τῶν
ἀσωμάτων νόησιϲ), acquired through his Platonist instruction, "quite overwhelmed me" (με ᾕρει σφόδρα),[48] and (in
the familiar phraseology of Plato) "the contemplation of
the [Platonic] forms furnished wings to my mind" (ἡ θεωρία
τῶν ἰδεῶν ἀνεπτέρου μοι τὴν φρόνησιν).[49] Justin says he
spent as much time as possible (συνδιέτριβον ὡϲ τὰ μάλιστα)
with the Platonist--he reports daily progress (ἑκάστηϲ
ἡμέραϲ, Dial. 2.6), suggesting the steady and frequent
contact with the teacher that would provide (in terms of
Lofland and Stark's paradigm of conversion) "affective
bonds" helping to bring him into the Platonic fold as well
as the "intensive interaction" important in making him the
exponent of Platonism he shows himself to be in his dialogue
with the old man (Lofland and Stark, 1973, 41-43, 45-47).
In the conceptuality of the sociology of knowledge, Justin's
Platonist teacher--this wise and eminent man (συνέτῳ ἀνδρὶ
καὶ προύχοντι) who is strongly reminiscent of Socrates (see
n. 40 of this chapter)--and the students who would
inevitably surround such a teacher constitute a plausibility structure for Justin the seeker, in contrast to the
Peripatetic who in Justin's eyes fails to act upon and
embody philosophy.

   From his Platonism Justin brings to Christianity a
doctrine of God in which deity is regarded as unchangeable
and as the cause of all things.[50] Among philosophically-
schooled Christians of the second and following centuries
this was a common view of God, almost de rigueur (see
Pohlenz, 1909, 17ff.; Pannenberg, 1959), and it is therefore

not surprising to hear that the old man with whom Justin is
carrying on the philosophical discussion is delighted
(ἐτέρπετο) when he hears Justin characterize God in this
way (*Dial.* 3.5). On epistemology and the nature of the
nature of the soul, however, the old man feels compelled to
waken Justin from his Platonic slumbers.[51] In addition he
introduces a conceptual element--prophecy and fulfillment--
which along with the true teaching on the nature of the
soul relativizes Justin's Platonism. In addition, it
entails, ultimately, the dependence of Platonism on Christianity's antecedents and makes credible many of the
miracle claims of Christian popular cultic piety. Whatever
one's judgment concerning the historicity of Justin's
conversion account, the importance of the schema of
prophecy-fulfillment in making Christian miracle traditions
credible for him must be conceded (see the explicit statement in *1 Apol.* 33.1-2; cf. also *Dial.* 84.2). In retrospect Justin describes the effect of his encounter with the
old man as the immediate enkindling of a fire in his soul
and the awakening of love for the prophets and the
followers of Christ (*Dial.* 8.1). The experience of warmth
or fire and the suddenness of the conversion are both
attested in conversion accounts, ancient and modern.[52]
Justin, on further reflection, as enjoined by the old man,
is led to the conclusion that "only this philosophy [Chris-
tianity] is trustworthy and beneficial."[53] The corollary is
that he should (in the terminology of sociology of knowledge) nihilate his former social and cultural worlds,
including their extraordinary phenomena. Such nihilation,
either in the form of outright rejection or of reorientation of pagan traditions, we have observed in a number of
passages. It is evident also in his conversion narrative:
"within a short time [of becoming a Platonist] I *supposed* I
had become wise, and *in my stupidity* I was expecting to
behold God at once."[54] In a passage in the *First Apology*
he formulates a hermeneutical principle for such nihilations: reason (ὁ λόγος) dictates that truly religious
persons and philosophers should honor and love only that
which is true and decline to follow the opinions of the

ancients if these are bad.[55] But what is "true," we have
seen, has a strong social and cultural element for Justin
(and for Celsus): the "true" is apt to be that which is
regarded as "true" within Justin's (or Celsus') social and
cultural matrix.[56]

That matrix is another factor in Justin's conversion to Christianity, as it was in his conversion to philosophy and as it is in conversions generally (above, pp. 84-85).
In a radical resocialization like conversion an important
role is played by "significant others" who form structures
in which the new mode of life and thought are' seen to be
plausible. The old man in Justin's account, through the
force of his arguments and perhaps because of his age, is
for Justin one·of those significant others. As in other
conversion accounts (Lofland and Stark, 1973, 42-43),
Justin's rapport with this representative of the new religion is almost instantaneous (*Dial*. 3.1-3). The old man's
general demeanor and his resemblance to Socrates (whom
Justin elsewhere treats with great respect: *1 Apol*. 5.3-4;
46.3; *2 Apol*. 7.3; 10.5-8) has already been noted.[57] In
addressing him Justin employs the language of primary
socialization: πάτερ.[58] That the old man is not the first
Christian[59] Justin would have encountered is evident, however, from a passage in the *Second Apology* where he says
that while still a Platonist he had heard Christians being
slandered (διαβαλλομένουſ) but seeing them unafraid of
death and unfettered by things temporal, reflected on how
such behavior contradicted the slander (*2 Apol*. 12.1-2).
Like Galen (see Walzer, 1949, 15), Justin is impressed by
the behavior and demeanor of Christians. Young has pointed
out that the martyrs' freedom and fearlessness recalls
Socrates' behavior, whereas the Platonists would not pass
Justin's test of dying for Socrates' teaching (*2 Apol*.
10.8; Young, 1971, 206-07; Skarsaune, 1976, 64-65). When,
as Justin says, love for the prophets comes to possess him,
it is coupled with love for the friends of Christ (*Dial*.
8.1; cf. above, p. 148). Justin's conversion, therefore,
is not only to a symbolic universe and a body of teachings
but to the group or groups who experienced those symbols

and teachings as real and made them seem plausible for
persons entering from the outside. In the group the
convert interacts with the members and the group's "perspective 'comes alive'" (Lofland and Stark, 1973, 45), even as
for Aelius Aristides his circle of friends in the Asclepius
temple imparted reality to the god and his revelations
(above, pp. 99-100).

For Justin such interaction seems to have begun
with his observation of Christians from afar while he was
still a Platonist, proceeded to direct encounter in
dialogue with Christians like the old man of his retrospective account, and developed through further contacts with
Christians in communal settings such as those on which
Justin reports in some detail in several well-known
passages (*1 Apol.* 65-67). That Justin was received into a
Christian community through a rite of entry seems likely
from the amount of space he devotes to baptismal ritual and
his use of the first-person plural pronoun in his description.[60] In another passage he seems to refer to initiation
as the next step after coming to know Christ.[61] He speaks
of baptism as an "enlightenment" (φωτισμόϛ), asserting that
those who are instructed for baptism are "enlightened in
their understanding" (φωτιζομένων τὴν διάνοιαν).[62] Talk of
enlightenment is not uncommon in the rhetoric and liturgical language of second-century Christianity.[63] The
importance of initiation and enlightenment for Justin,
personally and as a spokesman for Christianity, is suggested
not only by the stress he lays on them in *Dialogue* 61 but
also by the contrast we have observed between his
(enlightened) views of Jesus and Christianity after he
becomes a Christian and typically pagan and Middle
Platonist views of the same,[64] by the detailed contrast he
draws between the behavior of Christians before and after
conversion to Christianity (*1 Apol.* 14; cf. *2 Apol.* 2), and,
further, by the important role of initiation rites in
socialization and resocialization generally (see Eliade,
1958) as well as in Mediterranean antiquity down to
Justin's day.[65]

After Justin's reception into a Christian group the

communal activities and the significant others of that
group (or others like it) would play an important role in
the maintenance of the new reality (cf. above, p. 85).
Justin describes these communal activities in detail--the
initiations, the readings, the instruction, the prayers,
the ritual kiss, the rite of bread and cup, the offerings,
the aid to the poor--and the roles played by the actors in
these various dramas: the presider, the deacons, the
assembly, the God who is worshiped, and Christ, whose
example and commands legitimize various acts in the worship
(*1 Apol.* 61, 65-67). The importance of these groups and
their communal activities for Justin is evident from his
consistent identification with them: this is what "we" do
and the way "we" do it.

This broad context of resocialization and reality
maintenance should not be overlooked when viewing the way
in which the extraordinary phenomena in the Christian
tradition are viewed by Justin, this convert from paganism
and Middle Platonism to Christianity. As we noted earlier
(pp. 85-86) in citing an observation by Wayne Meeks, it is a
methodological mistake to interpret an early Christian ethical demand like "love one another as Christ loved you" in
isolation from its setting in Christian preaching and
ritual and the demonstration of such love. Similarly with
the extraordinary phenomena claimed for Christianity by
its followers: these phenomena are part of the story of
Jesus extending back to the prophets, on through the fulfillment of their divinely-inspired predictions, down to
the present day when extraordinary phenomena still occur in
his name among his followers, and into the future when at
his coming in glory the final wonders will occur. The
reading and exposition of that story and ritual response to
it were a regular feature of Christian assemblies, Justin
tells us. That he himself had pondered it long--alone or
in company with others--is clear from his writings, with
their extended exposition and defense of it, including its
extraordinary phenomena. Justin also reports that similar
phenomena occur in the present when, through the power of
Jesus' name, his followers drive out daemons who are

impervious to efforts of other exorcists and those who
employ incantations and drugs (*2 Apol.* 6.6; similarly, *Dial.*
30.3; 76.7; 85.2-3), or when prophecies by Jesus find their
fulfillment among Christians[66] or when prophetic gifts are
found among Christians (*Dial.* 82.1). Though Justin does
not mention healings or resurrections in his description of
Christian assemblies, it would not be unreasonable to infer
that these assemblies practiced rites of healing and resurrection similar to those reported by Irenaeus not many
years later (*Adv. h.* 2.31.2; Harvey ed., 2.48.2). The
relation between "then" and "now" was reciprocal and
mutually reinforcing: the extraordinary happenings in the
Jesus story made extraordinary happenings in the present
seem possible and plausible, and vice-versa, while exorcisms and healings reported in the Jesus story provided the
warrants and sometimes the techniques for exorcisms and
healings in the present.[67] On these and other grounds it
is not surprising, then, that for many early Christians
"All things are possible with God" is a frequent assertion,
almost an axiom, traceable to Jesus himself. Justin, as
we have seen, quotes it, citing Jesus as authority.[68] This
affirmation, and the affirmation of many of the extraordinary phenomena of Christian tradition, place his
attitude toward miracles in the category of popular cultic
piety, even as his thought generally is that of the
majority consensus emerging in second-century Christianity.[69] This is a position he did not find incompatible
with his training in philosophy, as did some other Christians acquainted with philosophy. His profession of
Christianity as the only trustworthy and beneficial philosophy (*Dial.* 2.1) does not entail for him a total disavowal
of Greek philosophy, like Celsus' of Christianity. He is
the first Christian we know of who views Greek philosophy
with some equanimity (see Bardy, 1949b, 100-02; Malingrey,
1961, 107-28; Waszink, 1963, 43-45, 47ff.), finding a niche
in Christianity for some of its representatives and its
teachings (above, p. 140), though, as we have seen, he
reorients and subordinates these to Christianity in accordance with his profession of Christianity's superiority.

As a sign of that profession he wore the philosopher's
robe,[70] and he philosophized in his writings and presumably
in the school he conducted at Rome.[71]

9.4 Celsus vs. Justin

Insofar as Celsus is in conflict with Christian popular
cultic piety over Christian miracle claims, he is implicitly in conflict with Justin concerning such of those
claims as Justin affirms. However, Celsus' selection of
materials and his manner of argumentation indicate that for
certain of these claims, such as virgin birth, incarnation,
and resurrection, he may have Justin specifically in mind.[72]
The antithetical nature of the philosophical elements in
the way each man views extraordinary phenomena also points
to polemic directed by Celsus specifically against Justin,
or if not him, then against the type of philosophical
thought he represents. Andresen's study of the two men has
done much to establish his contention that Celsus writes
with Justin in view as well as to identify social and
cultural aspects of the conflict between the two men.[73]
Our explication of the philosophical elements in their
conflict over miracle will take some cues from Andresen's
work while emphasizing and elaborating cultural and social
elements in the conflict.

        Justin shares with Celsus a belief in transcendent
deity but differs from him on the relation of this deity
to the world. Celsus insists on this transcendence (above,
p. 121), repeatedly urging over against Christians that
deity does not come down to earth as they say he has in the
incarnation and will again in the coming judgment.[74] If
even the least little thing on earth were altered, as would
happen were God to leave his throne, chaos would follow
(*C. Cels.* 4.5a, b). Miraculous interventions by deity in
human affairs are therefore precluded.

        For Justin such interventions come about through
the logos. Already prior to the incarnation the logos was
active, at the creation (*2 Apol.* 6.3; cf. *1 Apol.* 10.2;
59.1-5) and then subsequently among both pagans and Jews,[75]
the prophets predicting the incarnation of the logos, an

event which may thus be viewed as the climax of a series of
divine interventions which will one day culminate in
Christ's descending at his second parousia to raise the
dead and establish his thousand-year reign.[76] In Justin's
own words:

I have demonstrated that it was Jesus who, serving the will of the
Father, appeared to and spoke with Moses and Abraham and, in short, the
other patriarchs, and who came in order to be born a human being,
through the Virgin Mary, and who always is. He it is by and through
whom the Father is about to renew the heaven and earth.[77]

Why should one doubt that the logos, in accord with
the purpose of the Father of all things, was thus born of a
virgin when previously he had manifested himself in so many
forms (ἐν τοσαύταις μορφαῖς) to Abraham, Jacob, and Moses
(*Dial.* 75.4)?

The logos doctrine thus provides a comprehensive
warrant for Christian claims of miracles past, present, and
future, as well as a criterion for evaluating miracle
claims made by pagans: only those associated with Christ
the logos--preexistent or incarnate--are authentic; any
others are demonic imitations.[78] As if he were conversing
with a Middle Platonist, in himself or in the pagan world,
Justin employs the logos doctrine to preserve the divine
transcendence in reports of divine interventions, whether
at creation, in the history of the Jews, or in the incarnation. Similarly, the voice at Jesus' baptism, which Celsus
would later question on epistemological grounds (*C. Cels.*
1.41; above, pp. 107-08), is not that of God speaking directly
but of the logos which also spoke through the prophets and
through David (in the psalms) (*1 Apol.* 36.1-2; cf. 33.9;
Dial. 56.1; cf. Andresen's comments, 1955, 320-21).

A logos doctrine like Justin's is, for Celsus, at
best a corruption of true teaching about the logos. It is
what one might expect from Christianity which, along with
cults like those of Cybele, Mithras, and Sabazios, is a
religion devoid of logos and in which ignorant and impres-
sionable persons fall prey to scoundrels who palm off
divination and apparitions on them (*C. Cels.* 1.9; cf.
above, p. 112). Christians accept what they are told to

accept (above, p. 112), their stories of miracles associated
with Jesus offering egregious examples of their credulity
(above, pp. 106-07). Illustrating Christianity's corruption of the Greek logos is its claim that a man--indeed,
one of lowly origins and shameful career--is the logos
incarnate (above, p. 121). What a contradiction for Christians to claim uniqueness for Jesus as a divine messenger
(ἄγγελος) when their own traditions mention many such
messengers.[79] By contrast, Plato, whom Celsus cites (6.9)
as championing the ἀληθὴς λόγος, did not claim to have come
down from heaven (*C. Cels.* 6.10b; above, p. 114). While
there is some agreement between Celsus and Justin that the
logos was diffused among various peoples, there is disagreement on the identity of these peoples. Over against
Justin's teaching on this point, noted earlier (p. 140),
stands Celsus' insistence that the bearers of the logos
have been various wise men and peoples among whom the Jews
and their spokesmen are not numbered (*C. Cels.* 1.14, 16;
above, pp. 109-10, 115). For Celsus this alone would serve
to nihilate predictions in the Jewish scriptures, in which
Justin places so much stock as miraculous or as warrants
for the miraculous. However, these sources are in fact
derivative from the Greek logos: it is not Plato who
learned from Moses (as Justin asserts), but the reverse,[80]
while certain sayings of Jesus and Paul were stolen from
Plato and Heraclitus.[81] This reversal of one of Justin's
chief arguments is another reason for thinking that Celsus
knew Justin's work and directs much of his polemic at him
(cf. Andresen, 1955, 353-55; Chadwick, 1966, 23-24).

The logos of which Celsus speaks is a constituent
element of the ancient culture he sees himself called upon
to defend. Another such element, also a key term in
Celsus' polemic, is *nomos*, "custom" or "law."[82] In view of
the importance of logos and *nomos* in Greek thought and the
close relation between the two,[83] Justin's assertion that
Christ is *nomos*,[84] as well as logos, posed a challenge to
persons schooled in Greek culture. Measured by this *nomos*,
the "old," pagan *nomoi* are found wanting by Justin (cf.
above, p. 150), and entering the Christian fold means

breaking with the "old," inherited ways.[85]

Celsus is appalled by such a thought. Each people has its own distinctive *nomos*, he says,[86] and each person should be willing to serve his native country (τῆς πατρίδος) "for the sake of the preservation of *nomoi* and religion" (ἕνεκεν σωτηρίας νόμων καὶ εὐσεβείας).[87] Even the Jews whom, as we have noted, Celsus does not number among the bearers of the logos, have their own *nomos* (see n. 86 of this chapter). Where they err is in presumptuously thinking that their *nomos* is superior to those of other peoples, whereas the customs on which they pride themselves are paralleled among other peoples, and it is not to them alone that divine messengers have been sent (*C. Cels.* 5.41). Though Christians may have a few distinctive *nomoi* (see n. 86 of this chapter), unlike other peoples they possess no ancient *nomos*, which is not surprising since they originated in a revolt against the Jews, who themselves owe their origin as a people to rebellion against the Egyptians (see above, p. 111). Christians thus shut themselves off from "the common *nomos*" (τὸν κοινὸν νόμον, *C. Cels.* 1.1) and put forward a new *nomos* for which they claim superiority, exclusivity, and universal applicability.[88] Origen aptly summarizes Celsus' thinking: "all persons ought to live according to their ancestral ways [τὰ πάτρια] and should not be reproached for this; but Christians, who have forsaken ancestral ways and are not one, discrete people like the Jews, incur blame for assenting to the teaching of Jesus" (*C. Cels.* 5.35).

Seen against this background, Christianity's miracle claims are dubious on several counts. Measured by the public nature of *nomos* (cf. *C. Cels.* 1.1), some of the claims are suspect because the alleged miracles took place away from general scrutiny,[89] an assertion that goes counter to passages in Justin, indicating that for Justin the incarnation or virgin birth are matters of public record.[90] Christianity's association with magic (*C. Cels.* 1.6, 28, 71; cf. above, p. 56)--a charge firmly resisted by Justin (above, pp. 55-56)--is clearly contrary to *nomos*, i.e., it is illegal. Unlike Justin, to whom Christian miracle claims became credible when he forsook his ancestral *nomos* and who then consciously nihilated much in the

pagan and Jewish *nomoi* and insisted that converts
must make a break with their past, Celsus stands in horror
of conversion, whether from paganism to Judaism (*C. Cels.*
5.41, lines 1-3), or to Christianity (*C. Cels.* 8.69) or
from Judaism to Christianity (2.1; 2.4). Switching
allegiance to a *nomos* that claims to be superior is futile,
for *each* people claims its *nomos* is superior, says Celsus,
citing as authority a passage from Herodotus. The truth is
that "*nomos* is king": there is no people without a *nomos*,
and each gives allegiance to its own *nomos*.[91] Celsus thus
affirms Asclepius cult and its miracle accounts because
they belong to the Greek *nomos* while rejecting (as alien to
that *nomos*) the phenomenologically similar Jesus cult and
its miracle claims (above, pp. 105-06).

Celsus' impassioned rejection of Christianity and
his defense of pagan religions, despite his reservations
about some of their manifestations such as credulous acceptance of the wondrous, and his closing of philosophical
ranks over against Christianity so that he numbers even
Stoics--traditional bêtes noires of Platonists--among the
bearers of the ancient and true logos,[92] indicate that for
Celsus pagan culture--its religion and philosophy, its
nomos and logos--is ultimately one, at least vis-à-vis
Christianity. For Justin something similar is true: the
story of Christ, the logos and *nomos*, in its past, present,
and future, yields a culture in which pagan threads are
woven in subdued tones into a single Christian fabric;[93] to
tug at one thread of the fabric, such as miracle, would be
to begin to unravel the whole of Christianity as he has
come to know it.

This qualification--as he has come to know it--
bears stressing. Justin knows Christianity from the inside,
Celsus from the outside. The God Justin believes can do
the impossible is known to him socially--in relation to
persons like the old Christian in his conversion account or
those Christians glimpsed by him in their martyrdoms, and
in relation to groups whose communal activities he
describes. Experienced within the Christian fold, the
extraordinary phenomena of Christianity are regarded by

Justin as miracles, divine interventions in the course of
human affairs. Jesus, once dead, now lives, and will
return in glory. Safeguarding the divine transcendence
through his logos doctrine, Justin affirms the miracles of
Christian popular cultic piety even as, in contrast to
Celsus, he accepts (and regards as a virtue) the presence
of artisans, household slaves, and uneducated persons in
Christianity.[94] Celsus, on the other hand, knows Christians and their deity only from the outside: he reads the
Christians' scriptures and writings, hears reports of their
beliefs and behavior, and observes them (it seems) in
public places (*C. Cels*. 3.50, 52; cf. above, p. 112, and
ch. 8, n. 53). The pagan cultural and social worlds, however, he knows from the inside. Some of the extraordinary
phenomena of these worlds he affirms, many he rejects. But
those claimed by Christians he rejects *in toto*. Standing
outside the Christian fold, for him Jesus is dead (*C. Cels*.
7.36, 68; above, p. 107), whereas the Greek savior
Asclepius, familiar to him from Asclepius cult, lives and
appears to people in need (above, p. 107). Any other
stance toward Christian miracle claims seems unlikely. As
unlikely, perhaps, as for Aelius Aristides to have
encountered and accepted Asclepius as savior apart from the
imposing temple structure at Pergamum and its personnel and
rituals and the circle of distinguished men who gathered
there. Or as unlikely as for Justin to come to put
credence in a deity who does the impossible without having
undergone a resocialization that brought him inside a
matrix where that deity was honored and looked to for help.
As we encounter Celsus in the *Alethes Logos*, he is secure
in his place in pagan society and in his certainty of the
superiority of pagan culture. If he had ever been a seeker,
as Justin was, his searching seems to lie behind him.
Nothing moves him to give a hearing to Christianity, as
Justin did, and then to move from a hearing to an embrace
without which Christianity's miracle claims--even in
attenuated gnostic forms--appear as illusions of a people
devoid of logos and prone to fantasy.

10

ORACLES AND ASCLEPIUS:
ALEXANDER OF ABONOTEICHOS AND OTHERS

In Celsus' day, probably in the latter part of the reign of
Antoninus Pius (138-61 C.E.) and on into the reign of
Marcus Aurelius (d. 180 C.E.),[1] there was granted to the
little town of Abonoteichos in Paphlagonia on the Black Sea
a new manifestation of Asclepius, under the auspices of a
man named Alexander. Well-known in his own day, Alexander
has achieved lasting fame--or infamy--through a biting
satire by Lucian of Samosata with the unflattering title
Alexander the False Prophet. Alexander's deity, the "new"
(νέος, *Alex*. 43) Asclepius, represents another facet of
Asclepius piety in the second century--the giving of
oracles--in which there is implicit conflict with Christian
prophecy and, in Lucian's account, outright conflict with
Christians. His account is rich in details of the social
and cultural circumstances of this epiphany and, when
assessed in the light of other evidence, makes possible a
fruitful investigation of this conflict.

Lucian's account of Alexander and the Asclepius
cult he founded is briefly as follows. Alexander, a man of
unusual gifts and striking appearance, but an incorrigible
fraud and deceiver, conceives the idea of capitalizing on
his fellow Paphlogonians' credulity by establishing an
oracle in his home town of Abonoteichos. To this end he
stages an epiphany of the "new Asclepius"; having concealed
a small snake in a goose egg, he reveals the "new
Asclepius," which in a few days "grows" into an enormous
snake, acquired beforehand by Alexander and ready back-
stage. This snake, given the name Glycon, now appears to
the excited public in repeated "epiphanies." When Glycon
begins to give oracles, business is brisk. His fame soon

spreads through the empire. Even highly placed Roman
officials consult the oracle. Only the Christians and
Epicureans, but especially the latter, among whom Lucian
numbers himself, see through the trickery, and protest.
Alexander also institutes mysteries enacted by torchlight.
Lucian tells how he affronts Alexander, and how Alexander
in return makes an attempt on his life, which Lucian
manages to escape. Alexander, despite an oracle predicting
his deification, dies of natural causes.

   With respect to Lucian's vilification of Alexander
many scholars do not seem to have learned from modern
studies of Lucian and Lucian's piece (see App. F below)
that, as one scholar has put it, "Lucian liked few things
so much as the composition of an invective" (Baldwin, 1973,
104), and that as a general hermeneutical rule "It is
rarely safe to take him as gospel truth" (ibid.). Before
explicating the conflict of Alexander's Asclepius oracle
with Christian prophecy, we need to investigate Lucian's
treatment of Alexander and the oracle, for not until we
perceive Lucian's perception of these, and his skillful
manipulation of them for his own purposes, can we understand the conflict. At the same time, Lucian's conflict
with Alexander and the oracle--and by implication with
Christians and Christian miracle claims--is itself highly
instructive for our study.

10.1 <u>Lucian</u>: <u>Freedom from the Burden of the Contingent</u>
Lucian's *Alexander* is a striking example of a response to
"miracle" discussed at some length earlier: the dissolution of the wonder of a phenomenon regarded as a miracle by
denying any reference to deity and explaining it in a way
that makes such reference unnecessary (above, ch. 3.2).
Often a bitter foe of philosophy and philosophers, Lucian
appears in the *Alexander* as the self-conscious representative of certain traditions from the philosophical counterculture discussed in chapter 5.1; he draws on resources
from those traditions to nihilate the wonders ascribed to
the newborn Asclepius as well as the prophet and followers
of the god. A rhetorician, he wields weapons from the

rhetorical tradition to the same end.   Yet, however fierce
his attack, it is not sheer ridicule.   Like other satirists,
he writes from a platform, one he sometimes articulates but
which at other times must be reconstructed from the
Alexander or from others of his writings.   Unlike his
fellow rhetorician, Aelius Aristides, whom we saw to be a
devoted defender of Asclepius piety and the wonders associated with it, Lucian emerges in the *Alexander* as a determined
opponent of Asclepius piety, at least of the particular
brand promulgated by "the false prophet."

10.2   The Dissolution of Miracle

In a revealing passage in the *Alexander*, Lucian articulates
his point of departure in assessing extraordinary phenomena
like that of the wondrous epiphany of the snake in
Abonoteichos: one must approach them with the firm conviction that, even though one may be unable to discover how
they happen, yet they are fraudulent and impossible, and
one must view them with an adamantine mind, disbelieving on
principle and inferring what actually took place (*Alex*. 17).
        A good part of Lucian's tract is devoted to
exposing the "fraud" in the wonders associated with
Alexander's cult, i.e., to demonstrating how they can be
explained as something less and other than miracle.   Lest
readers be taken in by the epiphany scene and marvel at
this new manifestation of Asclepius, they are enlightened
in advance concerning the way in which Alexander had stage-
managed the whole performance, props and all (*Alex*. 7-17).
Readers' expectations of perhaps finding a holy spring at
the newly established temple at Abonoteichos are dampened
by Lucian's report (13) that the water has merely collected
of itself (αὐτόθεν) or from a rainfall (ἐξ οὐρανοῦ πεσόν),
while the mud that figures prominently in the account (13-
14) hardly serves as an announcement of sacredness in that
space and time, and Lucian's literary allusions (*Alex*. 14;
see the references in Harmon, 1925, 195, nn. 1, 2),
bagatellize the whole scene.[2]   Alexander's strange, even
ecstatic behavior prior to the epiphany, which is viewed
by the populace of Abonoteichos as divine authentication of

Alexander (*Alex.* 12: θεῖον τι καὶ φοβερόν), is given a
pedestrian interpretation by Lucian: the man sometimes
feigned madness (μεμηνέναι προσποιούμενοϳ ἐνίοτε), and to
make himself foam at the mouth he chewed on the root of the
soapwort (12). When the tiny snake that Alexander has
concealed in the egg he has hidden in the mud is then
revealed to the wondering crowd as Asclepius (14) and
shortly thereafter is displayed grown to great size (15)--
and with an anthroform head (12, 16: ἀνθρωπόμορφον)!--the
readers are not surprised: they have already been told
whence derive those remarkable components of this Asclepius
(7, 12, 13). Equally unsurprising are the origins of the
prophecies predicting the epiphany, which have raised the
populace's expectations in preparation for the epiphany:
they have been composed and conveniently "planted" by
Alexander and his fellow conspirator (10-11). Nor are
readers surprised to learn that sealed questions to the god
are returned with the seal unbroken but with an answer
within: they have been told in detail how Alexander
manages that (19-21) as well as autophone oracles (26).
The dim light in which the great snake with the strangely
human head is shown to devotees and the fact that Alexander
even allows them tactile contact with the deity help
account for the ease with which they interpret the display
as a manifestation of Asclepius (16). Along the way the
reader is entertained as well as enlightened--Alexander's
partner in crime, who has helped him concoct the idea of
founding an oracle and connecting with it the snake they
have acquired (7-8), remains behind in Chalcedon, "composing
ambiguous, equivocal, and oblique oracles, and shortly
thereafter died, bitten, I think, by a viper" (10).

  Much of Lucian's exposure of the alleged miracles
at Abonoteichos consists of exposing their perpetrator,
Alexander, as an unscrupulous charlatan of unsavory
morality, a man driven by greed. As a handsome boy,
Alexander sold his favors to others (*Alex.* 5). Later, as
the famous prophet, he himself corrupts handsome young boys
(41), to say nothing of his licentious relations with women
(42). Again, Lucian adds the humorous touch: many women

bragged that they had borne children by Alexander, and
their husbands attested that these boasts were true (42).
Alexander's unscrupulousness is seen in his blackmailing of
rich and powerful men who in submitting queries to the
oracle rendered themselves vulnerable by revealing damaging
secrets (32).   He has no compunctions about fabricating and
staging elaborate mysteries that enhance his reputation as
a prophet, indeed as divine (38-39), nor, if it serves his
purposes, does he scruple to put his enemies out of the way
(44-45; 46), including Lucian, whose murder he plots (55-
57).   The epiphany and the Asclepius oracle are hatched by
Alexander, we learn, as a money-making scheme (7ff.), and a
profitable one it is, with a huge clientele that produces a
handsome income,[3] even after one subtracts the wages of
Alexander's army of assistants (Lucian specifies these in
23 and 49).   He advertises his product by sending out
emissaries to various parts of the empire (24, 36) and by
prevailing on visitors from Rome to publicize the oracle on
their return home (31).   A marriage for Alexander's
daughter above her station (35) is one more link in Lucian's
chain of evidence as is guilt by association of Alexander
with the thaumaturge Apollonius of Tyana (5).   Terms of
obloquy almost seem to fail the skilled wordsmith in his
summary denigration of Alexander's character (4).

  The third main element in Lucian's dissolution of
the Asclepius miracles at Abonoteichos is the picture he
paints of the stupidity and gullibility of the *dramatis
personae*, with the exception of Alexander (an exception
that is part of Lucian's own scenario) along with Lucian
himself and certain Epicureans.   Alexander, we are told,
chooses Abonoteichos as the ideal locale to establish his
Asclepius oracle since the populace was thickheaded and
lacked sense (*Alex*. 9) while Paphlagonians[4] generally were
not only thickheaded and uneducated (17) but superstitious
and rich as well, ready to accord divine honors to any
traveling fortuneteller (9).   These "worthless" (ὄλεθροι)
Paphlagonians believe the oracle tracing Alexander's
descent to Apollo even though they know full well his
humble parentage (11).   At the epiphany of the newborn

Asclepius, they are "frantic with hopes" and begin to beg
treasures, riches, health, and other gifts from him (14).
The Paphlagonians who stream into Abonoteichos have already
taken leave of their senses and only in appearance do they
differ from animals (15). When this rabble is admitted to
view and touch the new Asclepius, now miraculously grown to
full size, it is in a fevered mood, astonished before the
fact and filled with high hopes (16). At the celebration
of the mysteries the Paphlagonians appear shod in coarse
shoes and breathing forth garlic odors, these strange
Eumolpids and Ceryces contrasting ludicrously with the
venerable priests of the Eleusinian rites (39). When certain Paphlagonians discuss subtleties of Alexander's
genealogy, Lucian dubs them "simple sages" (μωροσόφων, 40).

  Those of the oracle's clientele who are not Paphlagonians also receive short shrift. The Roman governor of
Cappadocia, who comes to the oracle for an autophone and,
bolstered by what he hears, goes down to defeat by the
Parthians in 161 C.E., is called a "foolish Celt" (*Alex.*
27). Lucian does not venture to pass judgment on the great
Marcus Aurelius, for whom an oracle from Alexander also
turns out to be a broken reed (48). But Rutilian,
Alexander's son-in-law and his influential advocate among
the most powerful and highest ranking citizens of Rome (30),
is not spared. Lucian admits that in other things Rutilian
was a good and honorable man who had acquitted himself well
in many Roman offices but in religious matters he was
"quite unwell" (πάνυ νοσῶν) and believed "strange things"
(ἀλλόκοτα) about the gods (30). On hearing of the oracle,
he comes close to deserting his office in order to fly off
to Abonoteichos (30). The glowing reports he receives of
the oracle inflame "the wretched old man" and throw him
into a tizzy (30). His unbounded adulation is then used by
Lucian to explain how it was that so many highly placed
Romans were taken in: Rutilian unsettles Rome, including
most of the people in the court, with the stories he lets
loose, so that these high-ranking Romans rush off to
Abonoteichos to secure oracles for themselves (31).

  Alongside this unflattering picture of the oracle's

clients and defenders Lucian places his portrayal of
Alexander as an imposing figure, distinguished by a handsome, even godlike (θεοπρεπής) appearance, intense, fervid
eyes (πολὺ τὸ γοργὸν καὶ 'ένθεον), a most pleasing and clear
voice (*Alex*. 3), and superior intelligence (4)--a person,
in short, capable of sweeping susceptible persons like
those described above from the solid ground of sense into
the slough of superstition. Their stupidity and naivete is
heightened by a quality they share with Alexander that makes
them an even easier prey to his wiles--greed. The epiphany
of the new Asclepius raises in the Paphlagonians wild hopes
of treasures, riches, health, and other divine gifts (14),
and Alexander appeals to this greed by advertising the
oracle as capable of locating buried treasures (24).

10.3 Lucian's Platform
When Lucian has finished with the new Asclepius, his
prophet, and his followers, nothing remains of the numinous
and the miraculous. It is not surprising that students of
Lucian have labeled him a second-century Voltaire (Hewitt,
1924-25) or a Heinrich Heine (Helm, 1927, 1772.20ff.) or
characterized him as "essentially one born out of due
time," "the only important exception to the credulity of
second-century writers" (R. M. Grant, 1952, 73, 71). These
hardly exhaust the estimates of Lucian. He has been vili-
fied as the antichrist (sources and discussion in Baldwin,
1973, 97-103), scolded as a cheap journalist who trims his
sails to every wind (Weinreich, 1921, 130; similarly, Helm,
1927, 1773.36ff.), viewed as an archaizing satirist,[5]
pigeonholed as "primarily an entertainer,"[6] and dismissed
as a man devoid of any sense of mystery (Caster, 1937, 332).
Betz points out that assessments of Lucian have varied so
widely because inappropriate criteria have been applied to
him (1961, 13; cf. Helm, 1927, 1772.2ff.). In our judgment,
"rhetorician" seems the least anachronistic, most appropriate, and most significant designation of a man who
regarded himself as such and earned his living and whatever
fame he acquired because he had learned rhetoric, which
equipped him to do public presentations as well as to serve

in public office.[7] The scope and complexity of rhetoric
required of the rhetor sufficient conversance with a
variety of fields of knowledge to be able to draw on their
various resources in public discourses. Aelius Aristides,
as we have noted (above, ch. 7, n. 4), was well acquainted
with Platonic philosophy. Although Lucian students rightly
assess him as not seriously interested in philosophical
thought, when it serves his purposes he can put it to work
for himself, as in the *Alexander*, where he pits against the
Asclepius cult in Abonoteichos certain elements in the
Epicurean and critical epistemological traditions. Whatever Lucian's personal commitments,[8] in the *Alexander* he
represents (in the terminology of our study) certain strands
of the philosophical counterculture that look behind the
divine reference commonly asserted of inexplicable extraordinary phenomena for "natural" explanations of them
(above, ch. 5.1). It is Lucian's defense of this ethics of
belief (entailing, in this case, disbelief), in the
Alexander and in writings such as the *Philopseudes*, that
has earned him designations such as "Voltaire" or a person
lacking in a sense of mystery. Lucian's defense of the
ethic is so deft, thanks to his rhetorical skills, that the
uncritical reader has difficulty seeing the Asclepius cult
at Abonoteichos as an example of popular cultic piety in
which the hopes, the fears, and the lust for the wondrous,
which Lucian rejects as tyrannical, are met and satisfied.
A valid and fruitful comparison and contrast with Christian
prophecy is thus rendered difficult. It is necessary,
therefore, first to dismantle some of the weaponry of
Lucian's polemic.

One of Lucian's rhetorical devices is to cast his
denigrations of the origins and operation of the Asclepius
cult into narrative form--disarming flashbacks reported as
though they were eyewitness accounts. He was hardly there,
however, to overhear the tête-à-tête connivings that he
reports between Alexander and his partner as they plot
their scheme to establish the Asclepius oracle (*Alex.* 8-10),
discussions that would have taken place (if they did take
place) when Alexander was an unknown and decades before

Lucian wrote his account. Nor would Lucian have been present to observe the manufacture and painting of the snake's head (12), the concealment of the tiny snake in the egg and the egg in the mud (13), and the techniques employed by Alexander and his assistants in unsealing scrolls (19-21). Reitzenstein put forward the hypothesis that Lucian employed written sources in composing his piece.[9] It is difficult to conceive that Alexander would have committed to writing, or communicated orally to anyone, such damning secrets from his past. At best, Lucian's account of them is based on gossip, or on contemporary instances of phenomena similar to those at Abonoteichos; much of his account is probably fabricated, with the deftness acquired from much practice in the invention of scenarios for rhetorical exercises.[10] Though it is possible that Lucian cultivated and/or bribed temple personnel into revealing some of the techniques of the oracle that amazed oracle seekers, there is no mention of that and no need to postulate it in view of the contemporary treatises on such techniques. Hippolytus' *Refutation of All Heresies* describes several of the techniques Lucian says were employed by Alexander,[11] and the book "against magicians" (κατὰ μάγων) that Lucian says was written by Celsus, the recipient of Lucian's *Alexander*, also evidently gave examples of such techniques (*Alex*. 21). Lucian's intent and his audience are clear here: he writes, not to inform Celsus who needs no such informing, but to enlighten (σωφρονίζειν, 21) his readers by dispelling the mystery in Alexander's miraculous oracle.

Another rhetorical device Lucian employs to denigrate the Abonoteichos cult is, as we have seen, the disparagement of its adherents. But there are other ways of construing Lucian's data. Aside from the fact that his portrayal of the Paphlagonians as gullible dolts is a cliche his audience would readily recognize (see Caster, 1938, 17-18), adherence to the cult is not limited to Paphlagonians. According to Lucian, the adherents came from many other geographical areas[12] and from a broad spectrum of society[13] and included persons schooled in philosophy (*Alex*. 25). Numismatic and inscriptional evidence attests the cult's geographical diffusion[14] and shows that the cult persisted well beyond Alexander's lifetime.[15] Seen in their own time, when canons of belief among the educated had relaxed considerably from earlier centuries,[16] and/or as representatives of popular cultic piety, the adherents of the cult are not egregiously credulous. Neither is the behavior of Alexander's devoted follower Rutilian as remarkable as Lucian suggests. Lucian's description of him resembles in part Theophrastus' portrait of the superstitious man (*Char*. 16), a similarity that would not be lost on a cultivated audience. It is at least an exaggeration when Lucian says that Rutilian, whose career in public office (*Alex*. 30; above, p. 164) is now attested from inscriptional evidence,[17] nearly deserts his post in order to hasten to Abonoteichos (30). It may also be an exaggeration when Lucian says that Rutilian thought that he had become one of the celestials through his marriage to Alexander's daughter, reputedly borne by Selene the moon (35); but for Rutilian to have thought some such thing is not implausible behavior if one recalls the familiar story of the seduction of a Roman noblewoman who believes she has had intercourse with Anubis and glories in the act as an epiphany (Josephus, *Ant*. 18.65ff.). That a high Roman official should marry the daughter of a religious figure on the advice of an oracle would also not seem to be implausible behavior in Rutilian's time.[18] Neither is it surprising, in view of the often less-than-critical stance of second-century philosophers and their religious concerns (above, pp. 104-05), that Platonists, Stoics, and Pythagoreans should be numbered among the adherents of the cult (25).

Taken by itself and read uncritically, Lucian's pejorative portrait of Alexander may seem self-evidently true, and since no other accounts of Alexander are extant, Lucian's has often been taken at face value. But one can compare Lucian's portrayals of other historical figures with other contemporary accounts of them as well as with one another, and the comparison does not inspire confidence

in Lucian's reporting. Lucian's Demonax, e.g., accuses a
certain philosopher of pursuing philosophy for the sake of
gain (*Demon.* 31), whereas Marcus Aurelius (*Medit.* 1.8)
praises the same philosopher in glowing terms. Peregrinus
is spoken of by Aulus Gellius, who says he knew him personally, as an earnest, steadfast, and wise person (*Noct.
Act.* 12.11), but Lucian portrays him as anything but that
and, in contrast to Philostratus' report that Peregrinus'
self-immolation demonstrated his courage as a philosopher
(*Vit.* 563), ascribes that act to base motives. Comparing
Lucian's denigrations of three different figures, one sees,
as Caster has shown, that Lucian makes virtually the same
accusations against all three[19] and that these are standard
polemical devices in the rhetorical tradition (Caster, 1938,
84-85). To take such charges literally is incautious,
therefore, also in the case of Alexander, including the
assertion of Alexander's attempt on Lucian's life (*Alex.*
56).[20]

10.4 The Asclepius Cult in Abonoteichos

We are now in a better position to reconstruct the Asclepius
cult in Abonoteichos which underlies Lucian's jaundiced
portrait and to see it as a plausibility structure that
stands in implicit and sometimes explicit conflict with
Christian communities and their prophets. A key element in
the success of the cult is Alexander himself, a truly
"significant other" for its adherents. Lucian has characterized him as an imposing figure, handsome even when past
his prime (*Alex.* 3, 5), of unusual innate intelligence (4),
and projecting a numinous presence the violation of which
is viewed by his followers as sacrilege (ἱερόσυλοſ, 55).
If Lucian's report of ecstatic behavior is to be trusted
(12-14), it would--whether genuine or contrived (as Lucian
alleged)--have added to the aura of numinosity. These
attributes complement Alexander's religious sensibilities
and his superb managerial gifts that result in his assuming
roles as Glycon's prophet, as his near relative, as the
impresario and writer, director, and protagonist in the
"mysteries" of the cult.

As prophet of Glycon,[21] Alexander utters the word
of this new Asclepius (*Alex.* 19). He is "a friend at court,
who has the ear of Glycon, and can give or withhold aid
. . . as both introducing and representing the new cult, he
stands between humanity and Glycon."[22] Alexander's role as
manager, to use an apt modern term,[23] is closely related to
his function as prophet and intermediary. He sends out
emissaries to proclaim the god's successes (24), i.e., his
ἀρεταί, arranges the epiphanies of Glycon (15-17, 26) and
the autophones (26-27), in both of which he is the key
figure though the ostensible focus is on Glycon, commands
and pays a small army of assistants in and outside the
temple (23, 24), and is the impresario of the mysteries
(38-40). In the mysteries especially we see Alexander as
a near relative of Glycon, the ritual dramas predicating
his divinity several times over.[24] The whole drama of the
new Asclepius gives impressive evidence of Alexander's
sense of ritual. The revelation of the new Asclepius as a
tiny snake, the subsequent theophanies, the audiences with
Alexander, the giving of the oracles, the autophones, all
convey to the participants a sense of contact with deity
near at hand. In the mysteries a crowd of already
persuaded people, assembled by torchlight, with non-
believers ritually excluded, sees enacted on three successive nights a complicated aetiology of the cult which
syncretizes various time-honored religious traditions[25] and
features the epiphany (ἐπιφάνεια, 38) of the god thus
honored (38-40). The rituals constitute powerful plausibility structures for the cult, its oracles, and its
prophet.[26]

To the degree that power confers social status,
Alexander is a man of considerable standing. The wariness
with which Roman officialdom treated him, according to
Lucian (*Alex.* 57), his success in petitioning the emperor
to rechristen Abonoteichos (58), and the minting of coins
honoring the cult, give some concrete indication of his
standing. One may infer also that the recognition and
prosperity that the oracle brought to Abonoteichos would
have earned him a considerable measure of civic gratitude

and influence. The presence of persons of high social
standing among the oracle's clientele and the marriage of
Alexander's daughter to a high Roman official (35) would
have enhanced the prophet's social status.

To place Alexander socially in the detailed way
that Peter Brown (1971) has done for holy men in Syria
would require more data than our sources provide. Unlike
those holy men, Alexander does not seem to have exercised
his power in order to help suppliants with the day-to-day
problems of disputes with neighbors, difficulties with
political authorities, and the like (Brown, 1971, 87ff.).
It is directed rather to persons in various contingency
situations of small or great moment--marriage (*Alex*. 35),
rearing of children (33), sickness (22, 24, 25), war (27,
28), natural disasters (36). To relieve their anxieties
people come to the oracle, to which there are differing
degrees of access carefully controlled by Alexander. At
the farthest reach are those who submit inquiries and
receive oracles in reply. Their belief in the oracle,
indicated by the considerable amount of money they invest
in the fee and often in travel, is reinforced by paying out
the money (and making the trip) and by the communication
from deity, miraculous both in its uncanny knowledge of the
unknown and its inexplicable mode of delivery (19-20, 26).
To cure disbelief Alexander sometimes exercises "therapy,"[27]
and to repair damage done by erroneous oracles[28] he issues
new oracles (28) or his followers obligingly provide recti-
fying interpretations (33). Participation in the mysteries
marks another degree of access to the deity as does visual
and tactile contact with the deity. Initially such
contacts are granted to the general public (17-18, 26);
later, except for those who can afford autophones (34) or
audiences (43), it seems that these theophanies are trans-
muted into public appearances of the now-divine prophet, at
which times the opportunity to kiss his hand is sometimes
offered (55; cf. 41), abuse of which is considered
sacrilege (55).

The most immediate access to deity is enjoyed by
"those within the kiss" (οἱ ἐντὸς τοῦ φιλήματος), i.e., a

kiss from the prophet's lips, which was restricted to boys
eighteen years of age or under (41). Lucian perceives lustful intent in Alexander's behavior, in hypocritical contrast
to Alexander's injunctions against pederasty (41). If
Alexander did engage in pederasty, he and his followers may
not have perceived his behavior as hypocritical: what was
denied (by some) to ordinary humanity was permitted to
deity, while sexually intimate contact with deity was
regarded as auspicious and an honor (42). Viewed sociologically, Alexander's kisses demarcate the bounds of his
inner ring, the occupants of which are selected for their
birth, youth, and good looks and serve the ritual function
of singing hymns to the deity (41). Their term of service
is three years (41), after which time they could be counted
on to carry the gospel of Glycon to their home environs or,
perhaps, to graduate into the ranks of Alexander's assistants in the operation of the oracle. Lucian says little
about the latter, though we are told that the rapid growth
of the oracle required a fair number and various kinds (23,
24). Even according to Lucian's account, Alexander's
treatment of them--dividing the proceeds according to each
person's worth rather than pocketing it all himself (23)--
would have pleased a modern labor leader.

      Lucian presents Alexander's motives as base and his
use of power as ruthless and self-aggrandizing, as indeed
it was when viewed from the standpoint of his opponents and
victims. That his followers viewed him and his actions
otherwise is clear, as we have seen. Confronted with
evidence of error in his oracles, they disbelieve the error
and spring to his defense (*Alex.* 33, 44-45); evidence that
he was a "false prophet" in the sense of giving spurious
answers to trick questions (53-54) would not have impressed
them--any more than non-fulfillment of Pauline or Synoptic
predictions of an imminent parousia of the Christ in glory
(or similar predictions by Christian leaders in the modern
era) did not result (and have not resulted) in mass defec-
tions. Even had they been confronted with evidence of
wrongdoing or hypocrisy on the part of Alexander, their
loyalty would probably have persisted, as it commonly does

in followers of modern religious leaders (examples in
Festinger, Reicken, Schachter, 1956; Gager, 1975, 39-40;
cf. Sanada, 1979).

For Lucian the people who thronged Abonoteichos
were tyrannized by empty hopes, fears, and the wondrous
(*Alex*. 47); Lucian professes to find emancipation from such
tyranny in the writings of Epicurus (47, 61), and reports
that Epicureans opposed the oracle (44) and were hated by
Alexander and his followers (25, 38, 45-47). Representing
the critical epistemological tradition of the philosophical
counterculture, Lucian, along with at least some philosophers,[29] finds the Asclepius oracle anything but plausible and rejects its wonders and its prophet. For the
throngs, however, the oracle continues a specific strand of
a long tradition of popular cultic piety and provides a
divine answer to just those questions of contingency that
Lucian eschews. For the way the oracle met and satisfied
certain religious needs and expectations of the latter half
of the second century, the credit must go largely to
Alexander. As Weinreich observed, only when one posits for
him a complex interweaving of natural endowments, religious
intuition, sensitivity to religious needs of the day, and
fanatic devotion to a self-appointed mission do his appeal
and that of the cult become intelligible (Weinreich, 1921,
151; similarly, Nock, 1928, 162; Nilsson, 1961, 474; cf.
also Caster, 1938, 102).

10.5 Asclepius Oracle and Christian Prophecy
Like Lucian, but for different reasons, the Christians in
Paphlagonia are portrayed by him as rejecting the prophet
and the oracle, which stand in conflict with their own
prophets and their own means for confronting the future and
other situations of contingency. Whether or not Lucian
accurately reports that Alexander ordered Christians stoned
(*Alex*. 25) or ritually excluded them from his nocturnal
mysteries (38), such actions are symbolically true: the
Asclepius social groupings in Abonoteichos described above
and Christian communities are rivals, and claims to
prophecy are part of that rivalry. The Asclepius groups

and Christian groups, structurally similar in a number of
ways, presuppose or foster loyalties that extend to, or
include, loyalty to prophecy in those groups. Christians
revere their apostles and leaders, even as the adherents of
the cult in Abonoteichos look to Alexander as its founder
and leader. Within both groups there are various means of
fostering and maintaining "reality": distinctive symbols,
rituals of inclusion and exclusion,[30] rites that enact and/
or recite basic aetiologies of the group, and nihilation of
potentially rival deities and cults. In the Asclepius cult
at Abonoteichos deity is present to communicate knowledge
of the unknown through a prophet. In Christian groups that
is the case at least some of the time. As regards knowledge of the future, however, there is a significant
difference and an implicit conflict: Christians know the
future on a cosmic scale, with Jesus coming in glory (later,
if not sooner) to deliver his followers. In the second
century no prophet was needed to reveal that to them--it
was common knowledge, thanks to oral and written traditions.
There are, however, two important second-century instances
in which certain strands of Christian prophecy show
affinities with and yet stand in implicit conflict with
the Asclepius cult of Abonoteichos. One of these concerns
the prophets described in the *Shepherd* of Hermas; the other
is the Montanist movement.

10.6 The Prophets in *Mandate* 11[31]

In the Eleventh *Mandate* of Hermas' *Shepherd* the social
situation envisaged is quite different from that in Abonoteichos: small assemblies of Christians as opposed to
crowds of heterogeneous humanity. However, the common
pagan phenomenon of oracle inquiry, represented in the
Asclepius cult at Abonoteichos, is also represented in the
Mandate, but as a foil to true prophecy. Some persons in
Christian assemblies, the author tells us, are seeking
answers to questions about the future (11.2), and a "false
prophet" (ψευδοφροφήτηϛ) undertakes to answer them. Most
of Hermas' description of the inquiries and their prophets
is devoted to nihilation of them. The inquirers are

members of the Christian community (11.1-2) but unstable
(δίψυχοι, 11.1, 2, 4) in their adherence to it. They are
empty persons (κένοι, 11.3) devoid of truth (11.4). In
bringing inquiries about the future they are following
their evil desires (11.2, 6). In short, they are behaving
like Gentiles who consult oracles (11.4). For Hermas such
inquiry is inextricably associated with pagan religion,[32]
and he therefore labels the inquirers idolators
(εἰδωλολατροῦντεϲ, 11.4). The countercultural nature of
Christianity noted in chapter 5.2 above is manifest in this
description. Hermas' polemic against oracle inquiry within
Christianity does not rest on doctrinal differences (cf.
Dibelius, 1923, 539; Bauer, 1971, 179, n. 66). He does not
advance substantive arguments against such inquiry, as does
Epictetus, for example, who, like Hermas, sees such inquiry
as catering to human desires, but, unlike him, offers basic
warrants deriving, in his case, from Stoic philosophy.[33]
Hermas might, for example, have cited divine providence or
election, an important element in Christian tradition (Mt.
6.25-34; Rom. 8.28-39), as a reason not to make inquiries
about the future. Instead, he pits one group--the true
Christian community and its gift of prophecy--against
another group--weak, wavering Christians and their prophet
--and, by inference, oracles like that at Abonoteichos.

        The first group Hermas characterizes as faithful
(πίστοι, 11.1) or strong in the faith (11.4), as righteous
(11.4) and clothed with truth (11.4). When this group
assembles, it possesses the divine Spirit,[34] and any member
of the assembly who is thus a bearer of that spirit may
begin to speak by the prophetic or holy Spirit[35] when that
Spirit's angel, latent in the person,[36] is activated by the
prayer of the assembly (11.9, ἔντευξιϲ γένηται κ. τ. λ.).
Because the prophet speaks not on human initiative (i.e.,
in response to inquirers), but as moved by the Spirit (11.5,
8-9), his prophecy is with power (11.5, 17, 20, 21), from
God (11.5, 8, 17), from above (ἄνωθεν, 11.5, 8, 20, 21)--it
is miraculous. His exemplary behavior follows from the
fact that he is one of the group in which true prophecy
occurs: the behavior reported for him (11.8, 12) is no

more (nor less) than that expected of other members of the
group (see Reiling, 1973, 49-50, 97).

In the midst of this assembly but distinct from it,
according to Hermas, are those persons who idolatrize by
inquiring of a prophet about the future, after the manner
of pagans. By ascribing to this prophet behavior characteristic of pagan prophets, Hermas judges him guilty by
association: he evidently exhibits mantic behavior,[37] prophesies only in response to inquiries (11.2, 3, 6),
requires a fee (11.12), and tells inquirers only what they
wish to hear (11.2, 3, 6). The reprehensibility of his
behaviour and of those who form his clientele is evident
from the fact that he prophesies "in a corner" (κατὰ
γωνίαν, 11.13) rather than in the assembly as a whole, as
true prophets do.[38] Should he venture to prophesy in the
assembly, he and his spirit are unmasked by the prayer of
the assembly (ἔντευξιϛ, 11.14) as empty (11.3, 14, 15, 17),
earthly (11.6, 11, 12, 14, 17, 19), powerless (11.2, 11,
14, 17, 19), and from the devil (11.3, 17)[39]--his pro-
phesying is not miraculous. Hermas does not deny that the
false prophet sometimes speaks the truth, but that is
because the evil spirit who fills him is capable of fore-
seeing some of the future (11.3).[40] The false prophet is
susceptible to invasion by the evil spirit because, unlike
the members of the true Christian assembly, in his usual
state he does not possess the divine spirit: he is empty,
a ready receptacle. Hermas employs the familiar category
of "the impossible" (ἀδύνατον, 11.19; cf. above, p. 7) to
mark true Christian prophecy off from the false prophet's
utterances: as the sky is beyond the reach of human
striving (11.18-19), so is true prophecy, which must come
as a gift from above with the power of the divine (11.20-
21).

Possession of the Spirit was a common claim among
early Christians. Opposed to Hermas' claim that the true
Christian assembly possesses the Spirit is the "false"
prophet's claim that he possesses it (11.16, πνευματοφόρον).
Against that claim Hermas can muster only experiential
evidence. His polemic shows clearly that foretelling of

the future, of the kind common in pagan oracles like that
in Abonoteichos, had penetrated Christian communities in
the second century. From his polemic one may infer what
his opinion of Alexander and the Abonoteichos oracle would
have been. Had Hermas been there, he would doubtless have
been numbered among the Christians who, according to
Lucian, reviled the oracle. Specifically, he would likely
have characterized the Asclepius oracle as demonic, the
label he applied to Christian prophecy of which he
disapproved. It is hard to imagine, on the other hand,
that Hermas would have found Lucian's polemic against the
oracle congenial. The reputation of Epicurus, to whom
Lucian appeals, would have sufficed to repel him while his
answer to the questions of hope and fear raised by Lucian
would have differed markedly from Lucian's.

Hermas' "false prophet" and those members of the
Christian community who address inquiries to him would
likely also have had little use for the Asclepius oracle
at Abonoteichos. If Alexander had not rejected them, they
might have rejected him--as redundant (they had their own
prophet to whom to address questions about the unknown)
and/or as superseded (cf. Reiling, 1973, 80), and/or as
false because Asclepius was a false god or no god--and
might have leveled at him the same charges of immorality
and evil inspiration that Hermas leveled at their prophet
and that were the common stock of rival groups in the
Greco-Roman world. At the same time, the presence within a
Christian community of a religious form at home in pagan
society and culture testifies to the appeal of such a form
to Christians. Their rejection of it in a pagan context
would vary with the depth of their loyalty to their Christian community and with their individual anxieties about
the future.

10.7 Montanism[41]

The other instance of implicit conflict with the Asclepius
cult at Abonoteichos is the contemporary[42] movement,
commonly called Montanism, in Phrygia, further west in Asia
Minor. Unlike Hermas' "false prophet," the Montanist
prophets are not accused of giving predictions in response
to inquiries. There are nonetheless certain affinities

between Montanism and the Asclepius oracle at Abonoteichos.
These affinities at the same time represent points of
conflict.

In both cases a familiar deity is regarded as manifesting himself anew.[43] And in both instances ecstasy
authenticates the manifestations, with the prophets of the
respective deities exhibiting abnormal behavior and
speaking in strange tongues.[44] The conflict between the
two cults becomes evident in the claims made by the deities
of each. "I am Glycon" (εἰμὶ Γλύκων, *Alex*. 18) and "I am
the new Asclepius" (ἐγὼ Ἀσκληπιὸς νεὸς, *Alex*. 43), says the
god who speaks as "I" through his prophet Alexander (*Alex*.
22) in identification and presentation formulas (see Betz,
1961, 139, n. 1). Likewise, the deity of the Montanist
prophets speaks in the first person (ἐγώ and ἐγὼ εἰμί), and
in similar formulas, but identifies himself as the Almighty,
the Lord God, the Father, the Son, the Spirit, the Paraclete, word, and power (Aland, 1960a, nos. 1-4, 16). While
the inclusiveness of pagan religion would not preclude
recognition by Alexander of the Montanist deity or his
prophets--Alexander made "referrals" to other oracles (*Alex*.
29)--his explicit exclusion of Christians from his cult
(above, p. 173) indicates (if Lucian's report is accurate)
that he would regard the Montanist prophets and their deity
as rivals rather than as kin or allies. For Alexander's
followers, for their part, to have turned to the Phrygian
movement for knowledge of the future would have required a
radical resocialization, a conversion. The suspicion
attaching to Christians as atheists[45] or as subversive of
pagan culture and society (which we observed in the case of
Celsus) would attach also to the Montanists. Moreover,
Montanist prophecy, as far as we know, did not deal in
day-to-day anxieties and hence would be of little interest
to persons who brought such concerns to Abonoteichos. On
the other hand, Montanist prophecy would doubtless have
incensed educated inquirers at the Abonoteichos oracle, if
one may extrapolate from Celsus' ridicule of Christian
eschatology of the kind that promised final bliss to Christians and blisters to others (*C. Cels*. 5.14). Montanist

prophecy falls in this category, the Jewish and Christian apocalyptic tradition which postulated a millennial kingdom of the glorious faithful centering in a Jerusalem come down to earth.[46]

For Montanists--persons awaiting the imminent consummation[47]--inquiries about the future of the kind submitted at Abonoteichos should have been matters of secondary importance at most. Moreover, for them the locus of revelation was not Abonoteichos but certain towns in Phrygia.[48] And if, as we have seen (above, pp. 172-73), the adherents of the cult of the new Asclepius exhibited a staunch loyalty to their prophet, so, too, the Montanists were fiercely loyal to their prophets, defending them again and again in face-to-face encounters with opponents.[49] With their own prophets, their own preachers (see n. 52) and martyrs,[50] their own scriptures,[51] their own system of finances,[52] a distinctive ethos,[53] and set off from their Phrygian environment[54] and strengthened in their convictions and loyalties by conflicts with other Christians,[55] the Montanists formed a cohesive group. Confronted with the claims of the new Asclepius and the ecstatic behavior and wondrous foreknowledge of his prophet, the Montanists would doubtless have employed the label that Christians commonly used to discredit prophecy other than that of their own tradition and their own group: "demonic."

It was thus that anti-Montanist Christians explained the ecstatic behavior of the Montanist prophets. Prophecy in the state of ecstasy was, according to anti-Montanist polemic recorded by Eusebius, a sign of demonic possession and was not attested for the Jewish and Christian prophets in the traditions to which these anti-Montanists were committed.[56] That this was a case of special pleading is clear from the fact that first-century Christian sources attest ecstatic Christian prophecy and that Christians not involved in the Montanist controversy interpreted them as doing so (see the sources cited in Schepelern, 1929, 132-33, 153-54). Though the early anti-Montanist writers suggest there were doctrinal differences between themselves and the Montanists, Eusebius does not record any.[57] Other

Christian writers make clear that Montanists and mainstream
Christianity were not divided by differences in doctrine
(sources in Schepelern, 1929, 25-26), and modern scholarship generally concurs (e.g., Schepelern, 1929, 134-35;
Opitz, 1933, 207-08; Lietzmann, 1953, 200). What the anti-
Montanists found offensive in the Montanist movement is
evident from the matters they considered worthy of mention
in their polemic. These turn out to be challenges to the
integrity and stability of mainstream Christian communities
and to the authority of their leadership: divine spokesmen
authenticated, not mediately by divinely-chosen mainstream
leaders, but directly by divine inspiration, and standing
outside their control and in continuity with early Christian prophecy;[58] a sizeable and devoted following defiant
of mainstream leaders;[59] new scriptures and the interpretation of existing Christian scriptures in a way that
legitimated Montanism;[60] an ethos seen as subversive of
mainstream life-style (see n. 53 of this chapter). Moreover, a Christianity learning to accommodate its thought
and practice to Greco-Roman culture and to imperial rule
found disturbing a movement that was devoid of rapprochement with that culture[61] and fostered apocalyptic expectations that implied a less-than-perfect order in the
Empire.[62] Mainstream Christianity's rejection of Montanism
is not surprising. That it would, in addition, reject a
pagan cult similar in some aspects to Montanism, such as
that in Abonoteichos, is a point that need not be belabored.

At issue in each of the conflicts examined here is
the miraculous nature of the utterances, i.e., whether
deity did in fact speak through the persons who made that
claim. Social and cultural factors, as we have seen,
figure into the answers given, which reflect, not only
diverse, often competing social and cultural worlds, but
changes in the social and cultural situations of the groups
represented in the conflicts. What had been acceptable for
nascent Christianity of the first century in Greece and
Asia Minor where new revelations and pneumatic manifestations and utterances were not uncommon, polity was fluid,
and the relation to Greco-Roman culture and the Empire were

still largely undefined, is unacceptable to mainstream
Christianity in the second half of the second century as it
sought to come to terms with that culture and the Empire
and increasingly located divine authority and possession of
the Spirit in its leaders standing in succession to the
apostles.[63] Montanism, on the other hand, originated in a
geographical area and an ecclesiastical milieu where
episcopal authority was evidently not great,[64] charismata
had not been routinized, and rapprochement with Greco-Roman
culture and imperial authorities was not of great concern.
In such a setting, spontaneous manifestations of the Spirit,
in evident continuation or renewal of such phenomena in
earliest Christianity, were not unexpected nor unwelcome.
In view of the tenacity of pagan popular cultic piety,
which we have observed repeatedly in this study, and the
countercultural nature of Christianity, the mutual opposition of Christians and Alexander of Abonoteichos is not
unexpected. What is somewhat surprising is to find
numbered among the cult's clientele representatives of
another counterculture, the philosophical tradition, with
only a few persons, including a non-philosopher, Lucian,
representing the critical epistemological aspect of that
tradition. Figuring into this change are shifts in the
climate of thought (cf. p. 104 above), in the composition
of social classes in the Empire (see, e.g., Gager, 1971),
and in the political situation (see, e.g., M. Grant, 1968,
13ff.). The gradual modification and metamorphosis of the
social and cultural worlds of paganism, which we have
observed in this study and which has been documented elsewhere (Dodds, 1970; Armstrong, 1967, parts 1-4), and the
growing intellectual and social power and influence of
Christianity portended that in time Christian miracles
would come to supplant pagan miracles, sometimes by coopting
them: in his triumph the Galilean claimed the Asclepius
legacy as one of the spoils of war.[65]

11

CONCLUSION

Studies of early Christian miracle accounts and claims
often view them against their "background" in paganism and
Judaism, as though there were sharply drawn lines of demarcation and/or Christianity were the dominant entity in the
Greco-Roman world. Even those studies that do not make
these assumptions often import modern definitions and
understandings of "miracle" into early Christian (and non-
Christian) texts. Another common assumption is that
ancients differentiated little among extraordinary phenomena and tended to ascribe them indiscriminately to super-
normal agency. Understanding of those texts, and of
conflict over miracle claims, has been skewed as a result.

Our study has challenged these assumptions by
turning to the texts again and asking on what bases persons
in the Greco-Roman world demarcated the extraordinary from
the ordinary and ascribed certain extraordinary phenomena
to divine agency. It was seen, on the one hand, that they
had various and differentiated canons by which to demarcate
extraordinary from ordinary phenomena and, on the other,
that they did not view every unusual phenomenon as worked
by divine agency, that is, as "miracle"--there were other
modes of explanation. The canons of the ordinary varied,
however, from one period to another, from one people and
group to another, and often within a group and with social
status, education, and profession. Here lay the seeds of
conflict, which could fall along any of these lines.
Viewed from the perspective of language, the conflicts can
be seen as competitions in naming: affirming miracle of
the extraordinary phenomena of one's own group and denying
the name to those of rival groups. That is a sociological
judgment, and our study has shown that social and cultural

182

factors play a basic role in such conflicts and should
figure into attempts to understand them.

While such insights from the sociology of knowledge
relativize the arguments put forth by proponents of rival
miracle claims in the period under study, they should not
be seen as diminishing the importance of those arguments
for those who mounted them or as rendering superfluous
analysis of those arguments. Such analysis has predominated
in study of conflicts over miracle, however, and, as we
have seen, has often led to aporias because social and
cultural elements were often unspoken and unrecognized
warrants in argument. Our study makes the picture more
complex but in doing so contributes to understanding.

The complexity of the picture applies also to the
early Christian sources we have examined. A comparison of
these sources with pagan miracle texts shows that on
becoming a member of an early Christian community one did
not leave behind the common Greco-Roman canons of the
ordinary. Yet, for pagans, entry to such communities
entailed acquiring new referents for miracles--displacing
pagan deities with the Christian deity--and nihilation, by
various means, of wonders ascribed to the old deities.
Even Christians such as Justin, standing in the philosophical tradition and therefore possessed of a wider range of
options for assessing--and often rejecting--reports of
extraordinary phenomena, are seen defending extraordinary
phenomena of the Christian variety but rejecting those that
belong to "them." "They," as we have seen, often includes
other Christians or Christian groups, however, thus con-
firming once again the picture of the diversity of early
Christianity that has emerged in much recent study. Again,
understanding of these conflicts--between pagan and Christian and between Christian and Christian (or between pagan
and pagan)--is enhanced by attention to social and cultural
factors. It helps explain, for example, why Celsus rejects
Christian miracle claims while affirming similar pagan
ones, or why mainstream Christians reject Montanist
prophecy despite its affinities with early Christian traditions accepted by mainstream Christians.

The affinities between early Christianity and paganism have often been pointed out by scholars. Our study provides yet another illustration of that. Yet, as we have seen, early Christianity in many ways was distinctive enough to constitute a kind of counterculture. One means of Christian self-definition was polemic, including polemic over miracle claims. Precisely because early Christians were part of the Greco-Roman world, however, their polemic--and pagan counter-polemic--had to be sharp enough to establish differences and to legitimate the identities of what were rival social groups. And once again social and cultural elements are often discernible as unspoken warrants in the argumentation. In the light of the present study it would be interesting to pursue pagan-Christian conflict over miracle into subsequent centuries examining, for example, Origen's argument with Celsus, or Porphyry's with Origen and other Christians, or Augustine's with Porphyry. In doing so, attention should be paid to the changing social status of Christians and the changing nature of both Christianity and paganism over the decades. Some of the findings of our study might profitably be applied to investigation of conflict over miracle in the modern period.

For the study of ancient medicine and historiography it would be illuminating to explore in greater detail than was possible here the relation between ancient medicine and accounts of wondrous healings and the way historians, pagan and Christian, viewed and treated reports of extraordinary phenomena.

Neglected in our study, for the most part, for reasons of space, are the miracle accounts and claims in Jewish sources of the period. Investigation of these along the lines of the present study would make an important contribution to study of miracle texts.

Whatever the reasons and motives--propagandizing for a deity, the contingency of the human condition, a lust (and capacity) for wonder, the love of story--miracle accounts and claims bulk large in Greco-Roman sources and give substance to Goethe's dictum that "Miracle is faith's dearest child."

APPENDICES

A
HERODOTUS AND THE WONDROUS[1]

Herodotus is often dismissed as simply credulous and naive.
Such judgments fail to take account of the many times he
distances himself from what he is reporting through use of
indirect discourse (cf. the comments of A. D. Godley in the
Loeb edition, Vol. 1, xxiff.) or by explicit statements of
disbelief or suspension of belief (e.g., 1.5; 1.182; 2.123;
7.191; 8.8). He possesses a vocabulary for distinguishing
credible from incredible phenomena (e.g., 1.122-23, φάτις;
4.191, ἀκατάψευστος) albeit no real hierarchy of canons of
belief. For example, he suspends belief on whether the
young women on a certain island actually use feathers
smeared with pitch to collect gold dust from the mud, but
then says that anything can happen (εἴη δ᾽ ἂν πᾶν) and goes
on to report that he himself saw pitch taken from a pool of
water in Zacynthus (4.195). The canons he operates with
are mainly the unselfconscious kind noted in chapter two
(pp. 24-25), which inhere in the reports he simply records,
often without passing judgment, as part of his method
(2.123).

As to the divine as an explanatory factor, it
appears frequently in the traditions Herodotus reports,
which represent and reflect popular cultic piety, which
still has such force that it is more than once reported as
impeding military operations (7.205-06; 8.72; 9.7). He
shares that piety. In Book 2, e.g., he sometimes says he
will not name the name of a certain deity, and a similar
reverence is manifested in 9.65 where he attributes to
Demeter the θῶμα that in a battle fought near her grove
none of the Persians appeared (ἐφάνη) to have entered into
the sacred area (τέμενος) or died there. "I judge--if one
must make a judgment on divine affairs [εἴ τι περὶ τῶν

189

θείων πρηγμάτων δοκέειν δεῖ]--that the deity herself did
not receive them because they had burnt her temple, her
dwelling at Eleusis." Although Herodotus says that in his
history he will mention the gods only as necessary (2.3,
65), that proves to be quite frequently, both in the wonders
he reports and in his own interpretation of events. The
gods punish injustice (8.106) and are jealous of human
success (3.40); it is *nemesis* that causes Croesus' downfall
(1.34). One of the chief explanations (if not the chief
one) of the defeat of the Persians is their *asebeia* in
violating Greek land and Greek sanctuaries (see 8.109, 143-
44; 9.76; cf. 9.7). The social and cultural contexts of
such judgments are explored further in chapters five and
following of this study.

B
DIVINATION AND CULTURAL DIFFUSION[1]

Divination, which in English usage includes both prediction
of the future as well as discovery of hidden knowledge, is
an example both of diffusion of a cultural phenomenon and
of independent production of it in areas widely separated
in time and space.

On a functionalist view, divination exists in so
many cultures because it answers a definite human need.
Ecstatic prophecy, for example, which might be accounted
for on a diffusionist hypothesis in the ancient Near East
(Lindblom, 1962, 29ff.) or in ancient Greece (Fascher,
1927, 55-56), is a universal phenomenon, both synchroni-
cally and diachronically (see Lindblom, 1962, ch. 1; I. M.
Lewis, 1971) and is difficult to explain simply as diffusion. (Ecstasy, though admittedly catching, is not *that*
contagious.) The liver models used in hepatoscopy, on the
other hand, with their stylized features--and simply
through the fact of their existence--may plausibly be
regarded as an example of diffusion of a particular kind of
divination.

Discrete and independent or competing traditions of
divination are readily explicable on a functionalist view.
This discreteness is illustrated by a comparison of divination among the neighboring Etruscans and Romans (see
Bouché-Leclerq, 1963, vol. 4; Bloch, 1963, parts 2-3) and
by the Romans' consultation of the Etruscan specialists
(cf. the general statement in Livy 5.15.1 and the example
in Cicero, *De div*. 2.18.43). However, the Romans also
appropriated and indigenized (as well as rejected) Etruscan
and other non-Roman elements of divination (see the reconstruction in Bloch, 1963).

In the Greco-Roman world Stoicism's espousal of

191

divination did much to diffuse knowledge of it. Cicero, for example, drew on Posidonius (see Pohlenz, 1970, vol. 2, 117) as well as on his own training and experience as an augur.

C

THE IGNORANCE OF BYGONE AGES CONTRASTED WITH
PRESENT KNOWLEDGE IN THE UNDERSTANDING OF MIRACLE[1]

This theme, common in much modern discussion of miracle,
may be illustrated by a few significant examples.

Kant on the one hand sees no need to question the
Gospel miracles. On the other hand, his characterization
of them as *Hütte* that served the historical purpose of
introducing Christian doctrine, which really has no need
of them (Kant, 1907, 85; E.T., 1934, 79-80), accords with
his polemic against those who regard as miracles phenomena
that are (at least for the time being) inexplicable in
light of causation as presently understood (1907, 89; E.T.,
1934, 83, n.). "Wunder thun nichts zur Sache; sie dienen
nur, Lehren zu introduciren, die sonst sich auf Vernunft
gründen und, wenn sie einmal daseyn, sich auch wie ein
Gebäude bey Wegräumung des Gerüstes von selbst erhalten.
Es sind nicht Facta, sondern übernatürliche Deutungen von
Factis; denn die Bestimmung der Ursachen beruht immer auf
Vernunft."[2]

Schleiermacher's influential redefinition of miracle
proceeds from the assumption of a strict causal nexus
(*Naturzusammenhang*) of which ancients and traditional Christian interpretations were unaware, with the result that
they posited *absolute Wunder*, events allegedly occurring
outside that nexus ("etwas erfolgen soll, was aus der
Gesammtheit der endlichen Ursachen nicht zu begreifen ist")
(see Schleiermacher, 1960, paras. 14, 34, 47; 1958, 88-89,
115).

The programmatic statement by the well-known
rationalist H. E. G. Paulus (1828, vol. 1/1, 362, 364)
aptly characterizes much historical study of early Christian
miracles:

Ist nämlich aus der Erzählung deutlich, dass der Aufbewahrer
selbst und die Überlieferer der Erfolge sie mit Verwunderung als Etwas,
dessen Ursache sie sich nicht zu erklären vermochten, uns aufbewahrten,
so wird die historische Erklärungsweise, welche sich zuvörderst soviel
möglich in die Gedanken und Umstände der Augenzeugen und der Erzähler
zurückzuversetzen sucht, aus dergleichen Aufbewahrungen ohne allen
Anstand folgern, dass die Thataschen damals nach ihrem Ursprung
unerklärbar waren und daher als Wunder von den Erzählern mit
Verwunderung der Nachwelt übergeben worden sind. Bey dergleichen
historisch gegebenen Wundern zweifelt, wer die Quellen so nimmt, wie
sie da sind, mit Recht keinen Augenblick, dass sie ihrem Zeitalter und
den Geschichts-schreibern, der Ursache nach, unerklärbar und daher
Gegenstände der Verwunderung oder Wunder waren.
　　Dadurch, dass viele Erfolge mit Verwunderung erzählt sind, weil
ihre tiefere Ursachen *damals nicht* zu erforschen und nach den
Kenntnissen und Umständen des Zeitalters nicht zu erklären waren, kann
doch verständiger Weise kein Gränzstein gesetzt seyn, welcher sagte:
Das Geschehen *war* unerklärbar, also--wird, darf, soll es nie erklärt
werden.

That Paulus' view of the difference between ancient
and modern understanding of miracles has become common
property, even of many theologians dedicated to exposition
of the Christian faith, is shown by Michael Schmaus's
acceptance of the ever-widening province of scientific
explanations of extraordinary phenomena, thus reducing the
number of miracles (1969, 110-11).

D

ON THE DEFINITION OF "GNOSTIC"

In our text (ch. 8.3) the term "gnostic" is employed, in
accord with common usage, ancient and modern, to refer to
Christians and groups who prized special knowledge (*gnosis*)
postulating a downward movement of the divine that entraps
part of the divine, which must then be freed so it may
return to its origin.[1] Among ancient illustrations of such
usage one may refer to Origen's concession to Celsus that
there are self-professed "gnostic" Christians,[2] examples of
which are cited by Irenaeus, referring to Carpocratians,[3]
by Clement of Alexandria, referring to followers of
Prodicus "who falsely style themselves γνωστικούϛ" (*Strom.*
3.30.1), and by Hippolytus, referring to Naasenes.[4]

Many years ago R. P. Casey (1935), following R. A.
Lipsius (1875), sought to demonstrate that Ophites were the
original referents in Irenaeus' use of the term "gnostic."
Such a theory of Ophite priority in Irenaeus breaks down on
closer examination of the passages in which "gnostic"
(γνωστικοί, *gnostici, agnitores*) occurs. The term sometimes refers to a distinct group or stands in contrast to
other persons or groups,[5] but it is not all evident that
these "gnostics" are Ophites. Irenaeus can report that
"gnostics" were prior to the Valentinians,[6] but he also
asserts that a certain group--commonly identified as
Ophites (see above, ch. 8, n. 86)--derives from the Valentinians ("de Valentini schola generata est"; *Adv. h.* 1.30.
15; Harvey ed., 1.28.8) and that "gnostics" originated with
Menander, the disciple of Simon (3.4.3; Harvey ed., 3.4.3),
or with Simon himself.[7] Imprecision also marks Irenaeus'
usage in a number of other passages where the phrases
reliqui gnostici or *reliqui gnosticorum* function like "et
cetera," namely, as a concluding, catchall term in a

195

recital of errorist groups, some of which Irenaeus otherwise contrasts with "gnostics" but which he here groups
with them.[8] Or Irenaeus describes "gnostics" as many and
diverse;[9] that is, he does not have only one group in view
when he uses the term.

Casey is probably right in saying (1935, 50) that
"polemic zeal" "prompted Irenaeus to apply it carelessly
and in an ironical sense to sects who never employed it of
themselves." In any case, Irenaeus employs "gnostic" as a
general designation of diverse groups with some common
characteristics, a usage found also in Epiphanius (*Pan.*
25.2.1; 26.4.6; 31.7.8) and common among modern interpreters. In accord with such usage the persons Plotinus
attacks in *Enneads* 2.9 are designated "gnostics" by his
original editor Porphyry,[10] who in referring to what is
evidently *Enneads* 2.9 describes it as directed against
those who say that the maker of the cosmos and the cosmos
itself are evil,[11] that is, against persons with "gnostic"
traits, though Plotinus himself does not actually use the
term.

E
PLOTINUS AND GNOSTIC THAUMATURGY[1]

Though Plotinus never explicitly refers to "gnostics" in
the treatise commonly entitled *Against the Gnostics* (*Enn.*
2.9),[2] the treatise was understood by his first and subsequent editors as directed against them (see above, App. D),
and his description of the objects of his polemic accords
with general gnostic characteristics we observed in chapter
eight. Because Celsus and Plotinus both mount their arguments from Platonist platforms, Plotinus' treatise illuminates the implicit conflict we observed in chapter 8.3
between Celsus and Christian gnostics practicing thaumaturgy.

   Plotinus' polemic takes its start from first-hand
acquaintance with gnostics (*Enn.* 2.9.10.3-4; see p. 201
below) and with gnostic writings.[3] He looks with scorn on
what he labels the practice of magic (μαγεύειν) by gnostics
--their use of chants, charms, enchantments, suasions,
sounds, breathings, hissings.[4] He also ridicules the
gnostics' claim that they free from disease by ridding the
diseased, with a word (ἐξαιρεῖν λόγῳ), of the evil daemons
which supposedly cause disease (*Enn.* 2.9.14.11-15). Such
claims and practices Plotinus lumps with the feats
performed by magicians which cause the masses to marvel.[5]

   Plotinus' scorn has a familiar ring when one
recalls our analysis of "miracle" in the traditions of
Greek medicine and philosophy or Celsus' objections to
miracle claims in Jewish and Christian traditions.

   Plotinus' argument against what he reports as the
gnostics' view of the cause and cure of disease recalls the
Hippocratic polemic against the popular cultic view of
epilepsy as a "sacred disease" (above, p. 38). Like the
Hippocratic author, Plotinus argues that disease has

readily discernible causes and need not be attributed to
evil daemons; the cures of diseases demonstrate the same
thing (*Enn.* 2.9.14.17-23). By various *reductiones ad
absurdum* Plotinus demonstrates that the theory of demonic
causation of disease and the gnostic view of its cure are
logically unnecessary (2.4.14.23-25). Plotinus contrasts
such muddled and arrogant thinking with "our" philosophy,
with its straightforwardness, clarity, stability, and dis-
cretion, and its pursuit of a reverent rather than an
arrogant disposition (τὸ σέμνον, οὐ τὸ αὔθαδεϛ) (2.9.14.38-
43). This philosophy is the standard by which to measure
the views of others,[6] such as gnostic teachings, which are,
throughout, diametrically opposed to it.[7] In his polemic
Plotinus demonstrates how his philosophy is employed to
take the measure of gnostic "magic." To show the absurdity
and arrogance of gnostic chants and the like Plotinus asks
how sounds can affect incorporeal beings.[8] And what
presumption to address such chants to the higher powers
with the intent of making them obey their (the gnostics')
will (2.9.14.1-8)! To do so is to diminish the majesty of
those powers (2.9.14.9-11). As a foil to such practices
Plotinus puts forward the self-control and well-ordered
life-style advocated by philosophers and, as already noted,
the superior nature and goals of his philosophy (2.9.14.12-
13).

Even as Platonic philosophy is the context that
informs Plotinus' attack on gnostic "magic," so Greek
culture is the context of that philosophy, and, like
Celsus, Plotinus is a self-conscious representative of both.
This self-consciousness is seen in Plotinus' assertion that
the gnostics' thaumaturgical practices, while appealing to
the masses, do not deceive persons schooled in Greek
culture, of which Greek philosophy is the capstone.[9] It is
seen also when Plotinus, like Celsus (above, pp. 109-10),
assumes that that ancient culture and its authentic representatives, past and present, are superior to persons like
the gnostics who, while clearly indebted to that culture,
nonetheless ridicule and pervert it. Thus, while gnostics
may correctly derive some of their teachings from Plato and

other divine men of the past,[10] the things they have taken
from the ancients (τοῖς παλαιοῖς) have taken on some additions that are not fitting.[11] Such new teachings "have
been found outside the truth."[12] Plotinus summarizes some
of these points where the gnostics stand in opposition
(ἐναντιοῦσθαι) to the ancients: "they introduce becomings
and dissolutions of all kinds, find fault with the universe,
censure the soul for its association with the body, criticize the one who directs the universe, identify the demiurge
with Soul, and ascribe to the latter the same properties as
those possessed by individual souls."[13] Even when the
gnostics draw on Plato they misread him in constructing
their cosmogony[14] and cosmology[15] and their teachings on
soul[16] and the noetic realities.[17] The gnostics' assertion
that the association of the soul with the body is not to
the soul's advantage originated, not with them (2.9.7.2-4),
but with Plato (2.9.17.1-4). They misread him, however, in
simply hating the body (ibid.) rather than accepting the
necessity of remaining in the body, living in houses prepared by a good sister soul[18] and learning to take off this
bodily nature in thought in order to behold the noetic
sphere.[19] And rather than viewing the visible cosmos as
wicked and the celestial bodies as hostile,[20] they should
follow Plato (or Plotinus) in viewing this world as a
beautiful image of the higher world (*Enn.* 2.9.4.22ff.; see
n. 15 above) and the celestial bodies as beneficent
deities.[21]

Plotinus' annoyance with the gnostics is in part
the annoyance of the professional philosopher with dilet-
tantes who fail to carry premises and assertions through to
their logical conclusions. If the gnostics don't perceive
where the rashness of their cosmic pessimism leads (οὐδ'
ὅπου τὸ θράσος αὐτοῦ τοῦτο χωρεῖ), Plotinus does, and
demonstrates the untenability of such pessimism (2.9.13.
1ff.) as well as of their cosmogony (2.9.12.33ff.), their
view of the cure of disease (2.9.14.24-35), their denial of
providence (2.9.16.14ff.), and their despising of the celestial bodies (2.9.16.1-14). It is persons unskilled in
argumentation and ignorant of educated *gnosis*, i.e., Greek

philosophical tradition, who would be fearful of the fiery spheres in the sky.[22] Their ignorance is shown also by their talk of virtue without defining it or ever having written on the subject and without explaining *how* one attains virtue (2.9.15.27ff.). It is seen also in their clumsy behavior in setting forth their teachings: rather than demonstrating these in a friendly, philosophical, and even-handed way (εὐμενῶς καὶ φιλοσόφως . . . δικαίως), they ridicule and insult those who differ with them (2.9.6. 35ff.).

In part, however, Plotinus' polemic against the gnostics may represent an effort to purge himself of positions that were once close to his own or to suppress a continuing tension in his own thought, or both. The tension is generally acknowledged by scholars (e.g., those cited in Dodds, 1970, 25, n. 1). In the formulation of Dodds and Armstrong, it is the tension between the cosmology of the *Timaeus* (with its affirmation of the visible cosmos as an admirable product of soul) and the psychology of the *Phaedo* and the *Phaedrus* (with their view of the soul's descent into human form as unfortunate, the result of the soul's loss of its "wings") (cf. Dodds, 1970, 25; Armstrong, 1967, 230). Scholars who have attended to the chronological order of Plotinus' treatises and/or to a genetic study of his thought[23] see his attack on the gnostic view that arrogance and audacity (*tolma*) motivate the soul in its task of making[24] as a disowning of a view which he himself once held,[25] which he found in Plato (*Enn.* 4.8.1), and which he had once tried to reconcile with the cosmogony of the *Timaeus* (*Enn.* 4.8.5; cf. Dodds, 1970, 25). Plotinus moved, it seems, from ascribing the soul's descent to *tolma*, to rejection of that view and ascription of it to the gnostics, to a positive view of the descent (see the references cited in Dodds, 1970, 25-26). "Whatever his earlier doubts, Plotinus emerges in the end as the upholder of Hellenic rationalism,"[26] affirming the goodness of the visible cosmos and the culture predicated on that traditional Greek affirmation.[27]

The gnostics' thaumaturgical claims and their view

of the cause and cure of disease are only egregious aspects
of what Plotinus sees as a threat to that culture. He
defends it, as we have seen, against gnostic perversion and
subversion. It is evident from the foregoing that such
defense is a concern Plotinus shares with Celsus. And even
as Celsus views Christians as an alien body in pagan
society (above, pp. 109ff.), so Plotinus finds in his
gnostic opponents some of the same alienating traits
adduced by Celsus in his polemic. The gnostics' pessimistic
otherworldliness (above, p. 199) and their absurd elitism
and narcissism[28] set them apart from traditional pagan
society, as do their disrespect for traditional deities,[29]
their abdication of responsibility for persons outside
their own circle,[30] and their disdain for "all laws in this
world and for the virtue won long ago."[31] Such disdain
subverts the socialization processes that sustain culture
and society.[32] It accords with this that gnostics nihilate
the founders and foremost representatives of pagan culture
(2.9.6.36, 44, 49-51) and that, far from being an elite
group, as they imagine, embrace the worst sort of people,[33]
to the detriment of society.

    While Plotinus' polemic is sharp at times, it is
not as shrill as that of Celsus. Plotinus' ultimate
attitude to his opponents (though not to their teachings)
is one of resignation. *"What is one to say"* (τί ἄν τιſ
εἴποι), asks Plotinus, in face of some of the gnostics'
hopelessly muddled notions about the soul (2.9.5.22-23)?
The gnostics need to be taught--*"if they would bear with it
in good spirit"* (εἰ εὐγνωμόνωſ ἀνέχοιντο)--the nature of
soul and of the demiurge (2.9.8.1-6). In an obvious
reference to his opponents, he asks whether anyone--*"unless
he had gone daft"*--would put up with the thought that human
wisdom is superior to that of the celestial deities.[34] At
one point Plotinus pauses to profess compunctions about
continuing his detailed refutation of gnostic teachings:
he has gnostic friends, and he has no hope of convincing
them of their error in any case. They "chanced upon this
teaching before they became our friends," and now "a certain regard for them possesses us."[35] "I do not know how

they persist in it [gnostic teaching]," he confesses.[36]
Plotinus' treatise, then, is directed not *to* gnostics but
against them, for the sake of his pupils: "The things we
have said are addressed to our pupils, not to them [the
gnostics]--for there is nothing more that might be done to
persuade them--in order that they [the pupils] may not be
disturbed by them [the gnostics], who do not provide proofs
(for how could they?) but, rather, make audacious assertions. . . ."[37]

      Plotinus' attitude to his gnostic opponents is, at
least, an implicit recognition that what is in conflict
between him and them is not simply discrete issues or prac-
tices--"magic," cosmogony and cosmology, anthropology--but
whole ways of constructing reality, social and cultural
"worlds" (for this terminology see Berger, 1969, ch. 1).
Thus, while Plotinus may have denigrated some of the
gnostics' beliefs and practices as "magic," this does not
mean he rejects them simply because they are "magic."
Certain passages, both in Porphyry and in Plotinus, support
the claim that Plotinus, like others in his day (e.g.,
Origen; above, p. 58), believed in the efficacy of practices designated as "magic" (see the passages and scholarly
discussion cited in Armstrong, 1967, 207-09). His objection to the gnostic variety, as we have seen, was to the
premises that were operative and the use to which it was
put; gnostic "magic" was part of the gnostic "world," a
world Plotinus found incompatible with his own.[38]

F

STUDIES OF LUCIAN'S *ALEXANDER THE FALSE PROPHET*

Until inscriptions and coins bearing on Alexander and his
deity were discovered and catalogued, Lucian's account was
the only certain evidence on the subject.[1] Consequently,
estimates of Alexander and his cult generally took their
cue from Lucian's interpretation of them. A notable
example is Cumont's essay of 1887, written at the age of
19. Thirty-five years later, in another essay on Alexander,
written to atone for "un péché de jeunesse," Cumont characterized his earlier work as "d'une érudition un peu super-
ficielle" (1922, 202). During the period between these two
essays, estimates of Alexander and his cult and Lucian's
treatment of them had begun to change, with Lucian's stock
falling. Three years after the publication of Cumont's
first essay, A. Thimme (1890) sought to rehabilitate
Alexander and his cult, but his effort was vitiated by the
fact that it argued solely from the text of Lucian. Otto
Weinreich's groundbreaking study of 1921 was notable for
its use of the inscriptional and numismatic evidence now
available and the way it drew on that evidence to address
fresh questions to Lucian's account.[2] He drew attention to
the disparity between the evident success of this new
Asclepius cult, as attested by the new evidence, and what
he regarded as Lucian's maliciously simplistic explanation
of that success. He also sought to understand Alexander
and the cult in the context of second-century religiosity,
asking what religious needs they satisfied and which
religious forms they utilized. Cumont, in his second
essay, paid tribute to Weinreich's study, and A. D. Nock
modestly characterized his own brief but learned and
suggestive essay as "in the nature of a supplement to his
admirable paper."[3]

Weinreich's disdain for Lucian (1921, 130) is exceeded, perhaps, only by Lucian's hatred of Alexander. M. Caster's edition and translation of Lucian's piece (1938), with its extended commentary and detailed assessments, deals more adequately both with Lucian and Alexander. Since Caster's dissertation was a detailed study of *Lucien et le pensée religieuse de son temps* (1937), he brought to his study of Lucian's *Alexander* thorough knowledge of the Lucianic corpus. Accordingly, his work affords many fresh insights.

Subsequent literature on Lucian and Alexander reveals its indebtedness to these studies,[4] though, as is noted in chapter ten above, the hermeneutical conclusions are sometimes not drawn by scholars.

N O T E S

Notes to Preface

[1] In English, *inter alia*, Gager, 1975, the works by R. M. Grant, A. Malherbe, and G. Theissen reviewed by Gager, 1979; also Hock, 1979; Kee, 1980; Elliott, 1981. In German the studies by Gerd Theissen have been groundbreaking; they are noted in the pages that follow or in the works just cited. My investigation, undertaken and carried through largely independently of these works, has at many points been confirmed by and has benefited from subsequent examination of them; that there are differences in approach and interpretation between these studies and my own is also clear.

[2] See, e.g., Bieler, 1967, vol. 1, 84-87; von Wetter, 1916, 73-82; R. M. Grant, 1966, 93 (". . . in polemical writing, your magic is my miracle, and vice-versa"); Kolenkow, 1976; J. Z. Smith, 1975; Herzog, 1931, 140 ("Aberglaube ist immer der Glaube der Anderen; für den römischen Staat waren das die Christen, für die Christen waren es die Altglaübigen"); Theissen, 1974b, 230 ("'Aberglaube' ist dann der in einer Gesellschaft abgelehnte Glaube, 'Glaube', so könnte man ironisch formulieren, der offiziell anerkannte Aberglaube. Wo die Grenze zu ziehen ist, bestimmen die massgeblichen Kreise").

[3] Cf. Elliott's remarks, 1978, 592, and the comments of Theissen, 1975a, regarding the sociological study of conflicts in early Christianity.

[4] Here and throughout the study I use "pagan," non-pejoratively, to designate persons in the ancient Mediterranean world who were neither Jews nor followers of Christ; so also Dodds, 1970.

Notes to Chapter 1

[1] On definitions and terminology see further, ch. 4 below. Ancient examples of etymological definitions of miracle are given in Thulin, 1905, 194ff.

[2] According to Pliny (*N.H.* 2.53), Gallus published an explanation of solar and lunar eclipses. Cicero, *De Senec.* 14.49, describes Gallus as a geometer and astronomer who predicted solar and lunar eclipses. Cicero, *De div.* 2.6.17, amounts to a summary of what an educated person of his day might be expected to know about the causes of eclipses and other celestial phenomena; such knowledge makes them predictable. Cf. further Seneca, *N.Q.* 7.25.3.

[3] Livy records other situations where eclipses are reported as *prodigia* (7.28.7; 22.1.9; 30.38.8); he is probably being faithful to his sources here. A solar eclipse which he presents as caused by the moon's shadow he does not label a *prodigium* (37.4.4).

[4] See below, ch. 6.1, on "significant others."

[5] Herodotus, 1.74, similarly juxtaposes two traditions of knowledge: a solar eclipse takes the warring Lydian and Medean armies unawares, moving them to make peace; Thales of Miletus, on the other

hand, has predicted the eclipse to the Ionians. Plutarch offers
several such examples of eclipses explained by reference to deity, on
the one hand, and, on the other, as caused by alignment of earth, sun,
and moon; e.g., *De superstit.* 169A-B, *De fac. lun.* 931Dff.

Notes to Chapter 2

[1]See the brief exposition in R. M. Grant, 1952, 57-58, and the
studies cited there. Some examples of *adynata* are rivers flowing up-
stream, night not following day, the sun changing its course, trees in
the sea, fish on land.

[2]For an overview see Ziegler, 1949, 1137-66; more recently,
Giannini, 1963, 1964. The first modern collection, A. Westermann,
Paradoxographoi: Scriptores Rerum Mirabilium Graeci (Braunschweig,
1839), was not accessible to me. The most recent edition (with Latin
translation) is Giannini, *Paradoxographorum.*

[3]*Att. noct.* 9.4.2 (libri Graeci miraculorum fabularumque pleni,
res inauditae, incredulae . . .).

[4]In Origen, *C. Cels.* 2.55; 3.26, 32-33; see further, ch. 8
below.

[5]Chadwick, *Contra Celsum,* 149, n. 1, gives some of the sources
plus secondary literature.

[6]For example, chapters 2-6 of Apollonius, *Mirabilia,* which
Ziegler, 1949, 1152, and Giannini, 1963, 122, place in the second
century B.C.E.; Greek text with Latin translation in Giannini, *Paradoxographorum,* 120-27; E. T. (and unidentified Greek text) in Tiede,
1972, 313-16. Also Ps.-Aristotle, *De mirabilibus auscultationibus*
839a; also in Gianinni; the collection is variously dated: Ziegler,
1949, 1151, Hellenistic period; G. E. L. Owen in *Oxford Classical
Dictionary* ([2]1970), 115, the second to the sixth century. Phlegon, *De
mirabilibus* 1 (early second century; in Giannini, *Paradoxographorum,*
170-78), recounts the story (only partially preserved) of nocturnal
visits by a dead girl, which Ziegler, 1949, 1157, includes among
"Gespenstergeschichten"; however, this "ghost" has nightly intercourse
with a young male guest in the house and, when surprised by her parents
and after a valediction, "immediately became dead and her body was
stretched, visible, on the couch" (1.12). Chapter 3 is also a revivification account (ἀνέστη ὁ βούπλαγοϛ ἐκ τῶν νεκρῶν, ἔχων τραύματα
δέκα δύο, 3.4, line 239) while chapter 2 is indeed a *Gespenster-
geschichte.*

[7]An instructive summary that bears on some of the points of our
discussion is Talbert, 1975.

[8]See below, ch. 3.1.1, on reproduction, and cf. the virgin
birth accounts and controversies (below, ch. 8.1). Helen of Troy, in
Euripides, *Helen* 256, says that her birth (from an egg) has made her
ἀνθρώποιϛ τέραϛ; cf. P. Stein, 1909, 13, 20. In demarcating
Jesus' birth Origen uses "marriage that is customary for humans"
(συνήθων ἀνθρώποιϛ γαμῶν, *C. Cels.* 1.32) as a canon. Lucian's account

of reproduction on the moon, *Ver. hist.* 1.22, is a satire on accounts of odd modes of regeneration, such as Dionysus' from Zeus's thigh or insemination by the wind (see below, ch. 3.1.1.2): men have intercourse with men and conceive in the thigh, whence the child is delivered stillborn, and, placed facing into the wind, comes to life.

⁹Hence the accounts of the precociousness of certain more-than-human figures: for Jesus, see the references in Bauer, 1909, 92ff.; for pagan figures, Bieler, 1967, vol. 1, 34-35; in contemporary Jewish literature: Moses in Philo's *Vita Mos.* 1.18-21; Noah, *1 En.* 106.3, 11; *4 Ez.* 6.21 interprets such precociousness as an omen.

¹⁰Apparitions in dreams or otherwise are therefore frequently larger than life; see *Poim.* 1 (ὑπερμεγέθη μέτρῳ ἀπεριορίστῳ) and the further references in H. C. Puech's note *ad loc.* in Nock and Festugière, 1960, and some of the examples cited in Krauss, 1930, 139-61, to which may be added, from classical literature, Herodotus 5.55-56 and 7.12 (ἄνδρα μέγαν); 6.117 (a φάσμα appears: ἄνδρα . . . ὁπλίτην . . . μέγαν); 8.38 (two hoplites μέζοναʃ ἢ κατ' ἀνθρώπην φύσιν ἔχονταʃ assist the Greeks against the Persians); and Suetonius, *Jul.* 32 (*eximia magnitudine*); from Christian literature, Rev. 10.2; from Jewish (?) literature, *2 En.* 1.4 (two men bigger than any ever seen on earth). The stories of giants and reports of huge footprints in rock (Herodotus 4.82) or of unearthing of hugh bones or corpses (Herodotus 1.67-68; Pliny, *N.H.* 7.73) also belong here; see further, Rohde, 1966, vol. 1, 143, n. 35.

¹¹Redundant, deficient, and malformed parts were all taken cognizance of. Reports of hybrids--dogheaded men, headless men, etc.-- were the stock in trade of ethnography (Herodotus 4.191 is a good example) and of paradoxography. With apparitions, unusual appearance is frequently noted (often along with size, see the Herodotus and Suetonius references in the preceding note), e.g., Mk. 9.3 par.; Rev. 1.13-16; Tacitus, *Ann.* 11.21 ("species muliebris ultra modum humanum"); P. Oxy. 11.1381. 119-20 (λαμπ[ρ]αῖʃ ἠμφιεσμένοʃ). See further, below, n. 46.

¹²E.g., Homer, *Od.* 11.215ff.; Herodotus 3.62; "Palaephatus" (Grant, 1952, 47-48); Pliny, *N.H.* 2.27; 7.189; Mk. 5.40 par.; Acts 17.32; Jn. 11.39; *Acts Thom.* 9.96. The souls of the dead may return but only for a time, as when Agamemnon says he will return to assist in the revenge of his murder (Aeschylus, *Choeph.* 459f.; *Eum.* 578; Euripides, *Herc. Fur.* 492); cf. also Phlegon, *Mirab.* 2 (in Giannini, *Paradoxographorum*, 180, lines 143-44, 164-65): the ghost says the lords of the underworld permit her only a limited stay. Metempsychosis is a return, but with one's former identity erased, while survival after death is not a return at all.

¹³For varieties of peoples see the references in M. Smith, 1971, 174-88; for groupings, ibid., 181-82.

¹⁴Heroes and deities are distinguished from one another in some texts that list them side by side, e.g., Herodotus 8.109 and Arrian, *Anab.* 4.11.3; other references in Eitrem, 1912, 1112; on θεοῖʃ ἡρώσιʃ = *dis Manibus* in epitaphs, ibid., 1139, and Lattimore, 1942, 99. Roloff, 1970, concludes that in some respects (good looks, size, strength, courage) the heroes in the Homeric and Hesiodic mold (p. 3) are different from gods only quantitatively, but in others

(vulnerability, imperfection, and immortality) differ qualitatively (p. 79); he cites as a paradigm Bellerophon's futile attempt to storm Olympus (p. 131). There were varieties of heroes, however. Some were spoken of as gods and "received the sacrifice appropriate to a god"; Nock, 1944, 144; in Nock, 1972, vol. 2, 578. Cf. further Nock's observation (p. 162 = p. 593) "that the term *heros* often meant 'minor deity' and not 'man who lived and died and subsequently received veneration'"; and Farnell's first type of hero (Farnell, 1921). In speaking of heroes, the "human" canon of judgment is sometimes explicitly stated; see above, n. 10 (Herodotus 8.38).

[15] Eitrem, 1912, provides an overview; further, Rohde, 1966, vol. 1, 121ff.; and Nock, 1944.

[16] See Lattimore, 1942, 97. Eitrem, 1912, 1138, interprets this democratization of the term as a return to the starting point of hero cult: the hero is "die mächtige Totenseele." This seems to me to go beyond the evidence.

[17] See ibid., 1131ff., for references.

[18] E.g., good looks (Herodotus 5.47). Oracles frequently played a part in heroization, advising it as a solution to some difficulty plaguing a locality. Cf. Rohde, 1966, vol. 1, 128-31.

[19] This is a long and wide stream of tradition, both in paganism and Christianity; see the references in Pease, Cicero, *De div.* 1.30.63 (pp. 206-07). In the Jewish antecedents of Christianity further testament literature, such as *Testaments of the Twelve Patriarchs*, may be added to the canonical references Pease cites. Early Christian examples not noted in Pease include the passion predictions and the apocalyptic discourses in the Synoptic gospels and the farewell discourse in the Fourth Gospel as well as Ignatius, *Trall.* 5.2; *Mart. Polyc.* 5.2; 12.3.

[20] See the Christian martyr acts. Jewish antecedents: *Asc. Isa.* 5.14; 4 Macc. 6.5ff.; 9.21ff. Cf. in H. A. Musurillo (ed.), *Acts of the Pagan Martyrs: Acta Alexandrinorum* (Oxford: Clarendon, 1954), P. Oxy. 1242, lines 40ff. (p. 48).

[21] See Eitrem, 1912, 1112ff., for pagan references; cf. Guthrie, 1954, 232ff. Though the description of a Christian's tomb as ἡρῷον was not necessarily significant (Lattimore, 1942, 316), the great attention paid to martyrs' remains (as early as *Mart. Polycarp.* 17.1, 18.2 [cf. the transference of heroes' bones, in Rohde, 1966, vol. 1, 143, nn. 35-37], though adumbrated already in passages such as Mk. 5.25ff. parr., 6.56 par., Acts 19.12) and the importance of saints' and martyrs' tombs (in R. M. Grant's succinct paraphrase: *cujus tumulus, ejus religio*) have strong affinities with pagan hero cult. A summary comparison of pagan and Christian beliefs and practices concerning the tombs and remains of heroes and Christian martyrs is given in Pfister, 1909, ch. 14.

[22] See Cerfaux and Tondriau, 1956, and the sources and secondary literature cited there, to which may be added the important article by Nock, 1957 (in Nock, 1972, vol. 2, 833-46), which is a partial corrective to one of the statements in Nock, 1952, 481.

[23]Pyrrhus possesses δύναμιν θεῖαν in his big toe (Plutarch, *Pyrrhus* 3.4-5); the infant Augustus quiets the frogs on his grandfather's estate (Suetonius, *Aug.* 94.7); Vespasian performs two healings (Tacitus, *Hist.* 4.81; Suetonius, *Vesp.* 7; Dio Cassius, *Rom. Hist.* 65.8). Nock's assertion, 1957, 118 (1972, vol. 2, 838), that Augustus' command here "can hardly be regarded as a deliberate action" (as in a similar account in *Acts Jn.* 60), ignores the traditions of precocious infants; see n. 9 above. The Vespasian accounts perhaps stem from a Sarapis aretalogy (cf. Nock, ibid.), but in their present form they also clearly glorify Vespasian.

[24]Herodotus 7.203 (οὐ γὰρ θεὸν εἶναι . . . ἀλλ᾽ ἄνθρωπον).

[25]See Cerfaux and Tondriau, 1956, 139-40, and the sources cited there. Callisthenes' speech against prostration to Alexander (Arrian, *Anab.* 4.11.1-12.2) argues from Macedonian law (νόμῳ Μακεδόνων, 4.11.6) and the distinction between gods and mortals (ἄνθρωποι, 4.11.2-5).

[26]Hymn to Demetrius Poliorcetes, in Athenaeus, *Deipnos.* 6.63. 253d-f.

[27]Suetonius, *Aug.* 53; *Vesp.* 12; cf. Vespasian's joke when his death is near, "Vae, puto deus fio" (ibid., 23.4).

[28]Tertullian, *Apol.* 33.4: in triumphs the emperor is reminded by a call from behind him, "Respice post te! hominem te memento!"

[29]Cicero, *Phil.* 1.6.13; Pliny, *N.H.* 7.188, though not referring explicitly to the emperor, rejects the practice of making a god of a person who already has ceased to be even a human ("deumque faciendo qui iam etiam esse desierit"); Pliny the Younger, *Paneg. for Trajan*: Trajan is "sanctus et diis simillimus princeps" (7), with divine power (4), but he should never forget that he is a human and rules over other humans (2; cf. 52, 54).

[30]Nero is honored with a statue as large as that of Mars (Tacitus, *Ann.* 13.8). Domitian employs the title (and is acclaimed as) "Dominus et deus noster" (Suetonius, *Dom.* 13.1-2).

[31]The passages refer to traditional (generally Homeric) designations of Zeus as a sovereign (*First Discourse* 39) or of good rulers as sons of Zeus (*Fourth Discourse* 27) or reared by or dear to Zeus (ibid., 41; *First Discourse* 38) or like to Zeus in counsel (ibid., 38); royalty (βασιλεία) is called a child of King Zeus (ibid., 73). Popular feeling is evident in the belief in *Nero redivivus*, which, though not limited to the provinces (see Suetonius, *Nero* 57.1), is especially strong there; pagan sources in Cerfaux and Tondriau, 1956, 353, n. 3; Jewish and Christian sources in Reicke, 1968, 243. On the belief among pagans, Jews, and Christians in a world deliverer see Nilsson, 1961, 390-92; the nature of this deliverer--divine, human, or both--is a notoriously complex question.

[32]Philo, *Leg. ad. G.* 75: Gaius (Caligula) "no longer considered it worthy to remain within the bounds of human nature [ἐν τοῖς τῆς ἀνθρωπίνης φύσεως ὅροις] but overstepped them since he was eager to be considered a god [θεός]." He gives as his reason the necessity to be different as measured by the canon of the majority of humans (μὴ κατ᾽ ἄνθρωπον εἶναι), even as men in charge of herds are not themselves

members of the herd (76). However, says Philo, compared with the gods or demigods, Gaius is different in his nature, essence, and character (114, φύσιϳ, οὐσία, προαίρεσιϳ).

[33]Rom. 13.1ff. (on ἐξουσίαι as referring both to human and more-than-human authorities, see Cullmann, 1956, 95-114, and Käsemann, 1959; 1 Tim. 2.1ff.; Tit. 3.1; 1 Pet. 2.13ff.; Polycarp, *Phil.* 12.3.

[34]On the difficulty of making sharp distinctions here, however, see M. Smith, 1971, 187.

[35]See ibid., 182, and sources and literature cited there; Bieler, 1967, passim.

[36]For the variety of terms designating likeness to deity in a number of classical sources see Roloff, 1970, 3ff.

[37]Cf. Celsus (*C. Cels.* 7.9): "It is common and customary for each of the prophets just mentioned to say, 'I am God, or a son of God, or a divine spirit' [ἐγὼ ὁ θεόϳ εἰμι ἢ θεοῦ παῖϳ ἢ πνεῦμα θεῖον]."

[38]In the documentation that follows I cite sources about Jesus and, to indicate that the particular trait is not peculiar to Christian sources or idiosyncratic in the Greco-Roman world, also pagan sources on similar phenomena.

[39]On reproduction in the ordinary way as the canon see n. 8 above. The Matthean and Lucan genealogies trace Jesus' ancestry to David through Joseph, an embarrassment to the virgin-birth traditions which stimulated efforts to trace it through Mary; see Bauer, 1909, 13ff.; on attempts to harmonize the two genealogies, Jeremias, 1969, 290; Johnson, 1969, 140-45. In Ebionite traditions, Jesus' human origin is assumed; see the references in Bauer, 1909, 30ff. In Marcion's denial of a human origin for Jesus, the ordinary means of reproduction are presupposed, as something unworthy of an extraordinary being like a deity (references, ibid., 34). Pagan changes of Mary's adultery: *C. Cels.* 1.28, 32.

[40]See *C. Cels.* 1.66: blood, not ichor, flowed in Jesus' veins (quoting Homer *Il.* 5.340); also 1.70; etc.; see below, ch. 8.

[41]Except for the references to overcoming of death, I exclude the post-resurrection appearances.

[42]Walking on the sea, Mk. 6.45-52 par.; pagan parallels in Bultmann, 1957, 251-52.

[43]Lk. 4.30; Jn. 8.59; 10.39. Cf. Philostratus' Apolloniu; who tells Nero's interrogator that his is a body no one can bind (4.44) and who is able to remove his foot from fetters and reinsert it at will (7.38; 8.13).

[44]Jn. 6.21; cf. Acts 8.39-40. Pagan parallels in Bultmann, 1956, *ad* 6.21, n. See also Philostratus, *Apoll.* 4.10; 8.8, 12.

[45]On mortality as the general lot of humans cf. above, n. 12. Jesus "could not be held by death" (Acts 2.24) may be taken as the

motif of the Christian resurrection accounts. Pagan parallels in the classical period, in Roloff, 1970, 124-30, 150-56. In the Greco-Roman period, see above, p. 9, and Lucian, *Peregrinus* 6; 27-29; *Alex.* 40; Philostratus, *Apoll.* 8.30-31; cf. Talbert, 1975.

[46]Mk. 9.2-8 par.; on the recent discussion of this pericope see Robinson and Koester, 1971, 49, n. 43. Pfister, 1924a, 314-16, outlines the typical characteristics of epiphanies; the canon is the ordinary human in respect of size and appearance.

[47]In the canonical gospels: Mk. 2.8; Lk. 6.8; Matt. 12.25//Lk. 11.17; the passion predictions and the apocalypses; Jn. 1.48; 2.25, etc., and the farewell discourses. On special knowledge as a mark of divinity cf. Roloff, 1970, 111-12.

[48]The astonishment at both the content and the manner of Jesus' teaching, attested both in the synoptic (Mk. 1.22 par.; Mk. 6.2//Mt. 13.54; Mk. 11.18) and Johannine (Jn. 7.15) traditions, implies the speech of ordinary humans as a canon. Sometimes the canon is more explicitly stated: Lk. 4.22; Jn. 7.46. Cf. Pliny, *N.H.*, Pref., 29 (Theophrastus was a man so great in oratory that he won the title *divinum*); Plutarch, *Marius* 44; other pagan sources in Bieler, 1967, vol. 1, 54-55.

[49]An unusual display of power evokes the question of the person's nature (Mt. 8.27: ποταπός ἐστιν οὗτος). When Paul and Barnabas are placed in the category of Olympian gods because of a healing they have performed, they measure themselves and their worshipers by the canon of ᾰνθρωπος (Acts 14.15). In certain of the Acts speeches, on the other hand, the wonders Jesus performed do not remove him from the category of "man" (ἀνήρ); rather the operative power is ascribed to God (2.22-23; 10.38).

[50]Virtue: obedience to God (Mk. 1.9-11 par.; Mk. 14.32-42 par.; Heb. 4.15), in fulfillment of the divine will expressed in the scriptures (1 Cor. 15.3-4, and the speeches in Acts). Beneficence: Acts 10.38 may be taken as the motif of the miracles in the Synoptics and John, where people flock to Jesus for help. The infancy gospels, on the other hand, contain *Strafwunder*. Origen uses the argument from virtue and beneficence to dissociate Jesus from Celsus' charges against him, e.g., 1.63-68. On virtue and beneficence as marks of divinity see Talbert, 1975.

[51]See Bieler, 1967, vol. 1, 51ff.; Roloff, 1970, 103ff.; cf. *C. Cels.* 6.75.

[52]The application of Isa. 52.14 and 53.2-3 to Jesus may have led to the description of him as ugly; *C. Cels.* 6.75; Clement Alex., *Paed.* 3.3, 2 (explicitly quoting Isa., viz., 53.2); *Acts Pet.* 24 ("another prophet says" = Isa. 53.2). In a series of contradictory epiphanies of the earthly Jesus in *Acts Jn.*, Jesus is described as handsome (88) and enormously tall (90) but also as small and ugly (89).

[53]Cf. Justin, *Dial.* 48.3 (ᾰνθρωπος ὁμοιοπαθής ἡμῖν and ᾰνθρωπος ἐξ ἀνθρώπων).

[54]Pliny, *N.H.* 10.3-5, reporting many of the customary details about the phoenix as an Arabian bird, says he does not know whether the

bird is *fabulose*, but he is certain that a supposed phoenix brought to
Rome in his lifetime was a phony (*falsum*, 10.5).

[55]A concise treatment, rich in source material, is to be found
in Bernert, 1941, 1129-30, and Leisegang, 1941, 1130-64 (older secondary
literature cited, 1131-32, et passim). More recent, and with citation
of other important treatments, are R. M. Grant, 1952, ch. 1, and
Koester, 1969, 246-71.

[56]Photius (followed by the Suda), s.v. τέραϳ: παραπλάσμα· παρὰ
φύσιν τεχθέν; the Suda, further: τὸ παρὰ φύσιν γενόμενον. *Etymologicon
Magnum*, s.v. τέραϳ: τέραϳ λέγεται τὸ παρὰ φύσιν γενόμενον πρᾶγμα.

[57]Cf. Plato, *Cratyl.* 393B, 394D; Suetonius, *Claud.* 3.2:
Claudius' mother said he was a portent of a man, not finished by nature,
but only begun ("portentum eum hominis . . . nec absolutum a natura, sed
tantum incohatum").

[58]ἡ φύσιϳ ἡ ἀνθρωπίνη; see the pagan and Christian examples in
BAG, s.v. φύσιϳ, 2; cf. also n. 68 below. For the participial form,
cf. Xenophon, *Cyr.* 1.1.3, ᾶνθρωποϳ πεφυκώϳ, the human being as he is
(or: is as a result of his origins). Cf. Empedocles (in H. Diels and
W. Kranz [eds.], *Fragmente der Vorsokratiker: griechisch und deutsch,*
Vol. 1 [Berlin: Weidmann, 6̄1951], 31A71; in *De prisc. med.* 20, in the
Hippocratic corpus), who in his treatise περὶ φύσεωϳ described the
nature of humans thus: ἐξ ἀρχῆϳ ᾽ὅ τί ἐστιν ᾽ἄνθρωποϳ, καί ᾽ὅπωϳ ἐγένετο
πρῶτον καὶ ὁπόθεν συνεπάγη. On the relation between γένεσιϳ and φύσιϳ,
γίνεσθαι and φύεσθαι, see Leisegang, 1941, passim.

[59]φύσιϳ is used to denote the sex of a person and, frequently,
the distinguishing gential organ; see LSJ, s.v. φύσιϳ, VII, and
φυσικλεΐδιον; similarly *naturalia* = genital parts of a person, Celsus,
De medic. (Teubner and Loeb numbering), 1. Pref. 49; 5.21.1; 7.18.1;
7.28.1; referring to an animal, Columella 6.27.10. φύσιϳ as applied to
the nature of animals with respect to their sex: Ps.-Barnabas, *Ep.*
10.7; Clement Alex., *Paed.* 2.84; 2.85.2.

[60]Cf. Xenophon, *Cyn.* 1.3: no one should marvel that Asclepius
and other famous heroes died, even though they were pleasing to the
gods, "for that is nature" (τοῦτο μὲν γὰρ ἡ φύσιϳ). Aelian, *V.H.* 8.11:
τῶν ἀνθρώπων φύσιϳ θνητή. Cicero, *Pro Clu.* 10.29: "naturae
satisfacere" = to die. Pliny, *N.H.* 7.179: cases of persons returning
from the dead are *prodigia* and not *naturae opera*. Θνητὴ φύσιϳ, "humankind": Sophocles, *Frag.* 590; cf. Philo. *V. Mos.* 1.158 (on the mount
Moses sees τὰ ἀθέατα φύσει θνητῇ), and *PGM* 4.607 (the operator invokes
names that have never before entered εἰϳ θνητὴν φύσιν).

[61]See below, ch. 3; cf. Origen, *C. Cels.* 1.27, Jesus ventured
and achieved things "greater than human nature" (μείζω τῆϳ ἀνθρωπίνηϳ
φύσεωϳ); 1.45, about Moses and Jesus there have been recorded "wonders
beyond human nature" (παράδοξα καὶ ὑπὲρ τὴν ἀνθρωπίνην φύσιν).

[62]Pagan and Christian examples in BAG, s.v. φύσιϳ, 1; Latin
sources in LS, s.v. *natura*, II, A, 2. Synonyms are ᾽ἔθοϳ (Julian, *Mis.*
353A, ᾽ἔθοϳ, φασί, δευτέρη φύσιϳ) and ᾗθοϳ; cf. Holl, 1928, 255: ᾗθοϳ =
"Gemütsart."

[63]This summary is based on Leisegang, 1941, 1139-43, which

draws primarily on the Hippocratic corpus but also notes continuities
and discontinuities with the later empirical school and with Galen, who
explicates the concept of nature with reference both to the Hippocratics
and to philosophy. On Celsus' use of the Hippocratic corpus cf.
Spencer, 1935, vol. 1, ix, xii. Other pertinent material on nature and
medicine in Galen and other physicians is found in R. M. Grant, 1952,
11ff.

[64]The body and/or its ill member are ἔξω τῆς φύσιος. A sprain
or a dislocation is a springing away (ἀποπηδᾶν) from nature or a being
torn away from the original sound condition (ἀποσπάσθαι ἀπὸ τῆς ἀρχαίης
φύσιος). Nature figures as the norm in the terminology designating
unusual states of the body: μᾶλλον τῆς φύσιος, θερμότερον τῆς φύσιος,
ὑγρότερον τῆς φύσιος, etc. Leisegang, 1941, 1141-42.

[65]Leisegang, 1941, 1142: ἄγειν or παράγειν ἐς τὴν φύσιν, ἐς
τὴν ἑαυτοῦ φύσιν, ἐς τὴν φύσιν τὴν δικαίην; καθιστάναι ἐς τὴν ἀρχαίην
φύσιν.

[66]Cf. in the Hippocratic corpus, Loc. hom. 2 (in Littré ed.,
vol. 6, 278): φύσις δὲ τοῦ σώματος, ἀρχὴ τοῦ ἐν ἰητρικῇ λόγου. See
further, Leisegang, 1941, 1140, 9-35.

[67]Leisegang, 1941, 1139-40. Cf. below (p. 19) on nature as
personified and deified and as a creative, shaping force.

[68]On the necessity to know the nature of the disease, see
Leisegang, 1941, 1139, 20-23. The treatise Ancient Medicine (in Loeb
edition of the Hippocratic corpus, vol. 1) shows how the physician
needs to know the nature of humans generally (14; 20), of the individual
patient (12-13), and of both in relation to each other (20). Health,
i.e., φύσις (though the treatise does not use that term here), is an
equilibrium of forces (δυνάμεις) in the body (19; 24).

[69]Herodotus 1.19: the king of Lydia turns to the oracle at
Delphi when his illness persists.

[70]Mk. 5.26//Lk. 8.43. Aelius Aristides, see below, ch. 7. See
further the pagan and Christian sources in Weinreich, 1909, App. 1,
"Die Kunst der Ärzte versagt."

[71]See the preceding note, but also the ailments commonly mentioned in the healing accounts in the Asclepius inscriptions at
Epidaurus, in pagan literature, and in Christian accounts: lameness,
blindness, deafness, paralysis, infertility, etc. The Epidaurus
sources in Edelstein, Asclepius 1, T. 423ff. (texts and E. T.);
P. Fiebig, Antike Wundergeschichten (Kleine Texte, 79; Bonn: Marcus
and Weber, 1911), 3ff. (texts); 2nd ed., G. Delling (1960), 20ff.;
selections in E. T. in D. R. Cartlidge and D. L. Dungan (eds. and
trans.), Documents for the Study of the Gospels (Cleveland et al.:
Collins, 1980), 151-53.

[72]See Edelstein, Asclepius 2, 116-17; 174-78; G. Theissen,
1974, 233-36.

[73]On the relation between medicine and healing miracles, see
below, ch. 3.2.3.

[74]Censorinus, *De die nat.* 23 (3d c. C.E.), where the contrast is the day established by human decree, *dies civilis*.

[75]Prior to Aristotle it is attested only in Xenophon; it does not occur in Plato; LSJ, s.v., I.

[76]LSJ, s.v., II, 2. It also denoted, of course, anyone who studies *physis*. Guthrie's comment, 1962, 40: "It is to Aristotle in the first place that we owe the distinction between those who described the world in terms of myth and the supernatural, and those who first attempted to account for it by natural causes. The former he calls *theologi*, the latter *physici* or *physiologi*, and he ascribes the beginning of the new, 'physical' outlook to Thales and his successors at Miletus . . ." (*Metaph*. 983b20).

[77]Sources in LSJ, s.v., φύσιſ, IV, 3; cf. Leisegang, 1941, 1135-36.

[78]Cf. Plato, *Leg*. 10.888D, 889A-b; other, pre-Socratic sources in Leisegang, 1941, 1133, 29ff.

[79]See Guthrie, 1954, 135-37, and 1962, 4, 65, 87-89, 142-43.

[80]Guthrie, 1962, chs. 1-3, is a lucid, detailed exposition of the contribution of the Ionian thinkers in this respect.

[81]E.g., Ex. 9.23; 1 Kg. 18.38; 2 Kg. 1.10. Seneca, *N.Q.* 2.24, 2.58, offers explanations of why *fulmina* move downward or obliquely when the nature of fire is to rise.

[82]Zeno, *SVF* 1.45; cf. Aristotle, *Post. An.* 105b.20. On the history of the division see Pohlenz, 1970, vol. 1, 33.

[83]His detailed accounting (*N.H.* 1) of the number of *res* reported in each book would suggest a disinclination to reduce the total by omitting any. According to his nephew, Pliny the Younger (*Ep.* 3.5), Pliny believed that no book was so bad that it did not have something worthwhile in it. At many points it is clear that he cannot resist repeating an interesting marvel, and at places his table of contents reads like that of a paradoxography (e.g., 1.7.iiff., xlviif., liiff.; further examples in Ziegler, 1949, 1166. Unlike Seneca, he also includes material from the world of human affairs (Bk. 7). In scope his work actually comes closer to being an encyclopedia in the modern sense; Pliny mentions the Greek ἡ ἐγκυκλιόſ παιδεία in discussing his subject matter (Pref., 14), but he does not seem to have taken it as a model, if he intended by that term the *trivium* and *quadrivium* of ancient education; see Marrou, 1964, 244 and 527, nn. 2-5.

[84]In Bk. 7, e.g., he surveys various explanations of comets and, despite the authority of persons like Aristotle, proposes instead that comets appear because they travel in orbits; see 7.27.7 and Corcoran's exposition, 1971 (vol. 1), xxiii-iv.

[85]*N.H.* 2.149 ("quod si quis praedictum credat, simul fateatur necesse est maioris miraculi divinitatem Anaxagorae fuisse, solvique rerum naturae intellectum et confundi omnia si aut ipse sol lapis esse aut umquam lapidem in eo fuisse credatur").

[86]Similar expressions of such an ethics of belief are Galen's statement that extraordinary phenomena should not be allowed to deter one from seeing that in the majority of cases nature produces normal offspring or phenomena (see R. M. Grant, 1952, 13-14) and Seneca's advice (*N.Q.* 2.55.3) that one should look for "naturalem causam . . . et assiduam, non raram fortuitamque." Cf. also Aristotle, below, ch. 4, n. 5.

[87]Examples in R. M. Grant, 1952, 14, to which may be added Cicero, *De div.* 2.63.129: "Which is more worthy of philosophy, to interpret those things [i.e., visions in sleep] by means of the superstition of diviners or by an explanation from nature [*sagarum superstitione . . . naturae*]?"

[88]Roman examples in LS, s.v. *natura*, II, B, 3. The Stoic equation of *physis* with Zeus, *logos*, *pronoia*, and *heimarmenē* excluded from possibility anything (alleged to be) contrary to *physis*; sources in Leisegang, 1941, 1153.40ff. Cf. especially *SVF* 2.1000 (Aulus Gellius, *N.A.* 7.2): "In Book 4 of his work *On Providence*, [Chrysippos] says fate is a certain natural ordering of all things [φυσικήν τινα σύνταξιν τῶν ὅλων]. . . ." Also *SVF* 2.938 (Servius on Vergil, *Aen.* 3.90): Stoics and Academics say that "those things which are contrary to nature [*contra naturam*] do not happen but [only] seem to happen"; 2.937 (Chrysippus). R. M. Grant, 1952, 14, draws attention also to Alexander of Aphrodisias (*De fato* 27.197.31), who identifies nature with fate and views it as a measure of the possible.

[89]*N.H.* 2.27: "ne deum quidem posse omnia." This statement occurs in a section (2.14-27) that takes up the subject of the gods, only to conclude that since they are subordinate to nature they need not be treated in a work on nature.

[90]Ibid. ("naturae potentia, idque esse quod deum vocamus").

[91]*N.H.* 2.113 ("illa vero faticida ex alto, statisque de causis et ex suis venire sideribus").

[92]*Gen. an.* 739b.19-20 (ἡ δὲ φύσιϲ οὐδὲν ποιεῖ περίεργον). Ibid., 741b.4 (ἡ δὲ φύσιϲ οὐδὲν ποιεῖ μάτην).

[93]*Phys.* 252a.11-12 (ἀλλὰ μὴν οὐδέν γε ἄτακτον τῶν φύσει καὶ κατὰ φύσιν· ἡ γὰρ φύσιϲ αἰτία πᾶσι τάξεωϲ).

[94]*Rer. nat.* 2.1101-02; 6.396, 398, 404-05; cf. Cicero, *De div.* 219.45, and Seneca, *N.Q.* 2.42.1.

[95]The identification is not univocal (see the commentary *ad* 1.1ff. by C. Bailey in his edition of *De rerum natura* [Oxford: Clarendon Press, 1947]); natural theology (*rerum natura creatrix*, 1.629; 2.1117; 5.1362) is mingled with traditional Roman mythology (*Aeneadum genetrix*, 1.1). The identification of nature with Venus/Aphrodite is attested in *PGM* (references in Leisegang, 1941, 1162, who also cites Latin inscriptions with *Venus Fisica = Physika?*).

[96]*De usu partium* 11.14; I cite and translate from the text in Walzer, 1949, 12-13.

[97]Cf. Galen's comments on Christians, in Walzer, 1949, 14-15.

[98]"Law(s) of nature" and "natural law" occur more commonly in treatments of miracle in the modern period than in earlier sources. Augustine occasionally uses *lex naturae* in connection with miracle (*Civ. D.* 21.8; *C. Faust.* 26.3), and *lex naturae* and *lex naturalis* are used frequently by Aquinas (see Deferrari and Barry, 1948-53, 633, col. 2, a²), but in the discussions devoted explicitly to miracle he employs (depending on the objections he is meeting) terms such as *contra* or *praeter naturam*, *praeter* or *mutare ordinem naturae*, *contra* or *praeter ordinem rerum*, *naturae ordo a Deo rebus inditus*, *praeter ordinem naturalem rerum*, *contra inclinationem naturae*, *supra potentiam naturalem*, *supra* or *excedens facultatem naturae*, *per necessitatem naturae*, *sine operatione principiorum naturae*, *supernaturalis*; see *S.T.* 1.105.6-7; 1/2.113.10; 2/2.178; 3.43.2; *Summa c.G.* 101. *Principia naturae* would seem to approximate to *leges naturae*; cf. Minucius Felix, *Octav.* 19.10 (*SVF* 1.162): "Zeno naturalem legem atque divinam . . . omnium esse principium." This Aristotelian conceptuality--each object has a characteristic nature and a variety of different causes act upon it--contrasts with the mathematical and mechanical model of nature in the Newtonian tradition that underlies the terms "law(s) of nature" and "natural law" in many of the modern treatments of miracle; cf. Randall, 1940, ch. 11; Swinburne, 1970, 1-3. Hume's definition of miracle as a violation of a law of nature (*Enquiry Concerning Human Understanding*, sec. 10, pt. 1) is perhaps the most famous definition employing the new conceptuality, but the same or similar definitions occur repeatedly in writers before and after him. The terms "law(s) of nature" or "natural law," and perhaps inevitably modern conceptuality, are then read into ancient sources, by dogmaticians (e.g., Shedd, 1888, 534, 540; Pieper, 1951, 300, n. 23, "laws of nature," but in the German original, 1917, 356, "Weltregiment") and apologists (Ramm, 1955, 58, "The Bible clearly teaches that . . . the laws of Nature are the laws of God") but also by philologists (P. Stein, 1909, 17) and biblical scholars (Schmid, 1965, 1255, citing without further justification Philo, *Vit. M.* 1.174f., 2.261, where there is in fact no reference to "Naturgesetz"; Pritchard, 1950, 97, "Miracles cannot be brushed aside with the remark that the ancient Israelite was ignorant of the laws of nature").

[99]E.g., Cornford, as cited in n. 105 below. Lembert, 1905, 5-6 (there is "eine tiefe Kluft" between ancient and modern understandings of miracle "einfach aus dem Grunde, weil der Begriff der Naturgesetze in unserem heutigen Sinne nicht vorhanden war"). Vögtle, 1972, 211 ("Einmal hat die Welt des Neuen Testamentes den modernen Begriff des Naturgesetzes, sei es im Sinne eines absoluten Determinismus, sei es im relativierten einer statistischen Gegebenheit, noch nicht gekannt"). Rahner, 1962, 525 ("Von daher ist es gar nicht sonderlich gut, wenn wir diese Heilungswunder, die der Glaube wirkt, von vornherein aus dem Gesamt einer menschlichen Geschichte herausrücken, hinein in die Isolierung der selektiven Betrachtungsweise einer naturwissenschaft-lichen Physik und Medizin und in dieser künstlichen Isoliertheit dann fragen, ob in ihnen die Naturgesetze 'aufgehoben' seien oder nicht").

[100]A thoroughgoing treatment is Tennant, 1925. More recently, Smart, 1964, ch. 2; Holland, 1965; Schmaus, 1969, 106, 111.

[101]R. M. Grant, 1952, ch. 2; Koester, 1968; Watson, 1971. On Philo, Goodenough, 1935, 50ff.; Delling, 1970, esp. 89ff.

[102]The two words came to be defined over against each other, beginning at least with the Sophists, perhaps before; see Koester, 1968, 524-26; Watson, 1971, 218-19; Guthrie, 1969, 55-134.

[103]See Plato, *Gorgias* 483E; further references in R. M. Grant, 1952, 22, n. 1 (discussion in Koester, 1968, 523); Zeno, *SVF* 1.162, is dubious; see Grant, 21, and below, n. 121. For the late first century C.E., Dio Chrysostom, *Or.* 80.5; Epictetus, *Diss.* 1.29.9; 2.17.6.

[104]Aristotle, *De cael.* 268a.13, referring to the Pythagoreans.

[105]Plato, *Tim.* 83E: παρὰ τοὺς τῆς φύσεως νόμους. Cornford, 1937, *ad loc.*: "'contrary to the laws of nature' is a mistranslation. All that is meant is the customary and normal process by which blood is healthily formed."

[106]Cleanthes, *Hymn to Zeus*, SVF 1.537; the passage does not actually have νόμος φύσεως but is very close to it: Ζεῦ, φύσεως ἀρχηγέ, νόμου μετὰ πάντα κυβερνῶν, χαῖρε.

[107]*BJ* 3.370 (φύσιως γὰρ νόμος ἰσχυρὸς ἐν ἅπασιν τὸ ζῆν ἐθέλειν).

[108]*De op. mundi* 171 (φύσεως νόμοις καὶ θεσμοῖς). See further *Spec. leg.* 4.232ff.

[109]Posidonius is a possible exception in Stoicism, depending on how one reads him; see R. M. Grant, 1952, 22-23. Similarly with Philo; contrast Leisegang, 1941, 1160, 64ff., with R. M. Grant, 1952, 15; Goodenough, 1935, 51-52; 1962, 99; Delling, 1970, 91-92, 94-95, and n. 72. Goodenough and Delling make the point that God and *physis* function as equivalents in Philo, but the two terms, because of their Philonic setting, do not have the same meaning as in Stoicism: for Philo God is transcendent and personal. Not to be overlooked, of course, in characterizing the Stoic deity as immanent and impersonal is the religious feeling evident, e.g., in a piece like Cleanthes' *Hymn to Zeus*, with its address to Zeus as "father" and its prayer for under-standing; cf. Pohlenz, 1970, vol. 1, 108-10.

[110]These are called φύσεως προθεσμία (*Spec. Leg.* 4.208), φύσεως νόμιμα (4.212), φύσεως θεσμοί (4.215); Koester, 1968, 538.

[111]*Praem.* 108 (the command to reproduce is a νόμος φύσεως); *Aet.* 57-59 (see next note).

[112]*Spec. Leg.* 4.204-05 (the νόμος φύσεως permits only animals of like species to mate or be yoked together in work). *Aet.* 57-59: since the "laws of nature, immutable statutes" (νόμους φύσεως, θεσμοὺς ἀκίνητους), do not permit reproduction of full-grown offspring, the story of the Myrmidons, sprung full-blown from the earth, is a mythic fabrication (μύθου πλάσμα).

[113]Another way of expressing the relation between the cosmic order and God is that of Delling, 1970, 91-95 (with full citation of sources): If φύσις is a functional equivalent of God (see n. 109 above), then νόμος φύσεως is God's will for the cosmos, and departures from it, as measured by ordinary human experience and expectations, do not really go against the law of nature. "Für Philon besteht kein

Gegensatz zwischen Gott und Natur. . . . Wunder--jedenfalls biblische
--sind für Philon wider die Erwartung, aber nicht wider die Natur" (95).

[114]Translations of νόμοϛ ἔμψυχοϛ vary. Colson, 1935, renders
"living law." Goodenough, 1935, 186, renders it "incarnate law" (V.
Mos. 1.162), but, as Georgi points out (1964, 160, n. 3), "incarnate"
is misleading since the stress is on the soul, not the body. On other
occasions Goodenough's rendering is "animate law" (thus in 1928, 1938).
In 1962, 34, "incarnate" appears directly alongside lex animata.

[115]Another possible rendering of λογικόϛ, other than the
familiar and inadequate "rational" and "spiritual," is "vocal" (Goodenough, 1962, 34; 1935, 186), which Goodenough justifies by reference
to "the common Hellenistic notion that the king's business was to make
articulate the divine realm and will into which he could penetrate"
(1935, 186, n. 36, with the sources cited). In 1935, 332 he translates
λογικὸν ζῷον as "a reasonable animal"; on p. 51 his exposition suggests
"reasoning power" as a rendering of λογικὴ φύσιϛ.

[116]V. Mos. 2.48. Cf. 2.51: Moses began his writing by
relating, not the founding of a city made with human hands, but rather
the origin of the cosmos (τῆϛ μεγαλοπόλεωϛ), since he considered the
laws (that he would record later) to be "the truest likeness of the
governance of the cosmos" (ἐμφερεστάτην εἰκόνα τῆϛ τοῦ κόσμου
πολιτείαϛ).

[117]Philo offers other such explanations on his own, in V. Mos.
2.253-55, 267, 282-87.

[118]V. Mos. 2.63-64, where the term ἰσότηϛ is not used, but the
idea is certainly present in the description of the subsiding of the
rain and the floodwaters in the days of Noah, with the conclusion:
"For as though God had commanded it, each kind--seas and springs and
rivers--received back what it had granted as a sort of necessary loan,
for each stream subsided into its own place." Then the humans and the
animals emerge from the ark to an earth that bears a likeness to the
earth when it was first created.

[119]Cf. Philo, Quis heres 144-45, and above, p. 21, and n. 104,
on νόμοϛ φύσεωϛ as designating the Pythagoreans' view of numerical
relations.

[120]Goodenough, 1932; 1935, 64-68. Cf. V. Mos. 2.7, where the
union of kingship, lawgiving, priesthood, and prophecy is praised and
compared with the Graces whom an "immutable law of nature" (νόμοϛ
φύσεωϛ ἀκίνητοϛ) does not permit to be separated.

[121]Cf. Goodenough, 1935, 56ff.; Delling, 1970, 91. Koester,
1968, 529, observes that in the Cicero quotation (De nat. deor.
1.36 = SVF 1.162) that is the only evidence for the possible use by
Zeno of νόμοϛ φύσεωϛ, Cicero's translation--lex naturalis-- is more
likely a rendering of λόγοϛ φύσεωϛ, which Stoics commonly posited as
the νόμοϛ of the cosmos (references in Koester, 529, n. 7, including
Philo, Jos. 29); "the precise translation ratio naturae seems to be
absent in Latin Stoic sources." On the Stoic ὀρθὸϛ λόγοϛ cf. the
sources and comments in Goodenough, 1935, 56; Pohlenz, 1970, vol. 1,
index, s.v.

[122]Whether Philo is idiosyncratic, and what predecessors and like-minded contemporaries he had, are questions answered more by inference than by direct evidence. One argument against mere idiosyncrasy is that Philo could not have moved with such assurance and finesse over such a vast body of material, integrating Greek philosophical and biblical traditions, unless he had had predecessors; he refers to such in *V. Mos.* 1.4, and Goodenough, 1935, chs. 10-11, has sought to identify some. Another argument is that Philo's complex expositions, presented without detailed explanation and defense of the underlying presuppositions, all the while Philo remained a respected leader and spokesman of the Jewish community in Alexandria, render it unlikely that his interpretations, including his usage of νόμος φύσεως, are simply private.

[123]*De res.* 42 ("a divinis viribus, non a naturalibus legibus").

[124]*De an.* 2.2 ("nihil divinae licentiae servat, leges naturae opiniones suas fecit"); *licentiae* here may be equivalent to *potestati*; see Waszink *ad loc.*

[125]See R. M. Grant, 1952, 21, 25; Watson, 1971, passim, and p. 234 (*lex naturae* in Cicero is "often better translated rationality or morality").

[126]*Georg.* 1.60-61 ("continuo has leges aeternaque foedera certis/imposuit natura locis").

[127]*Phars.* 6.462 ("legi non paruit aether").

[128]*De clem.* 1.19.1; the Greeks and Romans thought the dominant bee in the colony was male.

[129]*ex more*; cf. ἐξ ἠθέων in the Herodotus passage (2.142) in the text.

[130]Cf. above, p. 5. Another manuscript tradition reads *trepidat* for *strepitat*; see note in Loeb ed., *ad loc.* Seneca continues in the same vein, 7.3ff.; cf. 7.16.1 where he contrasts *cotidiana* and *miraculum*. The theme of nature as wondrous but disregarded because it is so familiar appears also in Plotinus (see Dodds, 1951, 286) and is important in Augustine's view of miracle (see *In Ioh. Ev. Tract.* 24.1; *Civ. D.* 21.4.4).

[131]The certainty that the dead remain dead (see above, p. 9, and n. 12) is used to good literary effect in Herodotus 3.62 and *Acts Thom.* 9.96. Similarly, blindness and the restoring of sight in Jn. 9.32.

[132]Herodotus 1.165: the Phocaeans, having abandoned their town (in Ionia), sink some iron in the sea and swear not to return before the iron appears again, i.e., never. 4.201: When besieging Barea (in North Africa), the Persians dig and conceal a trench at night, then stand on it and swear to keep a peace treaty with the townspeople as long as the ground they stand on remains unchanged, i.e., always; when the Bareans open their gates, the Persians break through the boards covering the trench and take over the city. 6.37: the unchanging (and therefore predictable) nature of the pine tree (πίτυς) is interpreted

as the key to a threat by Croesus. 8.143: The Athenians promise not to make an agreement with Xerxes as long as the sun runs its regular course.

On the iron incident cf. Pritchard, 1950, 97, alluding to 2 Kg. 6.1-7: "The very fact that the story of the floating iron was told to honor the prophet makes it clear that the average Israelite knew that the iron was heavier--always heavier--than water. . . ."

[133]Cf. the precautions taken against fraud in the dispensing of oracles (W. Dittenberger [ed.], *Sylloge Inscriptionum Graecarum*, Vol. 3, [Leipzig, [3]1920; reprinted, Hildesheim: Olms, 1960], no. 1157; E. T. in F. C. Grant, 1953, 35-36; cf. Herodotus 7.6) and testing of oracles (e.g., Herodotus 1.47-48 and the sources cited in Pease, Cicero, *De div.*, 336-37, *qui sibi*). Dreams and visions are another example. One expected to dream, so that Herodotus singles out for mention a people reported to have no dreams (4.184). The reporting of predictive dreams in the ancient sources may leave one with the impression that the ancients viewed all dreams as predictive, a special case of the claim that "Wunder geschah all Tage." But the predictive ones are reported precisely because they are extraordinary. Again the foil is the ordinary, the many dreams that were not predictive. The first intent of the dream books and dream interpreters in antiquity was to separate predictive or significant dreams from non-predictive or non-significant dreams; see the brief history of ancient interpretation of dreams in Behr, 1968, 171ff.; cf. Dodds, 1951, 106-07.

A waking vision would be more extraordinary than a dream because much rarer. Though it is often difficult to distinguish these two in the sources (see Michaelis, 1954, 372, n. 4), at least some persons in antiquity recognized the importance of doing so. Thus Oxy. P. 11, 1381.91ff., tells of a mother sitting unsleeping by the side of her sick son, when "suddenly she beheld--it was not a dream or sleep, for her eyes were opened immovably but not seeing clearly, for a divine, terrifying apparition came to her . . ." (εἶτ' ἐξαπ[ί]νηϛ ἑώρα-- οὔτ' ὄναρ οὔθ' ὕπνοϛ, ὀφθαλμοὶ γὰρ ἦσαν ἀκείνητοι διηνυγμένοι, βλέποντεϛ μὲν οὐκ ἀκρειβῶϛ, θ[.]εία γὰρ αὐτὴν μετὰ δέ[ο]υϛ εἰσῄει φαντασία[ν], lines 107-14). The distinction between a waking and a dream vision is also expressed in the terminology employed or the description of the circumstances; e.g., Acts 10.3, εἶδεν ἐν ὁράματι φανερῶϛ, ὡσεὶ περὶ ὥραν ἐνάτην τῆϛ ἡμέραϛ; 10.10, ἐγένετο ἐπ' αὐτὸν ἔκστασιϛ. Awareness of the distinction between vision and actual event is expressed in passages like 2 Cor. 12.2-3 and Acts 12.9. For pagan sources, see Wikenhauser, 1939, 320-33.

In the philosophical tradition, Socrates' *daimonion* is cited as proof of the sage's ability to hear the divine voice in a waking state; Holl, 1928, 260.

[134]The sympathy-empathy concept, for example; see Reinhardt, 1926, with the comments of Pohlenz, 1970, vol. 2, 58, 108; R. M. Grant, 1952, index, s.v. "Sympathy." Power was seen as residing in names, plants, stones, metals, statues, the stars, etc.; see Nilsson, 1948a, 103ff., 171. The power in humans is evident in healing narratives (e.g., Mk. 5.21-43), or in accounts of the famous rhetorician whom many kissed on the chest and hands because they thought him possessed of divine potency (Nilsson, 1948a, 168), or in the story of Plotinus' repelling of an attempt to visit a sunstroke on him (Porphyry, *Vita Plot.* 10). Among the Neoplatonists, Iamblichus, *De myst.* 4-6, offers a carefully articulated theory of power.

Notes to Chapter 3

[1]Cf. Edelstein, *Asclepius* 2, 156-57: ". . . the ancients, even scientists and philosophers, did not debate so much the possibility of miracles, as their actuality."

[2]*Pace* LSJ, which lists this reference under "sign from heaven, portent, omen." φάσμα does not in itself imply reference to the divine (see the citations in LSV, s.v., 2), and when Herodotus wishes the word to imply such reference he makes it quite evident (e.g., 4.79; 7.37-38; 8.37).

[3]Ps-Aristotle, *De mirab.* 846a (in Giannini, *Paradoxographorum*, 306): during an eruption of Aetna the deity causes the streams of lava to divide and flow around pious persons bearing their aged parents to safety on their shoulders.

[4]*De generatione animalium*; he also treats reproduction in connection with the animals discussed in *Historia animalium*. In *Gen. an.* he frequently takes up predecessors' theories. For modern studies of ancient views of reproduction see the literature cited in the Loeb edition of *Gen. an.*, xvii, xxxv.

[5]See the agricultural treatises by Cato the Censor, Varro, Vergil, and Columella, each of which reveals indebtedness, often explicitly, to the agricultural tradition.

[6]There is a convenient catalog of ancient reports of extraordinary reproductions in Pease, Cicero, *De div.*, pp. 262-63 (*ad hominum pecudumve*, etc.).

[7]See the list of sources in Pease, Cicero, *De div. ad* 1.36 (p. 154). In the Aristotle references, *Gen. an.* 755b.18 is dubious; Varro, *Rer. rust.* 2.1.26, should be added; "Justin Martyr," *De res.* 3, should doubtless be Ps-Justin.

[8]Herodotus 3.151; Suetonius, *Galba* 4.2; Juvenal 13.66. Cf. Cicero, *De div.* 2.28.61: "I think a mule has foaled more frequently than a [Stoic] sage has existed" ("saepius enim mulam peperisse arbitror quam sapientem fuisse").

[9]Herodotus 3.153; 7.57 (τέραϝ in both cases); Livy 26.23; 37.3 (*prodigia* both times); Varro 2.1.26 (*portentum*), followed by Columella (6.37.3 (*prodigiosos*); Pliny *N.H.* 8.173, "In our annals mules have often foaled, but it was regarded as a portent" (*prodigii*); Suetonius, *Galba* 4.2 (*obscaenum ostentum*).

[10]*Cappadocia*: Pliny, *N.H.* 8.173, citing Theophrastus; Ps-Aristotle, *Mirab.* 69 (835b.1). *Syria*: Aristotle, *Hist. An.* 6.24 (577b.24-26), though this kind of mule is said to be different. *Africa*: Varro, *Rer. rust.* 2.1.27 (Columella 6.37.3, citing Varro, supplies the place).

[11]Varro, 2.1.26. However, repugnance toward the mule itself, as a mixture of species, may have been a factor; alongside rarity of reported occurrences, in the ill omening of reports of mules foaling; see Pease, Cicero, De div., loc. cit., n. 7 above.

[12]Aristotle, Gen. an. 747b.26-27, says the female mule is totally nonreproductive (ἄγονος ὅλως), though he also says that conceptions occur but are never brought to completion.

[13]O. Zirkle, 1936, 95-130, surveys the subject from ancient to modern times, giving many of the ancient sources but sometimes inadequately or erroneously identified and with trivial conclusions. The sources arranged by categories and, so far as possible, chronologically, include the following:
Wind impregnation of mares: Homer, Il. 16.150ff.; 20.221ff.; Aristotle, Hist. an. 572a.13ff.; Varro, Rer. rust. 2.1.19; Vergil, Georg. 3.267-83; Columella 6.27.3-7; Pliny, N.H. 8.166 and 16.93-94; Silius Italicus, Punica 3.378.83 and 16.363-65; Aelian, Nat. an. 4.6; Caius Iulius Solinus, Collectanea rerum mirabilium 23.7; Justinus, De hist. Philip. 44.3; Augustine, Civ. D. 21.5.
Of ewes: Pliny, N.H. 8.189 (the wind plays a role in the determination of a lamb's sex); Aelian, Nat. an. 7.27 (the wind aids fertility rather than actually impregnating).
Of tigresses: Oppian, Cynegetica 1.323 and 3.353-60; Claudian, De rapt. Proserp. 3.262-67.
Of nymphs: Ovid, Fasti 5.195ff. Of animals generally: Lactantius, Div. Inst. 4.12.2.
Of fowl: "wind eggs" (ὑπηνέμια): Aristophanes, Birds 695; Aristotle, Hist. An. 559b.27ff. (description); Gen. An. 749b35ff., 750b.2ff. (explanation); Varro and Columella, loc. cit.; Pliny, N.H. 10.106; Athenaeus, Deipn. 2.57e; Ps.-Clement, Recog. 8.25.5. Partridges: Aristotle, Hist. An. 541a.26ff., 560b.10ff. Wind impregnation or self-propagation of vultures (γύψ, vultur): Plutarch, Mor. 286c; Ps.-Aristotle, De mirab. 835a.1ff.; Aelian, Nat. an. 2.46; Tertullian, Adv. Val. 10; Origen, C. Cels. 1.37; Eusebius, Praep. Ev. 3.12; Basil the Great, Hexaem. 8.6; Ambrose, Hexaem. 5.20; further references in D. W. Thompson, Glossary of Greek Birds (Oxford: Clarendon, [2]1936), s.v. γύψ; Aristotle, Hist. An. 563a, and Pliny, N.H. 10.19, do not mention self-impregnation of the vulture but reject other theories positing an extraordinary origin for them.
In Orphic thought see Guthrie, 1952, 94-95, and ch. 4, n. 17; also the discussion in Guthrie, 1954, 138-43.
Wind/spirit in connection with human pregnancy or birth: the virgin birth accounts in early Christian sources; Lucian, Ver. hist. 1.22 (see above, ch. 2, n. 8).

[14]E.g., Aristotle, Hist. an. 572a.13ff., and the Roman agricultural treatises (Varro, Vergil, Columella).

[15]E.g., Varro (res incredibilis . . . sed est vera); Vergil and Silius Italicus (16.363) (mirabile dictu); Solinus (mira fecunditate).

[16]Aristotle, Hist. an. 572a.14; Pliny, N.H. 8.163; the Roman agricultural treatises, reflecting common agricultural lore (Vergil, sine ullis coniugis; Columella, etiam si marem non habeant . . . sine coitu; Silius Italicus, nullus erat pater). In Hist. an. 539b.14ff.

coition of male and female animals is presented by Aristotle as the
ordinary means of reproduction; the exceptions noted in *Gen. an.* 715a.
18ff. are mainly among the bloodless animals (ἔναιμα); similarly,
Pliny, *N.H.*, bks. 8 and 10 (quadrupeds and humans; among aquatic creatures those originating spontaneously, 9.160-61, and by self-propagation, 9.166, are noted). Ps.-Clement, *Recog.* 8.25.5-6, gives a catalog
of paradoxographical reproductions, which are characterized as
occurring *mutato ordine* (25.5).

[17]E.g., Aristotle, *Hist. an.* 748a.21ff.; *Gen. an.* 737a.18ff.;
et passim; cf. Pliny, *N.H.* 7.64-66.

[18]Homer; Pliny (8.166); Silius Italicus (3.384-85); Justinus.
The same comparison with the speed of the wind is found in the Oppian
and Claudian accounts of tigresses.

[19]Aristotle, *Hist. an.* 572.9ff.; Vergil; Columella; Aelian
(citing Aristotle); Solinus.

[20]All the accounts presuppose this, but some mention it
explicitly (Pliny, 8.166, *animalem spiritum*; 16.193, *genitalis spiritus
mundi*; Silius Italicus, *genitali concipit aura*; cf. Lucretius, *De rer.
nat.* 1.11, *genitalibus aura favoni*).

[21]"Alongside the stream Oceanus," *Il.* 16.151. *Crete:* Aris-
totle, *Hist. an.* 572a.14. *Asia Minor:* Vergil. *Spain:* Varro (in
Lusitania, at the ocean, near Lisbon on Mt. Tagrus); similarly Pliny,
Columella, Silius Italicus, Solinus, Justinus. *Cappadocia:* Augustine.
"Certain regions" (*aliquot regionibus*): Columella.

[22]In mating season (Aristotle, *Hist. an.* 573a.13) specified
as spring (Vergil; Pliny, 16.93; Columella; Silius Italicus). Varro,
"at a certain time" (*certo tempore*).

[23]Three years: Varro, Pliny (8.166), Columella, Augustine.
Seven years: Silius Italicus.

[24]See above, n. 13. On the mares' impregnation through the
mouth cf. the similar assertion concerning weasels, *Barn.* 10.8, Ps.-
Clement, *Recog.* 8.25.5. In the case of vultures, inexplicability plays
a role in the accounts of their wind impregnation or self-propagation:
Since no one had ever seen a vulture's nest (which Aristotle and Pliny
deny), and/or there was no male vulture, or if there were, it did not
play a part in reproduction, how did the species survive? Inexplicable
foalings, seemingly apart from contact with stallions, may have
figured into the origin of stories about wind impregnation of mares
too, as is reported in a seventeenth-century account concerning one of
the regions where such impregnations were reported to occur in antiquity; see Zirkle, 1936, 104.

[25]Homer (cited in Aelian's prose account and probably followed
by Silius Italicus, 16.364-65); Vergil, who draws on Aristotle (see
W. Richter [ed.], *Vergil: Georgica* [Munich: Huebert, 1957], 294-95)
but incorporates this into a long discourse on love (3.242ff.).

[26]Ovid, *Fasti* 5.195ff. (an aetiology for the spring festival of Floralia).

[27]8.25.4-5: "So that it will not seem, as people think, that this [*scil.* ordinary reproduction] comes about by some order of nature and not by the ordering of the creator [*naturae quodam ordine et non dispensatione fieri conditoris*], he commanded a few animals to preserve their kind on earth by a change in the order [*mutato ordine*], as an indication and proof of his providence."

[28]Democritus (in Aristotle, *Gen. an.* 769b.31ff. = H. Diels and W. Kranz [eds.], *Fragmente der Vorsokratiker: griechisch und deutsch*, Vol. 2 [Berlin: Weidmann, [6]1952], 68A.146). Herodotus 3.108. Xenophon, *Cyneget.* 5.13. Aristotle, *Gen. an.* 773a.33ff. Archelaus (3d c. B.C.E.), Ἰδιοφυῆ (fragments in Varro, *Rer. rust.* 3.12.3, and Pliny, *N.H.* 8.218; both in Giannini [ed.], *Paradoxographorum*, 25). Pliny, *N.H.* 7.48-49; 8.219; 10.179. *Barn.* 10.6. Clement of Alexandria, *Paedag.* 88. Julius Pollux, *Onomasticon* (late 2 c. A.D.) 5.73. Aelian, *De nat. an.* 2.12. Oppian(?) (ca. 200 C.E.), *Cyneget.* 3.515ff. Athenaeus, *Deipn.* 9.400. "Eratosthenes," *Catasterismi* 34. "Hippocrates," *Superfetatio* 1.

[29]The verbs are ἐπικυΐσκεσθαι and *superfetare*. Democritus and Aristotle (*Gen. an.*) discuss the subject in relation to τέρατα; see below, pp. 31-32.

[30]*Superfetatio* (περὶ ἐπικυήσιοⲥ), in E. Littré (ed. and trans.), *Oeuvres completes d'Hippocrate*, Vol. 8 (Paris, 1853; reprinted, Amsterdam: Hakkert, 1962), 472-509. Only sec. 1 of the treatise takes up superfetation; the rest, much of which repeats portions of other treatises in the corpus, instructs in various kinds of deliveries.

[31]773a.33f., where the technical term ἐπικυΐσκεσθαι is employed. See sec. b below.

[32]*Gen. an.* 770a.10 (ἀλλὰ καὶ τῷ πολλὰ ἅμα ἔχειν κυήματα).

[33]770a.14 (διόπερ καὶ πολλὰ δίδυμα τίκτουσιν).

[34]770a.18 (περιττὸν οὐδὲν ἔχοντεⲥ).

[35]772a.35ff.; see further, below p. 50.

[36]The Democritus passage (*Gen. an.* 769b.32-34) is uncertain textually at one point, but the general sense is clear. Again the term ἐπικυΐσκεσθαι is not employed but the meaning is clearly present: two sperm enter the uterus at different times and the resulting fetations then grow together producing a τέραⲥ. Aristotle rejects this view on the ground that it does not allow for malformations resulting when two sperm enter the uterus at the same time (770a.1ff.).

[37]Phlegon, *Mir.* 28 (Antigonus: 20 infants from four pregnancies, a tradition attested in Aristotle, *Hist. An.* 584b.33ff.). He

also reports 50 sons born to one woman (30; source: Hippostratus) and
50 daughters to another (31; source: Danaus) but does not claim them
all for one delivery.

[38]*N.H.* 7.33. As a specific example of superfetation Pliny
(7.48) cites the case of twelve infants stillborn to one mother.

[39]*N.H.* 7.49: a woman's husband and an adulterer, a slave
woman's master and his steward. He reports, further, twins born two
months apart, and triplets, two of which were delivered three months
after the first; he does not say whether these infants had the same or
different fathers. In 7.51 he ascribes differences in twins'
appearance to their resemblance to father or mother.

[40]On the subject of such twins see especially the works by
Harris, 1903; 1906; 1913; 1927, 23-38 et passim. For the pagan sources
see the handbooks on mythology.
    The traditions, of course, are not uniform: some assert divine
paternity for both twins, some only for one, some for neither; some do
not even mention twinship in connection with the figures. What is
evident is that twins are considered τερατώδη, as Aristotle said, and are
apt to be, either one or both, associated with deity, in their birth,
prowess, and/or invulnerability to death.
    On Jesus and Judas Thomas see the Greek version of the *Acts of
Thomas* (Lipsius and Bonnet [eds.], *Acta Apostolorum*, Vol. 2/2 [1903],
99-291; E. T., Hennecke-Schneemelcher, *New Testament Apocrypha*, 425-31),
where Judas is called ὁ δίδυμος τοῦ χριστοῦ (31; 39); in the extant
Syriac version the first reference has been corrected to "ocean flood"
(*thoma* to *tehoma*) but the second has been allowed to stand. The
similarity of Jesus and Judas is stressed (11; 45), but also their
dissimilarity: Judas is only a man (66; 140); he is not Jesus but
Jesus' servant (160) whose more than human authority and power derive
from Jesus. That is to say, the two are twins but not identical twins,
even though they are very similar in appearance (11; 45). As with the
pagan twins cited above, the question of paternity is left in doubt.
Jesus once says he is "the son of Joseph the carpenter" (2), though
this occurs in a legal document where he could hardly name a divine
father; otherwise he is addressed as God and consistently portrayed as
more than human. Judas, on the other hand, can be worshiped as a god
(106) and achieves the immortality denied, e.g., to Remus and granted
only on alternate days to Castor (*Od.* 11.300ff.).

[41]773b.7-8: "Where there are many young, one is a superfetation in relation to the other" (διὰ τὸ καὶ τῶν πλειόνων τοῦ ἑνὸς εἶναι
θατέρῳ θάτερον ἐπικύημα); in 772a.34 and 772b.13-14 he mentions twins
specifically (see above, p. 32).

[42]Impregnations with a long interval between are infrequent
because the mouth of the uterus usually closes during pregnancy, but
they do occur (*Gen. an.* 773b.13-16), evidently when the uterus remains
open; however, that is παρὰ φύσιν and the fetation suffers as a result
(774a.27-31).

[43]Varro: "Who does not know that if one puts in [to the
warren] a few hares, male and female, in a short time it will be
filled? Such is the fecundity of this quadruped." An exception to

this view is Antigonus, who reports (*Historiarum mirabilium collectio* 11; in Giannini, *Paradoxographorum*, 36) that on the island of Ithaca hares do not reproduce; the context of his statement is a paradoxographical list of such examples, the necessary premise of which is that any species needs to reproduce in order to survive, especially on an island.

[44]Pliny, similarly, ascribes the fecundity of harmless, edible animals to *benigna natura* (8.219; cf. 10.143), which he elsewhere deifies (*N.H.* 2.27; see above, p. 18); for Pliny's Stoic interpretation of *natura* and *mundus* see *N.H.* 2.1-2. Aristotle, *Gen. an.* 771a.18ff., interprets the same data physiologically: large animals produce few offspring because in them the nutriment goes into producing the bulk required by the σῶμα, whereas in small animals it goes into nourishing many fetations.

[45]It has many anal (or vaginal? see Archelaus and Varro) openings; it is hermaphroditic; it bears offspring once a month; it is awake when it is sleeping.

[46]The intent of the passage (10.6) is unclear, nor is it apparent whether superfetation is implied (R. A. Kraft, 1965, 111-12). What is evident is the letter's use of paradoxographical traditions as the basis of ethical exhortation; there is no interest in explaining them.

[47]Lev. 11.5 (LXX; MT 11.6); Dt. 14.7. On this exegetical tradition see R. A. Kraft, 1965, 110ff.

[48]In fact to do so would raise questions about God's nature or wisdom in constituting the hare such a lustful creature when lust is, after all, παρὰ φύσιν.

[49]*De div.* 2.28.61. The argument is presented as the hypothetical viewpoint of Chrysippus ("si a Chrysippo quaeram"). This is partly correct: Chrysippus along with other Stoics affirmed *heimarmenē* and a strict nexus of causes (*SVF* 2.913, 918); on the other hand, he also affirmed divination (*SVF* 2.1187, 1191, 1192), which he and other Stoics sought to reconcile with *heimarmenē* (cf. Cicero, *De div.* 1.52.118, and Pohlenz, 1970, vol. 1, 106-07).

[50]*De div.* 2.28.61 (". . . nihil enim fieri sine causa potest; nec quicquam fit quod fieri non potest; nec, si id factum est quod potuit fieri, portentum debet videri; nulla igitur portenta sunt"). Cf. further 2.22.49. A modern version of this argument that whatever happens is what can happen, therefore there are no departures from what can happen ("natural law"), is given by McKinnon, 1967.

[51]See the references in Pease, Cicero, *De div.*, *ad loc.*, to which may be added Aristotle, *Gen. an.* 771a.1ff.

[52]*De div.* 2.28.60 ("Quicquid enim oritur, qualecumque est, causam habeat a natura necesse est, ut, etiamsi praeter consuetudinem exiterit, praeter naturam tamen non possit existere").

[53]Ibid. ("in re nova atque admirabili"). Cf. Theophrastus' negative characterization of a *teras*: τὸ γὰρ εἰωθὸς οὐ τέρας (*De caus. plant.* 5.3.1); cf. below, p. 49.

[54]Seneca, *N.Q.* 7.16.1. Lucian's *True History* parodies this characteristic of the genre.

[55]The meteoric rise of the Romans to dominance of the *oikoumene* (1.1.5) is connected by Polybius with τύχη, whose operations he presents as offering an explanatory principle enabling him to give a single synoptic view (ὑπὸ μίαν σύνοψιν, 1.4.2) in the hitherto unattempted history of the whole process that he sets as his task (1.4.2-11). Cf. Petzold, 1969, 11, n. 3.

[56]M, Codex Vaticanus 73; printed in the edition of F. Hultsch, *Historiae*, Vol. 3 (Berlin: Weidmann, 1870), as Bk. 37.9, but omitted in more recent editions of Polybius. It is cited in R. M. Grant, 1952, 52, but without reference to the textual problem. If not authentic, the passage is nonetheless representative of Polybius.

[57]5.15.1-2 ("sine ullis caelestibus aquis causave qua alia quae rem miraculo eximeret").

[58]*Hist.* 2.50.4; Tacitus includes the account of an omen because he does not venture "to refuse credence to things that are so widely reported and disseminated" ("ita vulgatis traditisque demere fidem non ausim"). 4.81: eyewitnesses continue to testify to Vespasian's healings of two men sent to him by Sarapis even now when the emperor is dead and they can expect no monetary or other gain from it.

[59]*Ann.* 14.12. the *prodigia* must have come about *sine cura deum* because Nero continued his rule and his crimes after the appearance of the *prodigia*.

[60]*Hist.* 1.86 ("a fortuitis vel naturalibus causis in prodigium et omen imminentium cladium vertebatur").

[61]Cato's treatise on agriculture offers many home remedies the *Sitz im Leben* of which is the daily treatment of illness on the self-sufficient farming establishment; Varro's treatise presupposes Cato but also recommends calling a physician (1.16.4; 2.1.21) when home remedies are inadequate.

[62]*Flor.* 19 (*quibusdam medicamentis*). Earlier but briefer accounts of the same incident: Celsus, *De medic.* 2.6.15 (Teubner and Loeb numbering); Pliny, *N.H.* 7.124.

[63]The horror with which persons of uncertain or dual sex were commonly viewed is indicated by Livy's list of *prodigia* in 31.12 (*ante omnia abominati semimares*; they are thrown into the sea and an elaborate expiation is ordered) and Phlegon, *Mir.* 6.1-4 (such a phenomenon is a φάσμα and some of the diviners recommend burning both the

mother and infant). Other references, ancient and modern, in Pease, Cicero, *De div.*, p. 272; de Saint-Denis, 1942.

[64]32.12.1. Cf. his further strictures against the misconceptions and misguided reactions of popular cultic piety in 32.12.2-3.

[65]See Edelstein, *Asclepius* 2, ch. 4, "Temple Medicine," and Dodds, 1951, 115, who notes that though strange prescriptions and treatments like some of those prescribed in the Epidaurian inscriptions still figured in medicine generally, "there remains the important difference that in the medical schools they were subject, in principle at least, to rational criticism, whereas in dreams, as Aristotle said, the element of judgment (τὸ ἐπικρῖνον) is absent." Cf. further Behr, 1968, 35-36.

[66]ἰατρόʃ: Clement of Alexandria, *Protr.* 4.54; Aelian, *Var. hist.* 12.51; the Suda, s.v. Μενεκράτηʃ; ἰατρική: Athenaeus, *Deipnos.* 7.289A, D. The sources are collected in Weinreich, 1933, App. 1.

[67]Athenaeus, *Deipnos.* 7.289D; Weinreich, 1933, 27, suggests the latter offer concerned diet or other practical measures.

[68]A stock motif; see above, ch. 2, pp. 15-16 and n. 70.

[69]See the sources cited in n. 66. Weinreich, 1933, 4, notes that many physicians excluded epileptics from their practice. However, the Hippocratic treatise *The Sacred Disease* does not do so (see above, p. 38). M. Smith, 1971, 187, seems to imply that epilepsy was the *only* malady Menekrates healed; the sources do not say that and suggest the contrary. How he accomplished the healings of epilepsy, whether by the practice of medicine, as in the Hippocratic treatise, or by incantations and purifications (see the same treatise), or both, is not told us. His claim to divinity was credited by some but rejected as madness by many others (see Weinreich, 1933, 19-22, 26-27), another instance of the functioning of the canon of the ordinary human.

[70]A commonplace in agricultural lore; see Varro, *Rer. rust.* 3.16.4.

[71]Cf. Ninian Smart's characterization of miracle as something experimentally unrepeatable (1964, ch. 2). Vergil prescribes no rites that would connect the operation with the aetiology and return it to *illud tempus*, which Eliade, 1961, 80ff., sees as a paradigm for such activities. The proper context for viewing Vergil's description of the technique is agricultural folklore (cf. Judg. 14.14-18) and the Roman tradition of agriculture as a *scientia* (Varro, *Rer. rust.* 1.31.1; 2.1.11, 21; *disciplina*, 3.3.1) with its detailing of one technique after another; Varro, *Rer. rust.* 2.5.5 and 3.16.4, refers to the generation of bees in this way. The aetiology has been interpreted as political allegory, with various contemporary referents postulated; see Coleiro, 1971, esp. 117ff. Such interpretations, whatever their merits, do not annul the *aition*'s function as poetic conclusion (in a customary Vergilian adaptation of motifs from Greek literature) to Vergil's account of beekeeping; see Wilkinson, 1961, 113-14.

[72] Studies of Greco-Roman daimonology are many. Chapter 1 of Tambornino, 1909, is a "Testimoniorum collectio." Many texts are cited and discussed in Andres, 1918, and Foerster, 1935, with bibliography. More recent studies include Skovgaard Jensen, 1966; Wey, 1957; Böcher, 1972, for which "das religionsgeschichtliche Vergleichsmaterial" (ibid., 5) is provided by his 1970 volume. A perceptive theoretical statement, with affinities to the approach taken here and with citation of recent literature, is J. Z. Smith, 1978. On Christian demonizing of pagan miracle claims see further, below, ch. 9, p. 139 and n. 16.

[73] I use "demon" to indicate the pejorative sense and "daimon" or "daemon" the neutral sense of the Greek and Latin terms.

[74] Conceived of as the soul of a dead person, a daimon might grant favors (Lucian, *Peregr.* 27, is a good example) or harass and torment the living (examples in Andres, 1918, 275-76). Δαίμων could also denote deities, major or minor (including tutelary deities), or divine power; see LSJ, s.v., and, in the magical papyri, Foerster, 1935, 8. As such they expected to be paid the proper honors and would cause trouble if they were not; Dio Chrysostom, *Or.* 32.76, offers a late first-century example.

[75] Plato, *Symp.* 202D-203A, provided the focus for this tradition; its history is indicated in Nilsson, 1961, 254-57; Pohlenz, 1909, 132ff.; Skovgaard Jensen, 1966, ch. 5. In Middle Platonism in the second century, with its transcendent deity, this tradition plays an important role; e.g., Plutarch, *Is. et Os.* 360E; *De def. or.* 415ff.; Apuleius, *De deo Socr.* 4-6 (citing the *Symp.* passage), on which Augustine, *Civ. D.*, Bk. 8 et passim, provides a penetrating Christian commentary.

[76] Celsus (in *C. Cels.* 7.9) makes a number of the same complaints about persons claiming divine inspiration. On Alexander see further, ch. 10 below.

[77] The anonymous writer in Eusebius, *H.E.* 5.16.1ff., and Apollonius of Asia Minor, 5.18.1ff. On the date and place, and further discussion of Montanism, see ch. 10.7 below.

[78] *H.E.* 5.16.7, 9; cf. the Montanists' own oracles, *H.E.* 5.16.17; Epiphanius, *Pan.* 48.4, 11; 49.1.

[79] *H.E.* 5.16.10 (ψευδοπροφητικὸν πνεῦμα); 5.16.8 and 5.17.2 (ψευδοπροφήτης); cf. 5.16.14 (τῆς κατ᾽αὐτοὺς λεγομένης προφητείας).

[80] 5.16.8 (τῶν νόθων ἐκφωνημάτων); 5.16.9 (τοῦ νόθου πνεύματος).

[81] 5.16.9 (ἐκφρόνως).

[82] 5.16.8 (τοὺς ὄχλους ταρράττοντι; τὸ βλαψίφρον πνεῦμα) (also 5.16.13).

[83] 5.16.8 (τὸ λαοπλάνον πνεῦμα . . . πλανώμενοι ὑπ' αὐτοῦ).

[84] Apollonius dwells on this; see 5.18.2-11, with the conclusion that if they are guilty as charged, "they are not prophets" (οὐκ εἰσὶ προφῆται).

[85] 5.16.7, Montanus prophesies "contrary to the custom of the church from the beginning in its tradition and succession" (παρὰ τὸ κατὰ παράδοσιν καὶ κατὰ διαδοχὴν ἄνωθεν τῆς ἐκκλησίας ᾽ἔθος δῆθεν); cf. 5.16.9, the prophetesses speak ἀλλοτριοτρόπως. They blaspheme the whole church (5.16.9) and against the Lord and the apostles (5.18.5), set up their own ethic (5.18.2), pass on the spirit to others in their following (5.16.9) and give their movement organizational form (5.18.2).

[86] Cf. Mk. 13.22//Mt. 24.24 (deceit); Mt. 7.15.23 (inauthentic prophecy); Acts 8.20 (defective motivation; cf. 1 Cor. 13.2); 13.6, 10 (deceit); 2 Thess. 2.9-10 and Rev. 13.11ff. (deceit and diabolic agency); *Did.* 11.8-12 (deceit and greed); 16.3-4 (deceit, reprehensible behavior, inauthentic wonders); Hermas, *Mand.* 11 (reprehensible motivation and behavior, harmful and deceitful predictions, deficient group loyalty; cf. further ch. 10.6 below); *Act. Pet.* 4 (Lipsius and Bonnet ed., vol. 1, 49.13: *magus, planus*).

[87] τοῖς θείοις, a term which makes explicit the divine reference of σημεῖον in this account. Plutarch's contemporary, Arrian, uses θεῖον regularly to designate divine omens; *Anab.* 1.18.6; 1.25.6-7; 1.26.2; 2.3.3; etc.; see below, p. 46.

[88] The point is that these are all σημεῖα.

[89] Hipparchus, the Hellenistic astronomer (d. ca. 125 B.C.E.), adhered to the geocentric system despite Aristarchus' espousal of the heliocentric hypothesis, because the latter did not account for the data as fully as the former did; one must "save the phenomena" (data), he said (see Tarn and Griffith, 1961, 297, and Farrington, 1969, 115-16). "His theory also had the advantage of not offending popular prejudice by removing the earth from its traditional place at the centre of the universe" (Farrington, 116). Similar motivations and results are often discernible, *mutatis mutandis*, with respect to miracles.

[90] *N.H.* 2.191. This was a common element in explanations of earthquakes; e.g., Anaxagoras (in Aristotle, *Meteor.* 2.365a); Aristotle, ibid., 366; Lucretius, *De rer. nat.* 6.535ff.

[91] Like Aristotle, who on this point, however, can offer only a few general statements (*Meteor.* 367a-368a).

[92] *N.H.* 2.191: the various theories must be left for each person to decide; as for himself, he attributes them to the winds.

[93] An examination of some of the philosophical and theological issues involved in coincidence construed as miracle is Holland, 1965, 43-51.

[94]The time of Herodotus (from whom an example is cited in our text) is also the age of Pericles, with its many public works. In the building boom fostered by the Hellenistic rulers advanced technology was employed. Vitruvius' first century (B.C.E.) work on architecture is a repository of Greek and Roman knowledge of the subject (cf. Pliny, *N.H.* 35-36). In the Roman agricultural tradition, knowledge of construction technique was detailed (e.g., Cato, *De agric.* 14-15; 18-22; 38). An elementary structural principle is implicit in a statement like Seneca's (*N.Q.* 7.14.1-4) that the theory of a solid sky overhead is untenable because there is nothing that would support such weight. In the Synoptic tradition (from which an example is cited in our text), cf. Mt. 7.24-27.

[95]The relation between the cause of an event and the sign that foreshadows the event was much discussed by the savants of antiquity. See Cicero, *De div.* 1.16.29, and Pease's note (pp. 139-40). For the Stoics, whose teachings on fate and divination raised the question of determinism, see the sections on fate and divination in *SVF* and Pohlenz, 1970, vol. 1, 101-08, and the index, s.v., "Heimarmene." In the texts we are considering the philosophical issues implicit in them are not taken up.

[96]In Suetonius' account of the collapse of an amphitheater, killing 20,000 spectators, his interest is solely in Tiberius' help to the survivors, and he says nothing about their interpretation of the event (*Tib.* 40). There are also explicit miracle stories, of course, where a building collapses in direct response to the activity of a thaumaturgist, e.g., *Act. Ioan.* 42.

[97]Cf. Herodotus 4.28: in Scythia there are many thunderstorms in the summer, "but if a thunderstorm comes during the winter, it is considered a divine sign [τέραϛ], to be marveled at. If an earthquake occurs, whether during the summer or the winter, it is considered a divine sign [τέραϛ] in Scythia."

[98]Other examples of extraordinary phenomena interpreted in favor of one group and to the discrediting of another, rival group are given in Theissen, 1974, 232-33, with the apt comment, "Erhalten haben sich oft nur die Interpretationen der Sieger" (p. 232).

[99]*Anab.* 2.3.8. Cf. Homer, *Od.* 21.413, where thunder authenticates the hero Odysseus, and the comment by P. Stein, 1909, 34: "In itself thunder is not a prodigy; but when it thunders at the very time that Odysseus is making ready for the great affair he is able to believe that Zeus--whose sign is thunder--is indicating to him through the thunder that the affair will end well." Similarly, *Od.* 20.100ff., where Zeus responds with thunder to Odysseus' request for a *teras*, and a servant woman recognizes it as a *teras* from Zeus since the sky is clear.

[100]On the eagle as the bird of Zeus see LSJ, s.v., ἀετόϛ, and P. Stein, 1909, 35, 43-44, 57-58; in Latin literature, Krauss, 1930, 98-101.

Notes to Chapter 4

[1] The Suda, s.v. τέραʃ: 'ἡ σημεῖον. *Etymologican Magnum*, s.v. τέραʃ: τὸ σημεῖον. For τεράστια the Suda gives: σημεῖα, θαύματα.

[2] The *Etymol. Magn.*, s.v. τέραʃ, differentiates τέραʃ as τὸ παρὰ φύσιν γενόμενον πρᾶγμα from σημεῖον as τὸ παρὰ τὴν κοινὴν συνήθειαν γινόμενον. The distinction here is probably between cosmic order and common social custom, mores (τὴν κοινὴν συνήθειαν). When Herodotus labels as a *teras* a case of a woman's having public intercourse with a goat (2.46) it is surely because it is contrary to common mores; it would also have been considered παρὰ φύσιν in an ethical sense (cf. above, p. 34). The interchangeability of *teras* and *semeion* (when applied to extraordinary phenomena) has been denied by a number of scholars who contend that *semeion* characteristically serves to distinguish Christian miracles from extraordinary phenomena in pagan sources, which are designated as *terata*. To enter into this dispute here goes beyond the scope of this study; as I have sought to show elsewhere (Remus, 1982), such a distinction is contradicted by ancient usage.

[3] *Gen. an.* 770b.5 (ἔστι δὲ καὶ τὸ τέραʃ τῶν ἀναμοίων).

[4] 769b.7ff. (οὐδὲ ἄνθρωποʃ ἀλλὰ ζῷόν τι μόνον); cf. above, ch. 2.2, on *anthropos* as a canon of the ordinary. Phlegon's paradoxographical work, *De mira.* 22-24, 26-27 (Giannini, *Paradoxographorum*, 212ff.), collects reports of human mothers' giving birth to animals or part animals; cf. also Pliny, *N.H.* 7.34-35.

[5] 770b.10ff.: "A *teras* belongs to the class of things contrary to nature--contrary to nature, yet not to all of nature, but rather to nature in the majority of instances [ὡʃ ἐπὶ τὸ πολὺ], for as regards the nature which is always and by necessity [τὴν ἀεὶ καὶ τὴν ἐξ ἀνάγκηʃ] nothing occurs 'contrary to nature'; rather, what is contrary to nature is found among those things that occur as they do in the majority of instances [ὡʃ ἐπὶ τὸ πολύ] but may possibly occur otherwise. Even among the latter what takes place contrary to this particular order, yet not randomly [μὴ τυχόντωʃ], seems to be less of a *teras* because even what is contrary to nature is in some way according to nature, whenever formal nature does not gain control over material nature. Therefore people do not call such things τέρατα, just as they do not in those other cases where something takes place with regularity [εἴωθε], as with fruit." Aristotle then cites the case of the "smoky" vine and its variably colored grapes: "people do not consider that a *teras* because it does this frequently and with regularity" [διὰ τὸ πλειστάκιʃ εἰωθέναι]. And Aristotle at least can give a further explanation in terms of *physis*: "The reason is that in its nature it [the vine] is between white and black so that the change is not great nor, as it were, contrary to nature, for it is not a change to another nature." Aristotle also speaks of "transgressing nature," which is a synonym of "contrary to nature" (771a.12ff.): unusual fetal formations that "transgress nature a little ordinarily live, but those that transgress it more do not live whenever that which is contrary to nature occurs in the parts that govern life" (τὰ μὲν οὖν μικρὸν παρεκβαίνοντα τὴν φύσιν ζῆν εἴωθεν, τὰ δὲ πλεῖον οὐ ζῆν ὅταν ἐν τοῖʃ κυρῖοιʃ τοῦ

ζῆν γένηται τὸ παρὰ φύσιν). For Aristotle's "statistical" definition of monstrous genetic formations see also 772a.36-39.

[6]771a.23ff.: *physis* operates in fetation to produce the right number of offspring in the size proper to the parents. Similarly 772a.10ff.: male semen will not produce an embryo larger or smaller than is natural (τοῦ πεφυκότοʃ). On *physis* as artist or craftsman in Aristotle see the references in the Loeb edition of *Gen. an.*, pp. xlvi-xlvii; on *physis* generally in Aristotle, see above, pp. 16-17.

[7]Older works useful for their rich collection of data include Luterbacher, 1904; Wülker, 1903; Thulin, 1905. More recently see Bloch, 1963, a concise treatment, with bibliography, and Händel, 1959, 2283-96.

[8]Bloch, 1963, 119-28, gives a lucid outline; more details are supplied by Luterbacher, 1904, and de Saint-Denis, 1942. Wülker, 1903, 86-92, gives a chronological list (with sources) of public Roman prodigies for the years 496 B.C.E.-292 C.E. Livy is the chief source for the pre-Christian era. For the 3d and 2d centuries B.C.E. he reports prodigies annually, apparently drawing on official publication of prodigies reported for each year; see Luterbacher, 1904, 13-14; de Saint-Denis, 1942, 126, 128ff.; Bloch, 1963, 112-14, 145-46; his accounts thus reflect the attitude both of the general populace and of the authorities.

[9]These divisions are modern; ancient attempts at classification are various and not very successful.

[10]*De div.* 2.27.58. He appeals to Thales and Anaxagoras as persons who would not have believed such reports. Pease, Cicero, *De div.*, *ad* 1.98 (pp. 271-73), lists many of the ancient and modern reports of bleeding rivers and sweating statues, including ancient criticisms of such reports, to which may be added Augustine, *Civ. D.* 3.11, who ascribes weeping of statues to demons.

[11]Pliny, *N.H.* 2.104. Neither the Cicero nor the Pliny passages actually use the term *prodigium*, but it and similar words (see below) are commonly applied to such phenomena.

[12]See Bloch, 1963, 145-46, and cf. Livy 43.13.1: "I am not unaware that, because of the same neglect by which people commonly believe the gods provide no portents [*nihil deos portendere*] in our day, no prodigies [*prodigia*] whatever are reported to the state or recorded in the annals." That prodigies continued to be reported unofficially is evident from Suetonius and Tacitus and from the list in Wülker, 1903. Tacitus notes a change in attitude toward them, however; see above, p. 37.

[13]For "explanation" of wonders by restricting them geographically, see above, ch. 3, passim.

[14]*Rer. rust.* 2.1.26; see above, p. 29. Augustine, *Civ. D.* 21.8, after quoting Varro's account of a *portentum*, gives what amounts

to a definition: "It is certain that an author such as Varro would not call it a portent unless it seemed to be contrary to nature" ("Hoc certe Varro tantus auctor portentum non appellaret, nisi esse contra naturam videretur").

[15] Cf. Varro, according to Servius, *ad Aen.* 3.366: *miraculum, quod mirum est.* It occurs frequently in this sense in Livy: 1.47.9, summoned by the usurper Tarquin, the senators are astounded at the unaccustomed and wondrous sight of him as king (*novitate ac miraculo attoniti*); acts of Roman hardihood (2.13.13, a soldier holds his hand in a fire without flinching) or daring (5.46.3, a Roman passes openly through enemy lines to offer a sacrifice) are labeled *miracula*; 6.12.2, where the Volsci get all those soldiers to wage their many wars is a *miraculum* to Livy; etc. Another instance without divine reference is 4.35.9 where Livy uses *miraculum* (along with *portentum*) to designate what is normally considered impossible (that a plebeian should be fit for high office). Many further examples, from both pagan and Christian sources, covering events, phenomena in nature, and human constructions (e.g., the seven wonders of the world), in *Thesaurus Linguae Latinae*, s.v., I/1.

[16] The inexplicability is stated clearly by Valerius Maximus (fl. time of Tiberius), 1.8 (p. 43, lines 23-25 in Kempf ed.): "Those things are justly called *miracula* for which it is difficult to discern whence they originate or why they persist" ("quae, quia unde manauerint aut qua constiterint dinoscere arduum est, merito miracula uocentur"). He then offers examples. For another example see above, pp. 36-37 (Livy, 5.15.1-2). Livy, 2.36.7, reports a miracle sequence similar to those in Christian (Lk. 1.20-22, 62-66) and pagan literature (Oxy. P. 11, 1381; E. T. in F. C. Grant, 1953, 124-27, and Nock, 1933a, 86-88): a man stricken with illness for failing to report a dream to the authorities is healed--*ecce, aliud miraculum*--when he finally does so. Tacitus, *Hist.* 4.81, uses *miraculum* to designate a healing miracle performed by Vespasian and showing the divine favor toward the emperor (cf. above, ch. 2, n. 23), and Apuleius, *Met.* 2.28, to designate a resurrection by an Egyptian *propheta.* *Miraculum* is used by Christian writers to designate the wondrous events in the story of Christ and the wonders he worked as well as those recorded in the martyr acts; see *Thesaurus Linguae Latinae*, s.v., 1056.14ff.

Miraculum in the sense of a coincidence that is interpreted as a divine sign is found in Tacitus, *Hist.* 2.50, and *Ann.* 13.41, in connection with emperors, much as θεῖον is in Arrian in connection with Alexander (see above, p. 46).

An example of usage in which the divine referent is not the deity of cultic piety but of Stoic theology (cf. above, p. 18) is *N.H.* 2.206ff., where Pliny lists wonders of the earth (*terrae miracula*)-- mines yielding richly despite human depletion and luxurious consumption, the great variety of gems, caves whose exhalations produce prophecy, et al.--and interprets these as manifestations of the divine sway of nature in the cosmos.

[17] Rainbows as a τέραϛ: Homer, *Il.* 11.26-28; 17.548.

[18] Cf. Aristotle, *Meteor.* 371bff.; Pliny observes that rainbows are *frequentes*; Aristotle's observation that rainbows caused by the moon are rare does not lead him, as it often does others in such cases, to ascribe them to deity.

[19]Cf. Ps.-Quintilian, *Decl.* 10.5: "Magus est, cuius ars est
ire contra naturam." In the Androcles story as told by Aelian, *Anim.*
7.48, when the lion recognizes Androcles and fawns on him, the spectators think he is a γόης.

[20]A survey of various anthropological viewpoints through 1937
(with extensive bibliography) is provided by Benedict, 1937. More
recently, R. and M. Wax, 1962, 1963; Douglas, 1966, ch. 4, et passim.;
Marwick, 1970; Kiev, 1964.

[21]Cf., e.g., Webster, 1948, who follows Frazer, 1911, 220, in
defining magic as the manipulation, effective *ex opere operato*, of an
impersonal power "exhibiting uniform invariable tendencies" (p. 38),
whereas religion (in this case, animism) has to do with "a power manifested capriciously toward man by spiritual beings" (p. 38); but
"Spiritual beings are often credited with a knowledge of magic" and
"hand it down to men and sometimes use it in their relations with men"
(p. 39), and though this distinction may be "clear and definite . . .
for us, it remains vague and fluid for primitive thought" (p. 39), and
magic and animism "merge insensibly into each other" (p. 39). Webster
ends up speaking of "magico-animistic observances in which spiritual
beings are definitely regarded as under the operator's control" (p. 54),
which is probably a fair description of the rites, but one wonders how
much the original distinction contributes to the understanding of them.
    Many more recent anthropologists are disinclined to draw a
sharp distinction between magic and religion and instead prefer to
place magic, sorcery, witchcraft, and religion on a single continuum,
with the "primarily magical" at one end, the "primarily religious" at
the other, and "magico-religious" or "religio-magical" in between; thus
Firth, 1956, 156-57, 166-70, followed by Worsley, 1968, xxviii, n. 2,
who also notes the permeability of the "mundane" and the "magical"
(xxvii). The definitional problems in classical and more recent theory
are discussed further in Douglas, 1966, 74ff.
    The disciplines in which investigators stand influence defini-
tions and terminology. Where historians of religion are apt to think
of rituals as belonging to "religion," anthropologists and sociologists
are apt to speak of the same kind of rituals as "magical" or "magico-
religious." Thus the Wax's, 1962, 184, speak of certain rituals of
"the magical world view" as intended to return one to the *illud tempus*,
to use Eliade's term, whereas Eliade (1961, 80ff.) thinks of such
rituals as religious. One suspects that among anthropologists, whatever the modifications in theory and conceptuality, as far as terminology is concerned the tradition of Hubert and Mauss lingers, where
"magic" serves to connote "the whole corpus of ritual and belief of
primitive peoples" (Douglas, 1966, 74).
    The lack of consensus regarding terminology and conceptuality
indicated in these examples, to say nothing of the no less conflicting
views in historical and exegetical studies of the Greco-Roman world,
underlines the importance of attempting to listen afresh to the ancient
sources themselves.

[22]The necessity of attending to the chronological and social
locations of the use of the term "magic" is increasingly recognized by
investigators, e.g., Segal, 1981, a study, undertaken independently of
my own, which operates with a similar methodology and comes to similar
conclusions regarding the use of the term in the Greco-Roman period;

similarly Peters, 1978, xvii, 9-10, etc., takes account of the social
location of charges of "magic" in the medieval period.

[23]On the history of the word *magos* and *magus* see Abt, 1908,
106-08; Pease, Cicero, *De div.*, pp. 175, 178; Tavenner, 1916, 1ff.;
Bidez and Cumont, 1938.

[24]Older literature in the commentaries and in BAG, s.v. μάγοſ;
more recently, Mann, 1958; Hengel and Merkel, 1973; Hull, 1974, 122-28.

[25]Ignatius, *Eph.* 19.3; Justin, *Dial.* 77.4; 78.1, 7, 9; 88.1;
102.2-4; Irenaeus, *Adv. h.* 3.9.2 (Harvey ed., 3.10.1); Tertullian, *De
Idol.* 9. Cf. also Origen, *C. Cels.* 1.60, in response to Celsus' charge
(1.58) that at Jesus' birth χαλδαῖοι appeared; Origen seeks to distinguish *magoi* and *Chaldaioi* (1.58), but the two were commonly identified
(see Bidez and Cumont, 1938, vol. 1, 33-36).

[26]In the Two Ways material in *Did.* and *Barn.*: *Did.* 2.2, οὐ
μαγεύσειſ, οὐ φαρμακεύσειſ; 5.1, μαγεῖαι and φαρμακίαι; cf. *Barn.* 20.1,
μαγεία; *Did.* 3.4 lumps the following together: οἰωνοσκόποſ, ἐπαοιδόſ,
μαθηματικόſ, περικαθαίρων.

[27]*2 Apol.* 5.3; cf. Gen. 6.1ff.; for other Jewish and Christian
testimonies to this tradition see R. H. Charles (ed. and trans.), *The
Apocrypha and Pseudepigrapha of the Old Testament in English with
Introductions and Explanatory Notes to the Several Books*, Vol. 2,
Pseudepigrapha (Oxford: Clarendon Press, 1913), 191, *ad 1 En.* 6.2.

[28]The subject of the sentence is left in doubt; for Satan as
the subject see J. H. Waszink, Tertullian, *De anima* (Amsterdam:
Meulenhoff, 1947), 577. The close association of magic, demons, and
Satan in Tertullian's exposition suggests that the ambiguity is not a
serious difficulty in interpretation.

[29]*De anim.* 57.2 ("multiformem luem mentis humanae, totius
erroris artificem, salutis pariter animaeque vastatorem").

[30]Ibid. 57.6, 9 (*phantasma*); *Apol.* 23.1 (*phantasmata*).

[31]*De anim.* 57.2, 5, 6, 12 (*fallacia*); 57.12 (*praestigias*);
Apol. 23.1 ("miracula circulatoriis praestigiis"); 23.7 ("magia aut
aliqua eiusmodi fallacia").

[32]In *Apol.* 22.7 Tertullian uses the same vocabulary to describe
the works of demons--*praestigiis falsis*--that he elsewhere uses to
describe magic. In *De anim.* 57 the wonders of necromancy are attributed to demonic power.

[33]At least some of the traditions may with some likelihood be
dated in the second century; Hennecke-Schneemelcher, *New Testament
Apocrypha* 2, 266, 275.

³⁴*Act. Pet.* 5 (Lipsius-Bonnet ed., vol. 1, 49.25) (*magum*);
Mart. Pet. 1 (1, 80.20)(μάγοſ); *Act. Pet.* 28 (1, 75.22) (*magus et
seductor*). By magic spell (*magico carmine*, ch. 6; Lipsius-Bonnet 1,
51.28) and magic art (*magica arte*, ch. 23 = 1, 71.12) he leads people
astray. When they see his marvels are not genuine, they turn away from
his *magia*, ch. 28 (1, 76.21).

³⁵Ibid. ch. 23 (1, 71.10-11) (*inposturas*); ch. 28 (1, 75.31-
76.23) (a resurrection worked by Simon turns out to be only apparent).
The πνεύματα he causes to appear are φαινόμενα μόνον, οὐκ ᾿όντα δὲ
ἀληθῶſ, *Mart. Pet.* 2 (1, 80.25); similarly, *Act. Pet.* 31 (1, 81.21ff.).
Yet it is said that Simon can fly (ibid. 4 and 32), a fact that is
called τὸ παράδοξον (*Mart. Pet.* 3 = 1, 82.20), causing Peter himself
to marvel (*Act. Pet.* 32 = 1, 83.13: "et ipse mirabatur talem visum").
There are canons of the ordinary here, but they are not very tight.

³⁶*Act. Pet.* 6; 17; 25; etc. The triumph of Christianity over
magic is seen also in the *Act. Ioan.* (for which the earliest certain
attestation is Eusebius, *H.E.* 3.25.6): the cult of Artemis of Ephesus,
which pagan tradition commonly associated with magic, is labeled
ἡ πολλὴ μαγεία καὶ ἡ ταύτῃ ἀδελφὴ φαρμακεία (43; Lipsius-Bonnet 2/1,
172.16-17) and the goddess is called a demon (42; 43); in response to
the apostle's prayer her altar and temple are destroyed or badly
damaged (42).

³⁷*1 Apol.* 26.2 (διὰ τῆſ τῶν ἐνεργούντων δαιμόνων τέχνηſ,
referring to Simon); 26.4 (διὰ μαγικῆſ τέχνηſ referring to Menander).
The charge that they deceive people, a common form of obloquy (cf.
above, p. 41) is noted in 26.4 and 56.1.

³⁸The designations μάγοſ, μαγεία, and related words function
to deny divine reference to the inexplicable phenomena worked by the
apostles, i.e., the phenomena are not miracles. In the *Act. Pl.* the
charge that Paul is a magician serves to explain his uncanny ability
to win women over to encratism (chs. 15; 20). The same theme recurs
in the *Act. Thom.* (probably to be dated in the first half of the third
century, Hennecke-Schneemelcher, *New Testament Apocrypha* 2, 441), chs.
99; 106; 134; 138; 152; in ch. 102 this power is specified as βάσκανοſ
ὀφθαλμόſ. The labels magician and magic are employed to explain other
extraordinary phenomena as well: healings, exorcisms, and wonders
arouse the suspicion that the apostle is a μάγοſ (*Act. Thom.* 20 =
Lipsius-Bonnet 3, 131.2); never before was it heard that anyone raised
a dead person, therefore the apostle did it τοῖſ ἔργοιſ τῆſ μαγείαſ
(96 = 3, 209.13); by τέχνῃ μαγικῇ Thomas, that φαρμακόſ (the Ω ms.
tradition; μάγοſ, P), opens the doors of the prison (162 = 3,372). In
addition to the labels μάγοſ (102; 104) and φαρμακόſ (98; 114; 116;
117; 123; 130) and the charge of the evil eye (see above), the apostle
is called a πλάνοſ (102 = 3,215.6) and a wicked man and home-wrecker
(106 = 3,218.11-12: πονηρὲ καὶ ἀφανιστὰ καὶ ἐχθρὲ τοῦ ἐμοῦ οἴκου),
and his ascetic virtues are turned into their opposites (96). In the
Clementine Recognitions (1.42.4 = GCS 51, 33) the guards at the tombs
say they are unable to prevent Jesus' resurrection because he was a
magus. The same labels used by Christians to designate opponents are
here put into the mouth of pagans to discredit Christians.

³⁹Justin, *1 Apol.* 30, against the suggestion that Jesus per-
formed his *dunameis* by magical art (μαγικῇ τέχνῃ); *Dial.* 69.7, the
Jews of Jesus' day said his healings and resurrections were φαντασία
μαγική and he was a μάγος and a λαοπλάνος. Tertullian, *Apol.*: Jesus
was a *magus*, 21.17 (say Jews), 23.12 (say pagan deities/demons); pagans
would presumably say that his followers exorcise through *magia* (23.7).
In a number of publications M. Smith has argued that Jesus was
a "magician" and that both he and his followers practiced "magic"; see
1973a, passim; 1973b, 101ff.; 1978. In 1973b, 220-22, his investigation of the meaning of the term "magic" shows that at least for some
ancients magic did not necessarily imply compulsion of the gods (cf.
below, sec. 4.3.2.2) and was "capable of prayer, of individual devotion
to the deity, and of considerable religious feeling" (p. 222), i.e.,
that it was on a continuum with "religion"; he also notes the social
conditioning of the use of the word ("a term of abuse" with connotations of "social subversion," 220), with assessments of thaumaturgists
varying with the person(s) doing the assessing (e.g., pp. 222, 227-29).
As to Smith's categorization of Jesus as a magician, one may note
Segal's observations (1981, 369-70): "The most interesting question
for scholarship, as I see it, is not whether the charge of magic
against Jesus is true or not. Since he does not claim the title, there
can be no possible demonstration or disproof of a charge which is a
matter of interpretation in the Hellenistic world. The most interesting question for scholarship is to define the social and cultural
conditions and presuppositions that allow such charges and counter-
charges to be made."

⁴⁰Tertullian, *De anim.* 57.2 (text in n. 96 below) is an
exception.

⁴¹I use the word "manipulations" in a neutral sense. They are
described in detail in T. Hopfner, 1928, 301ff.

⁴²On magic in *C. Cels.* see Miura-Stange, 1926; Bardy, 1928.

⁴³*C. Cels.* 4.33 (ἐν τοῖς μαγικοῖς συγγράμμασι). Pliny, *N.H.*
30.8-9, describes such books and traditions concerning others (30.4).
Cf. further Bidez and Cumont, 1938, vol. 1, Index Général, s.v.,
"Livres."

⁴⁴*C. Cels.* 1.6, where Celsus notes that ability to perform
paradoxa is grounds for claiming that one is acting τῷ θεοῦ δυνάμει;
similarly, 1.28 (where Origen adds that Jesus' wonders accord with his
status as son of God), 1.38 (where Origen interprets Celsus as
charging that Jesus' incredible manifestations of power were done ὡς
ἀπὸ μαγείας καὶ οὐ θείᾳ δυνάμει γεγενημένας), and 1.68 (where Celsus
asks whether the wonders worked by *goētes* warrant our regarding them
as υἱοὺς θεοῦ); in 2.49 Celsus turns Jesus' predictions of false prophets against him, asking if it is not a miserable argument for Christians to infer from the same works that he is God and they are *goētes*.
These passages illustrate von Wetter's thesis, 1916, 73-82, that a man
who was a son of God to his followers was apt to be a magician to his
enemies; cf. above, Preface, n. 2. In 2.51 Origen seems to imply that
Celsus does not acknowledge divine miracles; this is an untenable
accusation.

[45]Similarly in *C. Cels.* 2.50-51, where, however, Origen
mentions manipulations (ἐπαοιδέ*ς*, κατακλήσει*ς*, μαγγανεία) as characterizing μαγεία and γοητεία; though he does not undertake to show that
miracles claimed by Christians are free of such manipulations it is
implicit in his argument since such manipulations are associated with
demons and Christians have nothing to do with demons.

[46]Abgar correspondence, in Eusebius, *H.E.* 1.13.6 (ἄνευ φαρμάκων
καὶ βοτανῶν) and 18 (ἄνευ φαρμακεία*ς* καὶ βοτάνων). On the date of the
correspondence (probably 4th c.) see W. Bauer, in Hennecke-
Schneemelcher, *New Testament Apocrypha* 1, 437ff., and 1971, index,
s.v. "Abgar legend."

[47]See Hull, 1974, 128ff., with citation of earlier form- and
redaction-critical literature; Matthew's motives are variously
explained.

[48]Antithesis 14 in the reconstruction of Harnack, 1924a, 90,
based on Tertullian, *Adv. M.* 4.9.7 (see Harnack, 1924a, 282*).

[49]Cf. also Ps.(?)-Justin, *De res.* 4, where, however, the
assertion that Jesus healed with a word is not contrasted with magic.

[50]Grundmann, 1935, 303.6ff., exemplifies this view so far as
the synoptic miracle accounts are concerned; he is quoted with approval
by van der Loos, 1965, 324-25, who cites others holding similar views.
Grundmann's distinction between "das krafterfüllte Wort Jesu" and
"Zauberformeln" overlooks Jesus' utterance of foreign words in two
Marcan accounts (5.41; 7.34), presumably because for Jesus they were
not foreign. But for later followers they were, and their preservation has its own *Sitz im Leben*, namely, thaumaturgy that employed
nomina barbarica. Pagans could easily construe them and Christians'
use of the name Jesus in exorcisms, healings, and other settings as
"Zauberformeln"; such *nomina barbarica* are a standard feature of the
magical papyri, and Jewish names, including that of Jesus, are common
in the magical papyri; references in Nilsson, 1948b, 5-8; further Gager,
1972, ch. 4. Lucian, *Philops.* 12, gives a portrait of a Babylonian
magos in action; his technique involves recital of seven holy names
from an ancient book (ἱερατικά τινα ἐκ βίβλου παλαιᾶ*ς* ὀνόματα ἕπτα);
similarly the Babylonian *magos* in Lucian's *Menippus* 6-10; the figure
and technique were sufficiently stereotyped to be recognized when
parodied. On ῥῆσι*ς* βαρβαρική generally see the references in Bultmann,
1957, 238; Betz, 1961, 153-55; Nock, 1929, 229 (in Nock, 1972, vol. 1,
189).

[51]*Apol.* 21.17; cf. *Sib. Or.* 8.267, 285-86 (above, p. 59).

[52]Thus Grundmann, 1935, 303.1ff.; the "magische Züge (Speichel,
Betasten, usw)" in the accounts and "die substantiell-magischen
Vorstellungen" are circumscribed, he says, by the setting and by the
compelling power of the personality of the healer (p. 303, n. 67).

[53]For an answer to Grundmann see R. M. Grant, 1952, 172-73, and
his judicious summary (p. 173): "The fundamental difficulty with

Grundmann's arguments is due to his identification of (non-Christian) miracle with magic. This identification cannot be justified, and a thoroughgoing distinction between Christian and non-Christian miracle stories cannot be made. The contexts are different; the phenomena are somewhat similar."

[54]See Hull, 1974, especially chs. 5-7, with citation of older literature.

[55]See, e.g., Pliny the Younger, *Epp.* 10.33-34; 10.92-93; 10.96.7; Celsus in *C. Cels.* 1.1, 7; 8.17, 20; Tertullian, *Apol.* 38-39. Cf. Wilken, 1971, 279ff.

[56]E.g., Justin, *Dial.* 89ff. (cf. further, below, pp. 140-41); Tertullian, *Scorp.* 1.

[57]*De anim.* 57. On the terms ἄωροι and βιαιοθάνατοι see Hopfner, 1928, 306.

[58]*Met.* 3.17 ("hic nares et digiti, illic carnosi clavi pendentium").

[59]*Philops.* 29, ἀνεσκολοπίσθη, a synonym of ἀνασταυροῦν, as in *Pereg.* 11; other such passages in LSJ, s.v. ἀνασκολοπίζω.

[60]*Philops.* 17 (τὸν δακτύλιον . . . σιδήρου τοῦ ἐκ τῶν σταυρῶν πεποιημένον). On the apotropaic power of iron see Hopfner, 1928, 326; by way of comparison, Schienrl, 1980. Other texts mentioning use of *ousia*, Hopfner, 1928, 331.

[61]*Act. Thom.* 121. Cf. further chs. 132-33, where oil, water, and bread, and the pronouncing of the name of Jesus over the bread are all part of the rite of baptism; ch. 157, where a prayer is addressed to the oil with a petition to Jesus that his power would come into the oil, as it once had permeated the wood of the cross.

[62]References in Söder, 1932, 55, 57, 60, 67, 69, 71, 91, 93. On "cross mysticism" in these writings cf. von Wetter, 1921, 110ff., 124ff.

[63]On the sign of the cross as a baptismal seal see Dölger, 1911, 171-79. On exorcism in connection with baptism and the use of materials (salt, spit, oil) and manipulations (exsufflation, e.g.) see Dölger, 1909.

[64]Nilsson, 1961, 696-98. An example is offered by Goodenough, 1953, 155-56: a translator of Coptic *Zaubertexte* acknowledges that the distinction between supplication and compulsion is not absolute in the texts but feels the distinction ought to be observed--and therefore "translates a given Coptic imperative as *du sollst* when its association seems to him magical, and as *mögest du* when it seems to reflect ecclesiastical liturgy." That is to say, the distinction must be read into the texts.

[65]Nock, 1929, 230-31 (in 1972, vol. 1, 191-93). Borrowing a phrase from Lucan, he labeled the religious element *ignota pieta*.

[66]Nock, 1933b, 170 (in 1972, vol. 1, 314). He goes on to note the ambivalent nature of words like φίλτρον, φαρμακόν, and ἐπῳδή.

[67]Festugière, 1932, 289, 308-15 (the mysteries), 327-28 (Hermeticism and Christianity).

[68]Goodenough's own terms are "subjective" and "objective" judgments, according to "personal taste and sympathy" or psychological type or "grades of intelligence" or "levels of spiritual sensitivity" (1953, 159). But he also observes that "the practitioners of the 'higher' approaches to religion" are pitted against those of the "lower" or against "the lower levels of *other* religions," which they label "magic" or "superstition"; or the conquerors of a religion denigrate that religion as "superstition" (p. 159); i.e., Goodenough notes social and cultural distinctions.

[69]Goodenough, 1953, 157-59. Depending on one's perspective, Paul's statement that he no longer lives but Christ lives in him (Gal. 2.20) might be construed as "mystical" (A. Schweizer) or as "sacramental" (see Schlier, 1951, 63, n. 2) or as "magical," especially when coupled with his assertion that he was capable of *all* things (πάντα) through Christ who was giving him power (ἐνδυναμοῦντι, Phil. 4.13); magicians made similar claims (see R. M. Grant, 1952, 61, 128).

[70]Festugière, 1932, 290-92, gives a list, documented from the magical papyri.

[71]Goodenough, 1953, 157. The egoistic aspect of religion, with worshipers looking to their deities to supply what is useful to them, is developed and illustrated with quotations from pagan and Christian writers in Feuerbach, 1967, 51ff. Luther's definition of "to have a god" is a case in point: with sorcerers and practitioners of black magic, who contract with the devil to supply them with what they need and desire, he contrasts those who place their trust wholly in God, for a god is that which provides one with all good and helps in every distress (1959, First Commandment).

[72]Conversion and spiritual transformation as miraculous is a relatively late topos; cf. Origen, *C. Cels.* 1.43, 67 (implicitly); Augustine, *C. Dei* 22.5 (explicitly).

[73]Goodenough, 1953, 158; on the "mechanical efficacy" of sacraments in medieval Christianity see Thomas, 1971, 33ff.

[74]Weinreich, 1929, 9 (175), "'Zauberspruch,' der sich oft nur schwer vom Gebet unterscheiden lässt"; pp. 176-77 (342-43), in the magical papyri "gerade die eingehendsten Anweisungen für magisches Türöffnen nehmen ihre Zuflucht zum Gebet. Entweder unterstützt das Gebet den Zauber, oder der Zaubernde identifiziert sich mit einem Gott, der die Türöffnung vollbringen kann, so dass gewissermassen der Zauber das Wunder voraussetzt und es als Präzedenzfall benutzt. Wer sagt, der

Zauberer öffnet die Tür durch eine ἐπῳδή, sagt solange recht wenig,
als wir nicht wissen, wie die ἐπῳδή im einzelnen Falle beschaffen war.
Da wo wir welche kennen--eben aus den ausführlicheren Angaben der
Papyri--sind diese ἐπῳδαί eine Mischung von Gebet und Zauberspruch und
gelten deshalb als wirksam, weil der Zaubernde durch die Gebetsmacht
über die Kräfte eines Gottes mitverfügen kann." Weinreich gives
examples of doors opened by magic or spells, pp. 176-96 (342-62), then
of doors opened in response to prayer, pp. 197-200 (363-66).

[75]In principle he could see no distinction between spell and
magic or between magic and religion (1924b, 325: "kein prinzipieller
Unterschied zwischen Zauberspruch und Gebet so wenig wie zwischen
Zauberei und Religion"), a statement with which Nock (1933b, 172 =
1972, vol. 1, 315) agrees, adding that "incidental ancient attempts at
theoretical differentiations are clearly the products of individual
sophistication." Yet, though spell and cult served the same purposes,
Pfister sees the beneficent and sacramental purpose as more prominent
in the latter (1924b, 331). Pfister's evolutionary assumptions (ibid.,
336) would be difficult to establish; cf. Weinreich, 1929, 176 (342).

[76]Homer, *Od.* 19.457; Pindar, *Pyth.* 3.51; Plato, *Rep.* 426B;
Charm. 155B-C; Xenophon, *Mem.* 3.11.16f.

[77]Plato, *Theat.* 149C; the midwives who employ it are called
"respected" (σεμναί, 150A); in Socrates' own philosophical midwifery he
says he chants (ἐπᾴδω) to Theatatus (157C).

[78]Ibid. 2.3-4 (μάγοι τε καὶ καθάρται καὶ ἀγύρται καὶ ἀλαζόνεʃ).
The author describes them as claiming to accomplish through magic and
sacrifices the impossible things that tradition associated with persons
called magicians (cf. above, n. 69), such as drawing down the moon,
making the sun disappear, etc. (4.12ff.). Cf. further Sophocles, *Ajax*
581-82 (a wise physician doesn't chant ἐπῳδάʃ when a knife is called
for), and Euripides, *Suppl.* 1110, which speaks of persons who seek to
lengthen life through use of βρωτοῖσι καὶ ποτοῖσι καὶ μαγεύμασι.

[79]Cf. *Sacred Disease* 4.21ff.: the deities are identified from
the behavior of the sufferers.

[80]Ibid. 4.15-16 (ὑπὸ ἀνθρώπου γνώμηʃ, κρατεῖται καὶ
δεδούληται).

[81]Ibid. 4.11-12 (μαγεύων καὶ θύων).

[82]Ibid. 4.5-6 (εἴτε καὶ ἐκ τελετέων εἴτε καὶ ἐξ ἄλληʃ τινὸʃ
γνώμηʃ καὶ μελέτηʃ).

[83]On this "guilt culture" see Dodds, 1951, 35-36, 77-80.

[84]On this subject see Douglas, 1966.

[85]*Deisidaimonia* itself underwent a change from a term of honor
to one of abuse; see Nilsson, 1967, 796; Dodds, 1951, 35. Rengstorf,

1969, 117.18-20, characterizes the popular system as "Aberglaube" and associates this judgment with Plutarch; but that is not the whole story. In his well-known treatise on superstition it is the excess evident in superstition that Plutarch criticizes (cf. *De superstit.* 171F); elsewhere (see above, ch. 3.3.1 and *De Is. et Os.*) his desire to "save the phenomena" of cultic piety, including its myths, divination system, and marvels, manifests itself. Cf. in general Nilsson's remark (1967, 797): "Es bestand in den griechischen Religion nicht die glatte Scheidung die wir zwischen Religion and Aberglauben machen. . . . der Unterschied zwischen θεοσέβεια und δεισιδαιμονία war kein Wesensunterschied, sondern er lag in der Übertreibung, dem Zuviel."

[86] *Laws* 10.909B (θεοὺς ὑπισχνούμενοι πείθειν, ὥς θυσίαις τε καὶ εὐχαῖς καὶ ἐπῳδαῖς γοητεύοντες). Cf. further *Laws* 11.933A-E; *Rep.* 2.364B.

[87] Diodorus Siculus 4.43.2 (θεῶν προνοίᾳ) and 4.48.6 (the sea god Glaucus appears near the ship afterward).

[88] *PGM* 4.2976ff. Riesenfeld's stylistic comparison (1946) of two brief hymns in the magical papyri with hymns from Greek and Egyptian religion shows a continuity in both style and content between the two categories of hymns.

[89] Cf. Irenaeus, *Adv. h.* 3.32.5 (Harvey ed., 2.49.3): The church "does nothing through invocations of angels or incantations or out of any other perverse inquisitiveness; rather, addressing prayers in a pure, chaste, and open manner to the Lord, who made all things, and invoking the name of our Lord Jesus Christ, it has worked miracles, not to lead people astray, but for their benefit" ("Nec invocationibus angelicis facit aliquid, nec incantationibus, nec reliqua prava curiositate; sed munde et pure et manifeste orationes dirigentes [dirigens] ad Dominum, qui omnia fecit, et nomen Domini nostri Jesu Christi invocans, virtutes secundum utilitates hominum, sed non ad seductionem perfecit"). Origen, *C. Cels.* 7.4: Christians exorcise "not by use of anything curious and magical or any potion, but by prayer alone and the simplest adjurations" (οὐδενὶ περιέργῳ καὶ μαγικῷ ἤ φαρμακευτικῷ πράγματι ἀλλὰ μόνῃ εὐχῇ καὶ ὁρκώσεσιν ἁπλουστέραις); similarly 7.67 where Origen says Christians exorcise by prayers (εὐχαῖς)--but then adds, "and by formulas [μαθήμασιν] from the holy scriptures"; Celsus associates *mathemata* with sorcery (above, pp. 57-58).

[90] See the preceding note and Justin, *2 Apol.* 6.6; *Dial.* 30.3; 76.7; 85.2-3.

[91] Dibelius, 1966, 100, has stated in a general way how the telling of miracle stories provided thaumaturgists with both a model and instruction for their wonderworking. Various sources from the early centuries attest Christians' use of such stories or other elements of Christian credos in this way; see the Justin references cited in the preceding note and *Mart. Pet. et Paul* 56 (Lipsius-Bonnet, *Acta* 1, 166); *Act. Pet. et Paul* 77 (ibid., 211); *Act. Ioan.* 70 (ibid. 2/1, 190); *Act. Thom.* 47-48 (ibid. 2/2, 163-65); 141 (247-48); Origen, *C. Cels.* 1.6; 3.24; *PGM* 2 (pap. 3), 211; ibid. (pap. 4 and 5B), 211-13; ibid. (pap. 13), 220-21; ibid. (pap. 18), 227.

[92]Tertullian, *Apol.* 23.6 (a Christian who fails to achieve a demon's confession of his true identity should be put to death on the spot); cf. 1 Cor. 13.2; Mk. 11.23 par.

[93]Cf. Euripides, *Bacch.*: Dionysus, the new deity (line 219), is called a stranger (ξένοϛ, 233) and an incanting Lydian sorcerer (γόηϛ ἐπῳδόϛ λυδίαϛ ἀπὸ χθονόϛ, 234). Ovid, *Met.* 534: Dionysus is accused of *magica fraudes*. Pliny, *N.H.* 30.13, thinks of Druidism as magic and calls the Druids "hoc genus vatum medicorumque."

[94]Hopfner, 1928, 344–45, gives many further examples of compulsion and threatening of deity.

[95]Ostanes, Typhon, etc., *De anim.* 57.1; Waszink, Tertullian, *De anim.*, *ad loc.* (pp. 475–76), gives the primary and secondary literature identifying these figures and their association with magic.

[96]*De anim.* 57.a ("Quid ergo dicemus magian? Quod omnes paene, fallaciam. Sed ratio fallaciae solos non fugit Christianos . . .").

[97]Ibid. 57.7 ("sed Mosei veritas mendacium devorat").

[98]Ibid. 57.7 ("Multa utique et adversus apostolos Simon et Elymas magi; sed plaga caecitas de praestigiis non fuit").

[99]*Apol.* 22.11, following Mayor in reading *venefici* for *benefici*.

[100]Ibid. 22.10–11; the idea that magicians or the demons responsible for magic first injure people and then by withdrawing their injurious influence seem to heal them occurs in other second-century texts (Tatian, *Or.* 18; Irenaeus, *Adv. h.* 2.31.2, Harvey ed., 2.48.2) as well as in later fathers (references in Mayor ed. of Tertullian, *Apol.*, *ad loc.*, pp. 316–17).

[101]*Apol.* 22.12: the appearances of the Dioscuri, water carried in a sieve, a grounded ship pulled by a woman, a beard turned red at a touch (pagan sources in Mayor *ad loc.*, p. 318); 23.6 (Asclepius). The instance of the woman's pulling the ship is instructive: Roman authors present it as a test, familiar in Roman religion, of an accused woman's virtue (Pliny, *N.H.* 7.120, *religionis experimento*) which is vindicated in this marvelous way by the Mother of the Gods in response to the woman's prayer (Ovid, *Fasti* 4.305ff.); Tertullian ascribes the wonder to "ingeniis vel etiam viribus fallaciae spiritalis," worked so that stones might be thought to be deities (*Apol.* 2.12).

[102]*Apol.* 23.1–2; *De anim.* 57. The foil is Christian prophecy (*Apol.* 21.18).

[103]Celsus' charge that it is shoddy argumentation to infer from the same wonders that one thaumaturgist is divine and another a *goēs* (above, n. 44) is posed as an issue in a dialogue in the Clementine

Recognitions (3.57-58) where the disciple Niceta states that if she had been present to observe Moses competing with the magicians she would not have known whether Moses was a *magus* or the magi wrought their wonders by divine authority, for the wonders would have appeared the same, even though only Moses' were authentic. Why is it sinful to believe Simon's wonders and not sinful to believe the Lord's, when they are both so extraordinary? Peter's answer is to unveil the truth God has hidden except from his followers.

[104]See above, p. 55; cf., e.g., *1 Apol.* 14.1-2: we warn you (pagans) to be on your guard against demons who seek to enslave you through magic; through the *logos* we (Christians) are persuaded to avoid them, even though we formerly used magical arts.

[105]This was a traditional use of this passage; cf. Justin, *Dial.* 72, and ch. 9, n. 16, below.

[106]*Adv. h.* 1.13.1 (Harvey ed., 1.7.1), *magicae imposturae* (Epiphanius: μαγικῆϛ . . . κυβείαϛ). The Epiphanius (*Pan.* 34.1) and Hippolytus (*Ref.* 6.39) texts are in Harvey.

[107]Irenaeus (1.12.3; Harvey ed., 1.7.2) and Epiphanius say the cup(s) was (were) mixed with wine (*calice . . . vino mixto*; ποτήρια οἴνῳ κεκραμένα) whereas Hippolytus speaks simply of ποτήριον.

[108]Cf. Hippolytus, *Ref.* 4.28 (GCS 26, p. 56, line 31), on giving a liquid the appearance of blood. On the relation of this passage and Irenaeus' mention of Anaxilaos as Marcos' source (*Adv. h.* 1.13.2; Harvey ed., 1.7.2) to Anaxilaos of Larissa see Wellman, 1928, 62.

[109]What were his sources and how accurate were they and how adequate is his reporting?

[110]Marcus' followers, at any rate, regarded him as possessing "virtutam maximam ab invisibilibus et ab inenarrabilibus locis" (Epiphanius: δύναμιν τὴν μεγίστην ἀπὸ τῶν ἀοράτων καὶ ἀκατανομάστων τόπων) and as working *virtutes* (Epiphanius: δυνάμειϛ τιναϛ), *Adv. h.* 1.13.1 (Harvey ed., 1.7.1). Cf. further von Wetter, 1916, 76.

[111]*PGM* 4.2448 (τῆϛ θείαϛ αὐτοῦ μαγείαϛ); 1.127 (τῆϛ ἱερᾶϛ μαγείαϛ). Spells are called holy (1.318 and 322, ἱεραῖϛ ἐπαοιδαῖϛ; 2.82, ἱερηϛ ἀοιδῆϛ), and a particular *praxis* will have a holy effect (4.160, ἱερὰν . . . ἐνέργειαν).

[112]E.g., Hermes is said to be μάγων ἀρχηγέτηϛ (*PGM* 4.2289) or φαρμάκων <εὑρετά> (8.28); he reveals names used in magic (4.887) and sends oracles (5.412; 7.676).

[113]*Epp.* 16-17; on their authenticity see Petzke, 1970, 41-42, 48-49.

[114]References in Petzke, 1970, 6, 8, 10, 20-21, 42. Philostratus' life of Apollonius paints a different picture.

[115] *Ep.* 17 (μάγουϛ ὀνομάζουσι τοὺϛ θείουϛ οἱ πέρσαι). Against his opponent Euphrates he then draws the conclusion: "A *magos* is, therefore, a worshiper of the gods or divine in nature; you, however, are not a *magos* but godless" (μάγοϛ οὖν ὁ θεραπεύτηϛ τῶν θεῶν ἢ ὁ τὴν φύσιν θεῖοϛ, σὺ δ' οὐ μάγοϛ, ἀλλ᾽ ἄθεοϛ) (ibid.). *Ep.* 16 shows that the designation *magoi* is associated with τοὺϛ ἀπὸ πυθαγόρου φιλοσόφουϛ and with τοὺϛ ἀπὸ Ὀρφέωϛ. Petzke, 1970, 49, concludes that "Apollonius von Tyana war höchstwahrscheinlich ein Pythagoreer, möglicherweise sowohl im Sinne eines Magiers, der die Natur kennt and deshalb zu allerlei 'Zauberwerken' befähigt ist, als auch im Sinne des ethisch anspruchsvollen Reformators der Sitten und des Kultes."

[116] *Apol.* 25 (Helm ed., pp. 29-30): "Persarum lingua magus est qui nostra sacerdos"; see above, p. 55.

[117] *Alcib.* 1.121E, now generally considered a spurious writing; cited in *Apol.* 25 (Helm ed., pp. 30.4ff.).

[118] *Apol.* 26 (p. 31): "sin vero more vulgari eum isti proprie magum existimant, qui communione loquendi cum deis immortalibus ad omnia quae velit incredibili[a] quadam vi cantaminum polleat. . . ."

[119] Though second-century Christian usage is predominantly negative, the positive side of the tradition is also reflected. Among the gifts Tatian says the Greeks owe to barbarians is magic (*Or.* 1.1, μαγεύειν Πέρσαι); the negative side appears alongside, however (*Or.* 8.2; 17.1). As part of his argument from the relativity of pagan laws and mores Tatian observes that what the Greeks consider immoral (the Persian *magoi* practice intercourse with their mothers) the *magoi* esteem highly; this is a stock example in arguments on the relativity of mores; see Chadwick, 1947, 35.

[120] Nock, 1933b, 174-75 (1972, vol. 1, 318). Nock (n. 58) cites a passage (in Clement of Alexandria, *Protr.* 2.22, GCS 12, p. 16, lines 24ff.) in which Heraclitus links *magoi* with bacchants, maenads, and others whose rites he is unsympathetic toward. Herodotus, though noting the high social status of the *magoi* and their functions in sacrificial rites (1.132, 140; 7.43) or as interpreters of the king's dreams (1.107-08, 120, 128; 7.19) and of entrails (7.113) and extraordinary phenomena (7.37), sometimes employs language which, if not to him then to others, suggested rites associated with figures like Circe and Medea; their rites before the crossing of a river, e.g., are described as charming (φαρμακεύσαντεϛ) a river by sacrificing white horses and performing many similar rites (7.114.1), and to quiet a storm they offer a victim to the wind and chant to it with howls (7.191, καταείδοντεϛ βοῇσι οἱ Μάγοι τῷ ἀνέμῳ; the variant reading γόῃσι, for βοῇσι, would seem to be the *lectio facilior*). The fact that the *magoi* accompanied Xerxes into Greece (the tradition mentioned Ostanes by name; Pliny, *N.H.* 30.8) did not endear them to Athenians and other Greeks. Herodotus' contemporary, Sophocles (*Oed. Tyr.* 387), uses *magos* as a term of reproach, and Euripides, another contemporary, links potions and manipulations with *magoi* to explain an extraordinary event (*Orest.* 1496-97, ἤτοι φαρμάκοισιν ἢ μάγων τέχναισιν).

[121]Cf. Abt, 1908, 88, n. 1, and Sherwin-White, 1952, 211-12, where some of the pertinent legal sources are cited. Cf. Apuleius, *Apol.* 26 (Helm ed., p. 31.12), *discrimen capitis*; 100 (111.13), *capitis*. The legal basis of the accusation is set forth by Abt, 1908, 82-88 (the *Lex Cornelia de Sicariis et Veneficiis* of 81 B.C.E.); similarly Massoneau, 1934, 168. MacMullen, 1966, 124-26, specifies some of the Roman laws against magic and discusses their significance.

[122]Special kinds of fish were said to have been used as *materia magica* for this purpose; *Apol.* 29-33; 40.

[123]*Apol.* 9 (Helm ed., 10.6); 42 (49.4 and 20); 45 (52.15, 18, 21); 69 (78.5); 84 (93.5); 90 (99.13).

[124]Ibid. 69 (Helm ed., 78.5); 84 (93.5); 90 (99.13).

[125]Ibid. 57 (Helm ed., 65.5, *nocturna sacra*); 58 (66.8, the same). He is also accused of employing a secret process to make a *sigillum* which he addressed as βασιλέα and intended to use for harmful magical purposes (61, Helm ed., 69.8: "ad magica maleficia occulta fabrica").

[126]See the chronological survey of legal texts and prosecutions in Massoneau, 1934, 136ff.

[127]*Apol.* 61-66; Abt, 1908, 296-306, weighs the pro's and con's of the case.

[128]Apuleius, *Apol.* 49-50, draws on the *Timaeus* to explain his medical examination of the epileptic woman. In discussing the epileptic *puer* he uses the ambiguity of *puer* ("boy" or "slave") as an opportunity to display his knowledge of the use of boys as mediums, a standard practice.

[129]The accuser is a farmer (*Apol.* 16-17; 23) with a bourgeois ethic of property that contrasts with Apuleius' devotion to learning and to the philosophical devaluation of material possessions (17-23). Apuleius faults him for his poor Greek (87). The accuser has only recently come into wealth (23), whereas Apuleius inherited wealth (23) from a father who was a man of prominence in the colony of Madaura (24), a mantle that then fell to the son (24). Though Apuleius had subsequently gone through most of the inheritance (23), he retained his aristocratic standing, associating with Roman aristocracy (*Florida* 16-17) and receiving high honors from Carthage (ibid. 16).

[130]Though the present form of Apuleius' defense is an expanded version, with long rhetorical flights into literature and philosophy, it accords with his usual style as displayed in the *Florida*. Abuse of an adversary was a commonplace in rhetoric, but Apuleius' repeated lecturing of his accuser is an added feature which was probably not confined to his defense in court.

[131]See the observations of Theissen, 1974b, 236, 240.
Theissen's treatment, though different in approach from that followed
here, comes to a similar conclusion: apart from sociological distinc-
tions--social status, legitimation, and function--it is difficult to
discern differences between various kinds of thaumaturgy and thaumaturgists in the Greco-Roman world (ibid., 230ff.). On the question of
whether terminology serves to distinguish early Christian from pagan
miracles see Remus, 1982.

Notes to Chapter 5

[1]For this definition of culture see Malinowski, 1927, 621ff.;
Berger, 1969, 6 and n. 8.

[2]On the liver models and the bases and interpretive techniques
of hepatoscopy, which are found throughout the ancient Near East and
the Mediterranean world, see Pease, Cicero, *De div.*, pp. 95-98;
Landsberger and Tadmor, 1964; Dietrich and Loretz, 1969.

[3]I use "matrix" in the ordinary, dictionary sense, prescinding
from its more technical use in present form-critical studies (as in
Knight, 1974).

[4]The *physis* tradition (above, ch. 2.4-5), e.g., was a diffused
culture, but the feeling for cosmic order which it articulated into a
self-conscious ethic of belief is also observable as a general phenomenon manifested in rough-hewn canons of the ordinary which are
indigenous in various cultures and societies (see above, pp. 24-25).
On cultural diffusion see further, App. B.

[5]See LSJ and/or *TWNT* svv. "τρίβων," "πήρα/πηρίδιον," "ξύλον,"
"βάκτρον/βακτηρία," "σκῆπτρον"; Wendland, 1972, 86-91; Georgi, 1964,
193-95; Rengstorf, 1933, 408-12; Nock, 1933a, ch. 11.

[6]This long tradition is well delineated by Nock, 1933a.
Epictetus' sketch of the Cynic missionary philosopher (*Disc.* 3.22) and
his description of the profound effect his own teacher Musonius had on
his hearers (*Disc.* 3.23) have application beyond Cynicism and Stoicism;
cf. Lucian, *Nigrinus* 35, and Nock's characterization of the "simple
evangelical fervour" of Epicurus and his followers (1933a, 172), well
illustrated in Lucian, *Alex.* Philostratus' contrast between Apollonius
of Tyana's steadfastness in philosophy and his followers' wavering and
apostasy illustrates the ideal and its persistence.

[7]See Derenne, 1930; Nilsson, 1967, 767ff., 791. In the Greco-
Roman period Domitian's persecution of philosophers is well known; for
the Flavian period generally see MacMullen, 1966, ch. 2, "Philosophers." Apuleius' defense of philosophy in the course of defending
himself (*Apol.*) illustrates a common antipathy between philosophers and
those unversed in it.

[8]Cf. the polemics of the various schools against each other.
Lucian's caricatures of the different schools (e.g., *Zeus Catechized*,
Zeus Rants, *Philosophies for Sale*, *The Dead Come to Life*, *The Double
Indictment*) represent common notions of their distinguishing charac-
teristics.

[9]From Plato on, ἀρχαῖοι or παλαιοὶ μῦθοι refers primarily to
these stories (see Stählin, 1942, 775, n. 44), and though philosophers
were divided in their assessment of the value of myths, they shared
with many other educated persons a disbelief in the literal sense of
myths (cf. Stählin, 778-82). It was the philosophers who first provided comprehensive, cogent alternatives to the cosmogonies and cosmo-
logies of the myths, while their allegorizations offered a way to
affirm the myths while yet denying or ignoring their literal sense.
Cf. above, p. 16, and Steinhauser, 1911, 5ff., who outlines the
Auseinandersetzung of philosophy with cultic piety's referring of
extraordinary phenomena to the divine.

[10]Insofar as they reveal the genealogical and social relations
of the gods and something of the gods' characters and Greek myths
ordered the cosmos and offered guidance for relations with deity in
cult and behavior; yet the gods remained distinct from humans, and
their doings fundamentally as unpredictable as those of the Homeric
heroes or as the wind and weather. Cf. W. K. C. Guthrie, *The Greeks
and their Gods* (Boston: Beacon, [2]1954), 118ff., where correlations
between different kinds of Greek myths and different kinds of Greek
(or Mediterranean) societies are drawn.

[11]Nock, 1933a, 176. The trial of Apuleius on charges of magic
(see above, pp. 70-71) illustrates the attitude as well as the change
in philosophers noted in our text below. Similarly, Philostratus,
Apoll. 4.35: Nero opposed philosophy because he believed it was a
cover for divination (μαντικὴν συσκιάζοντεʃ). Nilsson, 1961, 528,
reverses Nock's equation: "Die griechischen Wundermänner der
Kaiserzeit waren ausgesprochen oder wenigstens halbwegs Philosophen;
sie predigten eine höhere Gotteserkenntnis, eine strengere Moral,
gerechte und strenge Lebensführung, sie verrichteten daneben auch
Wunder, heilten Kranke, erweckten sogar Tote, offenbarten sich an
entlegenen Plätzen. Sie waren θεῖοι ἄνδρεʃ."

[12]In the preceding chapters recall, *inter alia*, the Ionians,
Aristotle, Theophrastus, Cicero, Seneca, Pliny.

[13]Cf. Cicero, above, ch. 2, n. 87 (*dignius*); Seneca, *N.Q.*
6.3.4 (*satius, dignius*).

[14]Cf. above, p. 18, and Cicero's noting of the Stoics' inconsistencies, above, p. 43.

[15]Cf. *Coriolanus* 38.3: persons with good will and love toward
the deity are unable to reject or deny marvels such as talking statues
(above, p. 43).

[16]Pohlenz, 1970, vol. 1, 141-53, outlines the Stoic view, with reference to predecessors and opposing views; on the Roman translation and appropriation of the terms see ibid., 274 and 331, with the note on terminology in vol. 2, 163, para. 2; further references in Pease, Cicero, De div., pp. 450-51 (terrebunt).

[17]N.Q. 6.3, esp. 6.3.4. Included in the fears that Seneca seeks to dispel is the fear of death, to which he addresses himself in characteristic Stoic fashion (6.1.8ff.).

[18]Cf. Cicero's affirmations at the end of De div. (2.72.148-50), with the distinction between religio (which includes traditional rites, 2.72.148) and superstitio (associated with divination), which never permits one a secure existence, with a tranquil mind (2.72.149, quieta mente); on Cicero's support of the state religion for its social value see the passages noted in Pease, De div., p. 393 (rei publicae causa). Epicurus, in Usener (ed.), Epicurea, nos. 386-87; Lucretius, above p. 78. Cf. Polybius, 16.12.9, who excuses the reporting of marvels on the grounds that they support piety among the multitude (τὴν τοῦ πλήθουϛ εὐσέβειαν πρὸϛ τὸ θεῖον). See now Babut, 1974, which demonstrates the ambivalence of Greek philosophy to traditional religion, both attacking and defending it.

[19]Herodotus 3.38.1; he then cites Pindar (Frag. 169.1), νόμον πάντων βασιλέα (3.38.4).

Notes to Chapter 6

[1]Mannheim, 1936; see also Mannheim, 1925, 1931, and the study by Remmling, 1968. A brief retrospect of the discipline is offered by Berger and Luckmann, 1967, 4ff.; see also the overview in Lieber, 1974. In addition to the literature cited by Berger and Luckman, see Curtis and Petras, 1970, and the extensive bibliography of the sociology of knowledge in Gurvitch, 1971, 255-92.

[2]This is a view of long standing among students of early Christianity; see the overview in Kreissig, 1967, 93-95, and the literature cited in Gager, 1971, 119, n. 70. Recent research has challenged simplistic statements of this view in favor of a more nuanced interpretation that takes fuller, more careful account of the presence in early Christianity of influential members of the middle and upper ranks of Greco-Roman society; see inter alia Judge, 1960; Theissen, 1974a; Malherbe, 1977. In judging the social constituency of early Christianity the distinction between social class (in the Roman Empire, a legal classification) and social status (related to such matters as wealth, education, and associates) is worth observing; see, generally, Dubermann, 1976, 84-85, 94-97, and for the Roman Empire of the first two centuries Gager's review (1979, 180) of Malberbe, 1977, et al.

[3]Though caveats regarding the incautious use of the distinction between "epistle" and "letter" or the application of the term *Klein-literatur* to early Christian writings are in order (see, e.g., Neill, 1964, 241; Conzelmann, 1975, 6), they do not call in question the basic distinction between literature produced for an educated elite and exemplified by the Greek and Latin classics and more popular, occasional pieces intended for a broader spectrum of readers. Christian writings of the first two centuries fall largely in the latter category; see, recently, Malherbe, 1977, 18-19, and ch. 2.

[4]Nock, 1933a. Bardy's more recent, detailed study (1949a) confirms Nock's thesis.

[5]Cf. 1 Cor. 4.15-16; 11.1; 1 Thess. 1.6. The term "father" is found also in mystery religions; see Reitzenstein, 1966, 20, 40, 98-99; Vermaseren, 1963, 152-53.

[6]The imitation ethic is common in early Christian sources; see Heitmann, 1940; Larsson, 1962.

[7]E.g., 1 Cor. 14.24-25: when Christians prophesy in worship, Paul envisages that outsiders who enter will come to new self-knowledge through this communal witness and, falling on their faces, will worship God, proclaiming him to be present in the worshiping community.

[8]In addition to references in the New Testament (Mk. 10.27 parr.; Mk. 14.36; Lk. 1.37) and in the Jewish scriptures (Job 42.2), cf. the first- and second-century writers cited in Chadwick, 1948, 84, and R. M. Grant, 1952, ch. 9.

[9]The Stoa: Cicero, *De nat. deor.* 2.41.86 ("There is nothing, they say, which God is not able to accomplish" [Nihil est, inquiunt, quod deus efficere non possit]); similarly 3.39.92. Leiden Pap. J395 (3-4 c. C.E.), *PGM* 2, 119, lines 708ff.: a recipe designed to gain knowledge of the future instructs the operator not to despair if he receives a dire prediction but instead to ask the god to change it, for this god is capable of anything (δύναται γὰρ πάντα ὁ θεὸς οὗτος) (line 713).

[10]Berger and Luckmann, 1967, 5. The cultural and social dimensions of beliefs have been noted also by philosophical writers (Clifford, 1877; Wittgenstein, 1972, 21, nos. 143-44; Harvey, 1974, 408, 410).

[11]*Civ. d.* 3.15. As part of the self-education in astronomy that freed him from his belief in astrology (cf. *Conf.* 4.3.4-6), Augustine read books by astronomers that explained the causes of eclipses; see *Conf.* 5.4.6 and cf. O'Meara, 1965, 100.

[12]*S.T.* 1.105.7; ignorance of causes produces *admiratio*, which Aquinas takes as the root of the word *miraculum*. Similarly in *Summa c. G.* 3/2.101, where Aquinas uses the terms *ignarus* and *astrologus*.

[13]Rahner, 1962, 524-26; Rahner argues for a "three-dimensional" scientific methodology that allows for the possibility of the operation of "higher," spiritual forces. Similarly Metz, 1965; cf. his statement that "Wunder kann deshalb als solches nie in einem Welthorizont begegnen, der in seinem Entwurf diese von Freiheit getragene u. bestimmte Orientierung des Gesamtdaseins von vorherein (evtl. rein methodologisch, wie in den Naturwissenschaften) ausschliesst" (col. 1265). Also Schmaus, 1969, 110-11.

[14]Spinoza, 1883, ch. 6, "Of Miracles" (p. 84: "miracles were wrought according to the understanding of the masses, who are wholly ignorant of the workings of nature . . . the ancients took for a miracle whatever they could not explain by the method adopted by the unlearned in such cases"; pp. 92-93: narrators of events report, not "the plain facts seen or heard," but their own perception of them, which is often colored by self-interest, as when the Hebrews at the time of Joshua reported that the sun and moon stood still, thus "convincing and proving by experience to the Gentiles, who worshipped the sun, that the sun was under the control of another deity who could compel it to change its daily course"); Toland, 1696, para. 71 (p. 152) (marvellous accounts "may be met with among the *Papists*, the *Jews*, the *Bramins* [sic], the *Mahometans*, and in all places where the Credulity of the People makes 'em a Merchandize to their Priests"); para. 73 (p. 154) ("for it is very observable, that the more ignorant and barbarous any People remain, you shall find 'em most abound with Tales of this nature, and stand in far greater awe of Satan than Jehovah").
    In the same period John Locke, in defending Christian miracles, points to the evidential value of miracles for "the bulk of mankind," which has little education nor the leisure necessary to weigh abstract arguments; see 1958a, 66-67, 75-76; cf. 1958b, 85-86.

[15]Kant, 1907, 85-86 (E.T., 1934, 80-81): "Daher haben weise Regierungen jederzeit zwar eingeräumt, ja wohl gar unter die öffentlichen Religionslehren die Meinung gesetzlich aufgenommen, das *vor Alters* Wunder geschehen wären, *neue* Wunder aber nicht erlaubt. Denn die alten Wunder waren nach und nach so bestimmt und durch die Obrigkeit beschränkt, dass keine Verwirrung im gemeinen Wesen dadurch angerichtet werden konnte, wegen neuer Wunderthäter aber mussten sie allerdings der Wirkungen halber besorgt sein, die sie auf den öffentlichen Ruhestand und die eingeführte Ordnung haben könnten."

[16]This assumption underlies much of the discussion in the modern period; see App. C.

[17]See the works cited above in ch. 2, n. 100. An exception is the scientist Lunn, 1950, who regards the investigation of extraordinary phenomena "for the presence of supernatural agencies" as the most important task of scientists (p. 242). Lembert, 1905, 7, and Mensching, 1957, see the natural sciences as defining the limits of miracle precisely whereas for ancients the line was not thus demarcated.

[18]For example, Paley, 1884, 7, who argues for the evidential value of miracles but also asserts the priority of belief in God: of his "existence and power, not to say of whose presence and agency, we have previous and independent proof. . . . In a word, once believe

that there is a God, and miracles are not incredible"; Schleiermacher, 1960, 99-100; Strauss, 1972, 76, 419; Mill, 1872, 168; Tennant, 1925, 61-69, 86-89, 94; Taylor, 1934, 359-63; Bultmann, 1954, distinguishing *Wunder* and *Mirakel* and defining the former as *Offenbarung* and *Vergebung* (pp. 221, 226) and discernible only by faith (pp. 216, 219-21); Smart, 1964, 2.53 (p. 46), 2.58 (p. 49); Holland, 1965, 44 (referring to extraordinary coincidences); Swinburne, 1970, 46-47, 71. The Roman Catholic theologians cited in n. 13 above posit belief in God as prior to belief in miracle, rather than the reverse.

[19]Reimarus, 1897a, 335: "Ein jeder stelle sich unpartheyisch in die Stelle der Heyden, und urtheile denn, ob es wohl möglich sey, dass die durch gegründete Ueberführung zum Christemthume zu bringen sind. Sie sind erstlich von ihrer väterlichen Religion, so wie wir, von Jugend auf so eingenommen, dass sie sich um andere zu bekümmern so unnöthig als gefährlich halten. Wer ihnen dieses verargen wollte, der mag mir zuvor antworten, ob er den Talmud, die Misna und Gemara, den Alcoran, den Zendavesta des Zerduscht, den Sad-der der Destur, den Con-fu-zu und andere dergleichen Bücher gelesen? ob er Völker Religionen so genau zu kennen und so unpartheyisch zu untersuchen jemals Lust, Fähigkeit oder Zeit gehabt? ob er nicht glaube, die Religion, darin er erzogen worden, sey die einige wahre und seligmachende? ob er nicht daher unnöthig zu seyn glaube, sich um andere Religionen viel zu bekümmern? ja ob er es nicht fast für sündluch erachtet hätte, sich nach andern, als bessern, umzusehen, und aus Reizung zu denselben ihre Bücher zu lesen und nach ihren Lehrern zu laufen?"

[20]Ibid., 325: "Und siehe, sie [*scil.* die Kinder] nehmen ihn [*scil.* den Glauben ihrer Eltern], wie alle übrige Religionen und Secten, nach den Ehe-Pacten, nach dem Willen und Bestimmung ihrer Aeltern, nach dem Exempel ihrer Vorfahren, getrost an; *und können nicht anders handeln.* Wer kann von solchen Kindern eine Fähigkeit fordern, dass sie die Wahrheit dessen, was sie lernen beurtheilen, und so sie im Irrthume wären, eine bessere Religion suchen und finden sollten? Wer kann ihnen verdenken, dass sie bey dem Vertrauen, bey dem Gehorsame, so sie ihren Aeltern schuldig sind, auch derselben ihre Religion für wahr und für die beste halten? . . . und sie sind ohne das von selbst geneigt, was ihnen ihre Aeltern und Lehrmeister sagen, was alle bekannte und angesehene Leute glauben, *ohne Untersuchung blindlings für wahr zu halten.* . . . sie folgen den Aeltern so getrost auf dem unbekannten Wege zur Seligkeit, als auf einem unbetretenen Wege zu einem Luftschlosse" (emphases added).

[21]1897b, 316 (= 1970, 252). Persons who had a high regard for Jesus and had heard of his miracles would find it credible that Jesus was resurrected. "Dazu hatten die Apostel von ihrem Meister gelernet Wunder zu thun, oder wenigstens wie man es machen müsste um den Schein zu haben, und solches unter die Leute zu bringen, und ich habe anderwärts gezeiget, dass es gar keine Kunst sey, Wunder zu erzählen oder auch zu machen, wenn sich viele mit Mund und Hand hierin einander behülflich sind, und wenn sie mit einem Volke zu thun haben, des gewohnt und geneigt ist, Wunder zu glauben." In interpreting the miracle narratives in Acts as involving willful manipulation of beliefs, with an element of deception (cf. para. 60), Reimarus overlooks the function of social groups as plausibility structures; otherwise, however, his observations adumbrate modern anthropological and

sociological research on the social matrices of extraordinary phenomena; see below, p. 93.

[22]1897b, 303 (= 1970, 232). When "enlightened" (*verständige*) Jews, such as the scribes and authorities, demanded miracles of Jesus, so they could investigate them, he scolded them instead, "so dass kein Mensch von dieser Gattung an ihm glauben konnte" (1897b, 303-04 = 1970, 232-33).

[23]Reimarus, like his contemporary Hume (see above, p. 88), pits the Romans, as persons more sophisticated in assessing extra-ordinary phenomena, against other, non-"classical" peoples like the Jews; 1897b, 318 (= 1970, 255). Reimarus thus fails to distinguish between various social and cultural strata among the Romans, though he elsewhere (preceding note) distinguishes between educated and uneducated Jews.

[24]Strauss, 1972, para. 92, p. 420: Olshausen asks, "if the apostles were to enter our mad-houses, how would they name many of the inmates? We answer, they would to a certainty name many of them demoniacs, by reason of their participation in the ideas of their people and their age, not by reason of their apostolic illumination; and the official who acted as their conductor would very properly endeavour to set them right: whatever names therefore they might give to the inmates of our asylums, our conclusions as to the naturalness of the disorders of those inmates would not be at all affected."

[25]Ibid., para. 92, pp. 420-21. Strauss's strictures would apply to Reimarus who, rather than attempting to understand the original matrix of miracle accounts, faults the reporters for not meeting his own criteria of credibiilty; cf. Reimarus, 1897b, 303 (= 1970, 232); 326 (267).

[26]Strauss, 1972, para. 94, p. 438, contrasting Gibbon with Herodotus and faulting Paulus for not observing such distinctions.

[27]Cannon, 1942. Cannon's findings were tested on rats by Richter, 1957. Other pertinent anthropological studies (conveniently reprinted in Lessa and Vogt, 1965) of the relation between healing and social setting are Ackerknecht, 1942 (cf. esp. pp. 400-401 in Lessa and Vogt); Gillin, 1948. Jonathan Swift's "killing" of John Partridge, apparently contributing to the latter's death by effectively blotting his name from the roll of the living and robbing him of his livelihood, is an example of the effect of social reality on physical survival; the incident is described in Highet, 1962, 98-99.

[28]Lévi-Strauss, 1967, 169-73; Lévi-Strauss's dictum (which is taken from p. 174) is not an invariable maxim: demonstrations of power might be necessary to authenticate a shama; see the excerpt from Lowie, 1954, in Lessa and Vogt, 1965, 453.

[29]Mk. 6.5, which adds that Jesus did heal a few persons; see Bultmann's comments, 1957, 31; Matt. does not report the οὐκ ἐδύνατο.

[30]Mk. 2.3ff.; 7.24ff.; 9.14ff.; Mt. 8.5ff. Bultmann, 1957, 234-35, and Held, in Bornkamm, Barth, and Held, 1963, 278, cite such accounts in disproof of psychologizing explanations of healing stories. Such exegesis fails to perceive the importance in healings of community beliefs regarding the possibility of miracles and the power of the healer.

Notes to Chapter 7

[1]Dölger, 1950, treats the conflict from the time of Aristides (the Christian apologist) and Justin on into the fourth century. Earlier expositions are Harnack, 1892, 93ff.; 1924b, vol. 1, 133ff.; Edelstein, *Asclepius* 2, 132-38.

[2]The most complete edition of the Aristides corpus remains W. Dindorf's *Aristides* (3 vols.; Leipzig, 1829; reprinted, Hildesheim: Olms, 1964). Orations 17-53 (in Keil's numbering) are contained in B. Keil (ed.), *Aelii Aristidis Smyrnaei Quae Supersunt Omnia*, Vol. 2 (Berlin: Weidmann, [2]1958). The six *Hieroi Logoi* are numbered *Ors.* 47-52 in Keil; I cite them by consecutive number (1-6) rather than by oration number. Orations 1-2 (Keil's numbering) have now appeared in the first volume of the Loeb edition edited and translated by Behr, 1973. For the sake of convenience of reference, I sometimes give the Testimony number in Edelstein, *Asclepius* 1.

[3]Behr, 1968, has synthesized the literary and archeological data into a life of Aristides and an interpretation of his religion, the most prominent element of which is Asclepius piety.

[4]On Aristides' education see Behr, 1968, ch. 1, and 1973, vii-viii. Aristides' familiarity with Plato is evident in his style (see ibid., xiv) and in his defense of rhetoric against philosophy; one of these defenses, *Or.* 2, is a good illustration of "Aristides' thorough knowledge of Plato, which is apparent in his easy citation, innumerable allusions, and stylistic borrowings" (Behr, 1973, 278). Behr, 1968, 11, n. 28, catalogues Aristides' many references to Plato.

[5]See *Ors.* 2-4 (against philosophical detractors); 28, 33, and 34 (on rhetoric). On the opposition between rhetoric and philosophy see Marrou, 1964, Pt. 1, ch. 7 (in fifth- and fourth-century Athens), and Pt. 2, chs. 10-11 (the Greco-Roman period).

[6]Aristides is aware of Platonizing interpretations of Asclepius, as when, in one of Aristides' dreams, Pryallianus, a Platonist comrade at the Asclepius temple in Pergamum, points Aristides to the sky, where he sees Asclepius, "the soul of the universe" (τοῦ παντός ψυχήν) (*Hieroi Logoi* 4.56 = *Or.* 50.56, Keil ed.). In *Or.* 42.4, Keil ed. (Edelstein, *Asclepius* 1, T. 303, 317) Aristides assigns Asclepius cosmic functions. But a developed cosmic Asclepius theology, such as one finds in the Neoplatonists (see Edelstein, *Asclepius* 1, T. 304-309), is not where Aristides' interest lies, as the speech to Asclepius (*Or.*

42, Keil ed.; Edelstein, *Asclepius* 1, T. 317) makes clear: it is the healings and the advancement of his career that are focal. On cosmic Asclepius theology in Aristides' day see further Boulanger, 1923, 199 and 208, n. 1; Edelstein, *Asclepius* 2, 107-108; Behr, 1968, 158.

[7]The evidence is cited and interpreted in Behr, 1968, 37, 49, 55, 100, 168-69.

[8]On occasion he equated the two; see Behr, 1968, 62-63.

[9]See *Hieroi Logoi* 2.5 (Keil ed., p. 395, line 31). On such recourse to deity, see above, ch. 3.2.3.

[10]Behr, 1968, 27-30, brings together the literary and archaeological data and provides a plan.

[11]L. Sedatius Theophilus was of praetorian rank (τῶν ἐστρατηγηκότων ʽΡωμαίοιϛ), *Hieroi Logoi* 4.16 (Keil ed., p. 429, line 14). L. Claudius Paradalas was a strategus of Pergamum and an official at the Asclepius temple there (see Behr, 1968, 48, n. 28), "who, I would say, was foremost of the Greeks of our time in knowledge of letters" (*Hieroi Logoi* 4.27; Keil ed., p. 432, lines 21-22). L. Cuspius Pactumeius Rufinus was consul ordinarius in 142 C.E., "probably the foremost person in Pergamum in his day" (Behr, 1968, 48); he built the Asclepius temple in Pergamum and continued to endow it (*Hieroi Logoi* 4.28; Keil ed., p. 432, lines 28-30; further evidence in Behr, 1968, 48, n. 29). C. Julius Bassus Claudianus (*Hieroi Logoi* 1.21; 4.28) was a strategus of Pergamum (see Behr, 1968, 49, n. 30). Q. Tullius Maximus, a member of the Roman Senate (*Or.* 47, Dindorf ed., p. 414, lines 9ff.), figures in Aristides' therapy in the Asclepius temple, if Behr's emendation in *Hieroi Logoi* 4.18 (Keil ed., p. 430, lines 2ff.) is correct, as seems probable (see Behr, 1968, 48, n. 26, and 256, n. 58).

[12]*Hieroi Logoi* 4.16-17 (Keil ed., p. 429, lines 10ff.): Sedatius encourages the ailing Aristides to declaim, telling him a wondrous deed of the god (ἔργον τοῦ θεοῦ θαυμαστόν, 4.16; p. 429, lines 28-29), namely, how a sick man's exertions in obedience to Asclepius' behest caused him to perspire and ended his sickness. Ibid. 4.27 (Keil ed., p. 432, lines 20ff.): Pardalas assures Aristides his illness happened through some divine providence (τύχῃ τινὶ θείᾳ συμβῆναι) in order that associating with the god might improve his practice of rhetoric. Ibid. 4.43 (Keil ed., p. 436, lines 18ff.): Rufinus arrives at the temple, in response to Asclepius' invitation, at other than his usual hour in order to be present at a choral performance Aristides is giving. Ibid. 4.19-21 (Keil ed., pp. 430-31): Rosander, another temple companion, is described as devoted to the worship of Asclepius (4.19, περὶ τὴν τοῦ θεοῦ θεραπείαν ἐπιμελήϛ).

[13]Healing apart from physicians and their art: see, e.g., *Or.* 45 (Dindorf ed., p. 20), χωρὶϛ ἰατρῶν καὶ τέχνηϛ; other examples of similar unfavorable comparisons of divine and human healing in Behr, 1968, 55, n. 52; 169, nn. 23-24. Miracle terms: *thaumata, paradoxa, aretai, dynameis, terata, semeia*; sources in Behr, 1968, 35, n. 62.

[14]References in Behr, 1968, 152.

[15]*Or.* 45 (Keil ed., pp. 352ff.), εἰς Σαράπιν; *Or.* 36 (Keil ed., pp. 264ff.), Αἰγύπτοις; *Hieroi Logoi* 3.47-50 (Keil ed., pp. 424-25).

[16]*Or.* 40 (Keil ed., pp. 325ff.).

[17]*Or.* 37 (Keil ed., pp. 304ff.); *Hieroi Logoi* 2.41-42; 4.9 (Keil ed., pp. 403-404 and 428).

[18]*Hieroi Logoi* 2.10, 27 (Keil ed., pp. 397, 400-401); 3.15, 21-23 (pp. 417, 418-19); 4.16, 46 (pp. 429, 437). On the relation of Telesphorus to the Asclepius cult see Edelstein, *Asclepius* 2, 89, n. 50; Behr, 1968, 153.

[19]The absolute use of σωτήρ referring to Jesus: Quadratus, Justin, Tatian, Melito, Ptolemaeus, Heracleon, Naasenes, Clement of Alexandria. Referring to Asclepius: Aristides and others. Evidence in Dölger, 1950, 257-63; Latin equivalents, pp. 264ff.

[20]See *Oxford Classical Dictionary* ([2]1970), s.v. "Galen."

[21]*Or.* 46, Dindorf ed., pp. 399-405. The extent of the reference to Jews or Christians is disputed; at the least it includes the clauses alluding to "Palestine" on pp. 402-403: . . . τοῖς ἐν τῇ Παλαιστίνῃ δυσσέβεσι παραπλήσιοι τοὺς τρόπους. καὶ γὰρ ἐκείνοις τοῦτ᾽ ἐστὶ σύμβολον τῆς δυσσεβείας, ὅτι τοὺς κρείττους οὐ νομίζουσι. . . . (The "four" whom Aristides is defending—Miltiades, Themistocles, Pericles, Cimon [Dindorf ed., p. 157]—were a point of disagreement in the *Gorgias* 503C, 515Dff., 519A.)

[22]Most recently by Behr, 1968, 94, n. 2 (Christians). For earlier proponents of the view that Christians or Jews are being attacked, see the references in Boulanger, 1923, 258 and n. 4, and in de Labriolle, 1942, 81-82. Others have seen street philosophers such as the Cynics as the objects of Aristides' invective, apart from the allusion to "the impious persons in Palestine"; thus Boulanger, 1923, 259ff., citing a number of similar attacks on philosophers, and Wendland, 1972, 93. Harnack, 1924b, vol. 1, 517, leaves undecided whether Christians or Cynics are intended. Wendland, 1972, 93, n. 6, following E. Norden, observes that "Das fortdauernde Schwanken in der Frage, ob Aristides in seinen Gegnern Kyniker oder Christen schildere, zeigt . . . wie nah sich beide Richtungen berührten." De Labriolle, 1942, 83-87, develops this insight, suggesting that similarities between Cynics and Christians might lead contemporary observers to confuse the two.

[23]The context suggests that the referent of ἐκείνοις (Dindorf ed., p. 402, line 15; text cited above, n. 21) is the impious persons in Palestine (line 14) while the οὗτοι that follows (p. 403, line 1; text in n. 31 below) resumes the attack on philosophers (thus Boulanger, 1923, 259, n. 2). The aloofness of these οὗτοι from Greek ways accords with Cynic flouting of convention (cf. Diogenes Laertius

6.46, 58, 61, 69, 71); Jews and Christians were similarly accused, however, and have been taken as the referents here (Renan, in de Labriolle, 1942, 81).

[24] αὐθάδεια, Dindorf ed., p. 402, lines 14-15.

[25] ἀναισχυντία, p. 401, line 5.

[26] Disrespect for betters, p. 403, lines 1-3.

[27] λοιδορεῖν, p. 402, line 10; cf. παρρησιάζεσθαι, p. 401, line 6; προπηλακίζουσι, p. 402, line 12; διαβαλεῖν, p. 403, line 4.

[28] συγκραταπρᾶξαι μέν τι τῶν δεόντων ἁπάντων ἀχρηστόται, p. 403, lines 7-8.

[29] οὐ πανηγύρειϛ ἐκόσμησαν, οὐ θεοὺϛ ἐτίμησαν, οὐ πόλεσι συνεβούλευσαν, οὐ λυπουμένουϛ παρεμυθήσαντο, οὐ στασιάζονταϛ διήλλαξαν, οὐ προύτρεψαν νέουϛ, p. 404, lines 3-6.

[30] διορύξαι δ'οἰκίαν καὶ ταράξαι καὶ συγκροῦσαι τοὺϛ 'ἔνδον πρόϛ ἀλλήλουϛ, p. 403, line 8-p. 404, line 1.

[31] καὶ οὗτοι τρόπον τινὰ ἀφεστᾶσι τῶν Ἑλλήνων, μᾶλλον δὲ καὶ πάντων τῶν κρειττόνων, p. 403, lines 1-3.

[32] καταδύντεϛ δὲ εἰϛ τοὺϛ χηραμοὺϛ ἐκεῖ τὰ θαυμαστὰ σοφίζονται, p. 404, line 7-p. 405, line 1.

[33] On his socially prominent family see Behr, 1968, 1-4; this and his reputation as an orator gave him access to elite circles in Pergamum (ibid., 42, 57). He was honored by his home city Smyrna on more than one occasion (*Hieroi Logoi* 4.88, 95-104; Keil ed., pp. 447, 449-51), by Rhodes (*Or.* 24, Keil ed., pp. 54ff.; cf. Behr, 1968, 73-74), and by Roman officialdom (*Hieroi Logoi* 4.71ff.; Keil ed., pp. 443ff.). He was privileged to deliver his oration *To Rome* (*Or.* 26, Keil ed., pp. 91ff.) before the Roman court (cf. Behr, 1968, 88-89) and later to declaim before Marcus Aurelius (see ibid., 111).

[34] Aristides was careful to preserve the traditional Greek pantheon and hierarchy, subordinating even Asclepius, at least in theory, to Zeus and allotting the non-Greek Sarapis a place alongside, not within, the pantheon; see Behr, 1968, 148-58. A non-Greek deity like Christ would presumably have received similar treatment had his exclusivistic claims not precluded such coexistence.

[35] Asclepius' appearances contrasted with those of Jesus, *C. Cels.* 3.24; Jesus' ignoble death, 2.31; 7.53; his lowly and shameful origins, 1.28, 32, 39. See further below, ch. 8.

[36] On Christian use of these pagan texts see the references (including the second-century writers Aristides, Athenagoras, Clement

of Alexandria, Tertullian) in Dölger, "Heiland" (cited above, n. 2), 243-44.

[37] Behr, 1968, 155, notes that in his oration on Heracles (*Or.* 40, Keil ed., pp. 325ff.) Aristides omits any reference to "Heracles' conflict with Hera, which plays so prominent a part in the legend, Heracles' degrading labors, and his horrible self-immolation . . . in keeping with the conviction that the divine cannot be subject to such misfortunes." Cf. *Or.* 46.36 (Keil ed., p. 373), where Aristides says deity is impassible.

[38] See Weinreich, 1914. Aristides' hypochondria is not unusual for his time either; see the examples cited in Bowersock, 1969, 71-73, who observes that Aristides was "able to maintain his influential contacts without leaving the precinct of Asclepius at Pergamum."

[39] Sources on Asclepius sanctuaries are arranged geographically in Edelstein, *Asclepius* 1, ch. 7, and are discussed in chronological order in Edelstein, *Asclepius* 2, ch. 6; hundreds of temples are attested for the Greco-Roman period (ibid., 251ff.). The Pausanias excerpts in Edelstein, *Asclepius* 1, T. 718, 725-26, 739, etc., offer convenient reference to some of the Asclepius sanctuaries in the second century C.E.

[40] In addition to Aristides' friends at the Pergamum temple, upper-class Asclepius adherents in the second century include Marcus Aurelius (Edelstein, *Asclepius* 1, T. 407, 577) and Galen (T. 436, 458, 459; cf. above, p. 39); Edelstein, *Asclepius* 2, 117-18, cites examples of educated and/or upper-class Asclepius adherents from earlier centuries. Asclepius had a reputation for caring for the poor (Edelstein, *Asclepius* 1, T. 405; 423, no. 8; 482, lines 11-18, 79-81; cf. further, ibid. 2, 116-17, 175-78). The great number of Asclepius temples in the second century presupposes support among both the upper strata, who supplied money for the erection and maintenance of temples, and the lower strata, among which the Roman soldiers may be mentioned as important in the dissemination of the cult (Edelstein, *Asclepius* 2, 253); contrast the fourth century C.E. when popular support seems to have shifted from Asclepius to Christ (ibid., 256-57).

[41] Cf. Edelstein, *Asclepius* 2, 139-41; the tension between the practice of medicine and wondrous cures noted in ch. 3.2.3 above is reflected in an account reported in a fragment of Aelian (ibid. 1, T. 405) and in Aristides and his physicians (see Behr, 1968, 168-70).

[42] The Epidaurus inscriptions (Edelstein, *Asclepius* 1, T. 423) make this clear. Cf. further Edelstein, *Asclepius* 2, 112-113; Nilsson, 1967, 804ff.

[43] His career and self-esteem came to be inseparable from his belief in Asclepius; cf. Behr, 1973, xi.

Notes to Chapter 8

[1]Aristides mentions specifically Rosander (see above, ch. 7, n. 12); Euarestus of Crete, who came from Egypt to learn more about Asclepius (*Hieroi Logoi* 4.23; Keil ed., p. 431, lines 16-17); and Pryallianus, a Platonist (above, ch. 7, n. 6).

[2]In addition to the evidence cited by R. M. Grant, 1952, ch. 5, cf. Lucian's characterization (in *Philops.*) of philosophers in his day as credulous (cf. Nilsson's remarks, 1961, 521-22) and his statement (*Alex.* 25) that Platonists, Stoics, and Pythagoreans were receptive to Alexander of Abonoteichos, his cult and his wonders (see ch. 10 below); both descriptions must of course be assessed in light of Lucian's antipathy to philosophers (Demonax and Nigrinus are exceptions) and his admiration for the Epicurean tradition. Apuleius' great interest in the extraordinary is evident in the *Metamorphoses*.

[3]A fine summary is offered in Dörrie, 1960. Cf. further, Witt, 1937, 122-34 (p. 123, "It is therefore true to say that Platonism in the second century, if it had not become a religion, was characterized by its predominantly religious and theocentric world-view"); Andresen, 1952-53, e.g., 162, 166-67, 173, and 1955, 239ff.; Merlan, 1967, e.g., pp. 62-64 (Plutarch), 67 (Albinus); for Plutarch see also Nilsson, 1961, 402-13; for Maximus of Tyre the selections in de Vogel, 1964, 404-05.

[4]For Plutarch see above, ch. 3.3.1. The ambiguities in Apuleius' defense of himself against charges of magic have been noted by Abt, 1908; in the *Metam.* skepticism serves as the literary foil to the credulity presupposed in the book's many tales of the marvelous (e.g., 1.20), and the *curiositas* regarding the marvelous that leads to Lucius' degradation as an ass is labeled *sacrilega, inprospera*, and *temeraria*; see Wittman, 1938, 81-82. On Maximus of Tyre see the references cited in R. M. Grant, 1952, 69, and Grant's comments. On Celsus and Justin see below.

[5]Geffcken, 1907, 246; cf. also p. 245 ("einen gewaltigen Wirrwarr der Polemik") and p. 240, n. 12 ("das Gewirre dieses Kampfes").

[6]τερατευσαμένουϛ, *C. Cels.* 1.68; the negative connotations of the word are seen in its being coupled with ψεύδεσθαι; see LSJ s.v. τερατεύομαι. I cite Celsus, *Alethes Logos*, from Bader, *Alethes Logos* (using Bader's numbering), with reference also to the editions of P. Koetschau (ed.), *Origines Werke* 1-2 (GCS, 2-3; Leipzig: Hinrichs, 1899), and M. Borret (ed. and transl.), *Contre Celse* (Sources chrétiennes, 132, 136, 147, 150; Paris: Éditions du Cerf, 1967-69), and translation by Chadwick, *Contra Celsum*.

[7]*C. Cels.* 1.68 (such phenomena are the work of *goētes*; the banquet tables they seem to produce do not in fact exist [τὰ οὐκ ὄντα] and the extraordinary movement the *goētes* seem to impart to objects is a figment of the imagination); 1.6 (Jesus did his wonders by *goēteia*). Cf. above, p. 57.

[8]1.68 (marketplace wonderworkers [goētes] go through their paces in return for money); cf. 3.50, where Celsus compares Christians to such persons.

[9]Cf. Diodorus Siculus 4.71 where, observes Dölger (1950, 246), "die Art, wie Diodor das Gerücht von der Totenerweckungen bringt, zeigt deutlich, dass man sie im Volke annahm."

[10]Plato, Rep. 3.408B-C (Edelstein, Asclepius 1, T. 99); Sextus Empiricus, Adv. mathem. 1.260-62 (T. 69).

[11]7.35, Trophonius, Amphiaurus, and Mopsus, whose manifestations are not sham but visible and palpable (οὐ ψευδομένους ἀλλὰ καὶ ἐναργεῖς). The word ἐναργής is commonly used to designate divine manifestations as visible and palpable; see LSJ, s.v., and, e.g., Philo, Vita Mos. 1.289, who describes Balaam's vision of God as ἐναργῆ φαντασίαν.

[12]The general Greek meaning of eidōlon is "phantom" or "fancy" (of the mind), though it also means "image" or "likeness" (see LSJ, s.v.) and is thus employed in biblical Greek.

[13]2.55 (Γυνὴ πάροιστρος, ὥς φατε, καὶ εἴ τις ἄλλος τῶν ἐκ τῆς αὐτῆς γοητείας, ἤτοι κατά τινα διάθεσιν ὀνειρώξας καὶ κατὰ τὴν αὐτοῦ βούλησιν δόξῃ πεπλανημένῃ φαντασιωθείς, ὅπερ ἤδη μυρίοις συμβέβηκεν, ἢ, ὅπερ μᾶλλον, ἐπλῆξαι τοὺς λοιποὺς τῇ τερατείᾳ ταύτῃ θελήσας καὶ διὰ τοῦ τοιούτου ψεύσματος ἀφορμὴν ἄλλοις ἀγύρταις παρασχεῖν).

[14]If Celsus is aware of traditions such as 1 Cor. 15.6, Mt. 28.4, 11ff., or Ev. Pet. 9.35ff., where such public appearances, even to enemies, are reported, he ignores them.

[15]Origen, perhaps also for purposes of argumentation, supposes he does (3.27).

[16]Andresen, 1955, 47, gives other examples of wonders reported in pagen tradition that Celsus cites, sometimes in their most wondrous form.

[17]Celsus' answer to the possible objection that Asclepius' appearances were also only to his followers is implicit in his statement that a great multitude of people (πολὺ ἀνθρώπων πλῆθος), both Greeks and non-Greeks, saw and still see Asclepius and that an untold multitude (ἀμύθητον . . . πλῆθος) believe in him (3.24). Some of the Asclepius traditions tell how he overcomes disbelief by manifesting himself to the disbelievers; see Edelstein, Asclepius 1, T. 423, nos. 3, 4, 36.

[18]Harnack, 1892, 95; repeated verbatim in 1924b, vol. 1, 135. Similarly, Miura-Stange, 1926, 135ff., where she speaks of a "Mischung von Rationalismus und Aberglauben." More recently, Andresen, 1955, 46ff., explores in detail the contradictions in Celsus' polemic against Christians' miracle claims. Andresen's observation (p. 186) that scholars sometimes forget that Celsus writes as a polemicist and not as

an objective historian of religions is applicable to comments like
Harnack's and Miura-Stange's.

[19] Origen mentions the schools of Democritus, Epicurus, and
Aristotle. Cicero, *De div.* 1.3.5ff., gives a catalog of the views of
the philosophical schools on divination, on which Pease, pp. 53ff.,
gives a detailed commentary.

[20] See Pease, ibid. Among Middle Platonists, Plutarch's
treatises on oracles (*De def. orac.*; *De Pyth. orac.*) are well known.
Another Middle Platonist and a contemporary of Celsus, Maximus of Tyre,
reports that he saw Asclepius himself, not in a dream (εἶδον καὶ τὸν
Ἀσκληπιὸν ἀλλ' οὐχὶ 'ὄναρ, *Diss.* 9.7, Hobein ed., p. 110). Cf. further
Lucian's report that Platonists were among those philosophers receptive
to the oracles of Alexander of Abonoteichos (above, n. 2 of this
chapter, and below, ch. 10).

[21] Even among the Stoics, the traditional defenders of divination and oracles, one of its most distinguished scholars, Panaetius,
regarded these as dubious; cf. Pohlenz, 1970, vol. 1, 198, and vol. 2,
100 (at line 10), to which may be added Cicero, *Acad.* 2, 107.

[22] Andresen, 1955, 48, following Bader, *Alethes Logos*, 92,
interprets as pejorative Celsus' references (3.34b) to the cult of
various well-known heroes at oracle sites. This seems unwarranted.
The heroes Celsus cites were mortals who had wondrously been translated
(thus Amphiaraus and Trophonius; see Rohde, 1966, 89-90, 103, nn. 1-2)
or were worshiped as deities (ibid., 107-08, nn. 18-19) or both (for
Zalmoxis, also mentioned in Celsus' list, see Dodds, 1951, 166, n. 61).
The point of comparison, if Origen reproduces Celsus' thought
accurately, is that, like these heroes, Jesus, a mortal, receives cult;
this is Celsus' familiar technique of relativizing exclusivistic Christian claims by demonstrating their lack of uniqueness. Like Amphiaraus
and Trophonius, Jesus was persecuted by enemies; if Celsus intends this
comparison, it too could be a thrust at Jesus: they were translated,
but he is dead (above, p. 107). If the juxtaposition of Jesus with
these heroes is meant to imply that they, too, died, that in itself is
not necessarily pejorative, as the case of Asclepius shows (above,
p. 106); as I note in the text, Celsus elsewhere (7.45) speaks of these
heroes as alive and manifesting themselves.

[23] Celsus: some persons have experienced visible, palpable
apparitions (ἐναργῆ . . . φάσματα, 8.45); similarly, 7.35 (see above,
n. 11).

[24] See *C. Cels.* 6.19 and Praechter, 1926, 530, 536ff. (Celsus,
p. 550); Festugière, 1954, 92-140 (Celsus, pp. 115-23); Andresen, 1955,
52, 274-75, 299-300 (Celsus); Dörrie, 1960.

[25] *C. Cels.* 1.14a: Celsus sees a kinship among many peoples
with respect to this same doctrine (συγγένειαν παρὰ πολλοῖς τῶν ἐθνῶν
. . . εἶναι . . . τοῦ αὐτοῦ λόγου), i.e., the ancient doctrine of which
Celsus speaks later in 1.14c, which is also the "true doctrine" (Pref.,
4).

[26]Keim, 1873, 196ff., discerned a preface and four parts in
Celsus' treatise, a judgment concurred in by Koetschau, the editor of
the GCS edition (see his article, 1892), as well as by scholars
generally; see Andresen, 1955, 32, and Miura-Stange, 1926, 17-19.
Miura-Stange finds no order in Celsus' work but rather a "polemische
Planlosigkeit" (p. 18).

[27]Scholars have disputed the meaning of Celsus' statements
regarding the numerical growth and strength of the Christian movement
(3.10, 12, 73; other passages sometimes cited, such as 8.39 and 69
which speak of persecution, or 8.55 which states that such a despicable
group as the Christians deserves to die out, reveal little, if anything
about Celsus' view of the Christians' numerical strength); see Völker,
1928, 27-29. πλῆθος as a designation of Christian numbers (3.10, 12)
is an elastic term (see the examples cited in Völker, 28) and should
not be pressed too far. Moreover, the context of the contrast Celsus
draws between the Christians' meager beginnings (3.10, ἀρχομένοι . . .
ὀλίγοι τε ἦσαν) and the present πλῆθος of Christians, enough to divide
into competing factions, should be kept in mind: he is attempting to
demonstrate (Bk. 3) that Christianity originated in a revolt and is a
fissiparating movement (cf. Andresen, 1955, 39-40). Yet Celsus was
aware of Christian success in winning converts, as is indicated by
3.73b (τοῦ πλήθους τῶν προσερχομένων αὐτῷ [scil. τῷ λόγῳ]), is
suggested at least in part by the vehemence of his attack and would
seem to be substantiated by other sources (see the second-century texts
cited in Harnack, 1924b, vol. 2, 530ff., and the commentary, 546-48).
With these passages by Celsus one may compare Origen's statements in
the third century: the number of Christians in the Empire is still
only πάνυ ὀλίγοι (C. Cels. 8.69), but in comparison with their
beginnings they are (as Celsus says) a πλῆθος (3.10).

[28]8.2 (ἀποτειχιζόντων ἑαυτοὺς καὶ ἀπορρηγνύντων ἀπὸ τῶν λοίπων
ἀνθρώπων). Cf., similarly, Aristides, above, p. 101.

[29]8.75 (ἕνεκεν σωτηρίας νόμων καὶ εὐσεβείας). Celsus' exhortations here to Christians to participate in military and political life
and to offer sacrifice to the emperor and other rulers (8.63, 67) has
led some scholars (cited in Völker, 1928, 21, n. 22) to see the Alethes
Logos as motivated ultimately by political concern for constituted
authority and the empire. Celsus' argument ranges much more widely
than that, however, over pagan culture and society generally. For
Celsus there is a close tie between political authority, society, and
religion, as is evident in a number of passages (see below, p. 111
and n. 44). It would be exceptional for an ancient Greek or Roman not
to do so; see, e.g., Herodotus, below, App. A; on the Roman side, see
the study by C. Koch, 1954, and Augustine's perceptive observations in
Civ. d. 4. Second-century Christian apologists, for their part, sometimes contended that Christian presence in the Empire and prayers on
its behalf sustained it; see, e.g., Melito of Sardis, in Eusebius, H.E.
4.26.7-8; Tertullian, Apol. 5.6.

[30]1.1 (συνθήκας κρύβδην . . . παρὰ τὰ νενομισμένα [I concur
with Bader, Koetschau, and Borret, contrary to Chadwick, that this is a
statement by Celsus rather than by Origen] . . . αἱ δὲ ἀφανεῖς, ὅσαι
παρὰ τὰ νενομισμένα συντελοῦνται). Cf. 8.17 (text in n. 32 below). On

illegality of *collegia* see Trajan's letter to Pliny, in Pliny, *Epp.* 10.34, and the survey by Wilken, 1971.

[31]1.3 (κρύφα Χριστιανοὺς τὰ ἀρέσκοντα ἑαυτοῖς ποιεῖν καὶ διδάσκειν); 1.7 (κρύφιον τὸ δόγμα).

[32]8.17 (τὸ πίστον . . . ἀφανοῦς καὶ ἀπορρήτου κοινωνίας . . . σύνθημα).

[33]7.62 (οὐκ ἀνέχωνται νεὼς ὁρῶντες καὶ βωμοὺς καὶ ἀγάλματα).

[34]3.43, referring to the tradition and cult of Zeus's tomb on Crete. Celsus fails to mention that philosophy in the Academic mode also ridiculed these rites (see the sources cited in Chadwick, *Contra Celsum*, 157, n. 2). His charge that Christians do not understand these traditions and rites would apply also to this Academic polemic. This passage and Celsus' affirmation of oracles (above, p. 109) are illustrative of the Middle Platonists' attitude toward popular cultic piety, which, as was noted earlier, was more sympathetic than that of the Middle Academy. However, the passage also illustrates Celsus' readiness, noted earlier, to defend disputed aspects of pagan culture when confronted with Christian attacks on them, even though this may involve him in logical inconsistencies. On the apologists' similar stance vis-à-vis pagan and in defense of Christian culture see below, pp.

[35]3.19, referring to Christian ridicule of Egyptian animal deities. Again, Celsus fails to mention the commonplace criticism of these deities (by philosophers and educated persons generally, e.g., Sextus Empiricus, *Pyhrr.* 3.219, and *Adv. mathem.* 1.42; Josephus, *C. Ap.* 2.81; Lucian, *Parliam. of Gods* 10; Philostratus, *Apoll.* 6.19); he offers a Platonizing interpretation of them (honors paid them are to invisible forms [ἰδεῶν ἀϊδίων] and not to ephemeral creatures); cf. Plutarch's *De Is. et Os.* 355B-D.

[36]8.38 (Christians stand before images, blaspheme and strike them, and point out that they suffer no consequences); similarly, 8.41. For evidence that Celsus' description of such behavior toward images by some Christians is not without foundation see Völker, 1928, 19, n. 12. On Christian rejection of images see further *C. Cels.* 1.5a.

[37]εἴδωλα, 7.36 (cf. above, n. 12); 8.24.

[38]On daimons in pagan and Christian thought cf. above, pp. 40-41. Euhemerus ranked in antiquity "als erster unter den Atheisten" (Nilsson, 1961, 288), but euhemerism—the idea that gods were originally human— is found in much ancient mythology, Greek and non-Greek, with deities viewed as culture heroes (ibid., 284-86).

[39]Cf. 7.62: Christians' intolerance of pagan cult places them among other, similarly intolerant peoples, the most impious and most lawless sorts (τὰ δυσαγέστατα καὶ ἀνομώτατα); 5.25: even the Jews, for whom Celsus has no great sympathy, are like other peoples in having and

observing distinctive traditions (τὰ πάτρια) established for the common good (τὰ εἶς κοινὸν κεκυρωμένα).

^{40}3.5, 14; 5.33; 8.2, 49 (common to Christians is the disease of rebellion, τῇ στάσει συννοσοῦντεϳ).

^{41}5.41 (τὸν ἴδιον νόμον). In 5.25 Celsus states that the Jews, on becoming a distinct people (ἔθνοϳ ἴδιον), made laws befitting themselves (κατὰ τὸ ἐπιχώριον νόμουϳ θέμενοι), which they preserve along with their worship, as other persons do. Whatever else Jewish worship may be, it is traditional (ὁποίαν δή, πάτριον δ' οὖν). The foil is the Christians.

^{42}5.33 (πόθεν ἥκουσιν ἢ τίνα ἔχουσιν ἀρχηγέτην πατρίων νόμων. οὐδένα θήσουσιν). The foil to the Christians here is Plato; see 6.10b and below, p. 114.

^{43}3.5 (αἴτιον γεγονέναι τῆϳ καινοτομίαϳ τὸ στασιάζειν πρόϳ τὸ κοινόν).

^{44}That Celsus regards the cosmos, the various peoples of the earth, social institutions, and even parts of the body as allotted to the administration of deities or daimons is shown by 5.25; 7.68; 8.28, 35, 53, 58, 60, 63.

^{45}1.8; Origen, in accord with his belief (in the early part of the work) that Celsus is an Epicurean (see 1.8 and cf. Chadwick's treatment of this subject in *Contra Celsum*, xxivff.), thinks that Celsus is here merely pretending (προσποιεῖται) to espouse such typically Platonic teaching; for a similar such statement by Celsus see 8.63b; for its Platonic character cf. Chadwick, *Contra Celsum*, 11, n. 2.

^{46}1.9 (λόγῳ . . . καὶ λογικῷ ὁδηγῷ). In accord with 1.16b, which names a variety of persons as bearers of the ancient doctrine, Celsus in 7.41 lists various categories of guides (ὁδηγούϳ) whom Christians should follow in order to receive the instruction mentioned in 1.9: ἐθνέουϳ . . . ποιητὰϳ καὶ σοφοὺϳ καὶ φιλοσόφουϳ. It is noteworthy that these guides in the ancient doctrine represent various facets of pagan culture, and not just philosophy, as Bader's note on 1.9 (*Alethes Logos*, 42) suggests ("Die Philosophie ist die allein richtige Führerin"). The foils to these trustworthy guides are the deceivers and tricksters (οἱ πλάνοι καὶ γόητεϳ, 7.36; cf. 1.9).

^{47}1.9 (ὡϳ γὰρ ἐν ἐκείνοιϳ πολλάκιϳ μοχθηροὶ ἄνθρωποι ἐπιβαίνοντεϳ τῇ ἰδιωτείᾳ τῶν εὐεξαπατήτων ἄγουσιν αὐτοὺϳ ᾗ βούλονται). On the frequently pejorative meaning of ἰδιωτ- words see below, p. 115 and n. 67.

^{48}1.9 (τοὺϳ ἀλόγωϳ πιστεύονταϳ).

^{49}1.9 (φησὶ δὲ τιναϳ [scil. τῶν Χριστιανῶν] μηδὲ βουλομένουϳ διδόναι ἢ λαμβάνειν λόγον περὶ ὧν πιστεύουσι χρῆσθαι τῷ μὴ ἐξέταζε ἀλλὰ πίστευσον᾽ καὶ 'ἡ πίστιϛ σου σῶσει σέ'). Although Celsus in this passage does not draw the traditional Platonic distinction between *pistis*, resting on sense perception and belonging to the category of opinion (*doxa*), and knowledge (*epistēmē*), gained through the mind (*dianoia*) and *noēsis* (Plato, *Rep.* 509D-511E; 534A), in 7.36 he distinguishes, pejoratively, between sense perception (*aisthēsis*) and the beholding of God achieved through the *nous*; when confronted with a common Christian word like *pistis* he may well interpret it, pejoratively, from a Platonic standpoint.

[50] See 1.27; 3.44, 49, 50, 55, 59, 72, 74, 75; 6.12-14.

[51] λόγων τῶν ἀρίστων, though Origen's repetition later in 3.49 reads λόγων ἀρίστων; cf. Bader's note 1 ad loc.

[52] 3.49; Origen agrees that education is not bad and, indeed, is "the path to virtue" (ὁδὸϛ γὰρ ἐπ᾽ ἀρετήν ἐστιν ἡ παίδευσιϛ). On *paideia* as an ideal and as characteristic of the Hellenistic and Greco-Roman periods see Marrou, 1964, 142-44, 270.

[53] 3.50, οἰκοτρίβων. It is a question how Celsus (or his sources) would have been able to recognize such persons in the market-place as slaves since the latter were not distinguishable from freemen or freedmen in external appearance or by the company they kept. Slaves were found at all levels of society and in every sort of occupation, with the best of education or the worst. The line between slave and free or freed was not sharply drawn, even when *de jure*, as in Roman law, a sharp distinction was intended. As in social situations generally, slaves' associates were apt to be persons of similar education, occupation, and interests. The evidence and prior literature on the subject is reviewed in Bartchy, 1973, ch. 2. This is not to say that slavery or former slavery carried no social stigma. Even though entry into slavery could sometimes elevate one's social status (ibid., 46-47, 116), on the other hand social acceptance of slaves or freedmen might be withheld or grudgingly given (ibid., 82 and 84, n. 310). Celsus' view of the slaves mentioned in 3.50 is negative, but as is clear from the context (they are linked with adolescent boys and stupid people, μειράκια . . . καὶ ἀνοήτων; similarly, 6.13b; text cited in n. 59 below) and from other passages, what is important for Celsus is not slavery as such but social level (as indicated by occupation) and level of education; see below, pp. 113-14.

[54] Cf. Andresen's perceptive summary (1955, 174-78) of Celsus' sociological observations on Christians, to which I am indebted; more briefly, Völker, 1928, 30.

[55] 3.55 (τοὺϛ ἀπαιδευτάτουϛ τε καὶ ἀγροικοτάτουϛ); on the latter term, see below, p. 115.

[56] 3.55, δεσπότων, which according to common usage (see the examples in BAG, s.v.) and the context here is best rendered "owner." It is not the Christians' slave status as such that draws Celsus' attention but what he sees as their lack of education and their mental occupation, neither of which hinders them from making extravagant claims and venturing to instruct others in those claims.

⁵⁷3.55 (εἶς τὴν γυναικωνῖτιν ἢ τὸ σκυτεῖον ἢ τὸ κναφεῖον).
Greek practice allowed slaves to be employed outside their own households; see Bartchy, 1973, 41-42, 74.

⁵⁸See BAG, s.v. τέλειος.

⁵⁹6.13b (τοῖς ἀπαιδευτάτοις ἢ ἀνδραπόδοις ἢ ἀμαθεστάτοις
διέξεισι . . . τὰ περὶ τῆς θείας σοφίας. Ἀνδράποδον, though denoting
in the first place a person taken captive and sold into slavery, could
also be used as a simple term of opprobrium (Plato, Xenophon, Dio
Chrysostom); LSJ, s.v.

⁶⁰On Jesus' humble origins cf. further 1.39 and 2.32b where
Celsus contrasts these with Christian claims of his descent from Jewish
kings. On his illegitimate birth cf. further 1.32.

⁶¹In 4.36 Celsus also speaks of old women (γραυσί) in a deroga-
tory way. In the present passage his argument is *a minore ad majorem*,
the premise of which is the common view of old women as typically
credulous and as sources of unreliable information (Pease, Cicero, *De
div.* 1.7, n. *anili superstitione*, and 2.19, n. *anile*, gives examples
from Greek and Latin sources of the classical and Greco-Roman periods;
cf. further BAG, s.v. γραώδης). Celsus or Origen (6.37) describes the
old woman lulling the child to sleep as "drunk."

⁶²ἐν τοῖς ἀτίμοις, which may refer to the land where the Jews
settled, as Origen interprets it (Goshen: Γεσέμ; cf. Keim, 1873, 54,
"unangesehener Gegend," and Chadwick's translation, "land that was
valueless"), or to the conditions under which the Jews lived (Andresen,
1955, 177, n. 16: "unter schimpflichen Umständen").

⁶³οὔτ' ἐν λόγῳ οὔτ' ἐν ἀριθμῷ; the Greek background of this
phrase is traced in Chadwick, *Contra Celsum*, 206, n. 1.

⁶⁴Andresen, 1955, 177, n. 16. Andresen views Celsus as
employing "die Berichte der Genesis," as does Bader, *Alethes Logos*,
116, n. 17.

⁶⁵Cf. Andresen, 1955, 177: "Bedenkt man . . ., wie stark das
soziale Argument bei Kelsos ins Gewicht fällt, dann wird man
gleichfalls hierin ein negatives Standesurteil erblicken dürfen."

⁶⁶"Boor," in its older sense of "peasant" or "rustic," and
"yokel" would seem to render well the meaning of ἄγροικος in Celsus'
day.

⁶⁷Lucian, *Peregr.* 13, also uses ἰδιώτης to characterize Christians. For examples of the frequently pejorative connotations of
ἰδιώτης and ἰδιωτικός see LSJ, *s.vv.*; a contemporary instance is Lucian,
Alex. 30 (ἰδιῶται . . . οἰκέται). The combination οἱ ἰδιῶται καὶ
ἀγροικότεροι in 1.27 functions as a hendiadys, as in Lucian, *Hermot.* 81
(ἄγροικος ἄνθρωπος καὶ ἰδιώτης). Cf. further Andresen, 1955, 169.

[68]The question of which Christian groups and Christian sources
Celsus was acquainted with has been the subject of much discussion,
which is surveyed, along with the data, in Völker, 1926, 1928, and more
recently in Andresen, 1955. Völker's reconstruction of Celsus'
"Christian library" led him to conclude (1928, 81, 84, 88) that Celsus
was acquainted with the canonical Gospel of Matthew; however, Celsus
(in Origen's reproduction) makes no explicit citations of or references
to Matthew (as he does, e.g., to the *Dispute of Jason and Papiscus*, in
4.52). Similarly with Celsus' supposed reading of the apologists (thus
Chadwick, *Contra Celsum*, 157, n. 2), whom he also does not cite
explicitly. A sustained and instructive example of methodological
self-consciousness in regard to Celsus' acquaintance with Christian
writings, specifically Justin's, is Andresen, 1955.

[69](καὶ μετρίουϛ καὶ ἐπιεικεῖϛ καὶ συνετούϛ τιναϛ καὶ ἐπ'
ἀλληγορίαν ἑτοίμουϛ εἶναι ἐν αὐτοῖϛ).

[70]Cf. 5.65b and 6.1, the introduction to this section, and
Andresen, 1955, 184.

[71]Cf. also 3.16 with Chadwick's note, *Contra Celsum*, 138, n. 2.

[72]5.65a (πλεῖον Ἰουδαίων ἐπίστασθαι λέγουσιν ἑαυτοὺϛ οἱ ἐν τοῖϛ
λόγοιϛ διαβεβηκότεϛ Χριστιανοί). The referents of ἐν τοῖϛ λόγοιϛ are
uncertain, as is evident from Origen's connecting of the phrase with
interpretation of the Jewish scriptures (hence Borret's rendering [in
Sources chrétiennes 147, 175], "les Écritures") and from the diversity
of modern translations, e.g., "in ihren Reden" (Keim, 1873, 76), "in
education" (Chadwick, *Contra Celsum*, 314), "in den wissenschaftlichen
Lehren" (Andresen, 1955, 184).

[73]4.48 (οἱ ἐπιεικέστεροι Ἰουδαίων καὶ Χριστιανῶν πειρῶνται πωϛ
ἀλληγορεῖν αὐτά, 'ἔστι δ' οὐχ οἶα ἀλληγορίαν ἐπιδέχεσθαί τινα ἀλλ'
'ἄντικρυϛ εὐηθέστατα μεμυθολόγηται).

[74]4.51 (πολὺ τῶν μύθων αἰσχίουϛ εἰσὶ καὶ ἀτοπώτεραι).

[75]4.39 is regarded as a Celsus fragment by Koetschau, in his
GCS edition, but not by Chadwick, *Contra Celsum*, nor by Borret in
Sources chrétiennes; it repeats Celsus' statement about the serpent in
4.36 (cf. 6.42) and is, in any case, "ein indirektes Kelsosfragment"
(Bader, *Alethes Logos*, 112, n. 10).

[76]E.g., Justin, *1 Apol.* 21.5, 25; *2 Apol.* 12.5; Tatian, *Orat.*
3, 6, 8-10, 21, 24; cf. Chadwick, 1966, 11.

[77]Lucian's satires on the gods, such as *Zeus Catechized* or *Zeus
Rants*, presuppose widespread knowledge of such criticism. Cf., in
general, Decharme, 1904, and, more recently, the summaries in Nilsson,
1967, 742-43 (Xenophanes and Sophists), 748 (Pindar), 762, 765-66
(Herodotus), 767ff. (philosophy in ancient Ionia and Greece); 1961,
192ff. (the Hellenistic period), and Attridge, 1978.

[78]4.51 (τὰ μηδαμῇ μηδαμῶſ ἁρμοσθῆναι δυνάμενα θαυμαστῇ τινι καὶ παντάπασιν ἀναισθήτῳ μωρίᾳ συνάπτουσαι).

[79]4.52; on "Aristobulus" see the references in Chadwick, *Contra Celsum*, 226, n. 1.

[80]4.52a. That Origen is reproducing Celsus' argument in sequence here, so that his own observations are an interjection and Celsus' comments on the *Dispute* are his own elucidation of fragment 4.51, is shown by Origen's ἑξῆſ (4.52) and Celsus' οἵαν δὴ . . . ᾿έγνων (4.52a: "I know just such [an allegory]").

[81]In Christian sources the work is sometimes ascribed to Aristo of Pella and variously referred to as *altercatio*, διαλέξιſ, and ἀντιβολή (Celsus has ἀντιλογία), and the name Jason is placed first; texts collected in Harnack, 1958, 92-95.

[82]Celsus' own, contrasting position is introduced by ἀλλ' ἐκεῖνα μᾶλλον (4.52b).

[83]I follow Andresen, 1955, 44, n. 4, and 86, n. 12, in taking ἀθάνατα in 4.52b as the antecedent of ἐκείνων.

[84]Cf. Plato, *Tim.* 41A-D, 42D, 69C-D; discussion in Andresen, 1955, 86-87.

[85]See further below, ch. 9.4 (seen vis-à-vis Celsus' interpretation of Plato, Justin's readings of the philosopher are misreadings).

[86]Origen, noting that Celsus does not name the group from whom he derived his information about the diagram, connects it with "Ophians" (6.24). Irenaeus also does not name the group he describes in 1.30 (Harvey ed., 1.28); however, later sources, in view of the role played by the serpent (*ophis*) in rites and teachings of such groups, refer his description to Ophians or Ophites (Theodoret, *Haer. fab.* 1.14 [text in Harvey 1, 226]: οἱ δὲ Σηθιανοὶ οὓſ Οφιανοὺſ ᾿ἢ Οφίταſ τινεſ ὀνομάζουσιν) or designate them as Ophites (Epiphanius, *Pan.* 37.1ff.). With Celsus' account of the serpent as the bestower of knowledge of good and evil, resulting in the cursing of the serpent by the Demiurge and of the Demiurge by the Ophites (6.27-28), one may compare the somewhat different versions in Irenaeus, *Adv. h.* 1.30.5ff., 15 (Harvey ed., 1.28.3ff., 8) and Epiphanius, *Pan.* 37.1.2ff. (In the *Hypostasis of the Archons* the serpent is also the enlightener [89.31-90.10] but after its cursing plays only the quiescent role of awaiting its release by the consummate man [90.34-91.3].) Celsus' description (6.25) of the diagram, with its outermost circle and the soul of the universe designated as Leviathan (i.e., a serpent; cf. Isa. 27.1 LXX, τὸν δράκοντα ᾿ὄφιν for שׁרׁ נׁחׁשׁ), has parallels in various gnostic sources (cited in Chadwick, *Contra Celsum*, 340, n. 2) that picture the cosmos as encircled by a serpent.

On the relation between Ophites and Naasenes, whose name derives from their revering of the serpent (Hippolytus, *Ref.* 5.6.3), see Casey, 1925-26, and Bornkamm, 1939, 658.

[87]On Simon see Irenaeus, *Adv. h.*, passim, and App. D. On the other names see the references in Bader, *Alethes Logos*, 139, or Chadwick's notes, *Contra Celsum*, 312, and cf. below, nn. 129, 130.

[88]5.61b (τῶν ὀνομαζόντων ψυχικούς τινας καὶ πνευματικοὺς ἑτέρους).

[89]Evidence supporting Origen's inference is ample in Irenaeus, e.g., *Adv. h.* 1.5.6 (Harvey ed. 1.1.10), 1.6.2 (1.1.11), 1.7.1 (1.1.12), 1.7.5 (1.1.14), 1.8.3 (1.1.16). Later sources attest the terminology for the second-century gnostic Basilides (Hippolytus, *Ref.* 7.27.6), for Sethians (ibid., 5.21.6) and Naasenes (ibid., 5.7.40; 5.8.7, 18, 23, 44; 5.9.21) and at Nag Hammadi (*Hypostasis of the Archons* 87.18; 89.11; 90.15; *Treatise on the Resurrection* 45.40-46.1). The Valentinians (*Adv. h.* 1.5.6 = Harvey ed., 1.1.10) cite Paul's use of the terms (1 Cor. 2.14-15). Pearson, 1973, ch. 6, has sought to demonstrate that the *pneumatikos-psychikos* contrast "develops out of a Hellenistic-Jewish exegesis of Genesis 2.7 (in the Greek text)" (p. 51).

[90]5.54 and 6.52-53, two gods, the demiurge and a higher god, with the followers of the latter designated as "strangers" (οἱ ἀλλότριοι, 6.52-53); 6.74, two sons of Gods (a quotation occurring, according to Origen, in a context in which Celsus is discussing Marcionites); 7.18, antithesis between Moses and Jesus. On these as Marcionite motifs see the texts cited ad loc. in the various editions of *C. Cels.* Celsus' reference (2.27) to threefold, fourfold, and multiple modification of the original text of the gospel by some Christians (μεταχαράττειν ἐκ τῆς πρώτης γραφῆς τὸ εὐαγγέλιον τριχῇ καὶ τετραχῇ καὶ πολλαχῇ) and to alteration of it in order to counter refutations of it (μεταπλάττειν, ἵν᾽ ἔχοιεν πρὸς τοὺς ἐλέγχους ἀρνεῖσθαι) may have Marcion's redactions in mind, as Origen thinks (2.27), or it may simply have in view the variety of gospels used by Christians; cf. Völker, 1928, 89-90; McArthur, 1966, 29. According to Origen (6.74), Celsus "frequently" (πολλάκις) refers to Marcion's thought; one should bear in mind, of course, that the "frequently" would include passages labeled "Marcionite" by Origen (e.g., 2.27) but not necessarily by Celsus himself, judging from the extant fragments of his work. Harnack was concerned to read Celsus passages as referring to Marcion and assembled evidence to that end (1924a, 275*, 325*-327*).

[91]6.74: "Then, once again, he sets forth for himself the arguments for Marcion and those against him, saying, 'Certain of the criticisms [leveled at them] they escape, but others they succumb to'" (εἶτα πάλιν ἑαυτῷ ἐπιφέρει τὰ ὑπὲρ Μαρκίωνος καὶ τὰ κατ᾽ αὐτοῦ λέγων τίνα μὲν ἐκφεύγουσι τῶν ἐγκλημάτων τίσι δὲ περιπίπτουσι). Whether Celsus derives his knowledge of Marcionite teaching from Marcionite sources, oral or written, or from anti-Marcionite polemic by other Christians, as the present passage may suggest, or from both kinds of sources, is difficult to say.

[92]Harnack, 1924a, 196, n. 1. Recent interpreters who class Marcion with gnostics include Knox, 1942, 13-14; Blackman, 1948, 82ff.; R. M. Grant, 1966, 125-26; Jonas, 1964, 173-74; 1963, 137ff.; Bianchi, 1967a. Foerster, on the other hand, is reluctant to class Marcion as a gnostic; see his *Gnosis* 1, 44.

[93]Cf. Irenaeus' imprecise terminology (below, App. D) even while distinguishing and labeling various gnostic groups, and Bornkamm's comment, 1939, 658: "Die starken Berührungen mit anderen gnostischen Systemen und die erheblichen Differenzen innherhalb der ophitischen Lehre machen eine klare Grenzziehung unmöglich. Das ist bei diesen Produkten des religiösen Synkretismus auch nicht zu verwundern, bei denen Grenzlinien immer relativ unsichere, nachträglich gezeichnete Hilfslinien sind."

[94]There are two, parallel accounts of this christology: Irenaeus, *Adv. h.* 1.6.1 (Harvey ed., 1.1.11, with the Greek text supplied by Epiphanius, *Pan.* 31.20), and Clement of Alexandria, *Excerpta ex Theodoto* 59-62. The ascription to Ptolemaeus occurs in the Latin text of Irenaeus (1.8.5 = Harvey ed., 1.1.18: "Et Ptolemaeus quidem ita") and is commonly accepted, e.g., Harvey, Vol. 1, 80, n. 2; R. M. Grant, 1961, 162; Foerster, *Gnosis* 1, 145. On the distinctiveness of paras. 59-62 (as part of the section paras. 43-65) in the *Excerpta* and the general inclination of scholarship to see a common source underlying the two accounts see F. Sagnard (ed. and trans.), *Extraits de Théodote* (Sources chrétiennes, 23; Paris: Les Éditions du Cerf, [2]1970), 28-32, 35. I cite Irenaeus according to the Harvey edition, the *Excerpta* according to Sagnard, whose text is largely that of Stählin in GCS.

[95]Irenaeus, *Adv. h.* 1.6.1 (Harvey ed., 1.1.11; ἐνδεδύσθαι τὸν ψυχικὸν Χριστόν); *Exc. Theod.* 59.2 (εὗρεν Ἰησοῦς Χριστὸν ἐνδύσασθαι).

[96]*Exc. Theod.* 59.3 (οὗτος ὁ ψυχικὸς Χριστὸς ὃν ἐνεδύσατο, ἀόρατος ἦν). In Irenaeus' account, the fashioning of a visible, tangible body for the Christ (see Harvey's emendation and the Latin text) implies invisibility, as does the assertion that the Savior "took nothing material (καὶ ὑλικὸν δὲ οὐδ' ὁτιοῦν εἰληφέναι).

[97]On this body cf. E. H. Pagels, "Conflicting Versions of Valentinian Eschatology: Irenaeus' Treatise vs. the Excerpts from Theodotus," *Harvard Theological Review* 67 (1974), 48-49.

[98]*Exc. Theod.* 59.4 (δυνάμει δὲ θείας ἐγκατασκευῆς); in Irenaeus' account the body with psychic substance is said to derive ἀπὸ δὲ τῆς οἰκονομίας and is prepared ἀρρήτῳ τέχνῃ.

[99]*Exc. Theod.* 60, where Lk. 1.35 is interpreted to refer to God's shaping of the body of the psychic Christ in the (womb of the) virgin (τὴν μόρφωσιν δηλοῖ τοῦ θεοῦ, ἣν ἐνετύπωσεν τῷ σώμα <τι> ἐν τῇ παρθένῳ).

[100]See n. 98 above.

[101]*Exc. Theod.* 59.4 (σῶμα τοίνυν αὐτῷ ὑφαίνεται ἐκ τῆς ἀφανοῦς ψυχικῆς οὐσίας).

[102]Irenaeus, *Adv. h.* 1.30.11-12 (Harvey ed., 1.28.6).

[103]Ibid. ("mundialia enim remisisse eum in munda"); "the disciples thought he had risen with a worldly body [*in corpore mundiali*], not knowing that flesh and blood do not obtain the kingdom of God [1 Cor. 15.50]."

[104]In the account of Basilides' teaching in Irenaeus, *Adv. h.* 1.24.4 (Harvey ed., 1.19.2), Simon the Cyrenean, forced to carry Jesus' cross, is changed to look like Jesus and erroneously crucified in his stead while Jesus, taking on Simon's appearance, stands by laughing at the crucifiers' mistake. Hippolytus' account in the *Refutatio omnium haeresium* says nothing of this and indeed reports that Jesus suffered in his bodily part (*Ref*. 7.27.10, ἔπαθεν οὖν τοῦτο ὅπερ ἦν αὐτοῦ σωματικὸν μέροϲ), which is supported by Clement of Alexandria's report (*Strom*. 4.12.81-83) that Basilides did not view Jesus as an exception to the general principle that humans suffer for their sins or (like a child) at least for their sinfulness. For reasons such as this scholars generally regard Hippolytus as a more trustworthy witness of Basilides' teachings than Irenaeus who mingles Basilides' teachings with those of his followers or with those of other gnostics; cf. Waszink, 1950, 1220ff., and R. M. Grant, 1959, 121. My account is based on Hippolytus in the edition of P. Wendland, *Hippolytus Werke*, Vol. 3 (GCS, 26; Leipzig: Hinrichs, 1916); for another example of divergence between Hippolytus and Irenaeus cf. n. 109 below.

[105]Cf. Hippolytus, *Ref*. 7.20.2-3 and esp. 7.21.1, with its long list of negatives leading up to the designation of deity as οὐκ ὢν θεόϲ.

[106]Ibid. 7.27.8-12. The differentiation (φυλοκρίνησιϲ) of the cosmos--composed of Hebdomad, Ogdoad, and the formless space occupied by humans (7.27.9)--is effected through the death and resurrection of Jesus, which return his bodily part to the formlessness (εἰϲ τὴν ἀμορφίαν) whence it came, his psychic part to its origin, the Hebdomad, and the other parts to the Great Archon and to "the boundary spirit" (7.27.10; for "the boundary spirit" [τὸ μεθόριον πνεῦμα], which is the Holy Spirit, see 7.23.1-2; 7.27.1, 7). Jesus is thus the firstfruits of the differentiation (τῆϲ οὖν φυλοκρινήσεωϲ ἀπαρχή) and the pattern for the differentiation of the third sonship (ᾧ τρόπῳ καὶ ὁ Ἰησοῦϲ πεφυλοκρίνηται) (7.27.12).

[107]Hippolytus, *Ref*. 7.25.6 (ἦλθε δὲ ὄντωϲ, καὶ <τοι> οὐδὲν κατῆλθεν ἄνωθεν οὐδὲ ἐξέστη ἡ μακαρία υἱότηϲ ἐκείνου τοῦ ἀπερινοήτου καὶ μακαρίου οὐκ ὄντοϲ θεοῦ).

[108]This offers another instance of the tendency to locate extraordinary phenomena in remote places; cf. above, ch. 3.1.

[109]Hippolytus, *Ref*. 7.25.6 (οὕτω κάτωθεν ἀπὸ τῆϲ ἀμορφίαϲ τοῦ σωροῦ διήκουσιν αἱ δυνάμειϲ μέχριϲ ἄνω τοῦ υἱότητοϲ); on "the heap" (ὁ σωρόϲ) cf. 7.23.3; 7.24.5; 7.27.5. By contrast, Irenaeus presents a Basilidean schema of emanations (which include the Christ); cf. Waszink, 1950, 1223.

[110]Hippolytus, *Ref.* 7.25.7 (ἀπὸ τῆς μετὰ τὸ μεθόριον μακαρίας υἱότητος).

[111]The Holy Spirit is the boundary between these two regions (ibid. 7.23.2, τὸ δὲ μεταξὺ τοῦ κόσμου καὶ τῶν ὑπὲρ κοσμίων μεθόριον πνεῦμα τοῦτο, ὅπερ ἐστὶ καὶ ἅγιον . . .); cf. further, above, n. 106.

[112]Cf. ibid. 7.22.3, where, in commenting on the origin of light, Basilides again employs circumlocutions and paradoxes: the light came from nothing and is non-existent, for the text (Gen. 1.3) does not specify any origin for the light but only that it came from the voice of the speaker, and this speaker (as Basilides has already asserted) is non-existent and did not come into being (οὐ γὰρ γέγραπται, φησί, πόθεν, ἀλλ' αὐτὸ μόνον ἐκ τῆς φωνῆς τοῦ λέγοντος· ὁ δὲ λέγων, φησίν, οὐκ ἦν, οὐδὲ τὸ γενόμενον ἦν).

[113]*C. Cels.* 3.42b (ἀποθέμενος ταύτας), presumably a reference to Christian claims to a change in Jesus' status after his death; cf. the translations of Keim (1873, 39), Chadwick, and Borret, and the comment of Bader, *Alethes Logos*, 94, "Die Worte ἀποθέμενος ταύτας veranlassen Kelsos, das Grab Jesu noch mit dem Zeusgrab der Kreter zu vergleichen," i.e., in the continuation of 3.42 in 3.43.

[114]3.42b (ἀλλ' ἀποθέμενος ταύτας ἆρα ἔσται θεός· τί οὖν οὐχὶ μᾶλλον ὁ Ἀσκληπιὸς καὶ Διόνυσος καὶ Ἡρακλῆς;).

[115]Although the intellectual achievements of second-century Christian gnostics are commonly recognized by scholars, the correlation between them and social class is not necessarily a simple one, as we noted earlier (above, ch. 6, n. 2) and as is evident from recent discussions of the social location of gnostics; see Kippenberg, 1970, and the critique by Munz, 1972. However, if one is careful to keep in mind the distinction between social class and social status (above, ch. 6, n. 2), one can agree with Theissen's conclusion (1975b, 165-69) that such data as the magnitude and complexity of gnostics' literary production, their stress on knowledge, their elitist consciousness vis-à-vis Christian communities, and their openness to the pagan world point to considerable affluence and social standing.

[116]See n. 91 above. Present-day knowledge of Marcion is beset with the same difficulty, though much care has been exercised by modern scholarship in its efforts to distill Marcion's views from the morass of anti-Marcionite polemic. Harnack, e.g., in reconstructing the text of Marcion's gospel distinguishes between those witnesses who evidently had direct access to it and those who did not (1924a, 178*-183*); nonetheless, as Harnack admits (p. 183*), one has "keine Gewähr, dass alle Korrekturen von Marcion selbst stammen; selbst die Fassung, wie sie bei Tert. vorliegt, kann schon Korrekturen der Schüler enthalten" (cf. further, p. 66*); for an example see *Adv. Marc.* 4.38.7 where Tertullian is addressing Marcion (the verbs are second person singular), but then switches to verbs in the third person plural--i.e., Marcionites--in discussing changes made in the text of the Gospel of Luke. For our purposes this is not crucial inasmuch as the distinction between Marcion and Marcionites was not a matter of concern for Celsus. Since the Marcionite chain of tradition extended beyond Celsus' day, it is

attested, therefore, in post-Celsian, anti-Marcionite polemic. Though there is continuity in this tradition, our characterization of the teachings of Marcion(ites) will draw chiefly on Irenaeus, Clement of Alexandria, and Tertullian (citing his *Adversus Marcionem* in the edition by E. Evans, 2 vols. [Oxford: Clarendon Press, 1972]), all roughly contemporary with Celsus, with occasional citations from later sources that confirm or supplement these witnesses either because they are based on them or have independent knowledge (e.g., Epiphanius; see Harnack, 1924a, 64*-66*, 182*).

[117]This aversion is sometimes reported explicitly, as in Tertullian, *Adv. Marc.* 1.15.4-5 (the Creator constructed the world from matter, to which Marcion imputes evil: "malum materiae Marcion deputans"), and Clement, *Strom*. 3.12.1 (creation is a φύσις κακὴ ἔκ τε τῆς ὕλης κακῆς καὶ ἐκ δικαίου γενομένη δημιουργοῦ; Harnack, 1924a, 276*). It is evident in the Marcionites' desistance from use of the things of the world (spelled out in Clement, *Strom*. 3.3.12; 3.4.25; Hippolytus, *Ref*. 10.19.4 = GCS 26, 280), such as foods (Tertullian, *Adv. Marc*. 1.14.4-5) and marriage (Irenaeus, *Adv. h*. 1.28.1 = Harvey ed., 1.26.1; Clement, *Strom*. 3.3.12; Tertullian, *Adv. Marc*. 1.29.2, 5; 4.11.8), in the exclusion of married persons from the church and the restriction of baptism to unmarried or separated persons (ibid., 4.11.8), in the admittance of married couples to the eucharist only if they first entered into a mutual pact against the fruit of marriage (ibid. 4.34.5), and in the assertion that salvation is only for the soul, the body, since it is taken from the earth, being incapable of sharing in salvation (Irenaeus, *Adv. h*. 1.27.3 = Harvey ed., 1.25.2).

[118]Epiphanius, who states (*Pan*. 42.10.2; GCS 31, 106) that he had examined firsthand both Marcion's gospel and his "apostolikon" (i.e., the edited Pauline corpus), reports (42.11.4; GCS 31, 107) that the genealogy of Jesus was missing from the gospel. The omission is indirectly attested by Tertullian's assumption, in arguing against Marcion, that on Marcion's view Jesus' origins would be unknown to his contemporaries: "How was he able to be admitted to the synagogue, a man so unexpected, so unknown [*tam repentinus, tam ignotus*], of whose tribe, people, house . . . no one as yet was certain?" (*Adv. Marc*. 4.7.7). From Gal. 3.26 Marcion omits the reference to Christ as the seed of Abraham; see ibid., 5.4.2. Harnack, 1924a, 102*, cites Origen, *Comm. in Iohann*. 10.24, as evidence for Marcion's omission of the statement of Jesus' descent from David in Rom. 1.3; however, the passage is hardly explicit on this point.

[119]Epiphanius states (*Pan*. 42.11.5; GCS 31, 107-08) that Marcion's gospel began with "In the fifteenth year of Tiberius Caesar" (i.e., Lk. 3.1); this is substantiated by Irenaeus, *Adv. h*. 1.27.2 (Harvey ed., 1.25.1) and by reports that Marcion portrayed Jesus as having descended in the fifteenth year of Tiberius; thus Irenaeus, *Adv. h*. 1.27.2 (Harvey ed., 1.25.1); Tertullian, *Adv. Marc*. 1.19.2; 4.6.3; 4.7.1; Hippolytus, *Ref*. 7.31.5 (GCS 26, 217). Marcion also omitted the reference to Jesus' blood mother and relatives (Lk. 8.19) while retaining the interpretation of his true mother and relatives (Lk. 8.20-21); see Harnack, 1924a, 198*, for sources and comment. From Gal. 4.4 he evidently omitted the assertion of Jesus' birth from a woman; see ibid., 74*.

[120]Various verbs are used by the anti-Marcionites to describe Marcion's portrayal of Christ's first appearance on earth: *venientem* , *manifestatum*, Irenaeus, *Adv. h.* 1.27.2 (Harvey ed., 1.25.2); *manare*, Tertullian, *Adv. Marc.* 1.19.2; *revelatus*, ibid. 4.6.3; *descendisse*, ibid. 4.7.1; κατέρχεσθαι, Hippolytus, *Ref.* 7.31.5, 6 (GCS 26, 217). That Marcion viewed the movement as downward is indicated by Irenaeus' statement that Jesus "came from that Father who is above the God who is the maker of the world" ("ab eo Patre, qui est super mundi fabricatorem Deum, venientem") and by Tertullian's depiction (*Adv. Marc.* 4.7.1) of Christ as coming down to Galilee after first passing through the heaven of the Creator God ("eum descendisse in civitatem Galilaeae Capharnaum, utique de caelo creatoris, in quod de suo ante descendarat"); cf. ibid. 1.19.2 ("de caelo manare") and Tertullian's sarcastic statement in 4.22.7, "quia et ipse per caelum creatoris viam ruperat."

[121]Tertullian's designation of Marcion's Christ as a *phantasma* is probably on target; e.g., *Adv. Marc.* 3.8.1, "phantasma vindicans [scil. Marcion] Christum," would seem to be a direct statement or echo of Marcion's view, while in 3.9.1 Marcion's comparing of Christ's body to the angels of the Abraham and Lot story describes their appearance "quasi et illi phantasmate"; 5.14.1 is probably also formulated employing Marcion's terminology ("If the Father sent him [Christ] in likeness of flesh of sin, it should not therefore be said that the flesh which was seen in him was a phantasm [non ideo phantasma dicetur caro quae in illo videbatur]"). Tertullian, in discussing Marcionite interpretation of Philippians (*Adv. Marc.* 5.20), cites Phil. 2.7 and says that Marcionites think that Paul here supports their view of Christ's substance as a phantasm of flesh ("substantia Christi . . . phantasma carnis," 5.20.3). Other sources also refer to this passage, specifically the phrase ἐν ὁμοιώματι ἀνθρώπων γενόμενος, which Harnack (1924a, 126) regards as fundamental for Marcion as "biblischer Theologe"; thus Irenaeus, *Adv. h.* 1.27.2 (Harvey ed., 1.25.1), "in hominis forma manifestatum"; Chrysostom, commenting on Phil. 2.7, reports Marcion as saying, οὐκ ἐγένετο ἄνθρωπος, ἀλλ' ἐν ὁμοιώματι ἀνθρώπων γενόμενος (cited in Harnack, 1924a, 287).

The nature of Marcion's docetism will be discussed below; see n. 125. The motivation for it may be inferred from what was said earlier (n. 117) regarding his aversion to matter and its maker. It is summarized succinctly by Hippolytus, *Ref.* 7.31.6 (GCS 31, 217): "unbegotten, Jesus came down, he [Marcion] says, in order that he might be free from evil" (ἀγέννητος κατῆλθεν ὁ Ἰησοῦς, φησίν, ἵνα ᾖ πάσης ἀπηλλαγμένος κακίας). Tertullian, *Adv. Marc.* 3.8.2 and 3.11, goes into detail.

[122]Tertullian, *Adv. Marc.* 3.9.1; Ephraem, *Ev. Conc. Expos.*, p. 255 (cited in Harnack, 1924a, 286*).

[123]Tertullian, *Adv. Marc.* 4.9.7 (*verbo solo*).

[124]Celsus (*C. Cels.* 6.74) ridicules the conflict between two divine sons, evidently the two Christs of the Marcionites.

[125]As Evans remarks, in the introduction to his edition of Tertullian's *Adv. Marc.* (cited above, n. 116), xiii, "One might have expected that in consistency with himself he [Marcion] would have

excised the passion as well--or, as Tertullian suggests, even more so."
However, Marcion believed that his Christ was crucified, as is stated
plainly by Tertullian in *Adv. Marc.* 3.23.5 and 5.6.5 and implied in
passages like 3.18.1 and 5.3.10. Whether the crucifixion of a Christ
who was a phantasm (see above, n. 120) would occur with suffering is a
matter of dispute. Harnack, 1924a, 125, asserts that Marcion's
contemporaries did not draw from docetism the conclusions that moderns
do; he cites Marcion's comparison of Christ's body with those of the
angels who were Abraham's and Lot's guests (see above, n. 121) as
evidence that Marcion restricted his docetism to Christ's appearing to
have human flesh, so that he was indeed capable of suffering. On the
other hand, Harnack concedes that one cannot blame Marcion's opponents
for drawing the conclusion (which Harnack has just said they would not
draw) that the incarnation of Marcion's Christ was only apparent. Much
of Tertullian's controversy with Marcion centers on the nature and
authenticity of a Christ who was "flesh and not flesh, man and not man"
("caro nec caro, homo nec homo," 3.8.2); cf. 4.8.2-3; 4.9.5; 4.10.15-16;
4.20.13-14; 4.21.11-12 (Marcion's Christ had no reason to be ashamed of
the curse on crucifixion since he had no body, i.e., that would have
suffered); 4.42.6-8 (Tertullian raises some logical difficulties
connected with the crucifixion of a phantasm); 5.20.5 (Paul would not
have said Christ was obedient to death if Christ had been so constituted
as to be incapable of death, and he would not have praised Christ's
submission to death if his suffering had been an illusion).

[126]Addressed to Marcionite teaching? Origen puts it in this
context.

[127]6.74 (πόθεν ἀποδειχθήσεται θεοῦ παῖς ὁ τοιαῦτα κολασθείς);
the passage continues: "unless it had been predicted for him" (εἰ μὴ
περὶ τούτου προείρηται). Taken by itself, and in view of Celsus'
denial elsewhere both of Jesus' divine sonship and of proofs from
Jewish prophecy (see 1.50; 2.28; 3.1), the passage seems clear enough:
Celsus is denying divinity to Jesus since no son of God would have been
punished as he was (cf. 2.9, 31, and p. 106 above); only if his
punishment has been predicted (which it was not) would it constitute
proof of divine sonship. Origen's introduction to the passage, however,
puts a different interpretation on it: in order to discredit
Marcionites Celsus concurs with the assertion that Jesus was foretold
in prophecy. The tacit premise--that Marcionites do not accept such
proof from prophecy for their Christ--roots in their rejection of the
creator God. If Origen has given an accurate account of Celsus'
polemic, it would seem that Celsus is arguing ad hominem, affirming
here what he denies elsewhere in order to attack Marcionites at a
vulnerable point. If so, it would be another instance of Celsus'
determination to attack Christianity (and defend pagan culture) even at
the price of logical consistency.

[128]A brief characterization of gnostic exegesis, citing earlier
literature, is given in Wilson, 1968, ch. 3; for a case study
(Heracleon) see Pagels, 1973, 13ff. and passim.

[129]Or "Helenians," for their devotion to Helen (*C. Cels.*
5.62a), the consort of Simon.

[130]*Adv. h.* 2.31.2 (Harvey ed., 2.48.2); Irenaeus mentions
followers of Carpocrates as holding the same view (ibid.). Did Celsus

(or a source he was using) confuse Harpocrates (= the Egyptian god Horus) with Carpocrates, the early second-century gnostic? Cf. Nock, 1950, 50.

[131]See *Exegesis on the Soul* 134.10ff.; *Gospel of Philip*, sayings 21-23, 63; *Philip* also affirms resurrection in the flesh, however (saying 23).

[132]*Adv. h.* 1.2.4 (Harvey ed., 1.1.3); 1.4.1 (1.1.7).

[133]Ibid. 1.4.5 (1.1.8); 1.8.4 (1.1.17).

[134]Ibid. 1.8.2 (1.1.16) (καὶ εἰſ αἴσθησιν ἤγαγη τοῦ καταλιπόντοſ αὐτὴν φωτόſ).

[135]Ibid. 1.3.3 (1.1.5) (τὴν ἴασιν τοῦ πεπονθότοſ αἰῶνοſ).

[136]Ibid. (διδάσκοντα τοὺſ μαθητὰſ τὸ γεγονὸſ ἐν τοῖſ αἰῶσι μυστήριον).

[137]ὁ τῆſ Οὐαλεντίνου σχολῆſ δοκιμώτατοſ, Clement of Alexandria, *Strom.* 4.71 = Fragment 50 of Heracleon in W. Völker (ed.), *Quellen zur Geschichte der christlichen Gnosis* (Sammlung ausgewählter kirchen- und dogmengeschichtlicher Quellenschriften, New Series, 5; Tübingen: J. C. B. Mohr [Siebeck], 1932); unless otherwise indicated my citations from Heracleon are from Völker.

[138]In Origen, *Comm. in Iohann.* 13.60 (= Völker, Fr. 40); cf. the exposition in Pagels, 1973, 83-85.

[139]Origen, *Comm. in Iohann.* 13.11; see Pagels, *Johannine Gospel*, 80.

[140]Fr. 40 (καὶ δι' αἰσθήσεωſ πείθεσθαι καὶ οὐχὶ λόγῳ πιστεύειν).

[141]Above, p. 117. I have cited only examples of gnostic allegorizing of Jesus traditions; however, according to Irenaeus (*Adv. h.* 1.3.6; Harvey ed., 1.1.6), Ptolemaic Valentinians also interpreted to their own ends parables and allegories (παραβόλων καὶ ἀλληγορίων) found in "the Law and the Prophets."

[142]*Exegesis* 136.25ff., 137.1ff.; on the date and Valentinian nature of the *Exegesis* see M. Krause, in Foerster, *Gnosis* 2, 102-03.

[143]Fr. 21; the quotation from the *Kerygma* is found also in Clement Alex., *Strom.* 6.5.40-41 (E.T. in Hennecke-Schneemelcher, *New Testament Apocrypha* 2, 99-100).

[144]"Greeks" = hylics; cf. Pagels, 1973, 89.

[145]H. C. Puech, in Hennecke-Schneemelcher, *New Testament Apocrypha* 1, 248.

[146]Extant in the Berlin papyrus 8502 and in Codex III from Nag Hammadi; ibid., 244, and M. Krause in Foerster, *Gnosis* 2, 26, where there is an English translation (pp. 27ff.) of the *Letter of Eugnostus* as well as of the variants in the *Sophia*; English translation of both, by D. M. Parrott, in J. M. Robinson (ed.), *The Nag Hammadi Library in English*, translated by Members of the Coptic Gnostic Library Project of the Institute for Antiquity and Christianity (San Francisco et al.: Harper & Row, 1977), 207ff.

[147]The letter is probably the *Vorlage* of the *Sophia*, though scholarly opinion is divided on this point, as it is on the question of the Christian or non-Christian character of the *Letter*; see Puech in Hennecke-Schneemelcher, *New Testament Apocrypha* 1, 247-48, and the discussion and the literature cited in Wilson, 1968, 111ff., and by Krause in Foerster, *Gnosis* 2, 26-27. The Christian references in the *Sophia*, on the other hand, are explicit.

[148]*Letter of Eugnostus* 70.10ff. (E.T. in Foerster, *Gnosis* 2, 27-28); cf. also the obscure sally at philosophers "in this world" in another Nag Hammadi writing, *The Treatise on the Resurrection* 46.5ff. (E.T. in Foerster, *Gnosis* 2, 73).

[149]Above, p. 123. The evidence for Basilides' understanding of Jesus' miracles is scanty and indirect at best--Jesus' ministry took place in a way similar to what is recorded in the gospels (above, p. 123)--but the abstractness of his Jesus figure and of Jesus' ministry does not point to much interest in a literal view of the miracles.

[150]47.2ff. (E.T. in Foerster, *Gnosis* 2, 73): ". . . you received flesh when you came into the world. Why should you not receive flesh when you ascend into the aeon?"

[151]Saying 23. Wilson, 1962, 87-89, offers an explanation of the inconsistencies in the *Treatise* and in *Philip* ("flesh" may have more than one meaning, and resurrection in the flesh may be a prelude to putting off the flesh); there is also the possibility that the documents are composite works, with various (and sometimes conflicting) strands of thought interwoven.

[152]Irenaeus, *Adv. h.* 1.27.3 (Harvey ed., 1.25.2); Tertullian, *Adv. M.* 3.8.2 (the good God is neither the creator nor the resuscitator of flesh). Marcion evidently retained an edited version of Christ's reply to the Sadducees' question about resurrection (Lk. 20.34-36) though eliminating the verses (37-38) referring to the patriarchs and their God (evidence in Harnack, 1924a, 229*). Marcion's version of Christ's assertion of "the resurrection of the dead" appears to postulate something other than resurrection in the flesh: those who attain resurrection do not in fact die for they are like angels.

[153]*C. Cels.* 4.71, 73a; 6.53; deity, says Celsus, is ἔξω παντὸſ πάθουſ (6.65), ἔξω φθόνου (8.21), beyond the reach of hurt or pain (8.2).

[154]For an overview of the problem posed to some early Christians by divine anthropopathisms see Pohlenz, 1909, chs. 1-3; for details of Marcion's treatment of such traits see pp. 20-22.

[155]An instructive example is the differing interpretations which Marcion and Tertullian place on the sayings asserting hostility between David and the blind and lame of Jerusalem (2 Sam. 5.6ff.): Marcion takes the sayings literally, contrasting David's behavior toward the blind with Christ's healing of a blind man, while Tertullian sees in the blind a symbol of the Jewish people, who in their blindness denied entrance to the son of David (Tertullian, *Adv. Marc.* 4.36.13). Marcion's rejection of the God of the Jewish prophets would entail rejection of prophecies of the messiah of the good God; for specific examples see the texts cited in Harnack, 1924a, 290*-91*.

[156]Elisha uses water to heal the Syrian leper (2 Kgs. 5.9ff.) whereas Christ heals a leper through a word alone (Lk. 5.12ff.); Tertullian, *Adv. Marc.* 4.9.7. The prophet of the God of creation (Moses) stretched out his hands in order to kill many people in war (Ex. 17.8ff.) whereas Christ stretched out his hands (on the cross) in order to save; Megethius in Adamantius, *Dial.* 1.11 (text in Harnack, 1924a, 281*). The prophet of the God of creation (Joshua) caused the sun not to set until those warring against his people were killed (Josh. 10.12ff.) whereas the Lord says not to let the sun go down on your anger (Eph. 4.26); ibid., 1.13 (text in Harnack, 281*). The prophet of the God of creation (Elisha) has bears devour children (2 Kg. 2.24) whereas the Lord invites children to himself (Lk. 18.16); ibid., 1.16 (text in Harnack, 282*). At the request of Elijah, the Creator sends down a destructive fire (2 Kgs. 1.10ff.) whereas Christ forbids his disciples to ask for fire from heaven (Lk. 9.51ff.).

[157]On the sabbath Christ heals a man with a withered hand (Lk. 6.6-11; Tertullian, *Adv. Marc.* 4.12.9-15) and a crippled woman (Lk. 13.10-17; Tertullian, *Adv. Marc.* 4.30.1) and through contact, forbidden by the law, with the woman with the flow of blood heals her (Lk. 8.40-56; Tertullian, *Adv. Marc.* 4.20.7-14).

[158]My judgment of which miracle accounts were contained in Marcion's gospel and in what form is inferred from Tertullians' running dispute with Marcion's version of the gospel, in Bk. 4 of *Adv. Marc.*, compared against Harnack's reconstruction of Marcion's gospel from the same source as well as other sources (1924a, 183*ff.). As before (n. 116 above), there is no need to distinguish sharply between Marcion and his followers, except where these diverge significantly from him, as in the case of Apelles, discussed below.

[159]Tertullian, *Adv. Marc.* 4.9.3-15, 4.9.10, reports Marcion's interpretation of the healing account paraphrased in our text: "Nam et bonus, inquit [scil. Marcion, mentioned in the clause preceding], praeterea sciens omnem qui lepra esset liberatus solemnia legis executorum, ideo ita praecepit."

[160]See above, n. 155. The specifics of Marcion's interpretation of this miracle account are not easily distilled from Tertullian's polemic. However, that one of Marcion's Antitheses is at issue is clear from *Adv. Marc.* 4.36.13 where Tertullian states that he is refuting an Antithesis (*"antithesim* de suo retundam"); cf. also the clause, Christus *"ex diverso* [i.e., in contrast to David] caeco subvenit" (ibid.). The people's rebuke of the blind man calling Christ the son of David would lend itself to Marcionite interpretation, and Tertullian's challenge to Marcion to show that the rebuke was motivated by knowledge of Christ's true identity rather than by annoyance at the noise (4.36.9-10) suggests that Marcion interpreted their action to accord with his thought. Tertullian's assertion that he wishes to safeguard the Lord's patience from any implication by Marcion that the divine patience would tolerate error (4.36.10) suggests that Marcion said that Christ, being patient, did not disabuse the blind man of his error (4.36.10; note the syntax: *"Sed* patiens dominus [= Marcion's point]. *Non tamen* confirmator erroris [= Tertullian's riposte]").

[161]For example, the healing of the man with dropsy (Lk. 14.1-6); see Harnack, 1924a, 218*.

[162]Marcion even retains the feeding of the 5,000 (Tertullian, *Adv. Marc.* 4.21.3-5), which he might well have excised in view of his asceticism (above, n. 117). Had Marcion rejected miracle accounts on grounds of their incredibility, Tertullian would not argue, as he does in 3.2 and 3.3, that Marcion should not rest his case for Christ's deity on miracles.

[163]Cf. Tertullian, *Adv. Marc.* 3.2.1: since Marcion's Christ was a son, the father should have announced the son before the son announced the father; since he was sent, the sender should have authenticated the one sent.

[164]*Adv. Marc.* 3.3.1 ("Non fuit, inquis, ordo eiusmodi necessarius, quia statim se et filium et missum et dei Christum rebus ipsis esset probaturus per documenta virtutum").

[165]See Nilsson, 1961, 156-58; Weinreich, 1919, 3ff. (in 1969, 412ff.).

[166]The differences in thought between Apelles and Marcion are summarized by Harnack, 1924a, 188-89. Unlike Marcion, Apelles evidently allegorized on occasion; see Tertullian, *De carne* 8, which reports that Apelles interpreted "wandering sheep" allegorically (*figura*) of angels (text in Harnack, 1924a, 408). On the dating of Apelles to the second century see the evidence Harnack cites, 179-80.

[167]In Origen, *Hom. in Gen.* 2.2; Greek and Latin text in Harnack, 1924a, 413*.

[168]Ibid.: "Constat ergo fictam essa fabulam; quod si est, constat non esse a deo hanc scripturam." Cf. further Origen, *C. Cels.* 5.54: Apelles considers the writings of the Jews to be a fiction (μῦθον) and does not give credence to their reports of extraordinary

phenomena (ἀπιστοῦντα . . . ταῖſ παραδοξότερα ἀπαγγελλούσαιſ Ἰουδαίων γραφαῖſ). For other examples of Apelles' critique of the Jewish scriptures see Harnack, 1924a, 413*-16*; E.T. in R. M. Grant, 1957, 84-86. At the same time it should be noted that Apelles apparently did not reject everything in the Jewish scriptures and evidently ascribed some things in them to Christ; see Harnack, 1924a, 192, n. 1.

[169]Hippolytus, *Ref.* 7.38.4-5: after his resurrection in the flesh, showing that he was not a phantasm (οὐ φάντασμα, ἀλλὰ ἐνσαρκόſ), he dissolved his flesh into its earthly constituents (heat, cold, wet, dry).

[170]According to Rhodo, who reportedly knew Apelles and wrote a work against the Marcionites, from which Eusebius quotes, *H.E.* 5.13.2. Other references to the prophetess Philoumene include Tertullian, *De praeser.* 6 and 30; *Adv. Marc.* 3.11.2; *De carne* 7 (texts in Harnack, 1924a, 405*-07*); Hippolytus, *Ref.* 7.38; 10.20 (in Harnack, 411*-12*); Ps.-Tertullian, *Adv. omnes haer.* 6 (in Harnack, 409*).

[171]According to Tertullian, *De praeser.* 6 ("signis et praestigiis"; in Harnack, 405*); *Adv. Apelleiacos*, fragment preserved in a manuscript of Augustine, *De haer.* 24 (see Harnack, 178, n. 2, and 408*-09*, where the text is given; the fragment mentions *miracula* and specifically her subsisting on a large loaf of bread which she kept in a bottle with a narrow neck, from which she daily retrieved it whole).

[172]*Simon*: Acts 8.9-11; Justin, *Apology* 1.26.2-3; *Dial.* 120.6; Irenaeus, *Adv. h.* 1.23.1, 3-4 (Harvey ed., 1.16.1, 3); Clement Alex., *Strom.* 2.11 (52.2); Tertullian, *De anima* 34; Hippolytus, *Ref.* 6.19.4, 6; 6.20.2; Origen, *C. Cels.* 1.57.39-42; Ps.-Clement, *Hom.* 2.22, 24-26.
      Dositheus: Ps.-Clement, *Hom.* 2.24; cf. Origen, *C. Cels.* 1.57-26-29.
      Menander: Justin, *Apol.* 1.26.4; Irenaeus, *Adv. h.* 1.23.5 (Harvey ed., 1.17).
      Others: Irenaeus, *Adv. h.* 1.23.4 (Harvey ed., 1.16.3), where Irenaeus presents the Simonians' leaders, to whom he refers as "mystici sacerdotes," as performing "magias," etc. Useful collections of sources are Waitz, 1904; Lietzmann, 1927. Recent full-length studies of Simon include Salles Debadie, 1969; Beyschlag, 1974; Lüdemann, 1975; see also the review, by Meeks (1977), of these and other works on Simon.
      [173]Simon: Irenaeus, *Adv. h.* 1.23.2-3 (Harvey ed., 1.16.2). Menander: ibid. 1.23.5 (1.17).

[174]Thus Simon for the Simonians; ibid., 1.23.3 (1.16.2): "hominibus autem salutem praestaret *per suam agnitionem*" (Hippolytus, *Ref.* 6.19.5: διὰ τῆſ ἰδίαſ ἐπιγώσεωſ).

[175]Thus Menander who, according to Irenaeus, *Adv. h.* 1.23.5 (Harvey ed., 1.17), through his *magicam scientiam* overcomes the angels who made the world and by baptizing his disciples imparts resurrection to them (cf. Tertullian, *De anima* 50).

[176]Irenaeus, *Adv. h.* 1.25.2 (Harvey ed., 1.20.2) (Greek text in Hippolytus, *Ref.* 7.32.5: φάσκοντεϛ ἐξουσίαν ἔχειν πρὸϛ τὸ κυριεύειν ἤδη τῶν ἀρχόντων καὶ ποιητῶν τοῦδε τοῦ κόσμου, οὐ μὴν ἀλλὰ καὶ τῶν ἐν αὐτῷ ποιημάτων ἁπάντων).

[177]*C. Cels.* 7.9 (ἐγὼ ὁ θεόϛ εἰμι ἢ θεοῦ παῖϛ ἢ πνεῦμα θεῖον. ἤκω δέ).

[178]See the detailed treatment of Plotinus' treatise in App. E.

Notes to Chapter 9

[1]The literature on Justin Martyr is so extensive that one may justly speak of *Justinforschung*; thus van Winden, 1971, 1. See the bibliographies in Goodenough, 1923; Barnard, 1967; Hyldahl, 1966; Young, 1971; Trakatellis, 1976, who refers (p. x) to George Hunston William's "exhaustive bibliography on Justin Martyr" (unpublished).

[2]Wilken, 1971, 286; Wilken's phrasing is slightly different in the earlier version of the essay, 1970, 456.

[3]Cf. the remarks of Geffeken, 1907, 31-32, and the sources and studies cited there. More recently and in more detail see Nestle, 1941-42; Klein, 1967.

[4]*1 Apol.* 21.1-2; some of the same pagan accounts are cited in *Dial.* 67.2; 69.2-3. My citations from Justin are from E. J. Goodspeed (ed.), *Die ältesten Apologeten: Texte mit kurzen Einleitungen* (Göttingen: Vandenhoeck & Ruprecht, 1914).

[5]*1 Apol.* 22.2: "If we say that he [Jesus] was God's Logos, fathered by God in an unusual way, contrary to ordinary reproduction [ἰδίωϛ, παρὰ τὴν κοινὴν γένεσιν], as we stated earlier, let this be something shared [κοινόν] with you who say that Hermes is God's pro-clamatory Logos." 22.5: "And if we say that he was borne by a virgin, let this, too, be something shared [κοινόν] with us, in view of [the birth of] Perseus" (who was fathered by Zeus and borne by the virgin Danae). 22.6: "In that we say that he healed the lame and the para-lyzed and those suffering from the hour of birth, and raised dead persons, we shall seem to say the same things [ὅμοια . . . ταυτά] as those asserted to have happened through Asclepius." 23.1: "We say the same things [ταυτά]" (as pagans). 24.1: Christians say things "simi-lar to the Greeks" (τὰ ὅμοια τοῖϛ Ἕλλησι).

[6]*1 Apol.* 21.4 (πλὴν ὅτι εἰϛ διαφορὰν καὶ προτροπὴν τῶν ἐκ παιδευομένων ταῦτα γέγραπται· μιμητὰϛ γὰρ θεῶν καλὸν εἶναι πάντεϛ ἡγοῦνται).

[7]For Christians see Larsson, 1962, and the literature cited there. For pagans see the examples cited in Kittel, 1933, 210-11; BAG,

s.v. μιμέομαι, and cf. Euripides, *Ion* 5.436: "It is unjust to say humans act wickedly if we are imitating [μιμούμεθ] the 'good deeds' of the gods." Further material on both pagans and Christians is found in Heitmann, 1940 (Justin, pp. 79-89).

[8] *1 Apol.* 25.2: the Christian God was not guilty of adultery or sodomy nor was he possessed by the passions ascribed to Greek deities.

[9] Ibid. 23.3 (μόνοσ ἰδίωσ); in 22.2 the same word, ἰδίωσ, is used of Jesus' birth. Cf. further *Dial.* 66.3, where Justin asserts the singularity of virgin birth among Jews: only "our Christ" was born thus.

[10] In distinguishing extraordinary elements in the story of Jesus from the pagan counterparts discussed in *1 Apol.* 21-22, Justin does not refer to Christ's resurrection and ascension, but he mentions these at the beginning of the discussion (21.1), and their uniqueness for him may be inferred from his argument in ch. 23 and from his argument from prophecy to the reality of Christ's resurrection and ascension (ch. 45).

[11] *1 Apol.* 23.1 (πρεσβύτερα πάντων γεγενημένων συγγραφέων).

[12] Ibid. 59 (Justin cites Gen. 1), 60 (Plato was dependent on Moses but misread him).

[13] Ibid. 23.3. Cf. *Dial.* 69.1: among the Greeks the devil (ὁ διάβολοσ) worked wonders similar to the genuine, Christian wonders but did them falsely (παραποιήσασ); he also worked wonders through Egyptian magicians (μάγων) and through false prophets (ψευδοπροφητῶν) at the time of Elijah.

[14] Ibid. 54.2. For Justin's pejorative use of τερατολογία cf. *Dial.* 67.2, where Trypho accuses Justin of τερατολογία when Justin argues for the virgin birth of Jesus.

[15] Divine fatherhood or virgin birth: Dionysus (*Dial.* 69.2), Perseus (*1 Apol.* 54.8; *Dial.* 70.5). Resurrection and/or ascent to heaven: Dionysus (*1 Apol.* 54.6; *Dial.* 69.2), Perseus (*1 Apol.* 54.8), Bellerophon (ibid. 54.8).

[16] Key passages in the Jewish and Christian traditions are Ps. 95 [96].5 (in the Greek version, ὅτι πάντεσ οἱ θεοὶ τῶν ἐθνῶν δαιμόνια) and 1 Cor. 10.20 (cf. Rev. 9.20); cf. the survey of Jewish, Christian, and pagan traditions in Pohlenz, 1909, 129ff., and the studies cited above, in ch. 3, n. 72.

[17] *Dial.* 69.1 (ταῦτα βεβαίαν μου τὴν ἐν ταῖσ γραφαῖσ γνῶσιν καὶ πίστιν κατέστησεν); the premise of Justin's argument is that imitations (in this case, pagan phenomena) prove the genuineness of that which is imitated (i.e., prophecies in Christianity's scriptures).

[18] *1 Apol.* 46.2–3; among Greeks Justin mentions Socrates and Heraclitus, and among barbarians Abraham, Elijah, and the three men in the fiery furnace. In *2 Apol.* 8.1 Justin speaks of poets and philosophers such as Heraclitus and Musonius who were hated and put to death "because of the seed of truth implanted in every race of humans" (διὰ τὸ ἔμφυτον παντὶ γένει ἀνθρώπων σπέρμα τοῦ λόγου; cf. similarly ibid. 13.5, διὰ τῆς ἐνούσης ἐμφύτου τοῦ λόγου σπορᾶς); in ibid. 8.3 and 13.3 he uses the Stoic term σπερματικὸς λόγος; cf. similarly ibid. 10.2. On Justin's use of σπερματικὸς λόγος and τὸ σπέρμα τοῦ λόγου, and the distinctions between them, see the detailed studies by Holte, 1958, and Waszink, 1964, and the critique and exposition in Hyldahl, 1966, 70–85. Justin also claims for Christianity those Jews who, before Christ came, lived according to the law of Moses: at the resurrection they will be saved through him (*Dial.* 45.3–4).

[19] *1 Apol.* 55.3–8; Justin cites sailing, plowing, etc.

[20] Ibid. 55.6: the cross appears on trophies or standards used in processions and to it are affixed images of emperors after their death and deification.

[21] Ibid. 55.2 (τὸ μέγιστον σύμβολον τῆς ἰσχύος καὶ ἀρχῆς αὐτοῦ).

[22] *1 Apol.* 60.1–5, referring to *Tim.* 36B–C (specifically οἷον χεῖ in 36B); for other possible early Christian use of this Plato passage to refer to the cross see Daniélou, 1964, 285–87 (the *Tim.* passage is erroneously referred to as 26B).

[23] τὸ σχῆμα τοῦ σταυροῦ, *1 Apol.* 55.4; cf. 55.2; see Andresen's remarks, 1952–53, 193.

[24] Ibid. 55.4. This passage, in which the σχῆμα of the cross is seen in the human figure's erect posture, its ability to extend its hands, and its nose stretching down from the forehead and providing the channel for breath, is connected by Andresen (1952–53, 193 and n. 144) with somewhat similar thoughts in passages such as Cicero, *De nat. deor* 2.56, and (among Platonists) *Tim.* 90A and Ps.-Plutarch, *De exilio* 5 (600F). As a parallel to Justin's citing of the human being's erect posture as evidence of the σχῆμα of the cross Andresen (192–93) refers to Albinus, *Didask.* 23 (lines 11ff. in Hermann's Teubner edition), where the Middle Platonist speaks of the location of the head in the supreme position as a σχῆμα that imitates the σχῆμα of the universe.

[25] *1 Apol.* 55.2 (ἄνευ τοῦ σχήματος τούτου διοικεῖται ἡ κοινωνίαν ἔχειν δύναται).

[26] *1 Apol.* 54.1 (οἱ δὲ παραδιδόντες τὰ μυθοποιηθέντα ὑπὸ τῶν ποιητῶν οὐδεμίαν ἀπόδειξιν φέρουσι ἐκμανθάνουσι νέοις).

[27] Cf. the Galen excerpts cited and discussed by Walzer, 1949: Moses writes his books without demonstration, simply stating that God commanded, God spoke (pp. 11, 18); in the school (διατρίβη) of Moses and Christ one hears undemonstrated laws (νόμων ἀναποδείκτων)

(pp. 14, 46). Galen had written a book *On Demonstration*, and in criticizing Jewish and Christian teaching he assumes that logical demonstration is the way to knowledge; cf. Walzer, 45-48.

[28] *1 Apol.* 46.1. Chadwick, 1966, 19-20, aptly summarizes what I have called the axiomatic nature of Justin's argumentation: "Throughout his writing he invariably assumes that once the Christian position has been properly set out by an intelligent man, once its way of life has been seen in a faithful disciple, and once it has been seriously attended to by a sincere and open mind, the fulfillment of these three conditions can have only one consequence: the truth will be manifest and forthwith accepted. 'I have no need', he writes, 'of any sophistical ingenuity, but only to be candid and frank'" (*Dial.* 80.2; 120.6; 125.1).

Roger Brown's description (1969, 551) of the operation of the "consistency principle" in social relations is applicable to Justin's statements (as it is to a number of passages cited in this study): "It seems to be a general law of human thought that we expect people we like and respect to associate themselves with ideas we like and respect and to dissociate themselves or disagree with ideas from which we dissociate ourselves. These latter disapproved ideas we expect to find espoused by the wicked and the stupid--those we do not like or respect. The 'goods' in the world in the way of persons, things, and ideas are supposed to clump together and oppose the 'bads,' who are expected to form their own clump. This is a consistency principle. It describes the way the world ought to go, and as long as things work this way nothing much happens to our attitudes."

[29] Chadwick, 1966, 131, n. 53, referring to *Dial.* 38-39, 123.6, 125.5.

[30] *C. Cels.* 4.14 (μεταβολῆς δὲ ἐξ ἀγαθοῦ εἰς κακὸν καὶ ἐκ καλοῦ εἰς αἰσχρὸν καὶ ἐξ εὐδαιμονίας εἰς κακοδαιμονίαν καὶ ἐκ τοῦ ἀρίστου εἰς τὸ πονηρότατον). For the Platonic lineage of this passage see Bader's notes in *Alethes Logos*, ad loc.

[31] On the world as evil see *C. Cels.* 4.14 and the comments by Andresen, 1955, 94-96, showing *inter alia* the connections of Celsus' thought in this respect with that of other Middle Platonists. On evil as rooting in matter see *C. Cels.* 4.65 (ἐκ θεοῦ μὲν οὐκ ἔστι κακά, ὕλῃ δὲ πρόσκειται καὶ τοῖς θνητοῖς ἐμπολιτεύεται); for other Middle Platonists who associate matter or the body with evil see Witt, 1937, 121.

[32] *C. Cels.* 5.14; cf. 4.23 where, characterizing Christian thought, including its eschatology, as pitifully anthropocentric, Celsus compares Christians (and Jews) to self-important worms (or bats, ants, or frogs).

[33] *C. Cels.* 5.14. Celsus also attacks the Christian doctrine of the resurrection of the body in 8.49. For another attack by a Middle Platonist on the foolishness of belief in the resurrection of the body see Plutarch, *Rom.* 27-28.

[34]*1 Apol*. 18.6; also 19 (where Justin cites Jesus as saying, τὰ ἀδύνατα παρὰ ἀνθρώποιϲ δύνατα παρὰ θεῷ) and *Dial*. 69.

[35]The now classic exposition of this characterization is Andresen, 1952-53. A list of scholars who affirm Andresen's characterization, with or without qualification, is given in Hyldahl, 1966, 70, n. 61, to which may be added Daniélou, 1973, 107, 330-33, 346-47, and Chadwick, 1964-65, 280. Although one of Hyldahl's chief concerns is to distance Justin from Platonism, both before and after his conversion to Christianity, he acknowledges (pp. 68-69) that Andresen has demonstrated Middle Platonic influence on Justin. On pp. 43ff. Hyldahl traces some of the history of scholarship connecting Justin with Middle Platonism.

[36]That Justin was a follower of Platonism before his conversion is stated unambiguously in *2 Apol*. 12.1 (καὶ γὰρ αὐτὸϲ ἐγώ, τοῖϲ Πλάτωνοϲ χαίρων διδάγμασι, διαβαλλομένουϲ ἀκούων Χριστιανούϲ). Since the Platonism of Justin's day is generally characterized by scholars as "Middle Platonism," and Justin's writings have been shown to manifest various characteristic traits of Middle Platonism (see preceding note), scholars commonly (but not unanimously) identify the Platonism Justin professes in *2 Apol*. 12.1 (and *Dial*. 2.6, if one accepts it as an historical account; see n. 38 below) as Middle Platonism. It is somewhat incongruous of Hyldahl (1966) to acknowledge the first two points and even that Justin was a follower of Platonism before his conversion to Christianity (pp. 156-57, 175, 273, 292-93) and then to dispute that this Platonism was Middle Platonism (pp. 68-69, 273) or that Justin's attachment to this Platonism prior to conversion involved any systematic instruction in it (pp. 157, 273, 280, 288).

[37]Nock, 1956, 316, may be right in saying that some of Andresen's interpretations seem forced and that Platonists do not ignore history but, rather, find other things more important; the latter point Andresen demonstrates quite satisfactorily, it seems to me: history is important for Middle Platonists if a philosophical teaching can be found there (1955, 246ff.), and it is the latter which directs one's gaze from the transient to the transcendent (ibid., 263-75). Cf. Dörrie, 1957, 187, 194-95, who agrees that Middle Platonism had no real historical thought or philosophical reflection on history.

[38]Those viewing the account as substantially historical or as reflecting in some degree Justin's actual progress to Christianity include Nock, 1933a, 255, and 1954, 114; Chadwick, 1964-65, 280; Skarsaune, 1976, 67-68, 70-71; for others see Hyldahl's review of Justin research in the opening pages of 1966. Hyldahl argues at length that Justin's account of his conversion is a literary fiction and reviews earlier studies disputing its authenticity. Van Winden, whose 1971 study took its start from the preparation of a review of Hyldahl's book (see the comment in 1970, 309-10) and constitutes an extended dialogue with it, also considers the conversion account a literary fiction (see pp. 52, 63, 108-09, 118, 127) but qualifies and corrects much of the circular and confused reasoning in Hyldahl's otherwise valuable commentary on the opening chapters of the *Dialogue*. Young, 1971, unlike Hyldahl and more comprehensively than van Winden, whose work he did not have access to (see 1971, 5, n. 1), traces the argument in *Dial*. 1-8 step by step, concluding that the account is a

fiction; though acknowledging some indebtedness to Hyldahl, he, too, notes some major difficulties in Hyldahl's treatment.

[39]The retrospective nature of Justin's account of his conversion, which seems to have escaped Hyldahl, 1966, has often been noted, both by those who view the account as historical and by those who do not, e.g., Nock, 1933a, 255; Andresen, 1952-53, 160; Chadwick, 1964-65, 280; van Winden, 1971, 108-10, 127; Young, 1971, 201, 207; Waszink, 1965, 148; Skarsaune, 1976, 68, 70.

[40]Skarsaune, 1976, 70-71, suggests that the old man may indeed represent a historical figure; he points, e.g., to the casual mention of him in *Dial.* 23.3, where there is no literary motive for introducing him. On the modeling of the old man after Socrates see Young, 1971, 30, 32, 34, n. 2, 203-04, and Skarsaune, 1976, 69, and the secondary literature cited there.

[41]Young, 1971, 161-201, marshals evidence to show that while the old man may not wholly or precisely express Justin's viewpoint, neither does he express views in conflict with Justin's as attested outside the conversation with the old man. On Justin's activity as a Christian teacher see below, n. 71.

[42]Lofland and Stark, 1973, 38-40, with further bibliography, p. 40, n. 13.

[43]Nock, 1933a, 107ff.; the same texts are adduced by Hyldahl, 1966, 149ff. To these texts may be added Tatian, *Orat.* 29, with Hyldahl's commentary, 237, 240ff.

[44]Marrou, 1964, 285: "Some idea of the various philosophical doctrines was simply part of one's general culture: as can be seen in Galen's case, it could be quite the normal thing to make some sort of contact with the four main traditions of Hellenistic philosophy one after the other." Cf. Josephus' account (*Vita* 2) of his investigation of the three main "schools" in the Judaism of his day as well as of the hermit Bannus.

[45]*Dial.* 2.3: "I thought he was really not a philosopher" (μηδὲ φιλόσοφον οἰηθεὶς ὅλως). This rather typical criticism of philosophers is frequently satirized by Lucian, e.g., *Icaromenippus, The Dead Come to Life, Menippus*.

[46]*Dial.* 2.4-5; in demanding knowledge of music, astronomy, and geometry as prerequisite to the study of philosophy the Pythagorean is more "Platonist" (cf. Plato, *Rep.* 411Ef., 525Bff., 530Bf., referring to Pythagoreans) than the Platonist who becomes Justin's teacher.

[47]Lofland and Stark, 1973, 40-41; each potential convert "had come to a moment when old lines of action were complete, had failed or been disrupted, or were about to be so, and when they faced the opportunity (or necessity), and possibly the burden, of doing something different with their lives" (41). As in Justin's account, for many of the persons studied by Lofland and Stark the turning points had to do

with disappointments experienced in education (ibid.). Other examples of turning points in conversion accounts are given in James, 1958, e.g., 174, 177.

[48]The emendation ἦρε ("lifted me up"), for ἤρει, is proposed by Hyldahl, 1966, 146-47, followed by van Winden, 1971, 51, and may be preferable, but does not change the meaning much.

[49]*Dial.* 2.6; cf. *2 Apol.* 12.1, where Justin speaks of himself as "delighting in the teachings of Plato" (τοῖς Πλάτωνος χαίρων διδάγμασι).

[50]*Dial.* 3.5 (τὸ κατὰ τὰ αὐτὰ καὶ ὡσαύτως ἀεὶ ἔχον καὶ τοῦ εἶναι πᾶσι τοῖς ἄλλοις αἴτιον, τοῦτο δὴ ἐστιν ὁ θεός); I follow van Winden, 1971, 59-60, in retaining θεός in the text, pace Hyldahl, 1966, 185, et alii, though the preceding θεόν should probably be amended to τὸ ὄν. Cf. the similar assertions by Celsus: deity is unchangeable (*C. Cels.* 4.14), unaffected by hurt or pain (8.2), devoid of envy (8.21), the cause of all things and himself caused by none (6.65, ἐξ αὐτοῦ τά πάντα . . . ἐξ οὐδενὸς ὁ θεός).

[51]*Dial.* 3-5. Young, 1971, 74ff., gives a good exposition of the old man's refutation of the Platonic doctrine of the immortality of the soul and its kinship with deity.

[52]For the experience of warming or enkindling on the occasion of conversion to a new understanding or a new religion cf. Lk. 24.32, Augustine, *Conf.* 8.6 (*accendi*), and John Wesley's well-known report of his "heart strangely warmed." Young, 1971, 158, points to Plato, *Ep.* 7.341C-D, where the appropriation of Platonic teaching is compared to light ignited by a dancing fire (ἀπὸ πυρὸς πηδήσαντος ἐξαφθὲν φῶς). G. H. Williams (1974a, 22), pointing out that the expression Justin uses here in *Dial.* 8.1, πῦρ ἀνήφθη, is found also in his account of Jesus' baptism (*Dial.* 88.3), suggests that in *Dial.* 8.1 Justin "may well allude to his own baptismal conversion."

Suddenness of conversion is a common feature of conversion accounts, which are like miracle accounts in depicting dramatic divine intervention as the answer to a hopeless situation. Classic examples are, in early Christian literature, the conversion of Paul as reported in Acts, and, in pagan literature, the story of the drunken Polemo's conversion to philosophy (reported, e.g., in Diogenes Laertius, 4.16). For the modern period numerous examples are offered in James, 1958. Those conversion accounts that narrate struggles leading to the point of helplessness, when deity intervenes, strongly suggest that accounts which do not mention such struggles presuppose them. Prescinding from the question of the historicity of Justin's conversion account as a whole, the suddenness of the conversion and its seemingly flimsy basis do not in themselves necessarily "pass credibility," as Young asserts (1971, 33; see above, p. 145). Young himself (pp. 206-08, referring to *2 Apol.* 12-13) rightly points to events in Justin's spiritual odyssey that prepared him for his embrace of Christianity; cf. also Skarsaune, 1976, 66. Plato, though indicating that illumination comes ἐξαίφνης (*Ep.* 7.341C; *Symp.* 210E), also notes that it is preceded by long acquaintance with a subject (πολλῆς συνουσίας, τοῦ συζῆν, *Ep.* 7.341C) and by instruction (παιδαγωγηθῇ, *Symp.* 210E). James, 1958, 148, n. 8, 177-83, gives examples of accounts in which preparation is specifically

mentioned as preceding conversion and offers an interpretation
(pp. 188ff.), based on the psychology of his day. Ramsey's discussion
of "discernment" and "disclosures" (1963) is helpful in interpreting
the phenomenon of sudden conversion.

[53]Dial 8.1 (ταύτην μόνην εὕρισκον φιλοσοφίαν ἀσφαλῆ τε καὶ
σύμφορον).

[54]Ibid., 2.6 (ὀλίγου τε ἐντὸς χρόνου ᾤμην σοφὸς γεγονέναι, καὶ
ὑπὸ βλακείας ἤλπιζον αὐτίκα κατόψεσθαι τὸν θεόν).

[55]1 Apol. 2.1 (παραιτουμένους δόξαις παλαιῶν ἐξακολουθεῖν ἂν
φαῦλαι ὦσιν).

[56]The Christian reference of "truth" for Justin is seen in
passages such as Dial. 110.6 where Justin describes conversion to
Christianity as ἐπιγνῶναι τὴν ἀλήθειαν τοῦ θεοῦ (cf. Dial. 8.2: if
Trypho is concerned about salvation and trusts in God, he should come
to know the Christ of God, ἐπιγνόντι σοι τὸν Χριστὸν τοῦ θεοῦ) and
Dial. 8.1 where he characterizes Christianity as the only trustworthy
and beneficial philosophy (text in n. 53 above).

[57]Cf. also Dial. 2.1, where the old man's appearance is described as "not contemptible" (οὐκ εὐκαταφρόνητος) and his demeanor as
"gentle and inspiring respect" (πρᾶον καὶ σεμνόν).

[58]Dial. 3.7; cf. above, p. 85 . That Justin should address the
old man as "father" is, in view of the latter's age and in the light of
Greco-Roman parallels (see n. 5 of ch. 6 above) and insights from the
sociology of knowledge, not "bemerkenswert und überraschend," as
Hyldahl maintains (1966, 191).

[59]Hyldahl, 1966, 161ff., argues at length that the old man of
the opening chapters of Justin's Dialogue is not to be understood as a
Christian but as a barbarian foreigner (βάρβαρος ξένος) who embodies
barbarian wisdom over against Greek philosophy; van Winden, 1971, 117-
18; Young, 1971, 173-74; and Skarsaune, 1976, 69, point out some of the
difficulties and confusions in Hyldahl's argument.

[60]1 Apol. 61; cf., e.g., 61.1, ἀνεθήκαμεν ἑαυτοὺς τῷ θεῷ
καινοποιηθέντες διὰ τοῦ Χριστοῦ, ἐξηγησόμεθα).

[61]Dial. 8.2, where τελείῳ γενομένῳ may refer to initiation.

[62]1 Apol. 61.12; that the φωτισμός refers to prebaptismal
instruction in specific Christian credenda and not to illumination
gained through the act of washing is indicated by 61.13: the person
who is enlightened is washed (ὁ φωτιζόμενος λούεται) in the name of
Jesus Christ, crucified under Pontius Pilate, and in the name of the
Holy Spirit, who through the prophets proclaimed beforehand all things
pertaining to Jesus. In other contexts Justin speaks of being
enlightened by the name of Christ (φωτιζόμενοι, Dial. 39.1) or by Jesus
(πεφωτισμένους, Dial. 122.1; cf. 122.5) and of the ability to

understand (correctly) the utterances of the prophets as a gift from God (*Dial*. 92.1), i.e., as divine enlightenment; similarly, *Dial*. 119.1.

[63]See BAG, s.v. φωτίζω, and Conzelmann, 1969, 348-49. *1 Clem*. 36.2, though it does not connect enlightenment with baptism as Justin does in the next century, is similar in thought and terminology to *1 Apol*. 61.12: ἠνεῴχθησαν ἡμῶν οἱ ὀφθαλμοὶ τῆς καρδίας . . . ἡ ἀσύνετος καὶ ἐσκοτωμένη διάνοια ἡμῶν ἀναθάλλει εἰς τὸ φῶς.

[64]Cf. Justin's own description of his change in attitude to Christianity and pagan opinions of it as a result of his conversion, *2 Apol*. 13.1.

[65]See, e.g., Nilsson, 1967, 653ff.; 1961, 679ff.; or the well-known enlightenment and initiation of Lucius in Apuleius, *Metam*. 11.

[66]*Dial*. 35.2-4 and 82.1-3: Christians are persecuted and false prophets have arisen in their midst, as predicted by Jesus.

[67]Cf. the comments by Dibelius, 1966, 100. Chadwick's assertion, 1964-65, 281, that Justin is "sensitive to the standing weakness of all arguments from miracles: they only carry conviction to those who are actual eye-witnesses of the miracle, and evoke no wonder in those who are dependent on second-hand testimony," is misleading. In *Dial*. 69.6 (which Chadwick cites) Justin indeed says that through his works (a series of gospel miracles has just been cited) Jesus disconcerted his contemporaries into acknowledging him (διὰ τῶν ἔργων ἐδυσώπει τοὺς τότε ὄντας ἀνθρώπους ἐπιγνῶναι αὐτόν), but in 69.7 he states that these same contemporaries discounted those works by attributing them to φαντασία μαγική, a common ploy, as we have observed in ch. 4; that is, the eyewitnesses refuse to acclaim as miracle extraordinary phenomena worked by someone rejected by them. Justin, on the other hand, was not an eyewitness of those phenomena but yet is convinced--after entering the Christian fold--that they happened.

[68]*1 Apol*. 19.6 (above, p. 144). On the axiom in early Christianity see above, ch. 6, n. 8.

[69]See the summary of Justin's teachings in Chadwick, 1966, 18-19, and compare the contrast between the teachings of this emerging mainstream majority Christianity and those of Valentinian gnostics in Pagels, 1973, 114ff.; cf. also Holte, 1958, 113, 117ff., who characterizes Justin as "a theological traditionalist," and Chadwick's observation that "Justin's theology deserves the epithet 'popular' in the sense that he wants to stress the points prominent in the mind of ordinary Christian folk. . . ."

[70]*Dial*. 1.2 (cf. 9.2); Eusebius, *H.E.* 4.11.8. The majority of scholars (see Hyldahl, 1966, 102) conclude from these passages (and others dependent on them) that Justin wore a philosopher's robe both before and after conversion to Christianity. Hyldahl (94-95, 102-12) argues that the robe, like the conversion account, is fictitious; van Winden, 1971, 28, points out the incongruity of treating the account as fictitious and yet arguing from it to Justin's behavior. Young, 1971,

6, regards Justin's wearing of the robe as historical, an expression of his conviction that Christianity is the only safe and helpful philosophy (*Dial.* 8.1-2).

[71]*Act. Iust.* 3; text in J. C. T. Otto (ed.), *Iustini Philosophi et Martyris Opera Quae Feruntur Omnia*, Vol. 2, *Opera Iustini Addubitata* (Corpus Apologetarum Christianorum Saeculi Secundi, 3; Jena, [3]1879; reprinted, Wiesbaden: Martin Sändig, 1971). The characterization of Justin's school by Williams, 1974, 108, seems apt: it "was something between an advanced catechetical center and a one-man philosophical hall"--Justin's pupils and fellow martyrs say they received Christian instruction from their parents and further instruction from Justin (*Acta Iust.* 4); that the philosophical argumentation in Justin's writings presupposes his teaching activity seems clear and is hinted by *Dial.* 50.1 where Trypho attributes Justin's ready answers to his participation in earlier disputes.

[72]For incarnation and resurrection see the cogent arguments in Andresen, 1955, 363-65, 367-69; for virgin birth note the comparison to Perseus both by Celsus' Jew (*C. Cels.* 1.67) and by Justin's Trypho (*Dial.* 67.2) and in *1 Apol.* 22.4.

[73]Andresen's argument (1955) is summarized, with general approval, by Chadwick, 1966, 132, n. 59, who also lists further affinities noted by himself and by Nock, 1956, 316, n. 4.

[74]*C. Cels.* 4.2ff.; Celsus' arguments are summarized and their Stoic and Platonic bases indicated in Andresen, 1955, 91-96.

[75]Above, p. 140 and n. 18; for a detailed listing of passages in which Justin sees the logos as active in Jewish history see Andresen, 1955, 315-16; cf. also Daniélou, 1973, 161: "The incarnation represents only the high point of a permanent οἰκονομία" (a term Justin employs in a number of passages).

[76]Andresen, 1955, 312-25, rehearses Justin's argument here and cites the pertinent passages.

[77]*Dial.* 113.4-5; similarly *1 Apol.* 63.10 where Jesus is specifically called logos.

[78]On the exclusivity of Christian miracle claims in Justin's thought cf. above, p. 138. With Justin's use of the logos doctrine to evaluate non-Christian miracle claims compare his use of "Christ as *nomos*" to assess non-Christian *nomoi* (below, pp. 155-56) and, in general his use of Christian teaching as a measure of Greek philosophy; see Chadwick, 1966, 20-21; Holte, 1958, 162ff.; *2 Apol.* 9.4 is a succinct statement of Justin's stance.

[79]*C. Cels.* 5.52. Völker, 1928, 62 (where older literature is also cited), relates the designation of Jesus as ἄγγελος to passages in Hebrews, Hermas' *Shepherd*, and Justin's *Dialogue* (56; 59; 103 [lege 113?]; 126; 127). Andresen, 1955, 102-03, regards other passages as more pertinent: in *1 Apol.* 62.5ff. Justin calls the logos ἄγγελος,

while in *1 Apol.* 22.2 he speaks of Hermes (by way of comparison with Jesus the logos) as λόγον τὸν παρὰ τοῦ θεοῦ ἀγγελτικόν. "Der Christus rückt durch die Angelosvorstellung in die Nähe des Götterboten (λόγος ἀγγελτικός) und wird so den griechischen Lesern verständlich. Kein geringerer als Kelsos beweist, dass tatsächlich nur unter diesem Aspekt ein Grieche die Logoschristologie verstehen kann" (103).

[80] *C. Cels.* 6.1-7.58; cf. 1.21, where Celsus says that Moses derived his teaching (τοῦ λόγου) from the wise peoples and preeminent men (mentioned in 1.14, 16).

[81] *C. Cels.* 6.16 (Jesus and Plato); 6.12 (Heraclitus and Plato in connection with the Christian teaching that human wisdom is foolishness with God; Paul is not mentioned in the fragment as preserved by Origen).

[82] In the terminology employed in this study, the *nomoi* of a people belong to what we have called social and cultural worlds; cf. Berger's use of the term *nomos* in describing "the socially constructed world" (1969, 19ff.).

[83] Andresen, 1955, 189, n. 1, and 191, n. 6, cites passages illustrating the tie between *logos* and *nomos*, from Heraclitus to Neoplatonism and including Christian apologists.

[84] *Dial.* 11.2, "to us was given an eternal and ultimate *nomos*, Christ" (αἰώνιός τε ἡμῖν νόμος καὶ τελευταῖος ὁ Χριστὸς ἐδόθη); 11.4, Christ is "the new *nomos* and the new covenant" (ὁ καινὸς νόμος καὶ ἡ καινὴ διαθήκη). Christian pairing of logos and *nomos* is often accompanied by citation of Isa. 2.3-4 in the Greek rendering (νόμος καὶ λόγος κυρίου), a passage cited also by Justin, *1 Apol.* 39.1 (*Dial.* 11.3 cites instead Isa. 51.4, which has νόμος . . . καὶ ἡ κρίσις); see the sources cited in Andresen, 1955, 191, n. 6; 326.

[85] *1 Apol.* 53.5 (τὰ πάλαια); *Dial.* 63.5 (τῶν παλαιῶν πατρῴων ἐθῶν); 119.5, Christians have departed from the kind of life in which they lived wickedly, following the customs (τὰ κοινά) of the other inhabitants of the earth; 123.5, they have turned away from the old wickedness of each race's way of life (ἀπὸ τῆς παλαιᾶς κακῆς ἑκάστου γένους πολιτείας).

[86] *C. Cels.* 5.34, a long quotation from Herodotus, is an extended statement of this; briefer statements, with the people and the terminology indicated, are, *for Jews*: 2.1 (τὸν πάτριον νόμον); 2.4a (*idem*): 5.25, line 2 in Bader's edition (νόμους); 5.41, line 2 (τὸν ἴδιον νόμον); *for Romans*: 8.69, line 2 (τῶν νενομισμένων); *generally*: 5.25, line 4 (τὰ πάτρια), line 11 (τὰ ἐξ ἀρχῆς κατὰ τόπους νενομισμένα); 8.75 (νόμων). In speaking of Christians Celsus seems to ascribe ancestral customs to them (5.33, πατρίων νόμων; 8.28, line 1, πάτριον), though the ascriptions may be rhetorical, for the sake of the argument (the first reference is in the form of a question, the second in a protasis).

[87] *C. Cels.* 8.75; cf. 5.25, lines 10-11: to do away with the customs established in each place from of old is impious (οὐχ ὅσιον).

[88]This is not stated in so many words by Celsus, but it may be inferred from passages in which he faults Christians for seeking to win converts (see below, p. 157), rather than acknowledging the legitimacy of each people's *nomos*, and from 8.72 which, whatever the difficulties connected with the passage (cf. Andresen, 1955, 190-92, 200, with Chadwick, *Contra Celsum*, 507, n. 1), clearly dismisses as impossible the hope of uniting all peoples in one *nomos* (εἰς ἕνα συμφρονῆσαι νόμον).

[89]Above, p. 107; *C. Cels.* 1.28 (Mary gave birth to Jesus "in secret," σκότιον).

[90]Jesus' birth was made public through the visit of the magi with Herod (*Dial.* 78) and can be verified from the census lists made under Quirinius (*1 Apol.* 34.2); his birth from a virgin was predicted so that it might be believed when it came to pass (*1 Apol.* 33.1; *Dial.* 84.2) and can now be publicly established from the same prophecies (*Dial.* 71.3).

[91]This is the way I understand Celsus' quotation of Herodotus quoting Pindar in *C. Cels.* 5.34, lines 40-41 (νόμον πάντων βασιλέα), in relation to Celsus' affirmation, on the one hand, of the distinctive nature of each people's *nomos* and, on the other, of τὸν κοινὸν νόμον (1.1).

[92]Cf. *C. Cels.* 5.20, where Origen reports that Celsus asserted that Zeno, Stoicism's founder, was wiser than Jesus. Because of the brevity of Origen's statement, Bader (*Alethos Logos*, 21) and other editors and students of Celsus have refrained from designating it as a passage from the *Alethes Logos*; Origen says enough, however, to show (as Andresen observes, 1955, 27) that "Kelsos im Kampf gegen das Christentum auch die Stoa beschwört" and "das er im seiner Abwehr sich nicht von dem schulphilosophischen Gegensatz des Platonikers zum Stoiker bestimmen lässt"; Andresen (pp. 26-27, 66, 72-77, 92-94) gives examples of such use by Celsus of Stoic teaching. Of these, *C. Cels.* 4.5a, b, the assertion that divine interruption of the cosmic order would produce chaos (above, p. 153), is pertinent to our study; it is a stock Stoic teaching but is attested also in the Middle Platonist, Maximus of Tyre (Andresen, 92-93).

[93]*Dial.* 2.1, where the old man asserts the oneness of ἐπιστήμη in contrast to the divisions within Greek philosophy.

[94]*2 Apol.* 10.8 (χειροτέχναι, ἰδιῶται); 12.4 (οἰκέτας); the theme of the inclusiveness of Christianity occurs in other patristic sources as well; see the second-century sources cited in Chadwick, 1964-65, 292, n. 2, and cf. further the sources cited in Holte, 1962, 161.

Notes to Chapter 10

[1]See the references to contemporary events and persons in
Lucian, *Alex*. 27, 30, 36, 48, 57. In *Alex*. 48 Lucian refers to Marcus
Aurelius as θεόſ, suggesting that he was dead and thus providing a
terminus a quo for Lucian's piece, which was written after Alexander's
death (*Alex*. 59-60), and an *ad quem* for that death. Cf. Cumont, 1887,
6 and n. 4; Caster, 1938, 6.

[2]Caster, 1938, 30-32, gives a detailed exposition of Lucian's
literary technique in the epiphany scene.

[3]In *Alex*. 15, 18, 49 Lucian describes the crowds in Abonoteichos. One derives another indication of the size of the clientele
from the annual income of 70,000-80,000 drachmas reported by Lucian
(*Alex*. 23) which, at the rate of about two drachmas per inquiry and
allowing for exaggeration by Lucian and for the fact that some persons
submitted more than one inquiry (*Alex*. 23), would have meant anywhere
from 10,000 to 20,000 inquirers annually.

[4]Lucian sometimes speaks of Abonoteichos as in Pontus (*Alex*.
10, 17, 25, 41, 43) and sometimes as in Paphlagonia or of Paphlagonians
(9, 11, 17, 39, 45). The confusing usage derives from mingling of
earlier (Paphlagonia) and later (Pontus) place names; see Cumont, 1887,
11, n. 2, and W. Smith, 1873, s.v. "Paphlagonia" and "Pontus."

[5]Highet, 1962, 42. Nilsson, 1961, 561, points out that
Lucian's choice of subjects for satire is dictated largely by classical
models.

[6]Baldwin, 1973, 103 (an old scholarly tradition); see Helm,
1927, 1770.3ff.; 1772.15ff. (P. Bayle).

[7]*Somn*. 10-15; *Bis acc*. 27-28; *Apol*. 12, 15; *Pisc*. 25. The
study of rhetoric prepared him for the duties he encountered when he
forsook rhetoric for a public office; cf. *Apol*. 12. In view of
passages such as *Apol*. 3, where Lucian speaks of public presentation of
one of his pieces, and *Her*. 7, where Lucian speaks of ceasing to give
declamations (τῶν ἐπιδείξεων πεπαυμένῳ), it is difficult to know what
Bowersock means when he says of Lucian that "there is no sign that he
had ever been a rhetorical performer" (1969, 114).

[8]These commitments would seem to be signaled in his portrait of
Denomax, his ideal philosopher, whom Lucian portrays as eschewing
thaumaturgy (*Dem*. 23, 25, 27), as living an exemplary (1-10) and
unpretentious life (5, 48, 58), as devoted to truth (3) and possessed
of a quick mind and ready wit--all traits that are foils to characteristics that Lucian satirizes in other writings.

[9]Reitzenstein, 1963, 38; he postulates ὑπομνήματα of Alexander
(though without offering any evidence of such), alongside the inscriptions mentioned by Lucian (if *Alex*. 43 refers to an inscription:
χρυσοῖſ γράμμασιν γεγραμμένον), but fails to take account of passages

that do in fact mention written sources (*Alex.* 4, 10). Caster, 1938, 19, 92, rightly labels the hypothesis very doubtful and fragile.

[10]Caster, 1938, 92, observes that the supposedly secret happenings in Lucian's account are narrated in much too great detail to be based on actual sources.

[11]Hippolytus, *Ref.* 4.29, describes the preparation of eggs for use by magicians (cf. *Alex.* 13); 4.34, on the unsealing and resealing of scrolls, corresponds at several points with *Alex.* 21; Alexander's autophone (*Alex.* 26) is paralleled in *Ref.* 4.28.41.

[12]Bithynia and Thrace (*Alex.* 18), Galatia (18, 30), Ionia, Cilicia, and Pamphylia (30), Rome (30-31), "the whole Roman Empire" (2, 36).

[13]The fact that Lucian reports no opposition to Alexander among the populace of Abonoteichos is made plausible by the renown and commerce the oracle brought to the town. At times Lucian's obloquy suggests only lower-class adherents (*Alex.* 17), but in other places he mentions persons of power and wealth (27, 30-32, 48).

[14]Two Latin inscriptions attest knowledge of the cult as far north and west as Dacia; *Corpus Inscriptionum Latinarum* 3, nos. 1021, 1022; texts in Caster, 1938, 96.

[15]Coins relating to the cult were minted under Geta (emperor with his brother Caracalla, 211-12 C.E.), Alexander Severus (emperor 222-35 C.E.), Gordian (emperor 238-44 C.E.), Gallus (emperor 251-53 C.E.); reproductions in Caster, 1938, preceding p.1; discussions, ibid., 96-97; Weinreich, 1921, 150; descriptions, discussions, and several reproductions in Babelon, 1900, 1-30.

[16]Contrast the examples of epistemological skepticism cited in ch. 3.2.1 above with the less-critical stance of second-century writers (e.g., Phlegon, above, ch. 4, n. 4; pp. 104-05) and in Nock, 1933a, 91, 128, and R. M. Grant, 1952, 41-77.

[17]*Corpus Inscriptionum Latinarum* 14, no. 3601; text and discussion in Cumont, 1887, 16, n. 2, and Caster, 1938, 52-53; another inscription (*CIL* 14, no. 4244) contains essentially the same data (Caster, 1938, 53, n. 2).

[18]According to accounts in the *Scriptores Historiae Augustae*, Septimus Severus, later emperor, married the daughter of a priest, on the advice of an oracle; she became the Empress Julia Domna; see Lampridius, *Sev. Alex.* 5.4, Spartianus, *Sev.* 3.9; cf. M. G. Williams, 1902, 254-60.

[19]Caster, 1938, 79-83, analyzing Lucian's polemic in *Adv. ind.*, *Pseudol.*, and *Rhet. praec.*

[20]Ibid., 87ff. In pillorying the rhetoric of his day, Lucian, *Rhet. praec.* 22, lists, as common practice, lying, slander, and plausible defamation (διαβολαὶ πιθαναί); was Lucian immune to this infection?

[21]*Alex.* 22, 55 (προφήτηϛ); 24 (ὑποφήτηϛ). Alexander's gift of prophecy is traced to his possession of the soul of Pythagoras (40).

[22]Nock, 1928, 162. Cf. *Alex.* 22: the god will grant favors if and when Alexander asks it of him.

[23]Caster, 1938, 42, 95, who derives the idea but not the term from Nock, 1928, 162.

[24]Alexander was fathered by Podaleirius, the son of Asclepius (*Alex.* 39), and is therefore related to Glycon, who is the new Asclepius and the grandson of Zeus (18); on his mother's side he is descended from Perseus, a son of Zeus (11); his golden thigh, bared in the mysteries (40), is a sign of divinity (cf. Nock, 1928, 164; Weinreich, 1921, 147); by Selene, the moon, he fathers his daughter (39).

[25]Among them: oracles, including contemporary ones (*Alex.* 29); the Asclepius traditions; Greek mythology and genealogy (*Alex.* 18, 38-39; for a possible connection of Alexander's ritual of his amour with Selene with the myth of Endymion and Selene and later ritual and religious interpretations of the myth see Cumont, 1922, 209-10, and Caster, 1938, 62-63); Sabazios cult (*Alex.* 15; cf. Weinreich, 1921, 133, and Caster, 1938, 15, 28-30); Pythagoreanism (*Alex.* 4, 33, 40; cf. Cumont, 1922, 206-07); Eleusinian mysteries (*Alex.* 38-40; cf. Caster, 1938, 61).

[26]There was ample precedent for ritual celebrations at Asclepius sanctuaries; in Asia Minor, e.g., at Pergamum (Edelstein, *Asclepius* 1, T. 570), Lampsacus (T. 572), Ephesus (T. 573).

[27]E.g., corporal punishment (*Alex.* 45), ostracism (46). On "therapy" see above, p. 85.

[28]Even the obscurity and ambiguity of the oracles did not preclude patent errors.

[29]*Alex.* 57; on Timocrates of Heraclea and his students see Philostratus, *Vit. Soph.*, Life of Polemo, and Caster, 1938, 75-76.

[30]The ritual kiss in Alexander's inmost circle is comparable to the ritual kiss in Christian communities; there is nothing, however, that would correspond to Christian baptism. Christian rituals of exclusion of the unworthy, like that mentioned in 1 Cor. 5 (above, p. 85) or Mt. 18.15-20, or perhaps connected with the eucharist (*Did.* 9.5; Justin, *1 Apol.* 66.1), compare in intent and result with Alexander's exclusion from the mysteries (*Alex.* 38); cf. Caster, 1938, 61.

[31]Basic studies of the *Shepherd* of Hermas, *Mand.* 11 (§43 in the GCS numbering), include Dibelius, 1923, 536-43; Opitz, 1960, 111-15; and especially now the commentary by Reiling, 1973, who cites other literature. My citations of the Greek text of *Mand.* are from M. Whittaker (ed.), *Der Hirt des Hermas* (Die apostolischen Väter, 1; GCS, 48; Berlin: Akademie Verlag, 1956); this text is printed (without apparatus) in Reiling, 177-79.

[32]The unstable Christians come "as to a diviner" (ὧς ἐπιμάντιν, 11.2; for the reading μάντιν rather than μάγον see Reiling, 1973, 34, n. 3); see also 11.4: μαντεύονται ὧς καὶ τὰ ἔθνη. See Reiling, 35, for other examples of Christian texts in which μάντιϛ refers to pagan diviners.

[33]Epictetus, *Disc.* 2.7. For other examples from pagan literature which report on diviners who tell inquirers what they want to hear, and persons who criticize such diviners, see Aune, 1978, 103-04. For examples from Jewish sources see Reiling, 1973, 36.

[34]11.9 (συναγωγὴν ἀνδρῶν δικαίων τῶν ἐχόντων πίστιν θείου πνεύματοϛ); 11.14 (συναγωγὴν πλήρη ἀνδρῶν δικαίων ἐχόντων πνεῦμα θεότητοϛ).

[35]11.9 (τοῦ πνεύματοϛ τοῦ προφητικοῦ . . . τῷ πνεύματι τῷ ἁγίῳ). For the distinction in Hermas between τὸ πνεῦμα τὸ θεῖον and τὸ πνεῦμα τὸ προφητικόν or τὸ ἅγιον see Reiling, *Hermas*, 112ff., 124.

[36]For this interpretation of ὁ ἄγγελοϛ τοῦ πνεύματοϛ τοῦ προφητικοῦ ὁ κείμενοϛ ἐπ' αὐτῷ (11.9) see Dibelius, 1923, 541 ad loc., and Reiling, 1973, 106-09, 124.

[37]This is a plausible interpretation of ἰταμόϛ . . . καὶ ἀναιδὴϛ καὶ πολύλαλοϛ in 11.12; see Reiling, 1973, 91-96.

[38]Cf. 11.8, where Hermas says the true prophet οὐδὲ καταμόναϛ λαλεῖ.

[39]On the label "diabolic" as a dissolution of miracle see above, ch. 3.2.5.

[40]This is a common notion in early Christianity; cf. above, p.139, and the sources cited in Reiling, 1973, 69, n. 4.

[41]Older studies of Montanism are cited in Aland, 1960b. Among the recent studies are Freeman-Granville, 1954; H. Kraft, 1955; Ford, 1956; Aland, 1955, 1960a; von Campenhausen, 1963, 198-210; R. M. Grant, 1970, ch. 9. In citing the Montanist oracles I employ the numbering of Aland's "Echte Orakel" (1960a, 143-46); Aland gives the corresponding numberings of the sayings in Bonwetsch, 1881, 197-200, and de Labriolle, 1913, 37-105.

[42]Scholars are still divided on whether to date the beginnings of the Montanist movement to the reign of Antoninus Pius, around 156 (thus Epiphanius), or to the latter part of the rule of Marcus Aurelius, around 172 (thus Eusebius); on either dating the movement is contemporaneous with the Asclepius cult at Abonoteichos (see n. 1 above). My concern is with this earlier Montanism in Asia Minor as attested by Eusebius' sources in *H.E.* 5.16ff. and certain passages in other Christian writers, rather than with the later manifestations of the movement.

[43]Lucian, *Alex.* 14, 43; the promised Paraclete speaks through Montanus (Aland, nos. 1, 2), and opponents refer (pejoratively) to Montanist prophecy as "new" (νέα; Anonymous, in Eusebius, *H.E.* 5.16.4; Serapion, in *H.E.* 5.19.2) while denying its divine inspiration.

[44]*Alex.* 12-14; Anonymous, in *H.E.* 5.16.7, 9; 5.17.2. The prophets' foreknowledge or knowledge of secret thoughts and deeds is perhaps also to be related to ecstasy; see Schepelern, 1929, 149-50.

[45]In *Alex.* 25 and 38 Christians are grouped with atheists (ἄθεοι).

[46]Aland, nos. 6, 12, 13; on Montanist eschatology see Schepelern, 1929, 28ff.; H. Kraft, 1955; Aland, 1960a.

[47]Cf. Aland, no. 13; Maximilla says, "After me there will not be another prophet, but consummation" (μετ' ἐμὲ προφήτηϛ οὐκέτι 'ἔσται, ἀλλὰ συντέλεια).

[48]Mentioned are Ardabau (Anonymous, in *H.E.* 5.16.7), which may be an apocalyptic place name, and Pepuza and Tymion (Apollonius, in *H.E.* 5.18.2; cf. Epiphanius, *Pan.* 49.1.2-3 = Aland, no. 12) between which may lie the mountain where the consummation would take place; see H. Kraft, 1955, 260-61.

[49]Examples in Anonymous, in *H.E.* 5.16.16, 17; Apollonius, in *H.E.* 5.18.13; Serapion, in *H.E.* 5.19.3.

[50]Anonymous, in *H.E.* 5.16.22; Apollonius, in *H.E.* 5.18.5-7.

[51]These would have consisted of sayings of the Montanist prophets (Anonymous, in *H.E.* 5.16.17), letters (Apollonius, in *H.E.* 5.18.5), and apologies (Anonymous, in *H.E.* 5.17.1); see further Schepelern, 1929, 13-14.

[52]Apollonius, in *H.E.* 5.18.4, 6, 11, accuses the Montanist prophets of taking gifts and says (5.18.2) that Montanus appointed administrators of Montanist assets (πρακτῆραϛ χρημάτων) who looked after collection of offerings (προσφορῶν) and paid Montanist preachers (ὃ σαλάρια χορηγῶν τοῖϛ κυρύσσουσιν αὐτοῦ τὸν λόγον).
The Montanists may have set other persons apart in positions of authority or honor. The term used by Anonymous (in *H.E.* 5.16.14), ἐπιτρόποϛ, should perhaps be taken literally, to denote an

administrative officer. Since παρθένοϳ as a designation of Montanist prophetesses was evidently not to be taken literally (see Apollonius, in *H.E.* 5.18.3), it may have denoted an order (cf. Ignatius, *Smyrn.* 13.1)--or the term may have been used by Montanists in imitation of tradition regarding earlier prophetesses (cf. Anonymous, in *H.E.* 5.17.3, and Acts 21.9) or in recognition of the prophetesses' encratism, or all of these.

[53]Dissolution of marriages and regulations for fasting, reported by Apollonius (in *H.E.* 5.18.2-3) of the Montanists, would accord with Montanist preparation for the eschaton and for reception of divine revelations; though mainstream Christianity prized virginity and asceticism, it differed from Montanism in the extent to which it made these obligatory or obligatory for all Christians. See the sources and discussion in Bonwetsch, 1881, 82-99; Schepelern, 1929, 53-59; H. Kraft, 1955, 258-59; Ford, 1956, 148.

[54]Schepelern's investigation (1929, 80-160) of the relation between Phrygian cults and Montanism discloses a number of affinities, not only with Phrygian religion, however, but also with Greco-Roman religions generally, including Judaism and Christianity; for early Montanism (our concern here) he found important differences between it and Phrygian cults (e.g., 129-30) and came to a generally negative conclusion (160) regarding early Montanism as an offshoot of those cults. Subsequent studies have investigated the Jewish and Christian roots of Montanism: see H. Kraft, 1955; Ford, 1956; Aland, 1960a.

[55]On this function of conflict see Coser, 1956, esp. chs. 2-3.

[56]Anonymous, in *H.E.* 5.16.7, 9; 5.17.2-4; Apollonius, in *H.E.* 5.18.3; Serapion, in *H.E.* 5.19.3.

[57]The vocabulary used by Eusebius' anti-Montanist sources in reporting encounters between Montanists and anti-Montanists is divided between the language of exorcism (Anonymous, in *H.E.* 5.16.8, ἐπιτίμων καὶ λαλεῖν ἐκώλυον; Serapion, in *H.E.* 5.19.3, ἐκβαλεῖν) and debate (διελέγχειν, Anonymous, in *H.E.* 5.16.4, 16, 17, and Apollonius, in *H.E.* 5.18.13; ἐλέγχειν, Anonymous in *H.E.* 5.16.17, 20). The latter imply doctrinal differences, as do the pejorative characterizations of the content of Montanist prophecy (Anonymous, in *H.E.* 5.16.3-4, 7-10, 12, 14) or writings (Apollonius, in *H.E.* 5.18.5). But any such differences are not specified, suggesting there were none or none worth mentioning; had there been any, it is unlikely Eusebius would have failed to bring to the notice of his readers this additional evidence of what he repeatedly refers to as the Montanist error.

[58]The ecstatic speech of the Montanist prophets and the attendant claim that the Christian deity spoke through them stands in the tradition of early Christian prophecy; in *H.E.* 5.17.3 Anonymous is at pains to refute any such claim to continuity (cf. also 5.16.7); cf. further von Campenhausen, 1963, 208-09.

[59]On the defiance see Anonymous, in *H.E.* 5.16.4, 5.16.16-17; Apollonius, in *H.E.* 5.18.13; Apollinarius, in *H.E.* 5.19.3. The size of

the Montanist following is suggested by the number of church leaders, from various localities, involved in the attacks on the Montanist prophets.

[60] For Montanist scriptures see n. 51 above; for interpretation of earlier Christian scriptures along Montanist lines see, e.g., Aland, 1960a, 131-32.

[61] Contrast the Montanist oracles with second-century Christian apologies such as Justin's or Athenagoras'.

[62] The Anonymous has a less dour view; noting the non-appearance of the wars and disturbances predicted by Maximilla, he sees God at work, not in such disturbances, but in the peace granted to Christians (in *H.E.* 5.16.19). On the desire of church leaders who opposed Montanism to avoid confrontation with the Empire see H. Kraft, 1955, 269-70, and R. M. Grant, 1970, 135-38.

[63] This trajectory may be traced through Luke-Acts with its stress on the Spirit's guidance of the apostles and its phrase, paradigmatic for subsequent generations--"it has seemed good to the Holy Spirit and to us" (Acts 15.28)--through Ignatius and the Pastorals to the first synods, convened in opposition to the Montanist threat to such views of divine authority and authentication; cf. Kretschmar, 1966, 1-11. On the superseding of prophets by teachers see von Campenhausen, 1963, 210ff.

[64] Cf. H. Kraft, 1955, 267-68; the strength of the episcopate in larger cities tended to fend off Montanism there (R. M. Grant, 1970, 141).

[65] For example, the continuity in the Christian and pagan practice of incubation has been documented by Hamilton, 1906.

Note to Appendix A

[1] See above, ch. 3, p. 36.

Note to Appendix B

[1] See above, ch. 5, p. 73.

Notes to Appendix C

[1]See above, ch. 6, p. 89.

[2]In Kant, 1913, 187. Whereas Kant's rather tolerant view of the Gospel miracles may have been directed against his older contemporary Reimarus (cf. Bohatec, 1938, 540), Lessing's similar interpretation of them as necessary to win acceptance for the new and alien teachings of Christianity is directed against Semler's reply to Reimarus; see Lessing in Chadwick, 1957, 55, and Chadwick's comments, p. 40.

Notes to Appendix D

[1]Cf. the definition of second-century gnosticism worked out by the conference on the origins of gnosticism, held in Messina, Sicily, in 1966, reproduced in Bianchi, 1966, 157, and reprinted in Bianchi, 1967b, xxvi-xxix.

[2]*C. Cels.* 5.61c (ἔστωσαν δέ τινεϛ καὶ ἐπαγγελλόμενοι εἶναι Γνωστικοί).

[3]*Adv. h.* 1.25.6 (Harvey ed., 1.20.4): "Gnosticos se autem vocant."

[4]*Ref.* 5.6.4 (μετὰ δὲ ταῦτα ἐπεκάλεσαν ἑαυτοὺϛ γνωστικούϛ, φάσκοντεϛ μόνοι τὰ βάθη γινώσκειν) and 5.11.1 (οἱ Νααϲηνοὶ . . . ἑαυτοὺϛ γνωστικοὺϛ ὀνομάζοντεϛ); cf. 5.8.29, where the Naasenes is reported as referring the conclusion of the parable of the sower to "gnostics," i.e., to themselves (τουτ''ἔστι, φησιν· οὐδείϛ τούτων τῶν μυστηρίων ἀκροατὴϛ γέγονεν εἰ μὴ μόνοι <οἱ> γνωστικοὶ τέλειοι).

[5]*Adv. h.* 1.11.1, 5 (Harvey ed., 1.5.1, 3); 3.11.2 (3.11.7); 4.33.3 (4.51.3).

[6]Ibid., 1.11.1 (Harvey ed., 1.5.1): ὁ μὲν γὰρ πρῶτοϛ, ἀπὸ τῆϛ λεγομένηϛ γνωστικῆϛ αἱρέσεωϛ τὰϛ ἀρχὰϛ εἰϛ ἴδιον χαρακτῆρα διδασκαλείου μεθαρμόσαϛ Οὐαλεντῖνοϛ).

[7]Ibid. 2. Pref. 1 (2. Pref.), "qui sunt ab eo Gnostici"; 4.33.3 (4.51.3), "Judicabit [scil. discipulus spiritalis (4.51.1 = Harvey ed., 4.50)] autem et vaniloquia pravorum Gnosticorum, Simonis eos Magi discipulos ostendens."

[8]Ibid. 2.13.8 (2.16.4), where Irenaeus says his polemic is applicable also to Basilideans "et adversus reliquos Gnosticos"; 2.31.1 (2.48.1), where he states that his polemic against Valentinians applies also to followers of Saturninus, Basilides, Carpocrates "et reliquos Gnosticorum, qui eadem similiter dicunt," and goes on to say that what he has said about emanations, aeons, etc., applies also to Basilides

"and all who are falsely called gnostics" ("et omnes qui falso cognominantur agnitores"); 4.6.4 (4.11.3), where Irenaeus regards as sharing an erroneous view of the Maker of heaven and earth Marcion, Valentinus, Basilides, Carpocrates, Simon, "or the remaining, falsely so-called gnostics" ("aut reliquis falso cognominatis Gnosticis"); 4.35.1 (4.57.1), where Irenaeus directs his polemic against Valentinians "et reliquos falsi nominis Gnosticos."

[9]Ibid. 2 Pref. 1 (2. Pref.): "Diximus quoque multitudinem eorum, qui sunt ab eo Gnostici, et differentias ipsorum, et doctrinas, et successiones annotavimus. . . ."

[10]*Vita Plot.* 16.11: βιβλίον ὅπερ "Πρὸς τοὺς Γνωστικούς" ἐπεγράψαμεν.

[11]Ibid. 24 (πρὸς τοὺς κακὸν τὸν δημιουργὸν τοῦ κόσμου καὶ τὸν κόσμον κακὸν εἶναι λέγοντας).

Notes to Appendix E

[1]See above, p. 135. Still useful as an extended treatment of Plotinus' treatise against the gnostics and its cultural setting is Schmidt, 1901.

[2]A phrase like τοὺς ἤδη ἐγνωκότας (*Enn.* 2.9.15.22-23) may refer to persons who lay claims to special knowledge, i.e., gnostics. This is as close as Plotinus comes to using the label. 2.9.13.10, where Plotinus sets forth educated and harmonious gnosis (πεπαιδευμένης . . . καὶ ἐμμελοῦς γνώσεως)--i.e., traditional Greek gnosis--as a foil to gnostics' fear of the celestial spheres, may be an oblique reference to the gnostics' supposed gnosis. Throughout I cite the *Enneads* and Porphyry's *Vita* from P. Henry and H.-R. Schwyzer (eds.), *Plotini Opera*, Vol. 1, *Porphyrii Vita Plotini*. *Enneades I-III*, and Vol. 2, *Enneades IV-V*. *Plotiniana Arabica ad Codicum Fidem Anglice Vertit Geoffrey Lewis* (Museum Lessianum, Series Philosophica, 33, 34; Paris: Desclée de Brouwer, and Brussels: L'Édition Universelle, 1951, 1959).

[3]*Enn.* 2.9.14.36-37: Plotinus leaves it to his readers to investigate the gnostics' other views by reading (ἀναγινώσκουσιν; scil. τὰς γραφὰς αὐτῶν).

[4]*Enn.* 2.9.14.4-8 (γοητείας καὶ θέλξεις καὶ πείσεις . . . καὶ ἤχους καὶ προσπνεύσεις καὶ σιγμοὺς τῆς φωνῆς καὶ τὰ ἄλλα, ὅσα ἐκεῖ μαγεύειν γέγραπται).

[5]*Enn.* 2.9.14.15-17 (ἐπαγγελλόμενοι σεμνότεροι μὲν ἂν εἶναι δόξαιεν παρὰ τοῖς πολλοῖς, οἱ τὰς παρὰ τοῖς μάγοις δυνάμεις θαυμάζουσι).

[6]*Enn.* 2.9.14.43 (τὰ δὲ ἄλλα τῷ τοιούτῳ παραβάλλειν).

[7]*Enn.* 2.9.14.43-44 (ἐναντιώτατα . . . διὰ πάντων).

[8]*Enn.* 2.9.14.8-9 (πῶς φωναῖς τὰ ἀσώματα;). Cf. *Enn.* 4.6.1 where Plotinus argues against theories of perception that posit a material impression of an external object on the soul.

[9]*Enn.* 2.9.14.15-18 (τοὺς μέντοι εὖ φρονοῦντος οὐκ ἂν πείθοιεν; the rest of the text is given in n. 5 above).

[10]The gnostics' general dependence on Plato and other "divine men": Plato, *Enn.* 2.9.6.10-11 (ὅλως γὰρ τὰ μὲν αὐτοῖς παρὰ τοῦ Πλάτωνος εἴληπται); "divine men" (τοὺς θείους ἄνδρας, 2.9.6.36), designated as "those more ancient persons" (ἐκείνων ὡς παλαιοτέρων, 2.9.6.37), including Plato (2.9.6.42); cf. 2.9.6.5-7, the gnostics contrive neologisms to commend their own school (τῆς ἰδίας αἱρέσεως) to others as though they (the gnostics) had no connection with "the ancient Greek school" (τῆς ἀρχαίας Ἑλληνικῆς). Specifically the gnostics are dependent on Plato for their teachings on "ascents from the cave" (ἀναβάσεις ἐκ τοῦ σπηλαίου, 2.9.6.8-9; cf. Plato, *Rep.* 7.514Aff.), "the judgments and the rivers in Hades and transmigrations" (αἱ δίκαι καὶ οἱ ποταμοὶ οἱ ἐν Ἅιδου καὶ αἱ μετενσωματώσεις, 2.9.6.13; cf. Plato, *Phaed.* 111Dff.), "immortality of the soul, the noetic cosmos, the first deity, the necessity for the soul to escape association with the body, separation from the body, flight from becoming to being--these things are posited in Plato" (ταῦτα γὰρ κείμενα παρὰ τῷ Πλάτωνι, 2.9.6.39-42); the gnostics "have heard Plato many times blaming the body for the sorts of impediments it offers to the soul" (2.9.17.2-3); the plurality of noetic entities (being, nous, demiurge, soul) in the gnostics' teaching derives from the *Timaeus* (*Enn.* 2.9.6.14-19; Plotinus cites from *Tim.* 39E 7-9).

[11]*Enn.* 2.9.6.55-57 (τὰ δ' ὕστερον τούτοις παρ' ἐκείνων ληφθέντα, προσθήκας δέ τινας οὐδὲν προσηκούσας εἰληφότα).

[12]*Enn.* 2.9.6.11-12 (ὅσα καινοτομοῦσιν . . . ταῦτα ἔξω τῆς ἀληθείας εὕρηται).

[13]*Enn.* 2.9.6.58-62 (γενέσεις καὶ φθορὰς εἰσάγοντες παντελεῖς καὶ μεμφόμενοι τῷδε τῷ παντὶ καὶ τὴν πρὸς τὸ σῶμα κοινωνίαν τῇ ψυχῇ αἰτιώμενοι καὶ τὸν διοικοῦντα τόδε τὸ πᾶν ψέγοντες καὶ εἰς ταὐτὸν ἄγοντες τὸν δημιουργὸν τῇ ψυχῇ καὶ τὰ αὐτὰ πάθη διδόντες, ἅπερ καὶ τοῖς ἐν μέρει).

[14]*Enn.* 2.9.4.2ff.: against the gnostic idea that the visible world resulted from the moral failure (σφαλεῖσαν) of soul, Plotinus argues that a soul that declined (ἔνευσε) would forget the things of the higher, noetic world (τῷ ἐπιλελῆσθαι δηλόντι τῶν ἐκεῖ); "if it forgot, how could it function as a craftsman, for whence does it fashion except from the things it beheld in that world?" (εἰ δὲ ἐπελάθετο, πῶς δημιουργεῖ; πόθεν γὰρ ποιεῖ ἢ ἐξ ὧν εἶδεν ἐκεῖ). The unspoken premise here is Plato's *Timaeus* where the demiurge fashions this world after the model of the living being (τὸ ζῷον; *Tim.* 30C-D; 39E). Similarly 2.9.6.24-25 (the gnostics give a false account of Plato's teaching on the way in which the world was fashioned).

[15]*Enn.* 2.9.4.22ff.: persons who find many vexatious things (πολλὰ . . . δυσχερῆ) in the visible world rate it too highly, thinking it should be the same as the noetic world rather than an image of it (εἰ ἀξοῦσι τὸν αὐτὸν εἶναι τῷ νοητῷ, ἀλλὰ μὴ εἰκόνα ἐκείνου)--even so, what more beautiful image of that world (καλλίων εἰκὼν ἐκείνου) could there be than this one? (Cf. *Tim.* 29D-30B.)

[16]*Enn.* 2.9.4.1-2: the gnostics' assertion that the soul made the world after it had shed its wings errs in referring this passage (Plato, *Phaedrus* 246C) to the soul of the All (ἡ τοῦ παντός) (rather than to individual souls). They err, too, in saying their own soul and that of the worst persons is divine (θείαν) but yet denying to the celestial bodies a share in the immortal soul (μὴ τῆς ἀθανάτου κεκοινωνηκέναι) (2.9.5.8-14).

[17]*Enn.* 2.9.6.16-21: the gnostics, not understanding (οὐ συνέντες) Plato (*Tim.* 39E 7-9), interpret him as positing three nous's; they think, moreover, that, according to Plato (κατὰ Πλάτωνα), the purposing nous (τὸν δὲ διανούμενον) is the demiurge, although they are far from knowing who the demiurge is and frequently identify soul with the demiurge.

[18]*Enn.* 2.9.18.14-16 (δεῖ δὲ μένειν μὲν ἐν οἴκοις σῶμα ἔχοντας κατασκευασθεῖσιν ἀπὸ ψυχῆς ἀδελφῆς ἀγαθῆς).

[19]*Enn.* 2.9.17.4-5 (ἐχρῆν ταύτην περιελόντας τῇ διανοίᾳ ἰδεῖν τὸ λοιπόν, σφαῖραν νοητήν).

[20]*Enn.* 2.9.15.21, nothing in this world is considered beautiful by gnostics (τούτων γὰρ οὐδὲν αὐτοῖς καλόν); 2.9.16.1-2, they despise the world and the gods and the other beautiful things in it (τὸ καταφρονῆσαι κόσμου καὶ θεῶν τῶν ἐν αὐτῷ καὶ τῶν ἄλλων καλῶν); 2.9.5.59, they find fault with the universe (text in n. 13 above); the celestial regions do not produce evil persons here below (2.9.8.34-35) and the cosmic spheres (ταῖς τοῦ κόσμου σφαίραις) are not to be feared, despite their fiery bodies (2.9.13.9ff.).

[21]Plotinus praises the celestial spheres for their beauty and for their contribution to the functioning of the All (*Enn.* 2.9.13.14-20; cf. Plato, *Tim.* 38C-E, where the celestial bodies perform their appointed tasks of marking off time), for their souls (*Enn.* 2.9.13.12-13; cf. *Tim.* 38E and *Laws* 10.898D), and for the reference that the stars' symmetry, good order, and form (εἶδος) have to their sources (*Enn.* 2.9.16.49-55; cf. *Laws*, where Plato infers to deity from the earth, sun, stars, and the ordering of seasons [10.886A] and from the orderly motion of the cosmos [10.896Dff.]).

[22]*Enn.* 2.9.13.9-10 (τί γὰρ φοβερὸν ἔχουσιν αὗται, ὡς φοβοῦσι τοὺς ἀπείρους λόγων καὶ πεπαιδευμένης ἀνηκόους καὶ ἐμμελοῦς γνώσεως;).

[23]Cf. the observations by H. C. Puech, R. Harder, and H. Dörrie in the discussion following the presentation by Puech, 1960, 183, 185, 190; Dodds, 1970, 25-26; Quispel, 1974, 160.

²⁴*Enn.* 2.9.11.21-22 (δι' ἀλαζονείαν καὶ τόλμαν ποιεῖ).

²⁵*Enn.* 4.7.13.11 (according to Porphyry, *Vita* 4.24-25, this treatise is the second in chronological order); 5.1.1.1-5 (chronologically the tenth treatise), where Plotinus says souls forgot the father because of evil rooting in audacity, birth, the assertion of differentiation, and the desire to be self-possessing (ἡ τόλμα καὶ ἡ γένεσιϛ καὶ ἡ πρώτη ἑτερότηϛ καὶ τὸ βουληθῆναι δὲ ἑαυτῶν εἶναι); cf. 4.8.5.9-10 (chronologically the sixth treatise), where Plotinus says the soul's descent may be marred by undue zeal (προθυμίᾳ . . . πλείονι).

²⁶Dodds, 1970, 26; cf. further Dodds, 1960, 22: Plotinus maintains "the rational Hellenic tradition against the pessimistic otherworldliness which found its fullest expression in Gnosticism." Cf. also R. Harder, who observes that Hellenistic cosmology, which perceived the cosmos as one great *polis*, is revived in Plotinus; his sharpest criticism of the gnostics is directed against their assertion that the world is evil. "Es ist ihm bewusst dass die Rettung der griechischen Bildung an die Wiedereinsetzung des Kosmos in seine Würde hängt. Diese Würde ist die des Notwendigen: ein klares, rational durchgeformtes Bild gegenüber Wirrnis und Willkür" (Harder, 1960a, 301-02; the quotation is from p. 302).

²⁷Even in the relatively late treatise (chronologically, number 33) against the gnostics, however, a tension persists between viewing any procession from the One or Nous as a declension (as gnostics said) and as good (as the *Timaeus* said); the latter we have noted (above, p. 199); for the former cf. *Enn.* 2.9.13.32-33, "there [in the higher world] soul is worse than Nous and Nous is less than something else" (καὶ γὰρ ἐκεῖ ψυχῇ χεῖρον νοῦ καὶ οὗτοϛ ἄλλου ἔλαττον). Armstrong, 1966, *ad loc.*, cites as further instances the late treatises 3.8.8.35-36 (chronologically, number 30) and 3.7.11.15ff. (chronologically, number 45).

²⁸*Enn.* 2.9.9.52ff.: "senseless persons" (ἄνθρωποι ἀνόηται) are persuaded by gnostics who tell them that they will be better, not only than humans, but also than gods, and that they are sons of God whereas those whom they honored as sons, according to tradition (ἐκ πατέρων), are not; the gnostics also tell them that even without exerting themselves they are better than heaven. *Enn.* 2.9.16.16-17: the gnostics say there is providential care of themselves alone (λέγουσι γὰρ αὐτῶν προνοεῖν αὖ μόνον). On such narcissism Plotinus comments (*Enn.* 2.9.9. 47-51) that to suppose there is room alongside God only for oneself is like flying in dreams and deprives one of the possibility of becoming divine, so far as that is possible for a human soul. Cf. Celsus' ridicule of what he regards as Jewish and Christian narcissism, *C. Cels.* 4.23 (above, p. 113).

²⁹*Enn.* 2.9.9.52ff. (see preceding note); 2.9.16.1ff.; 2.9.18. 17ff.

³⁰*Enn.* 2.9.15.18-20: seeing that they reject traditional virtue there remains for them only pleasure and what is not held in common with other persons and a concern for their needs alone (ὥστε αὐτοῖϛ καταλείπεσθαι τὴν ἡδονὴν καὶ τὸ περὶ αὐτοὺϛ καὶ τὸ οὗ κοινὸν

πρὸϛ 'άλλουϛ ἀνθρώπουϛ καὶ τὸ τῆϛ χρείαϛ μόνον). The foil to Plotinus'
perception of gnostic irresponsibility is his own civic consciousness
and influence, as reported by Porphyry and evidenced in his own affirmation of civic virtues; see the references and discussion in Harder,
1960b, 280ff.; Armstrong, 1967, 202-03, 229. Cf. also Harder's observations, 1960a, 302: "Scharfsichtig erkennt Plotin den tiefsten Mangel
der Gegner, ihr 'Nur mit sich selbst beschäftigt sein,' der Hang zum
'Nicht Gemeinsamen'; diese gemeinschaftswidrige Isoliertheit hindert
sie am Anerkennen, am Geltenlassen, führt sie zur Verachtung der andern
Wesen, welche Hybris ist. Plotin lehrt dagegen in neuem Sinne
Weltbürgertum. . . ."

[31]*Enn.* 2.9.15.12-13 (πάνταϛ νόμουϛ τοὺϛ ἐνταῦθα ἀτιμάσαϛ καὶ
τὴν ἀρετὴν τὴν ἐκ παντὸϛ τοῦ χρόνου ἀνηυρημένην).

[32]*Enn.* 2.9.15.15-17: "gnostic teaching does away with self-
control and with the righteousness implanted by mores and brought to
fulfillment by reason and by training"; in short, it nihilates the
things "by which a person might become morally excellent" (ἀνεῖλε τό τε
σωφρονεῖν καὶ τὴν ἐν τοῖϛ 'ήθεσι σύμφυτον δικαιοσύνην τὴν τελειουμένην
ἐκ λόγου καὶ ἀσκήσεωϛ καὶ 'όλωϛ καθ''ἃ σπουδαῖοϛ 'άνθρωποϛ 'ὰν γένοιτο).

[33]*Enn.* 2.9.5.8-9, gnostics say the souls of the most worthless
persons (τῶν φαυλοτάτων ἀνθρώπων) are immortal and divine; 2.9.18.17-18,
they call the most worthless persons (τοὺϛ φαυλοτάτουϛ) "brothers."

[34]*Enn.* 2.9.8.38-39 (ταῦτα τίϛ 'ὰν μὴ ἔκφρων γεγενημένοϛ
ἀνάσχοιτο;). Cf. also 2.9.9.52ff. (n. 28 above), where Plotinus calls
persons who fall for such assertions "senseless" (ἀνόηται).

[35]*Enn.* 2.9.10.3-4 (αἰδὼϛ γάρ τιϛ ἡμᾶϛ ἔχει πρόϛ τιναϛ τῶν
φίλων, οἱ τούτῳ τῷ λόγῳ ἐντυχόντεϛ πρότερον 'ἢ ἡμῖν φίλοι γενέσθαι).

[36]*Enn.* 2.9.10.5 (οὐκ οἶδ''ὅπωϛ ἐπ' αὐτοῦ μένουσι).

[37]*Enn.* 2.9.10.7-11 (ἀλλ' ἡμεῖϛ πρὸϛ τοὺϛ γνωρίμουϛ, οὐ πρὸϛ
αὐτοὺϛ λέγοντεϛ--πλέον γὰρ οὐδὲν 'ὰν γίγνοιτο πρὸϛ τὸ πείθειν αὐτοὺϛ--
'ίνα μὴ πρὸϛ αὐτῶν ἐνοχλοῖντο οὐκ ἀποδείξειϛ κομιζόντων--πῶϛ γὰρ;--ἀλλ'
ἀπαυδιζομένων, ταῦτα εἰρήκαμεν).

[38]This is true whether or not the gnostics whom Plotinus knew
professed some form of Christianity; on the construing of Porphyry's
syntax in *Vita* 16 (are the 'άλλοι, αἱρετικοί to be included among τῶν
Χριστιανῶν?) and the identification of the objects of Plotinus' polemic
in *Enn.* 2.9 see H. C. Puech, 1960.

Notes to Appendix F

[1]A non-Lucianic attestation of Alexander has been found by some
in Athenagoras, *Legatio pro Christianis* 26 (usually dated ca. 177-80

C.E., i.e., contemporary with Lucian's account), which tells of a
statue and cenotaph of "Alexander" at Parium in Troas (i.e., in Asia
Minor, a few hundred miles from Abonoteichos); see Cumont, 1887, 42,
and Weinreich, 1921, 135. Others refer the "Alexander of Athenagoras'
text to Priam's son Paris, who is the referent of the Homeric citation
(*Il*. 3.39) in the text, was called "Alexander" because of his valor,
and was said to have lived at Parium for a time; see A. Puech, 1912, 196,
n. 2; Caster, 1938, 95-96; Nock, 1928, 160, n. 3.

[2]Weinreich, 1921; see also the comments, anticipating this
essay, in 1914, 598-99.

[3]Nock, 1928, 160, n. 4. Nock discusses Alexander also in
1933a, 93-97.

[4]An exception is A. Stein, 1924. Stein identifies various
characters and some of the events in Lucian's account from numismatic,
inscriptional, and literary evidence; he betrays no knowledge of
Weinreich's study and acknowledges (p. 257, n. 2) that he had not had
access to Cumont, 1887.

ABBREVIATIONS
AND
REFERENCES

1. ABBREVIATIONS[1]

Bader, *Alethes Logos*	R. Bader (ed.), *Der Alethes Logos des Kelsos*
BAG	W. Bauer, *A Greek-English Lexicon of the New Testament*. . . . .; trans. by W. F. Arndt and F. W. Gingrich
Chadwick, *Contra Celsum*	H. Chadwick (trans.), *Contra Celsum*
Edelstein, *Asclepius* 1, 2	E. J. and L. Edelstein, *Asclepius: A Collection and Interpretation of the Testimonies*, Vols. 1, 2
E.T.	English translation
Foerster, *Gnosis* 1, 2	W. Foerster (ed.), *Gnosis: A Selection of Gnostic Sources*, Vols. 1, 2
FRLANT	Forschungen zur Religion und Literatur des Alten und Neuen Testaments
GCS	Die griechischen christlichen Schriftsteller der ersten drei Jahrhunderte
Giannini, *Paradoxographorum*	A. Giannini (ed. and trans.), *Paradoxographographorum Graecorum Reliquiae*
Hennecke-Schneemelcher, *New Testament Apocrypha* 1, 2	E. Hennecke and W. Schneemelcher (eds.), *New Testament Apocrypha*, Vols. 1, 2
JBL	*Journal of Biblical Literature*
LS	C. T. Lewis and C. Short, *A New Latin Dictionary*
LSJ	H. G. Liddell, R. Scott, H. S. Jones, and R. McKenzie, *A Greek-English Lexicon*

Pease, Cicero, *De div.*	A. S. Pease (ed.), *M. Tulli Ciceronis De Divinatione Libri Duo*
PGM	K. Preisendanz (ed. and trans.), *Papyri Graecae Magicae: Die griechischen Zauberpapyri*
P. Oxy.	*Oxyrhynchus Papyri*, edited and translated by B. P. Grenfell and A. S. Hunt
PW	G. Wissowa et alii (eds.), *Paulys Realencyclopädie der classischen Altertums-wissenschaft*
RVV	Religionsgeschichtliche Versuche und Vorarbeiten
SVF 1, 2, 3	H. F. A. von Arnim (ed.), *Stoicorum Veterum Fragmentum*, Vols. 1, 2, 3
T.	*See* Edelstein, *Asclepius*
TU	Texte und Untersuchungen zur Geschichte der altchristlichen Literatur
TWNT	*Theologisches Wörterbuch zum Neuen Testament*

---

[1]Full data on these works will be found in the References.

2. ANCIENT AND MEDIEVAL SOURCES

Acta Apostolorum Apocrypha. Vol. 1. Edited by R. A. Lipsius. Leipzig, 1891. Vols. 2/1 and 2/2. Edited by M. Bonnet. Leipzig, 1898, 1903. Reprinted, Hildesheim and New York: G. Olms Verlag, 1972.

Aelius Aristides. *Aristides.* Edited by W. Dindorf. 3 vols. Leipzig, 1829. Reprinted, Hildesheim: Olms, 1964.

_____. *Aelii Aristidis Smyrnaei Quae Supersunt Omnia.* Edited by B. Keil. Vol. 2. Berlin: Weidmann, 1898; reprinted, 1958.

Albinos. *Didaskalikos.* In *Platonis Dialogi secundum Thrasylli Tetralogias Dispositi.* Edited by C. F. Hermann. Vol. 6. Leipzig: Teubner, 1902. Pp. 152-89.

Ambrose. *Hexaemeron.* In *Opera*, Part 1. Edited by K. Schenkl. Corpus Scriptorum Ecclesiasticorum Latinorum, 32/1. Vienna and Prague: Tempsky, 1896.

Apelles. *Syllogisms.* In A. Harnack, *Marcion: Das Evangelium vom fremden Gott. Eine Monographie zur Geschichte der Grundlegung der katholischen Kirche. Neue Studien zu Marcion.* Leipzig: Hinrichs, [2]1924 (reprinted, Darmstadt: Wissenschaftliche Buchgesellschaft, 1960). Pp. 404-32. English translation in R. M. Grant (ed. and trans.), *Second Century Christianity: A Collection of Fragments.* Translations of Christian Literature, Series 6, Select Passages. London: SPCK, 1957.

Apocrypha and Pseudepigrapha. *See* Charles (ed. and trans.), *Apocrypha and Pseudepigrapha.*

Apologists. *See* Goodspeed (ed.), *Die ältesten Apologeten.*

Apostolic Fathers. *See* Bihlmeyer (ed.), *Die apostolischen Väter.*

Apuleius. *De deo Socratis.* In *Apulei Platonici Madaurensis Opera Quae Supersunt.* Vol. 3, *De Philosophia Libri.* Edited by P. Thomas. Leipzig: Teubner, 1908.

_____. *Florida.* Edited by R. Helm. Leipzig: Teubner, 1910.

_____. *Metamorphoseon Libri XI.* Edited by R. Helm. Leipzig: Teubner, 1913.

_____. *Pro se de Magia Liber (Apologia).* Edited by R. Helm. Leipzig: Teubner, 1912.

Ps.-Aristotle. *Mirabiles auscultationes*. In Giannini (ed. and trans.), *Paradoxographorum Graecorum Reliquiae*. Pp. 221-313.

Arnobius. *Adversus Nationes Libri VII*. Edited by A. Reifferscheid. Corpus Scriptorum Ecclesiasticorum Latinorum, 4. Vienna: Gerold, 1875.

Asclepius texts. *See* Edelstein, *Asclepius*, and Cartlidge and Dungan (eds. and trans.), *Documents*.

Athenagoras. *Legatio and De Resurrectione*. Edited and translated by W. R. Schoedel. Oxford Early Christian Texts. Oxford: Clarendon Press, 1972.

Augustine. *In Iohannis Evangelium Tractatus*. *Aurelii Augustini Opera*, Part 8. Edited by R. Willems. Corpus Christianorum, Series Latina, 36. Turnholt, Belgium: Typographi Brepols Editores Pontifici, 1954.

Barnabas. *See* Bihlmeyer (ed.), *Die apostolischen Väter*.

Basil the Great. *Hexaemeron*. In *Homélies sur l'Hexaéméron*. Edited and translated by S. Giet. Sources chrétiennes, 26. Paris: Editions du Cerf, 1949.

Bihlmeyer, K., editor. *Die apostolischen Väter: Neubearbeitung der Funkschen Ausgabe*. 2d ed., with a supplement by W. Schneemelcher. Part 1, *Didache, Barnabas, Klemens I und II, Ignatius, Polykarp, Papias, Quadratus, Diognetbrief*. Tübingen: J. C. B. Mohr (Siebeck), 1956.

Cartlidge, D. R., and D. L. Dungan, editors and translators. *Documents for the Study of the Gospels*. Cleveland et al.: Collins, 1980.

Celsus. *Der Alethes Logos des Kelsos*. Edited by R. Bader. Tübinger Beitrage zur Altertumswissenschaft, 33. Stuttgart and Berlin: Kohlhammer, 1940. *See also* under Origen.

Charles, R. H., editor and translator. *The Apocrypha and Pseudepigrapha of the Old Testament in English with Introductions and Explanatory Notes to the Several Books*. Vol. 2, *Pseudepigrapha*. Oxford: Clarendon Press, 1913.

Cicero. *De divinatione libri duo*. Edited by A. S. Pease, *M. Tulli Ciceronis De Divinatione Libri Duo*. Darmstadt: Wissenschaftliche Buchgesellschaft, 1963. Originally published in *University of Illinois Studies in Language and Literature* 6 (1920), 161-500, and 8 (1923), 153-474.

1 and 2 Clement. *See* Bihlmeyer (ed.), *Die apostolischen Väter*.

Clement of Alexandria. *Extraits de Théodote*. Edited and translated by F. Sagnard. Sources chrétiennes, 23. Paris: Les Editions du Cerf, [2]1970.

_____. *Le Pédagogue*. Edited [2] and translated by C. Mondésert and H. I. Marrou. Sources chrétiennes, 108.

_____. *Protrepticus*. In *Clemens Alexandrinus*. Vol. 1. Edited by O. Stählin. GCS, 12. Leipzig: Hinrichs, 1905.

Clement of Alexandria. *Stromata*. In *Clemens Alexandrinus*. Vols. 2, 3. Edited by O. Stählin. GCS, 15, 17. Leipzig: Hinrichs, 1906, 1909.

Ps.-Clement. *Die Pseudoklementinen*. Edited by B. Rehm and F. Paschke. Vol. 2, *Rekognitionen* (in Rufinus' translation). GCS, 51. Berlin: Akademie Verlag, 1965.

Didache. *See* Bihlmeyer (ed.), *Die Apostolischen Väter*.

Diels, H., and W. Kranz, editors and translators. *Die Fragmente der Vorsokratiker: griechisch und deutsch*. 3 vols. Berlin: Weidmann, [6]1951-1952.

Dittenberger, W., editor. *Sylloge Inscriptionum Graecarum*. 4 vols. Leipzig, [3]1915-24. Reprinted, Hildesheim: Olms, 1960.

Edelstein, E. J., and L. *Asclepius: A Collection and Interpretation of the Testimonies*. 2 vols. Publications of the Institute of the History of Medicine, Johns Hopkins University, 2d series: Texts and Documents, 2. Baltimore: Johns Hopkins University Press, 1945.

Epicurus. *Epicurea*. Edited by H. Usener. Leipzig: Teubner, 1887.

Epiphanius. *Ancoratus und Panarion*. Edited by K. Holl. GCS, 25, 31, 37. Leipzig: Hinrichs, 1915, 1922, 1933.

Ps.-Eratosthenes. *Pseudo-Eratosthenis: Catasterismi*. Edited by A. Olivieri. Mythographi Graeci, 3/1. Leipzig: Teubner, 1897.

Etymologicon Magnum seu verius lexicon saepissime vocabulorum origines indagans ex pluribus lexicis scholastis et grammaticis anonymi euisdam opera concinnatum. Edited by T. Gaisford. Oxford: Academicus, 1848.

Euripides. *Fabulae*. Vol. 2, *Supplices, Hercules, Ion, Troiades, Electra, Iphigenia, Taurica*. Edited by G. Murray. Scriptorum Classicorum Bibliotheca Oxoniensis. Oxford: Clarendon Press, [3]1913.

Eusebius. *Eusebius Werke*. Vol. 8/1, *Praeparatio Evangelica*. Edited by K. Mras. GCS 43/1. Berlin: Akademie Verlag, 1954.

Exegesis on the Soul. *See* Nag Hammadi treatises.

4 Ezra. *See* Charles (ed.), *Apocrypha and Pseudepigrapha*. Also G. H. Box (trans. and ed.), *The Ezra-Apocalypse. Being Chapters 3-14 of the Book Commonly Known as 4 Ezra (or 2 Esdras)*. London: Pitman, 1912.

Fiebig, P., editor. *Antike Wundergeschichten zum Studium der Wunder des Neuen Testaments*. Kleine Texte für Vorlesungen und Übungen, 79. Bonn: Marcus und Weber, 1911. 2nd ed. edited by G. Delling, *Antike Wundertexte*. Berlin: de Gruyter, 1960.

Foerster. *Gnosis*. *See* Nag Hammadi treatises.

Galen. *Galen on Jews and Christians*. By R. Walzer. Oxford Classical and Philosophical Monographs. London: Oxford University Press, 1949.

Giannini, A., editor and translator. *Paradoxographorum Graecorum Reliquiae.* Classici Greci e Latini, Sezione Testi e Commenti, 3. Milan: Istituto Editoriale Italiano, 1965.

Goodspeed, E. J., editor. *Die ältesten Apologeten: Texte mit kurzen Einleitungen.* Göttingen: Vandenhoeck & Ruprecht, 1914.

Gnostic Sources. *See* Völker (ed.), *Quellen,* and Nag Hammadi treatises.

Gospel of Peter. See Swete (ed.), *ΕΥΑΓΓΕΛΙΟΝ,* and Hennecke and Schneemelcher (eds.), *New Testament Apocrypha.*

Gospel of Philip. See Nag Hammadi treatises and Hennecke and Schneemelcher (eds.), *New Testament Apocrypha.*

Greek inscriptions. *See* Dittenberger (ed.), *Sylloge.*

Hennecke, E., and W. Schneemelcher, editors. *New Testament Apocrypha.* English translation edited by R. M. Wilson. Vol. 1, *Gospels and Related Writings.* Vol. 2, *Writings Relating to the Apostles; Apocalypses and Related Subjects.* Philadelphia: Westminster, 1963, 1965.

Hermas. *Die Apostolischen Väter.* Vol. 1, *Der Hirt des Hermas.* Edited by M. Whittaker. GCS, 48. Berlin: Akademie Verlag, 1956.

_____. *Le Pasteur.* Edited and translated by R. Joly. Sources chrétiennes, 53. Paris: Editions du Cerf, ^{2}1968.

Herodotus. *Herodoti Historiae.* Edited by C. Hude. Scriptorum Classicorum Bibliotheca Oxoniensis. 2 vols. Oxford: Clarendon Press, ^{3}1927.

Hippocratic treatises. *Oeuvres complètes d'Hippocrate.* Edited and translated by É. Littré. 10 vols. Paris, 1839-61. Reprinted, Amsterdam: Hakkert, 1962. Also, Loeb Classical Library: *Hippocrates.* 4 vols. Edited and translated by W. H. S. Jones. London: Heinemann, and Cambridge: Harvard University Press, 1923, 1923, 1928, 1931.

Hippolytus. *Hippolytus Werke.* Vol. 3, *Refutatio Omnium Haeresium.* Edited by P. Wendland. GCS, 26. Leipzig: Hinrichs, 1916.

Hypostasis of the Archons. See Nag Hammadi treatises.

Iamblichus. *Les mystères d'Égypte.* Edited and translated by E. des Places. Collection des Universités de France. Paris: Association Guillaume Budé, 1966.

Ignatius. *See* Bihlmeyer (ed.), *Die apostolischen Väter.*

Irenaeus. *Libros quinque adversus Haereses.* 2 vols. Edited by W. W. Harvey. Cambridge: Cambridge University Press, 1857. *Sancti Irenaei episcopi Lugdunensis quae supersunt omnia.* 2 vols. in 4. Edited by A. Stieren. Leipzig: Weigel, 1848-49.

Justin Martyr. *Apologies* 1 and 2. *Dialogue with Trypho.* *See* Goodspeed (ed.), *Die ältesten Apologeten.*

Justin Martyr. *Iustini Philosophi et Martyris Opera Quae Feruntur Omnia.* Edited by J. C. T. Otto. Vol. 2, *Opera Iustini Addubitata.* Corpus Apologetarum Christianorum Saeculi Secundi, 3. Jena, [3]1879. Reprinted, Wiesbaden: Martin Sändig, 1971.

Lactantius. *Opera Omnia.* 3 vols. in 2. Edited by S. Brandt and C. Laubmann. Corpus Scriptorum Ecclesiasticorum Latinorum, 19, 27. Vienna and Prague: Tempsky, and Leipzig: Freytag, 1890, 1897.

Letter of Eugnostus. See Nag Hammadi treatises.

Lucretius. *De rerum natura.* Edited and translated by C. Bailey. 3 vols. Oxford: Clarendon Press, 1947.

Magical texts. *See* Preisendanz, *Papyri Graecae Magicae.*

Maximus of Tyre. *Philosophumena.* Edited by H. Hobein. Leipzig: Teubner, 1910.

Masurillo, H. A., editor. *The Acts of the Pagan Martyrs: Acta Alexandrinorum.* Oxford: Clarendon, 1954.

Nag Hammadi treatises. *Exegesis on the Soul. Gospel of Philip. Hypostasis of the Archons. Letter of Eugnostus. Treatise on the Resurrection.* English translations in W. Foerster (ed.), *Gnosis: A Selection of Gnostic Texts,* Vol. 2, *Coptic and Mandean Sources.* English translation edited by R. M. Wilson. Oxford: Clarendon Press, 1974. Also in J. M. Robinson (ed.), *The Nag Hammadi Library in English.* Translated by Members of the Coptic Gnostic Library Project of the Institute for Antiquity and Christianity. San Francisco et al.: Harper and Row, 1977.

New Testament apocrypha. *See Acta Apostolorum Apocrypha* (ed. by Lipsius) and Hennecke and Schneemelcher (eds.), *New Testament Apocrypha.*

Origen. *Origen: Contra Celsum.* Translated and edited by H. Chadwick. Cambridge: Cambridge University Press, 1965.

_____. *Contre Celse.* Edited and translated by M. Borret. Sources chrétiennes, 132, 136, 147, 150. Paris: Éditions du Cerf, 1967-69.

_____. *Origenes Werke.* Vols. 1-2. Edited by P. Koetschau. GCS, 2, 3. Leipzig: Hinrichs, 1899.

Oxyrhynchus Papyri, The. Part [Vol.] 11. Edited and translated by B. P. Grenfell and A. S. Hunt. London: Oxford University Press, 1915. Text 1381.

Paradoxographa. See Giannini (ed. and trans.), *Paradoxographorum Graecorum Reliquiae.*

Phlegon. *De mirabilibus.* In Giannini (ed. and trans.), *Paradoxographorum Graecorum Reliquiae.* Pp. 169-219.

Photius. *Lexicon.* Edited by S. A. Naber. 2 vols. Leiden: E. J. Brill, 1865.

Pindar. *Carmina cum fragmentis.* Edited by C. M. Bowra. Oxford: Clarendon Press, 1935.

Plato. *Platonis Dialogi secundum Thrasylli Tetralogias dispositi.* Edited by M. Wohlrab and C. F. Hermann. 5 vols. Leipzig: Teubner, 1904-11.

Plotinus. *Plotini Opera.* Edited by P. Henry and H.-R. Schwyzer. Vol. 1, *Porphyrii Vita Plotini. Enneades I-III.* Vol. 2, *Enneades IV-V. Plotiniana Arabica ad Codicum Fidem Anglice Vertit Geoffrey Lewis.* Museum Lessianum, Series Philosophica, 33, 34. Paris: Desclée de Brouwer, and Brussels: L'Édition Universelle, 1951, 1959.

Pollux. *Pollvcis Onomasticon.* Edited by E. Bethe. Lexicographi Graeci, 9. Leipzig: Teubner, 1900.

Polybius. *Historiae.* Edited by F. Hultsch. Vol. 3. Berlin: Weidmann, 1870.

Porphyry. *Vita Plotini.* In Henry and Schwyzer (eds.), *Plotini Opera,* Vol. 1, q.v.

Preisendanz, K., editor and translator. *Papyri Graecae Magicae: Die griechischen Zauberpapryi.* 2 vols. Leipzig and Berlin: Teubner, 1928, 1931.

Pre-Socratics. *See* Diels-Kranz.

Pseudepigrapha. *See* Charles, *Apocrypha and Pseudepigrapha.*

Ps.-Quintilian. *Quintiliani quae feruntur Declamationes XIX Maiores.* Edited by G. Lehnert. Leipzig: Teubner, 1905.

Servius Grammaticus. *Servii Grammatici qui feruntur in Vergilii Carmina Commentarii.* Edited by G. Thilo and H. Hagen. 3 vols. Leipzig: Teubner, 1881, 1884, 1887, 1902.

Sibylline Oracles. *Die Oracula Sibyllina.* Edited by J. Geffcken. GCS, 8. Leipzig: Hinrichs, 1902.

Solinus, Gaius Iulius. *Collectanea Rerum Memorabilium.* Edited by T. Mommsen. Berlin: Weidmann, 1895.

Sophia Jesu Christi. English translation by D. M. Parrott in J. M. Robinson (ed.), *The Nag Hammadi Library in English.* Translated by Members of the Coptic Gnostic Library Project of the Institute for Antiquity and Christianity. San Francisco et al.: Harper & Row, 1977.

Stoic fragments. See von Arnim (ed.), *Stoicorum Veterum Fragmenta.*

Suidae Lexicon: Graece et Latine. Edited by G. Bernhardy. 2 vols. Halle and Braunschweig: Bruhn, 1843, 1853.

Swete, H. B., editor. *ΕΥΑΓΓΕΛΙΟΝ ΚΑΤΑ ΠΕΤΡΟΝ: The Akhmîm Fragment of the Apocryphal Gospel of St. Peter.* London and New York: Macmillan, 1893.

Tatian. *Oratio ad Graecos. See* Goodspeed, *Die ältesten Apologeten.*

Tertullian. *Adversus Marcionem.* Edited and translated by E. Evans. 2 vols. Oxford: Clarendon Press, 1972.

_____. *Adversus Valentinianos.* Edited by A. Kroymann. In *Tertulliani Opera.* Part 2, *Opera Montanistica.*

Corpus Christianorum, Series Latina, 2. Turnholt, Belgium: Typographi Brepols Editores Pontifici, 1954. Pp. 751-78.

Tertullian. *De anima.* Edited with introduction and commentary by J. H. Waszink. Amsterdam: Meulenhoff, 1947.

_____. *Q. Septimi Florentis Tertulliani Apologeticus.* The text of Oehler annotated with an introduction by J. E. B. Mayor. Translation by A. Souter. Cambridge: Cambridge University Press, 1917.

_____. *De Idolotria.* Edited by A. Reifferscheid and G. Wissowa. In *Tertulliani Opera.* Part 2, *Opera Montanistica.* Corpus Christianorum, Series Latina, 2. Turnholt, Belgium: Typographi Brepols Editores Pontifici, 1954. Pp. 1094-1124.

_____. *Scorpiace.* Edited by A. Reifferscheid and G. Wissowa. In *Tertulliani Opera.* Part 2, *Opera Montanistica.* Corpus Christianorum, Series Latina, 2. Turnholt, Belgium: Typographi Brepols Editores Pontifici, 1954. Pp. 1067-98.

_____. *Tertullian's Treatise on the Resurrection.* The text edited with an introduction, translation, and commentary by E. Evans. London: SPCK, 1960.

Theodotus. *See* Clement of Alexandria, *Extraits de Théodote.*

Theophrastus. *Theophrasti Eresii Opera, quae supersunt, Omnia.* Edited and translated by F. Wimmer. Paris, 1866. Reprinted, Frankurt am Main: Minerva, 1964.

Thomas Aquinas. *Summa Contra Gentiles.* Rome: apud Sedem Commissionis Leoniae et apud Libreriam Vaticanam, 1934.

_____. *Summa Theologiae.* 5 vols. Edited by Institute of Medieval Studies. Text of S. Pii Pp. V. Ottawa: Impensis Studii Generalis, 1941-1945.

Treatise on the Resurrection. *See* Nag Hammadi treatises.

Valerius Maximus. *Factorum et Dictorum Memorabilium Libri Novem.* Edited by C. Kempf. Leipzig: Teubner, 1888.

Vergil. *Vergil: Georgica.* Edited and commented by W. Richter. Das Wort der Antike, 5. Munich: Hueber, 1957.

Völker, W., editor. *Quellen zur Geschichte der christlichen Gnosis.* Sammlung ausgewählter kirchen- und dogmengeschichtlicher Quellenschriften, New Series, 5. Tübingen: J. C. B. Mohr (Siebeck), 1932.

von Arnim, H. F. A., editor. *Stoicorum Veterum Fragmenta.* 3 vols. Leipzig: Teubner, 1903, 1905.

For biblical texts the editions used were R. Kittel (ed.), *Biblia Hebraica* (Stuttgart: Priviligierte Württembergische Bibelanstalt, [3]1937), and E. and E. Nestle and K. Aland (eds.), *Novum Testamentum Graece* (Stuttgart: Württembergische Bibelanstalt, [25]1963).

For ancient sources not cited above the Loeb Classical Library editions were used.

All translations of Greek and Latin sources quoted in the text are my own.

3. LATER SOURCES AND MODERN STUDIES*

Abt, A. 1908 *Die Apologie des Apuleius von Madaura und die antike Zauberei: Beiträge zur Erlauterung der Schrift de magia*. RVV, 4/2. Giessen: Töpelmann.

Ackerknecht, E. H. 1942 "Problems of Primitive Medicine," *Bulletin of the History of Medicine* 11, 503-21. Reprinted in W. Lessa and E. Z. Vogt (eds.), *Reader in Comparative Religion: An Anthropological Approach*, 394-402. New York: Harper & Row, ²1965.

Aland, K. 1955 "Der Montanismus und die kleinasiatische Theologie," *Zeitschrift für die neutestamentliche Wissenschaft* 46, 109-16.

1960a "Bemerkungen zum Montanismus und zur frühchristlichen Eschatologie." In his *Kirchengeschichtliche Entwürfe*, 105-48. Gütersloh: Gütersloher Verlagshaus Gerd Mohn.

1960b "Montanismus." In K. Galling (ed.), *Die Religion in Geschichte und Gegenwart*. 3d ed. Vol. 4, 1117-18. Tübingen: J. C. B. Mohr (Siebeck).

Andres, F. 1918 "Daimon." In PW Suppl. 3, 267-322.

Andresen, C. 1952-53 "Justin und der mittlere Platonismus," *Zeitschrift für die neutestamentliche Wissenschaft* 44, 157-95.

1955 *Logos und Nomos: Die Polemik des Kelsos wider das Christentum*. Arbeiten zur Kirchengeschichte, 30. Berlin: de Gruyter.

Armstrong, A. H., editor. 1967 *The Cambridge History of Later Greek and Early Medieval Philosophy*. Cambridge: Cambridge University Press.

Armstrong, A. H., editor and translator. 1966 *Plotinus*. Loeb Classical Library. 3 vols. Cambridge: Harvard University Press, and London: Heinemann.

Attridge, H. W. 1978 "The Philosophical Critique of Religion under the Early Empire." In W. Haase (ed.), *Principat*. Vol. 16/1, 45-78. Aufstieg und Niedergang der römischen Welt: Geschichte und Kultur Roms im

---

*Ancient sources or collections or translations of ancient sources entered in this section and cited by the name of the editor/translator are cited in the text for comments, references, or specific renderings by the editor/translator.

Spiegel der neueren Forschung, Part 2. Berlin and New York: de Gruyter.

Aune, D. E. 1978 "Herm. Man. 11.2: Christian False Prophets Who Say What People Wish to Hear," *JBL* 97/1, 103-04.

Babelon, E. 1900 "Le faux prophète Alexandre d'Abono-tichos," *Revue numismatique* 4, 1-30.

Babut, D. 1974 *La religion des philosophes grecs de Thâles aux Stoiciens*. Vendome, France: Presses Universitaires de France.

Bader, R. *Alethes Logos. See* under Celsus.

Baldwin, B. 1973 *Studies in Lucian*. Toronto: Hakkert.

Bardy, G. 1928 "Origène et la magie," *Recherches de science religieuse* 18, 126-42.

1949a *La conversion au christianisme durant des premiers siècles*. Théologie, 15. Paris: Aubier, Editions Montaigne.

1949b "'Philosophie' et 'philosophe' dans le vocabulaire chrétien des premiers siècles," *Revue d'ascetique et de mystique* 25, 97-108.

Barnard, L. W. 1967 *Justin Martyr: His Life and Thought*. London: Cambridge University Press.

Bartchy, S. S. 1973 *First-Century Slavery and 2 Corinthians 7:21*. Society of Biblical Literature Dissertation Series, 11. Missoula, MT: Society of Biblical Literature.

Barth, C. 1911 *Die Interpretation des Neuen Testaments in der valentinianischen Gnosis*. TU, 37/3. Leipzig: Hinrichs.

Bauer, W. 1909 *Das Leben Jesu im Zeitalter der neutestamentlichen Apokryphen*. Tübingen: J. C. B. Mohr (Siebeck). Reprinted, Darmstadt: Wissenschaftliche Buchgesellschaft, 1967.

1957 ^{2}1979 *A Greek-English Lexicon of the New Testament and Other Early Christian Literature*. Translated and adapted from the 4th German edition (1952) by W. F. Arndt and F. W. Gingrich. Cambridge: Cambridge University Press, and Chicago: University of Chicago Press, 1957. 2d ed. revised and augmented by F. W. Gingrich and F. W. Danker from W. Bauer's 5th German edition (1958). Chicago and London: University of Chicago Press, 1979.

1971 *Orthodoxy and Heresy in Earliest Christianity*. 2d German ed., with added appendices, by G. Strecker. Translated by a team from the Philadelphia Seminar on Christian Origins and edited by R. A. Kraft and G. Krodel. Philadelphia: Fortress Press.

Behr, C. A. 1968 *Aelius Aristides and the Sacred Tales*. Amsterdam: Hakkert, and Chicago: Argonaut.

Behr, C. A., editor and translator. 1973 Aelius Aristides, *Panathenaic Oration and In Defence of Oratory*. Edited and translated by C. A. Behr. Loeb Classical Library. London: Heinemann, and Cambridge: Harvard University Press.

Benedict, R. "Magic." 1937 In E. R. A. Seligman (ed.), *Encyclopaedia of the Social Sciences*. Vol. 9, 39-44. New York: Macmillan.

Berger, P. L. 1969 *The Sacred Canopy: Elements of a Sociological Theory of Religion*. Garden City, NY: Doubleday Anchor Books.

Berger, P. L., and T. Luckmann. 1967 *The Social Construction of Reality: A Treatise in the Sociology of Knowledge*. Garden City, NY: Doubleday Anchor Books.

Bernert, E. "Physis." 1941 In PW 20/1, 1129-30.

Betz, H. D. 1961 *Lukian von Samosata und das Neue Testament: Religionsgeschichtliche und paränetische Parallelen. Ein Beitrag zum Corpus Hellenisticum Novi Testamenti*. TU, 76. Berlin: Akademie Verlag.

Beyschlag, K. 1974 *Simon Magus und die christliche Gnosis*. Wissenschaftliche Untersuchungen zum Neuen Testament, 16. Tübingen: J. C. B. Mohr (Siebeck).

Bianchi, U. 1966 "Le Colloque international sur les origines du gnosticisme (Messine, avril 1966)," *Numen* 13, 151-60.

1967a "Marcion: Théologien biblique ou docteur gnostique?" *Vigiliae Christianae* 21, 141-49 Reprinted in F. L. Cross (ed.), *Studia Evangelica 5* (TU, 103), 234-41. Berlin: Akademie Verlag, 1968.

Bianchi, U., editor. 1967b *Le Origini dello Gnosticismo/ The Origins of Gnosticism: Colloquium of Messina 13-18 April 1966*. Supplements to *Numen*, 12. Leiden: E. J. Brill.

Bidez, J., and F. Cumont. 1938 *Les mages hellénisés: Zoroastre, Ostanès et Hytaspe d'après la tradition grecque*. 2 vols. Vol. 1, *Introduction*. Vol. 2, *Les Textes*. Paris: Société d'éditions "Les Belles Lettres."

Bieler, L. 1967 ΘΕΙΟΣ ΑΝΗΡ: *Das Bild des "Göttlichen Menschen" in Spätantike und Frühchristentum*. 2 vols. Vienna: Höfels, 1935, 1936. Reprinted in one vol., Darmstadt: Wissenschaftliche Buchgesellschaft, 1967.

Blackman, E. C. 1948 *Marcion and his Influence*. New York: Macmillan.

Bloch, R. 1963 *Les prodiges dans l'antiquité classique (Grèce, Étrurie et Rome)*. Paris: Presses Universitaires de France.

Böcher, O. 1970 *Dämonenfurcht und Dämonenabwehr*. Beiträge zur Wissenschaft vom Alten und Neuen Testament, 90. Stuttgart et al.: Kohlhammer.

1972 *Christus Exorcista: Dämonismus und Taufe im Neuen Testament*. Beiträge zur Wissenschaft vom Alten und Neuen Testament, 96. Stuttgart et al.: Kohlhammer.

Bohatec, J. 1938 *Die Religionsphilosophie Kants in der "Religion innerhalb der Grenzen der blossen Vernunft." Mit besonderer Berücksichtigung ihrer theologisch-dogmatischen Quellen.* Hamburg: Hoffman und Campe.

Bonwetsch, G. N. 1881 *Die Geschichte des Montanismus.* Erlangen: Deichert.

Bornkamm, G. 1939 "Ophiten." In PW 18/1, 654-58.

Bornkamm, G., G. Barth, and H. J. Held. 1963 *Tradition and Interpretation in Matthew.* Translated by P. Scott. New Testament Library. London: SCM, and Philadelphia: Westminster Press.

Bouché-Leclerq, A. 1963 *Histoire de la divination dans l'antiquité.* 4 vols. Paris, 1879. Reprinted, Brussels: Culture et Civilisation.

Boulanger, A. 1923 *Aelius Aristide et la sophistique dans la province d'Asie au IIe siècle de notre ère.* Bibliothèque des Écoles Françaises d'Athènes et de Rome, 126. Paris: E. de Boccard.

Bowersock, G. W. 1969 *Greek Sophists in the Roman Empire.* Oxford: Clarendon Press.

Brown, P. 1971 "The Rise and Function of the Holy Man in Antiquity," *Journal of Roman Studies* 61, 80-101.

Brown, R. 1965 *Social Psychology.* New York: Free Press, and London: Collier-Macmillan.

Bultmann, R. 1954 "Zur Frage des Wunders." In Bultmann, *Glauben und Verstehen.* Vol. 1, 214-28. Tübingen: J. C. B. Mohr (Siebeck).

14 1956 *Das Evangelium des Johannes.* Kritisch-exegetischer Kommentar. Göttingen: Vandenhoeck & Ruprecht.

3 1957 *Die Geschichte der synoptischen Tradition.* FRLANT, 29. Göttingen: Vandenhoeck & Ruprecht.

Cannon, W. B. 1942 "'Voodoo' Death," *American Anthropologist* 44, 169-81. Reprinted in *Psychosomatic Medicine* 19/3 (1957), 182-90, and (in abridged form) in W. Lessa and E. Z. Vogt (eds.), *Reader in Comparative Religion: An Anthropological Approach* (New York: Harper & Row, ²1965), 321-27.

Casey, R. P. 1925-26 "Naasenes and Ophites," *Journal of Theological Studies* 27, 374-87.

1935 "The Study of Gnosticism," *Journal of Theological Studies* 36, 45-60.

Caster, M. 1937 *Lucien et la pensée religieuse de son temps.* Collection d'études anciennes. Paris: Société d'édition "Les belles lettres."

1938 *Études sur Alexandre ou le faut prophète de Lucien.* Collections d'études anciennes. Paris: Société d'édition "Les belles lettres."

Cerfaux, L., and J. Tondriau. 1956 *Le culte des souverains dans la civilisation grèco-romaine: Un concurrent du Christianisme.* Bibliothèque de Théologie, 3d series, Vol. 5. Tournai, Belgium: Desclée.

Chadwick, H. 1947 "Origen, Celsus, and the Stoa," *Journal of Theological Studies* 48, 34-49.

1948 "Origen, Celsus, and the Resurrection of the Body," *Harvard Theological Review* 41, 83-102.

1964-65 "Justin Martyr's Defence of Christianity," *Bulletin of the John Rylands Library* 47, 275-97.

1966 *Early Christian Thought and the Classical Tradition: Studies in Justin, Clement, and Origen.* Oxford: Clarendon.

Chadwick, H., editor and translator. 1957 *Lessing's Theological Writings.* A Library of Modern Religious Thought. Stanford: Stanford University Press.

Clifford, W. K. 1961 "The Ethics of Belief" (1877). Reprinted in W. Kaufman (ed.), *Religion from Tolstoy to Camus,* 201-20. New York: Harper.

Coleiro, E. 1971 "Allegory in the IVth Georgic." In H. Bardon and R. Verdière (eds.), *Vergiliana: Recherches sur Virgile* (Roma Aeterna, 3), 113-23. Leiden: Brill.

Colson, F. H., editor and translator. 1935 *Philo.* Loeb Classical Library. Vol. 6. London: Heinemann, and Cambridge: Harvard University Press.

Conzelmann, H. 1959 "φῶς, φωτίζω, φωτισμός, φωτεινός, φωσφόρος, φωστήρ, ἐπιφαύσκω, ἐπιφώσκω." In *TWNT* 9, 302-49.

1975 *1 Corinthians: A Commentary on the First Epistle to the Corinthians.* Translated by J. W. Leitch. Bibliography and references by J. W. Dunkly. Edited by G. MacRae. Hermeneia. Philadelphia: Fortress Press.

Corcoran, T. H., editor and translator. 1971, 1972 Seneca, *Naturales Quaestiones.* Loeb Classical Library. 2 vols. London: Heinemann, and Cambridge: Harvard University Press.

Cornford, F. M. 1937 *Plato's Cosmology: The Timaeus of Plato translated with a running commentary.* London: Kegan Paul, and New York: Harcourt, Brace. Reprinted, Library of Liberal Arts, Indianapolis and New York: Bobbs-Merrill, n.d.

Coser, L. 1956 *The Functions of Social Conflict.* Glencoe, IL: Free Press.

Cullmann, O. 1925 "Les récentes études sur la formation de la tradition évangélique," *Revue d'Histoire et de Philosophie religieuses* 5, 459-77, 564-79.

1956 *The State in the New Testament.* New York: Scribner.

Cumont, F. 1887 *Alexandre d'Abonotichos: Un épisode de l'histoire du paganisme au IIe siècle de notre ère.* Mémoires couronés et autres mémoires publiés par l'Académie Royale des sciences, des lettres et des beaux-arts de Belgique, 40. Brussels: Hayez.

Cumont, F. 1922 "Alexandre d'Abonotichos et le néo-Pythago-risme," *Revue de l'histoire des religions* 85-86, 202-10.

Curtis, J. E., and J. W. Petras, editors. 1970 *The Socio-logy of Knowledge: A Reader.* New York and Washington: Praeger.

Daniélou, J. 1964 *The Development of Christian Doctrine before the Council of Nicaea.* Vol. 1, *The Theology of Jewish Christianity.* Translated and edited by J. A. Baker. London: Darton, Longman, and Todd.

1973 *A History of Early Christian Doctrine before the Council of Nicaea.* Vol. 2, *Gospel Message and Hellenis-tic Culture.* Translated and edited by J. A. Baker. London: Darton, Longman and Todd, and Philadelphia: Westminster Press.

Decharme, P. 1904 *La Critique des Traditions religieuses chez les Grecs des origines au temps du Plutarque.* Paris: Picard.

Deferrari, R. J., and M. I. Barry. 1948-53 *A Lexikon of St. Thomas Aquinas Based on the* Summa Theologica *and Selected Passages of his Other Works.* Washington, DC: Catholic University of America Press.

Delling, G. 1970 "Wunder--Allegorie--Mythus bei Philon von Alexandria." Reprinted from *Wissenschaftliche Zeitschrift der Martin-Luther-Universität Halle-Wittenberg*, Gesellschafts- und sprachwissenschaftliche Reihe, 6 (1957), 713-39. In Delling, *Studien zum Neuen Testament und zum hellenistischen Judentum: Gesammelte Aufsätze 1950-1968*, edited by F. Hahn et al. Göttingen: Vandenhoeck & Ruprecht, 1970. Pp. 72-129.

Derenne, E. 1930 *Les procès d'impiété intentés aux philo-sophes à Athènes au Vme et au IVme siècles avant J.-C.* Bibliothèque de la Faculté de Philosophie et Lettres de l'Université de Liége, 45. Liége: Vaillant-Carmanne, and Paris: E. Champion.

Dibelius, M. 1923 *Der Hirt des Hermas.* Handbuch zum Neuen Testament, Supplementary Volume. Die apostolischen Väter, 4. Tübingen: J. C. B. Mohr (Siebeck).

⁵1966 *Die Formgeschichte des Evangeliums.* 5th ed., with an addition by G. Iber. Edited by G. Bornkamm. Tübingen: J. C. B. Mohr (Siebeck).

Dietrich, M., and O. Loretz. 1969 "Beschriftete Lungen- und Lebermodelle aus Ugarit." In *Ugaritica VI* (Mission de Ras Shamra, 17), 165-79. Paris: Mission Archéo-logique de Ras Shamra.

Dodds, E. R. 1951 *The Greeks and the Irrational.* Sather Classical Lectures, 25. Berkeley and Los Angeles: University of California Press.

1960 "Numenius and Ammonius." In E. R. Dodds et al., *Les sources de Plotin: Dix exposés et discussions* (Entretiens sur l'Antiquité classique, 5), 1-32. Geneva: Fondation Hardt.

1970 *Pagan and Christian in an Age of Anxiety: Some Aspects of Religious Experience from Marcus Aurelius to Constantine.* New York: Norton.

Dölger, F. J. 1909 *Der Exorcismus im altchristlichen Taufritual: Eine religionsgeschichtliche Studie.* Studien zur Geschichte und Kultur des Altertums, 3/1-2. Paderborn: Schöningh.

1911 *Sphragis: Eine altchristliche Taufbezeichnung in ihren Beziehungen zur profanen und religiösen Kultur des Altertums.* Studien zur Geschichte und Kultur des Altertums, 5/3-4. Paderborn: Schöningh.

1950 "Der Heiland." In his *Antike und Christentum: Kultur- und religionsgeschichtliche Studien* 6/4 (Münster: Aschendorff, 1950), 241-72.

Dörrie, H. 1957 Review of C. Andresen, *Logos und Nomos* (1955). In *Gnomon* 24, 185-96.

1960 "Die Frage nach dem Transzendenten im Mittelplatonismus." In E. R. Dodds et al., *Les sources de Plotin* (Entretiens sur l'Antiquité Classique, 5), 191-223 (discussion, 224-41). Geneva: Fondation Hardt.

Douglas, M. 1966 *Purity and Danger: An Analysis of Concepts of Pollution and Taboo.* Baltimore et al.: Penguin.

Dubermann, L. 1976 *Social Inequality: Class and Caste in America.* Philadelphia et al.: Lippincott.

Dubs, Homer H. 1950 "Miracles--A Contemporary Attitude," *Hibbert Journal* 48, 159-62.

Eitrem, S. 1912 "Heros." In PW 8/1, 1111-45.

Eliade, M. 1950 *Birth and Rebirth: The Religious Meanings of Initiation in Human Culture.* Translated by W. R. Trask. New York: Harper.

1961 *The Sacred and the Profane.* New York: Harper.

Elliott, J. H. 1978 Review of A. Schreiber, *Die Gemeinde in Korinth: Versuch einer gruppen-dynamischen Betrachtung der Entwicklung der Gemeinde von Korinth auf der Basis des ersten Korintherbriefes* (1977). In *Biblica* 59/4, 589-92.

1981 *A Home for the Homeless: A Sociological Exegesis of 1 Peter, its Situation and Strategy.* Philadelphia: Fortress Press.

Evans-Pritchard, E. E. 1937 *Witchcraft, Oracles and Magic Among the Azande.* Oxford: Clarendon Press.

Farnell, L. R. 1921 *Greek Hero Cults and Ideas of Immortality.* Gifford Lectures, 1920. Oxford: Clarendon.

Farrington, B. 21969 *Science in Antiquity.* London et al.: Oxford University Press.

Fascher, E. 1927 ΠΡΟΦΗΤΗΣ: *Eine sprach- und religionsgeschichtliche Untersuchung.* Giessen: Töpelmann.

Festinger, L., H. W. Riecken, and S. Schachter. 1956 *When Prophecy Fails: A Social and Psychological Study of a Modern Group that Predicted the Destruction of the World.* New York: Harper.

Festugière, A. J. 1932 *L'idéal religieuse des grecs et l'évangile*. Études bibliques. Paris: Librairie Lecoffre.

1954 *La révélation d'Hermes Trismegiste*. Vol. 4, *Le Dieu inconnu et la gnose*. Paris: Librairie Lecoffre.

Feuerbach, L. 1967 *Lectures on the Essence of Religion*. Translated by R. Manheim. New York et al.: Harper & Row.

Firth, R. [2]1956 *Human Types: An Introduction to Social Anthropology*. London et al.: Nelson.

Foerster, W. 1935 "δαίμων, δαιμόνιον, δαιμονίζομαι, δαιμονιώδης, δεισιδαίμων, δεισιδαιμονία." In *TWNT* 2, 1-21.

Ford, J. M. 1956 "Was Montanism a Jewish-Christian Heresy?," *Journal of Ecclesiastical History* 17, 145-58.

Frazer, J. G. [3]1911 *The Golden Bough: A Study in Magic and Religion*. Part 1, *The Magic Art and the Evolution of Kings*. 2 vols. London: Macmillan.

Freeman-Granville, G. S. P. 1954. "The Date of the Outbreak of Montanism," *Journal of Ecclesiastical History* 5, 7-15.

Gager, J. G. 1971 "Religion and Social Class in the Early Roman Empire." In S. Benko and J. J. O'Rourke (eds.), *The Catacombs and the Colosseum: The Roman Empire as the Setting of Primitive Christianity*, 99-120. Valley Forge, PA: Judson Press.

1972 *Moses in Greco-Roman Paganism*. Society of Biblical Literature Monograph Series, 16. Nashville and New York: Abingdon, 1972.

1975 *Kingdom and Community: The Social World of Early Christianity*. Prentice-Hall Studies in Religion Series. Englewood Cliffs, NJ: Prentice-Hall.

1979 Review of R. M. Grant, *Early Christianity and Society: Seven Studies* (1977), A. J. Malherbe, *Social Aspects of Early Christianity* (1977), and G. Theissen, *Sociology of Early Palestinian Christianity* (1977). In *Religious Studies Review* 5, 174-80.

Geffcken, J. 1907 *Zwei griechische Apologeten*. Sammlung wissenschaftlicher Kommentare zu griechischen und römischen Schriftstellern. Leipzig and Berlin: Teubner.

Georgi, D. 1964 *Die Gegner des Paulus im 2. Korintherbrief: Studien zur religiösen Propaganda in der Spätantike*. Wissenschaftliche Monographien zum Alten und Alten und Neuen Testament, 11. Neukirchen-Vluyn: Neukirchner Verlag.

Giannini, A. 1963 "Studi sulla paradossografia greca," Part 1, "Da Omero a Callimaco: motivi e forme del meraviglioso," *Istituto Lombardo* (Accademia di Scienze e Lettere Rendiconti, Classe di Lettere e Scienze Morali e Storiche) 97, 247-66.

1964 "Studi sulla paradossografia greca," Part 2, "Da Callimaco all'eta' imperiale: La letteratura

paradossografica," *Acme* (Annali della Facoltà di
Filosofia e Lettere dell' Università Statali di Milano)
17, 99-140.

Gillin, J. 1948 "Magical Fright," *Psychiatry* 11 (1948),
387-400. Reprinted (in abridged form) in W. Lessa and
E. Z. Vogt (eds.), *Reader in Comparative Religion: An
Anthropological Approach*. New York: Harper & Row,
²1965. Pp. 402-10.

Godley, A. D., editor and translator. 1921-25 *Herodotus*.
Loeb Classical Library. 4 vols. London: Heinemann, and
New York: Putnam.

Goodenough, E. R. 1923 *The Theology of Justin Martyr*.
Jena: Frommannsche Buchhandlung. Reprinted, Amsterdam:
Philo Press, 1968.

1928 "The Political Philosophy of Hellenistic Kingship,"
Yale Classical Studies 1, 53-102.

1932 "A Neo-Pythagorean Source in Philo Judaeus," *Yale
Classical Studies* 3, 115-64.

1935 *By Light, Light: The Mystic Gospel of Hellenistic
Judaism*. New Haven: Yale University Press. Reprinted,
Amsterdam: Philo Press, 1969.

1938 *The Politics of Philo Judaeus: Practice and Theory*.
New Haven: Yale University Press.

1953 *Jewish Symbols in the Greco-Roman Period*. Vol. 2,
The Archaeological Evidence from the Diaspora. Bollingen
Series, 37. New York: Pantheon Books.

²1962 *An Introduction to Philo Judaeus*. Oxford: Blackwell.

Grant, F. C., editor. 1953 *Hellenistic Religions: The
Age of Syncretism*. Library of Liberal Arts. Indianapolis and New York: Bobbs-Merrill.

Grant, M. 1968 *The Climax of Rome: The Final Achievements of the Ancient World A.D. 161-337*. New York,
Toronto, and London: New American Library.

Grant, R. M. 1952 *Miracle and Natural Law in Graeco-Roman
and Early Christian Thought*. Amsterdam: North-Holland
Publishing Co.

1959 "Gnostic Origins and the Basilideans of Irenaeus,"
Vigiliae Christianae 13, 121-25.

²1966 *Gnosticism and Early Christianity*. New York:
Harper & Row.

1970 *Augustus to Constantine: The Thrust of the Christian Movement into the Roman World*. New York: Harper &
Row.

Grant, R. M., editor. 1961 *Gnosticism: A Source Book of
Heretical Writings from the Early Christian Period*. New
York: Harper.

Grant, R. M., editor and translator. 1957 *Second Century
Christianity: A Collection of Fragments*. Translations
of Christian Literature, Series 6, Select Passages.
London: SPCK.

Grundmann, W. 1935 "δύναμαι, δύνατοƒ, δυνατέω, ἀδύνατοƒ, ἀδυνατέω, δύναμιƒ, δυνάστηƒ, δυναμόω, ἐνδυναμόω." In *TWNT* 2, 286-318.

Gurvitch, G. 1971 *The Social Frameworks of Knowledge.* Explorations in Interpretative Sociology. Translated by M. A. and K. A. Thompson. Oxford: Blackwell.

Guthrie, W. K. C. ²1952 *Orpheus and Greek Religion: A Study of the Orphic Movement.* London: Methuen.

²1954 *The Greeks and their Gods.* Boston: Beacon.

1962, 1969 *A History of Greek Philosophy.* Vol. 1, *The Earlier Presocratics and the Pythagoreans.* Vol. 3, *The Fifth-Century Enlightenment.* Cambridge: Cambridge University Press.

Hamilton, M. 1906 *Incubation or the Cure of Disease in Pagan Temples and Christian Churches.* St. Andrews: Henderson, and London: Simpkin, Marshall, Hamilton, Kent.

Hammond, N. G. L., and H. H. Scullard, editors. ²1970 *The Oxford Classical Dictionary.* Oxford: Clarendon Press.

Händel, P. 1959 "Prodigium." In PW 23/2, 2283-96.

Harder, R. 1960a "Plotinus Abhandlung gegen die Gnostiker." In his *Kleine Schriften,* 296-302. Edited by W. Marg. Munich: Beck, 1960. Originally published in *Die Antike* 5 (1929), 78-84.

1960b "Zur Biographie Plotins." In his *Kleine Schriften,* 275-95. Edited by W. Marg. Munich: Beck.

Hardon, J. A. 1954 "The Concept of Miracle from St. Augustine to Modern Apologetics," *Theological Studies* 15, 229-57.

Harmon, A. M., editor and translator. 1925 *Lucian.* Vol. 4. Loeb Classical Library. Cambridge: Harvard University Press, and London: Heinemann.

Harnack, A. 1892 *Medicinisches aus der ältesten Kirchengeschichte.* Leipzig: Hinrichs.

²1924a *Marcion: Das Evangelium vom fremden Gott. Eine Monographie zur Geschichte der Grundlegung der katholischen Kirche. Neue Studien zu Marcion.* Leipzig: Hinrichs. Reprinted, Darmstadt: Wissenschaftliche Buchgesellschaft, 1960.

⁴1924b *Mission und Ausbreitung des Christentums in den ersten drei Jahrhunderten.* 2 vols. Vol. 1, *Die Mission in Wort und Tat.* Vol. 2, *Die Verbreitung.* Leipzig: Hinrichs.

²1958 *Geschichte der altchristlichen Literatur bis Eusebius.* 2d, expanded edition by K. Aland. Vol. 1/1. Leipzig: Hinrichs.

Harris, J. R. 1903 *The Dioscuri in the Christian Legends.* London: Clay, and New York: Macmillan.

Harris, J. R. 1906 *The Cult of the Heavenly Twins.*
Cambridge: Cambridge University Press.

1913 *Boanerges.* Cambridge: Cambridge University Press.

1927 *The Twelve Apostles.* Cambridge: Heffer.

Harvey, V. A. 1961 "D. F. Strauss' *Life of Jesus*
Revisited," *Church History* 30, 191-211.

1966 *The Historian and the Believer: The Morality of
Historical Knowledge and Christian Belief.* New York:
Macmillan.

1969 "Is There an Ethics of Belief?" *Journal of
Religion* 49, 41-58.

1970 "The Alienated Theologian," *McCormick Quarterly* 23,
234-65.

1979 "The Ethics of Belief Reconsidered," *Journal of
Religion* 59, 406-20.

Heitmann, A. 1940 *Imitatio Dei: Die ethische Nachahmung
Gottes nach der Väterlehre der zwei ersten Jahrhunderte.*
Studia Anselmiana: Philosophica Theologica, 10. Rome:
Pontificium Institutum S. Anselmi.

Heitmüller, W. 1903 *"Im Namen Jesu": Eine sprach- und
religionsgeschichtliche Untersuchung zum Neuen Testament,
speziell zur christlichen Taufe.* FRLANT, 1/2. Göttingen:
Vandenhoeck & Ruprecht.

Helm, R. 1927 "Lukianos." In PW 13/2, 1725-77.

Hengel, M., and H. Merkel. 1973 "Die Magier aus dem Osten
und die Flucht nach Ägypten (Mt) im Rahmen der antiken
Religionsgeschichte und der Theologie des Matthäus." In
P. Hoffmann et al. (eds.), *Orientierung an Jesus: Zur
Theologie der Synoptiker: Für Joseph Schmid*, 139-69.
Freiburg et al.: Herder.

Herrmann, W. [2]1908 *Offenbarung und Wunder.* Vorträge der
theologischen Konferenz zu Giessen, 28. Giessen:
Töpelmann.

Herzog, R. 1931 *Die Wunderheilungen von Epidauros: Ein
Beitrag zur Geschichte der Medizin und der Religion.*
Philologus, Supplementary Vol. 22/3. Leipzig:
Dietrichs.

Hewitt, J. W. 1924-25 "A Second Century Voltaire,"
Classical Journal 20, 132-42.

Highet, G. 1962 *The Anatomy of Satire.* Princeton:
Princeton University Press.

Hock, R. J. 1979 *The Social Context of Paul's Ministry:
Tentmaking and Apostleship.* Philadelphia: Fortress
Press.

Holl, K. 1928 "Die schriftstellerische Form des
griechischen Heiligenlebens," *Neue Jahrbucher für das
klassische Altertum* 29 (1912), 406-27. Cited in text
from the reprinting in his *Gesammelte Aufsätze zur
Kirchengeschichte*, Vol. 2, *Der Osten* (Tübingen: J. C. B.
Mohr [Siebeck], 1928), 249-69.

334 / *Pagan-Christian Conflict Over Miracle*

Holland, R. F. 1965 "The Miraculous," *American Philosophical Quarterly* 2, 43-51.

Holte, R. 1958 "Logos Spermatikos: Christianity and Ancient Philosophy according to St. Justin's Apologies," *Studia Theologica* 12, 110-68.

1962 *Béatitude et sagesse: Saint Augustin et le problème de la fin de l'homme dans la philosophie ancienne.* Paris: Études augustiniennes, and Worcester, MA: Augustinian Studies, Assumption College.

Hopfner, T. 1928 "Mageia." In PW 14/1, 301-93.

Hull, J. M. 1974 *Hellenistic Magic and the Synoptic Tradition.* Studies in Biblical Theology, 2d ser., no. 28. London: SCM, and Naperville: Allenson.

Hume, David. 1894 *An Enquiry Concerning the Human Understanding, and An Enquiry Concerning the Principles of Morals.* Reprinted (from the edition of 1777) and edited by L. A. Selby-Bigge. Oxford: Clarendon Press.

Hyldahl, W. 1966 *Philosophie und Christentum: Eine Interpretation der Einleitung zum Dialog Justins.* Acta Theologica Danica, 9. Copenhagen: Munksgaard.

James, W. 1958 *The Varieties of Religious Experience: A Study in Human Nature . . . the Gifford Lectures . . . in 1901-1902.* Reprinted, New York: New American Library.

Jeremias, J. 1969 *Jerusalem in the Time of Jesus: An Investigation into Economic and Social Conditions during the New Testament Period.* Translated by F. H. and C. H. Cave from the author's revision of the 3d German edition. Philadelphia: Fortress Press.

Johnson, Marshall D. 1969 *The Purpose of the Biblical Genealogies, with Special Reference to the Setting of the Genealogies of Jesus.* Studiorum Novi Testamenti Societas Monograph Series, 8. Cambridge: University Press.

Jonas, H. [2]1963 *The Gnostic Religion: The Message of the Alien God and the Beginnings of Christianity.* Boston: Beacon Press.

[3]1964 *Gnosis und spätantiker Geist.* Part 1, *Die mythologische Gnosis mit einer Einleitung zur Geschichte und Methodologie der Forschung.* FRLANT, 51. Göttingen: Vandenhoeck & Ruprecht.

Judge, E. A. 1960 *The Social Pattern of the Christian Groups in the First Century: Some Prolegomena to the Study of New Testament Ideas of Obligation.* London: Tyndale Press.

Käsemann, E. 1959 "Römer 13, 1-7 in unserer Generation," *Zeitschrift für Theologie und Kirche* 56, 316-76.

Kant, I. 1907 *Die Religion innerhalb der Grenzen der blossen Vernunft. Die Metaphysik der Sitten. Kants gesammelte Schriften*, 1st division, *Werke*, Vol. 6. Edited by the Königlich Preussischen Akademie der Wissenschaften. Berlin: Reimer.

Kant, I.   1913   *Kants gesammelte Schriften*.   3d division,
Handschriftlicher Nachlass, Vol. 2/1, *Anthropologie:
Erste Hälfte*.   Edited by the Königlich Preussischen
Akademie der Wissenschaften.   Berlin: Reimer.

1934   *Religion Within the Limits of Reason Alone*.   Translated and edited by T. M. Greene and H. H. Hudson.
Chicago and London: Open Court.

Kee, H. C.   1980   *Christian Origins in Sociological Perspective: Methods and Resources*.   Philadelphia: Westminster
Press.

Keim, T.   1873   *Celsus' Wahres Wort: Ältester Streitschrift
antiker Weltanschauung gegen das Christentum vom Jahre
178 nach Christus.   Wiederhergestellt, aus dem
Griechischen übersetzt, untersucht und erläutert, mit
Lucian und Minucius Felix verglichen*.   Zurich.   Reprinted,
Aalen, Germany: Scientia Verlag, 1969.

Kiev, A., editor.   1964   *Magic, Faith, and Healing:
Studies in Primitive Psychiatry Today*.   London: Collier-
Macmillan, and New York: Free Press.

Kippenberg, H. G.   1970   "Versuch einer soziologischen
Verortung des antiken Gnostizismus," *Numen* 17, 211-31.

Kittel, G.   1933   "ἀκολουθέω, ἐξ-, παρ-, συνακολουθέω."   In
TWNT 1, 210-16.

Kittel, G., and G. Friedrich, editors.   1933-69
Theologisches Wörterbuch zum Neuen Testament.   9 vols.
Stuttgart: Kohlhammer.

Klein, G.   1967   "Der Synkretismus als theologisches
Problem in der ältesten christlichen Apologetik,"
Zeitschrift für Theologie und Kirche 64, 40-82.

Knight, D. A.   1974   "The Understanding of 'Sitz im Leben'
in Form Criticism."   In G. MacRae (ed.), *Society of
Biblical Literature 1974 Seminar Papers. . . .* Vol. 1,
105-25.   Cambridge, MA: Society of Biblical Literature.

Knox, J.   1942   *Marcion and the New Testament: An Essay in
the Early History of the Canon*.   Chicago: University of
Chicago Press.

Koch, C.   1954   "Der ältromische Staatskult im Spiegel
Augusteischer und spätrepublikanischer Apologetik."   In
Convivium (Festschrift for Konrat Zeigler; Stuttgart,
1954), 85-120.   Reprinted in Koch, *Religio: Studien zu
Kult und Glauben der Römer*.   Edited by O. Seel.   Erlanger
Beiträge zur Sprach- und Kunstwissenschaft, 7.   Nurem-
berg: Carl, 1960.   Pp. 176-206.

Koester, H.   1968   "ΝΟΜΟΣ ΦΥΣΕΩΣ: The Concept of Natural
Law in Greek Thought."   In J. Neusner (ed.), *Religions in
Antiquity: Essays in Memory of Erwin Ramsdell Goodenough*
(Studies in the History of Religions, 14), 521-41.
Leiden: E. J. Brill.

1969   "φύσις, φυσικός, φυσικῶς."   In *TWNT* 9, 246-71.

Koetschau, P.   1892   "Die Gliederung des ἀληθὴς λόγος des
Celsus," *Jahrbücher für protestantische Theologie* 18,
604-32.

Kolenkow, A. B. 1976 "A Problem of Power: How Miracle-Doers Counter Charges of Magic in the Hellenistic World." In G. MacRae (ed.), *Society of Biblical Literature 1976 Seminar Papers: One Hundred Twelfth Annual Meeting . . .*, 105-10. Missoula, MT: Scholars Press.

Kraft, H. 1955 "Die altkirchliche Prophetie und die Entstehung des Montanismus, *Theologische Zeitschrift* 11, 249-71.

Kraft, R. A., editor and translator. 1965 *The Didache and Barnabas*. The Apostolic Fathers, 3. New York: Nelson.

Krauss, F. B. 1930 *An Interpretation of the Omens, Portents, and Prodigies Recorded by Livy, Tacitus, and Suetonius*. Philadelphia: University of Pennsylvania dissertation.

Kreissig, H. 1967 "Zur socialen Zusammensetzung der frühchristlichen Gemeinden im ersten Jahrhundert u. Z.," *Eirene* 6, 91-100.

Kretschmar, G. 1966 "The Councils of the Ancient Church." In H. J. Margull (ed.), *The Councils of the Church*, 1-81. Translated by W. F. Bense. Philadelphia: Fortress Press.

de Labriolle, 1913 *La crise Montaniste*. Paris: E. Leroux.

1942 *La Réaction païenne: Étude sur la polémique anti-chrétienne du Ier au VIe siècle*. Paris: L'Artisan du Livre.

Landsberger, B., and H. Tadmor. 1964 "Fragments of Clay Liver Models at Hazor," *Israel Exploration Journal* 14, 201-17.

Larsson, E. 1962 *Christus als Vorbild: Eine Untersuchung zu den paulinischen Tauf- und Eikontexten*. Translated by B. Steiner. Acta Seminarii Neotestamentici Upsaliensis, 23. Uppsala: Almqvist & Wiksells, Lund: Gleerup, and Copenhagen: Munksgaard.

Lattimore, R. 1942 *Themes in Greek and Latin Epitaphs*. Illinois Studies in Language and Literature, 28/1-2. Urbana: University of Illinois Press.

Leisegang, H. 1941. "Physis." In PW 20/1, 1130-64.

Lembert, R. 1905 *Der Wunderglaube bei Römern und Griechen*. Part 1, *Das Wunder bei den romischen Historikern: Eine religionsgeschichtliche Studie*. Supplement to Jahres-Bericht über das Königliche Realgymnasium zu Augsburg im Schuljahr 1904/1905. Augsburg: Druck des Literar. Instituts von Haas & Bragherr.

Lessa, W., and E. Z. Vogt, editors. [3]1965 *Reader in Comparative Religions: An Anthropological Approach*. New York: Harper & Row.

Lévi-Strauss, C. 1967 *Structural Anthropology*. Translated by C. Jacobson and B. G. Schoepf. Basic Books, 1963. Reprinted, Garden City, NY: Doubleday Anchor Books, 1967.

Lewis, C. T., and C. Short. 1879 *Harpers' Latin Dictionary: A New Latin Dictionary Founded on the Translation of Freund's Latin-German Lexicon Edited by E. A. Andrews*. New York et al.: American Book Company.

Lewis, I. M. 1971 *Ecstatic Religion: An Anthropological Study of Spirit Possession and Shamanism.* Baltimore: et al.: Penguin.

Liddell, H. G., R. Scott, H. S. Jones, and R. McKenzie. [9]1940 *A Greek-English Lexicon.* Oxford: Clarendon Press. *A Supplement.* Edited by E. A. Barber et al. Oxford: Clarendon Press, 1968.

Lieber, H. J., editor. 1974 *Ideologienlehre und Wissenssoziologie: Die Diskussion um das Ideologieproblem in den 20er Jahren.* Wege der Forschung, 117. Darmstadt: Wissenschaftliche Buchgesellschaft.

Lietzmann, H. 1927 "Simon Magus." In PW, 2d series, 3A/1, 180-84.

[3]1953 *A History of the Early Church.* Translated by B. L. Woolf. Vol. 2, *The Founding of the Church Universal.* Cleveland: World.

Lindblom, J. 1962 *Prophecy in Ancient Israel.* Philadelphia: Fortress Press.

Lipsius, R. A. 1875 *Die Quellen der ältesten Ketzergeschichte neu untersucht.* Leipzig: Barth.

Locke, John. 1958a *The Reasonableness of Christianity.* [1]1695. Edited by I. T. Ramsey. A Library of Modern Religious Thought. Stanford: Stanford University Press.

1958b *A Discourse of Miracles.* [1]1706. Reprinted in Locke, 1958a, 78-87.

Lods, M. 1941 "Études sur les sources juives de la polémique de Celse contre les chrétiens," *Revue d'histoire et de philosophie religieuses* 21, 1-33.

Lofland, J., and R. Stark. 1973 "Becoming a World-Saver: A Theory of Conversion to a Deviant Perspective." In C. Y. Glock (ed.), *Religion in Sociological Perspective: Essays in the Empirical Study of Religion*, 28-47. The Wadsworth Series in Sociology. Belmont, CA: Wadsworth.

Lowie, R. H. 1954 *Indians of the Plains.* New York: McGraw-Hill.

Lüdemann, G. 1975 *Untersuchungen zur simonianischen Gnosis.* Göttinger Theologische Arbeiten, 1. Göttingen: Vandenhoeck & Ruprecht.

Lunn, Arnold. 1950 "Miracles--The Scientific Approach," *Hibbert Journal* 48, 240-46.

Luterbacher, F. [2]1904 *Der Prodigienglaube und Prodigienstil der Römer: Eine historisch-philologische Abhandlung in neuer Bearbeitung.* Beilage zum Jahresbericht über das Gymnasium in Burgdorf. Burgdorf: Eggenweiler.

Luther, M. 1959 *The Large Catechism.* In T. G. Tappert (ed. and trans.), *The Book of Concord: The Confessions of the Evangelical Lutheran Church*, 357-461. Philadelphia: Muhlenberg Press.

MacMullen, R. 1966 *Enemies of the Roman Order: Treason, Unrest, and Alienation in the Empire.* Cambridge: Harvard University Press.

Malherbe, A. J. 1977 *Social Aspects of Early Christianity*. Baton Rouge and London: Louisiana State University.

Malingrey, A.-M. 1961 *'Philosophia': Étude d'un groupe de mots dans la littérature grecque des Présocratiques au IVe siècle après J.-C.* Études et commentaires, 40. Paris: Klincksieck.

Malinowski, B. 1927 "Culture." In E. R. A. Seligman and A. Johnson (eds.), *Encyclopaedia of the Social Sciences*. Vol. 2, 621-45. New York: Macmillan.

Mann, C. S. 1958 "Wise Men or Charlatans," *Theology* 61, 495-500.

Mannheim, K. 1925 "Das Problem einer Soziologie des Wissens," *Archiv für Sozialwissenschaft und Sozialpolitik* 54, 577-652.

1931 "Wissenssoziologie." In A. Vierkandt (ed.), *Handwörterbuch der Soziologie*, 659-80. Stuttgart: F. Enke.

1936 *Ideology and Utopia: An Introduction to the Sociology of Knowledge*. Translated by L. Wirth and E. Shils. Reprinted, New York: Harcourt, Brace and World, n.d.

Marrou, H. I. 1964 *A History of Education in Antiquity*. Translated from the 3d French ed. by G. Lamb. 1956. Reprinted, New York: Mentor.

Marwick, M., editor. 1970 *Witchcraft and Sorcery: Selected Readings*. Baltimore: Penguin.

Massoneau, E. 1934 *La magie dans l'antiquité romaine: La magie dans la littérature et les moeurs romaines. La repression de la magie*. Paris: Librairie du recueil Sirey.

McArthur, H. K. 1966 *The Quest Through the Centuries*. Philadelphia: Fortress Press.

McKinnon, Alastair. 1967 "'Miracle' and 'Paradox,'" *American Philosophical Quarterly* 4, 308-14.

Meeks, W. 1973 Review of V. P. Furnish, *The Love Command in the New Testament* (1972). In *Interpretation* 27, 95-100.

1977 Review of J. M. A. Salles Debadie, *Recherches sur Simon le Mage I: L'"Apophasis Megalè"* (1969); K. Beyschlag, *Simon Magus und die christliche Gnosis* (1974); G. Lüdemann, *Untersuchungen zur simonianischen Gnosis* (1975). In *Religious Studies Review* 3/3, 137-42.

Mensching, G. 1957 *Das Wunder im Glauben und Aberglauben der Völker*. Leiden: E. J. Brill.

Merlan, P. 1967 "The Later Academy and Platonism." In A. H. Armstrong (ed.), *The Cambridge History of Later Greek and Early Medieval Philosophy*, 53-83. Cambridge: Cambridge University Press.

Merton, R. 1967 *On Theoretical Sociology: Five Essays, Old and New*. New York: Free Press, and London: Collier-Macmillan.

Metz, J. B. 1965 "Wunder: systematisch." In J. Höfer and K. Rahner (eds.), *Lexikon für Theologie und Kirche*. 2d ed. Vol. 10, 1263-65. Freiburg: Herder.

Michaelis, W. 1954 "ὅραμα." In *TWNT* 5, 372-73.

Mill, J. S. [8]1872 *A System of Logic, Ratiocinative and Inductive, Being a Connected View of the Principles of Evidence and the Methods of Scientific Investigation*. Vol. 2. London: Longmans, Green, Reader and Dyer.

"Miraculum." 1936-66 In *Thesaurus Linguae Latinae*. Vol. 8, 1054-59. Leipzig: Teubner.

Miura-Stange, A. 1926 *Celsus und Origenes: Das Gemeinsame ihrer Weltanschauung nach den acht Büchern des Origenes gegen Celsus. Eine Studie zur Religions- und Geistesgeschichte des 2. und 3. Jahrhunderts*. Beihefte zur *Zeitschrift für die neutestamentliche Wissenschaft*, 4. Giessen: Töpelmann.

Mozley, J. B. 1865 *Eight Lectures on Miracles*. Bampton Lectures, 1865. London: Rivingtons.

Munz, P. 1972 "The Problem of 'Die soziologische Verortung des antiken Gnostizismus,'" *Numen* 19, 41-51.

Neill, S. 1964 *The Interpretation of the New Testament 1869-1961: The Firth Lectures, 1962*. London et al.: Oxford University Press.

Nestle, W. 1941-42 "Die Haupteinwände des antiken Denkens gegen das Christentum," *Archiv für Religionswissenschaft* 37, 51-100.

Nilsson, M. P. 1948a *Greek Piety*. Translated by H. J. Rose. Oxford: Clarendon Press.

1948b *Die Religion in den griechischen Zauberpapyri*. Bulletin de la Société Royale des Lettres de Lund 1947-1948, 2. Lund: Gleerup.

[3]1967, [2]1961 *Geschichte der griechischen Religion*. Vol. 1, *Die Religion Griechenlands bis auf die griechische Weltherrschaft* ([3]1967). Vol. 2, *Die hellenistische und römische Zeit* ([2]1961). Handbuch der Altertumswissenschaft, 5/2. Munich: Beck.

Nock, A. D. 1928 "Alexander of Abonuteichos," *Classical Quarterly* 22, 160-62.

1929 "Greek Magical Papyri," *Journal of Egyptian Archaeology* 15, 219-35. Reprinted in Nock, *Essays*, Vol. 1, 176-94.

1933a *Conversion: The Old and New in Religion from Alexander the Great to Augustine of Hippo*. London et al.: Oxford University Press.

1933b "Paul and the Magus." In F. J. Foakes Jackson and K. Lake (eds.), *The Beginnings of Christianity*. Part 1, *The Acts of the Apostles*. Vol. 5, *Additional Notes to the Commentary*, 164-88. London: Macmillan. Reprinted in Nock, *Essays*, Vol. 1, 308-30.

Nock, A. D. 1944 "The Cult of Heroes," *Harvard Theological Review* 37, 141-74. Reprinted in Nock, *Essays*, Vol. 2, 576-602.

1948 Review of *Reallexikon für Antike und Christentum*, Lieferungen 1-7 (1941-44). In *JBL* 67, 251-60. Reprinted in Nock, *Essays*, Vol. 2, 676-81.

1950 Review of E. J. and L. Edelstein, *Asclepius*, in *Classical Philology* 45, 45-50.

[2]1952 "Religious Developments from the Close of the Republic to the Death of Nero." In *Cambridge Ancient History*. Vol. 10, *The Augustan Empire 44 B.C.-A.D. 70*, 465-511. Edited by S. A. Cook, F. E. Adcock, and M. P. Charlesworth. London et al.: Cambridge University Press.

1954 "Bekehrung." In *Reallexikon für Antike und Christentum* 2 (q. v.), 106-18.

1956 Review of C. Andresen, *Logos und Nomos* (1955). In *Journal of Theological Studies* N.S. 7, 314-17.

1957 "Deification and Julian," *Journal of Roman Studies* 47, 115-23. Reprinted in Nock, *Essays*, Vol. 2, 833-46.

1972 *Essays on Religion and the Ancient World*. Selected, edited, with an Introduction, Bibliography of Nock's writings, and Indexes, by Z. Stewart. 2 vols. Cambridge: Harvard University Press.

Nock, A. D., and A. J. Festugière, editors. [2]1960 *Corpus Hermeticum*. Vol. 1. Collection des Universités de France. Paris: Société d'Édition "Les Belles Lettres."

O'Meara, J. J. 1956 *The Young Augustine: The Growth of St. Augustine's Mind up to his Conversion*. London: Longmans, Green, 1954. Reprinted, New York: Alba House.

Opitz, H. G. 1933 "Montanus." In PW 16/1, 206-10.

1960 *Ursprünge frühkatholischer Pneumatologie: Ein Beitrag zur Entstehung der Lehre vom Heiligen Geist in der römischen Gemeinde unter Zugrundelegung des I. Clemens-Briefes und des "Hirten" des Hermas*. Theologische Arbeiten, 15. Berlin: Evangelische Verlagsanstalt, 1960.

Oxford Classical Dictionary, The. [2]1970 Edited by N. G. L. Hammond and H. H. Scullard. Oxford: Clarendon Press.

Pagels, E. 1973 *The Johannine Gospel in Gnostic Exegesis: Heracleon's Commentary on John*. Society of Biblical Literature Monograph Series, 17. Nashville and New York: Abingdon.

1974 "Conflicting Versions of Valentinian Eschatology: Irenaeus' Treatise vs. the Excerpts from Theodotus," *Harvard Theological Review* 67, 35-53.

Paley, W. [8]1884 *Paley's View of the Evidences of Christianity, comprising the Text of Paley, Verbatim; with Examination Questions, arranged at the foot of each page of the text, and a full analysis prefixed to each chapter*, by G. Fisk. Cambridge: Hall, and London: Simpkin,

Marshall, and Co., Whittaker and Co., and G. Bell and
Sons. The *Evidences* was originally published in 1794.

Pannenberg, W. 1959 "Die Aufnahme des philosophischen
Gottesbegriffs als dogmatisches Problem der frühchristlichen Theologie," *Zeitschrift für Kirchengeschichte* 70,
1-45.

Paulus, H. E. G. 1828 *Das Leben Jesu, als Grundlage einer
reinen Geschichte des Urchristentums*. 2 vols. in 3.
Heidelberg: Winter.

Pearson, B. A. 1973 *The Pneumatikos-Psychikos Terminology*.
Society of Biblical Literature Dissertation Series, 12.
Missoula, MT: Society of Biblical Literature.

Peters, E. 1978 *The Magician, the Witch and the Law*.
Philadelphia: University of Pennsylvania Press.

Petzke, G. 1970 *Die Traditionen über Apollonius von Tyana
und das Neue Testament*. Studia ad Corpus Hellenisticum
Novi Testamenti, 1. Leiden: E. J. Brill.

Petzold, K. E. 1969 *Studien zur Methode des Polybios und
zu ihrer historischen Auswertung*. Vestigia, Beiträge zu
alten Geschichte, 9. Munich: C. H. Beck.

Pfister, F. 1909 *Der Reliquienkult im Altertum*. First
half-vol., *Das Objekt des Reliquienkultes*. RVV, 5/1A.
Giessen: Töpelmann.

1922 "Kultus." In PW 11/2, Cols. 2106-2192.

1924a "Epiphanie." In PW Suppl. 4, 277-323.

1924b "Epode." In PW Suppl. 4, 323-44.

Pieper, F. 1917 *Christliche Dogmatik*. Vol. 2. St.
Louis: Concordia Publishing House.

1951 *Christian Dogmatics*. Vol. 2. Trans. by T.
Engelder and J. T. Mueller. St. Louis: Concordia
Publishing House.

Pohlenz, M. 1909 *Vom Zorne Gottes: Eine Studie über den
Einfluss der griechischen Philosophie auf das alte
Christentum*. FRLANT, 12. Göttingen: Vandenhoeck &
Ruprecht.

1970 *Die Stoa: Geschichte einer geistigen Bewegung*.
2 vols. Göttingen: Vandenhoeck & Ruprecht, 1948, 1949;
41970 (corrections, additions, index by H.-J. Johann).

Praechter, K., editor. 121926 *Friedrich Ueberwegs
Grundriss der Geschichte der Philosophie*. Vol. 1, *Die
Philosophie des Altertums*. Berlin: Mittler.

Pritchard, J. 1950 "Motifs of Old Testament Miracles,"
Crozer Quarterly 27, 97-109.

Puech, A. 1912 *Les apologistes grecs du IIe siècle de
notre ère*. Paris: Librarie Hachette.

Puech, H. C. 1960 "Plotin et les gnostiques." In E. R.
Dodds et al., *Les sources de Plotin: Dix exposes et
discussions* (Entretiens sur l'Antiquité classique, 4),
161-74 (discussion, 175-90). Geneva: Fondation Hardt.

Quispel, G. 1974 "From Mythos to Logos." In his *Gnostic Studies I* (Publications de l'Institut historique et archéologique néerlandais de Stamboul, 34/1), 158-69. Istanbul: Nederlands Historisch-Archeologisch Instuut in het Nabije Oosten, 1974. Originally published in *Eranos Jahrbuch* 39 (1970), 323-40.

Rahner, Karl. 1962 *Schriften zur Theologie*. Vol. 5, *Neuere Schriften*. Einsiedeln et al.: Benzinger.

Ramm, B. 1955 *The Christian View of Science and the Scriptures*. London: Paternoster.

Ramsey, I. T. 1963 *Religious Language: An Empirical Placing of Theological Phrases*. 1957. Reprinted, New York: Macmillan, 1963.

Randall, J. H., Jr. ²1940 *The Making of the Modern Mind: A Survey of the Intellectual Background of the Present Age*. Boston et al.: Houghton Mifflin.

Reallexikon für Antike und Christentum: Sachwörterbuch zur Auseinandersetzung des Christentums mit der antiken Welt. Edited by T. Klausen et al. Stuttgart: Hiersemann, 1950- .

Reicke, B. 1968 *The New Testament Era*. Translated by D. E. Green. Philadelphia: Fortress Press.

Reiling, J. 1973 *Hermas and Christian Prophecy: A Study of the Eleventh Mandate*. Supplements to *Novum Testamentum*, 37. Leiden: E. J. Brill.

Reimarus, H. S. 1897a "Unmöglichkeit einer Offenbarung, die alle Menschen auf eine gegründete Art glauben könnten." Braunschweig, 1777. In K. Lachmann (ed.), *Gotthold Ephraim Lessings Sämtliche Schriften*. 3d ed., revised by F. Muncker. Vol. 12, 316-58. Leipzig: Göschen'sche Verlagsbuchhandlung.

1897b "Von dem Zwecke Jesu und seiner Jünger." Parts 1 (paras. 1-33) and 2 (paras. 1-9, 33-60). Braunschweig, 1778. In K. Lachmann (ed.), *Gotthold Emphraim Lessings Sämtliche Schriften*. 3d ed., revised by F. Muncker. Vol. 13. Leipzig: Göschen'sche Verlagsbuchhandlung.

1970 *Reimarus: Fragments*. Edited by C. H. Talbert. Translated by R. S. Fraser. Lives of Jesus Series. Philadelphia: Fortress Press.

Reinhardt, K. 1926 *Kosmos und Sympathie: Neue Untersuchungen über Poseidonos*. Munich: Beck.

Reitzenstein, R. 1963 *Hellenistische Wundererzählungen*. Leipzig: Teubner. Reprinted, Darmstadt: Wissenschaftliche Buchgesellschaft, 1963.

1966 *Die hellenistischen Mysterienreligionen nach ihren Grundgedanken und Wirkungen*. Leipzig: Teubner, ³1927. Reprinted, Darmstadt: Wissenschaftliche Buchgesellschaft.

Remmling, G. W. 1968 *Wissenssoziologie und Gesellschaftsplanung: Das Werk Karl Mannheims*. Sozialwissenschaftliche Schriftenreihe, 6. Dortmund: Ruhfus.

Remus, Harold. "Does Terminology Distinguish Early Christian from Pagan Miracles?," *Journal of Biblical Literature* 101/4 (1982), 531-51.

Rengstorf, K. H. 1933 "ἀποστέλλω (πέμπω), ἐξαποστέλλω, ἀπόστολος, ψευδαπόστολος, ἀποστολή." In *TWNT* 1, 397-448.

1953 *Die Anfänge der Auseinandersetzung zwischen Christusglaube und Asklepiosfrömmigkeit.* Münster: Aschendorff.

1964 "σημεῖον, σημαίνω, σημειόω, ἄσημος, ἐπίσημος, εὔσημος, σύσσημον." In *TWNT* 7, 199-268.

1969 "τέρας." In *TWNT* 8, 113-27.

Richter, C. P. 1957 "On the Phenomenon of Sudden Death in Animals and Man," *Psychosomatic Medicine* 19/3, 191-98.

Riesenfeld, H. 1946 "Remarques sur les hymnes magiques," *Eranos* 44, 153-60.

Robinson, J. M., and H. Koester. 1971 *Trajectories through Early Christianity.* Philadelphia: Fortress Press.

Rohde, E. 1966 *Psyche: The Cult of Souls and Belief in Immortality among the Greeks.* Translated from the 8th German ed. by W. B. Hillis. London: Kegan Paul, Trench, Trübner, and New York: Harcourt, Brace, 1925. Reprinted in 2 vols., New York: Harper & Row.

Roloff, D. 1970 *Gottähnlichkeit, Vergöttlichung, und Erhöhung zu seligem Leben: Untersuchungen zur Herkunft der platonischen Angleichung an Gott.* Untersuchungen zur antiken Literatur und Geschichte, 4. Berlin: de Gruyter.

de Saint-Denis, E. 1942 "Les énumérations de prodiges dans l'oeuvre de Tite-Live," *Revue de Philologie* 68, 126-42.

Salles Debadie, J. M. A. 1969 *Recherches sur Simon le Mage I: L'"Apophasis Megalè."* Paris: Gabalda.

Sanada, Takaaki 1979 "After Prophecy Fails: A Reappraisal of a Japanese Case," *Japanese Journal of Religious Studies* 6/12, 217-37.

Scheler, M. 1960 "Probleme einer Soziologie des Wissens." In M. Scheler (ed.), *Versuche zu einer Soziologie des Wissens.* Schriften des Forschungsinstituts für Socialwissenschaften in Köln, 2. Munich: Duncker und Humblot, 1924. Revised and expanded version in Scheler, *Die Wissensformen und die Gesellschaft.* Leipzig: Neue Geist-Verlag, 1926. Reprinted in Scheler, *Gesammelte Werke.* Vol. 8, *Die Wissensformen und die Gesellschaft,* 15-190. 2d ed. edited, with additions, by M. Scheler. Bern and Munich: Francke Verlag, 1960.

Schepelern, W. 1929 *Der Montanismus und die phrygischen Kulte: Eine religionsgeschichtliche Untersuchung.* Translated by W. Baur. Tübingen: J. C. B. Mohr (Siebeck).

Schienrl, P. W. 1980 "Eisen als Kampfmittel gegen Dämonen: Manifestationen des Glaubens an seine magische Kraft im islamischen Amulettwesen," *Anthropos* 75/3-4, 486-522.

Schleiermacher, F. 1958 *On Religion: Speeches to its Cultured Despisers.* Translated by J. Oman from the 3d German edition. New York: Harper.

1960 *Der christliche Glaube nach den Grundsätzen der evangelischen Kirche im Zusammenhange dargestellt.* 7th ed. Vol. 1. Edited by M. Redeker. Berlin: de Gruyter.

Schlier, H. [11]1951 *Der Brief an die Galater.* Kritisch-exegetischer Kommentar über das Neue Testament. Göttingen: Vandenhoeck & Ruprecht.

Schmaus, M. 1969 *Der Glaube der Kirche: Handbuch katholischer Dogmatik.* Vol. 1. Munich: Max Hueber.

Schmid, J. 1965 "Wunder im Judentum." In J. Höfer and K. Rahner (eds.), *Lexikon für Theologie und Kirche.* 2d ed. Vol. 10, 1254-55. Freiburg: Herder.

Schmidt, C. 1901 *Plotins Stellung zum Gnosticismus und kirchlichen Christentum.* TU, 20/4. Leipzig: Hinrichs.

Schweitzer, A. 1910 *The Quest of the Historical Jesus: A Critical Study of its Progress from Reimarus to Wrede.* Translated from the 1st German edition by W. Montgomery. Reprinted, New York: Macmillan, 1955.

Segal, A. F. 1981 "Hellenistic Magic: Some Questions of Definitions." In R. van den Broek and M. J. Vermaseren (eds.), *Studies in Gnosticism and Hellenistic Religions Presented to Gilles Quispel on the Occasion of his 65th Birthday,* 349-75. Leiden: E. J. Brill.

Shedd, W. G. T. 1888 *Dogmatic Theology.* Vol. 1. New York: Scribner's.

Sherwin-White, A. N. 1952 "The Early Persecutions and Roman Law Again," *Journal of Theological Studies* N. S. 3, 199-213.

Skarsaune, O. 1976 "The Conversion of Justin Martyr," *Studia Theologica* 30, 53-73.

Skovgaard Jensen, S. 1966 *Dualism and Demonology: The Function of Demonology in Pythagorean and Platonic Thought.* Copenhagen: Munksgaard.

Smart, N. 1964 *Philosophers and Religious Truth.* London: SCM.

Smith, J. Z. 1975 "Good News is No News: Aretalogy and Gospel." In J. Neusner (ed.), *Christianity, Judaism and Other Greco-Roman Cults: Studies for Morton Smith at Sixty.* Part 1, *New Testament* (Studies in Judaism in Late Antiquity, 12), 21-38. Leiden: E. J. Brill.

1978 "Towards Interpreting Demonic Powers in Hellenistic and Roman Antiquity." In W. Haase (ed.), *Principat.* Vol. 16/1, 425-39. Aufstieg und Niedergang der römischen Welt: Geschichte und Kultur Roms im Spiegel der neueren Forschung, Part 2. Berlin and New York: de Gruyter.

Smith, M. 1971 "Prolegomena to a Discussion of Areta-logies, Divine Men, the Gospels and Jesus," *JBL* 90, 174-99.

Smith, M. 1973a *Clement of Alexandria and a Secret Gospel of Mark*. Cambridge: Harvard University Press.

1973b *The Secret Gospel: The Discovery and Interpretation of the Secret Gospel According to Mark*. New York et al.: Harper & Row.

1978 *Jesus the Magician*. New York et al.: Harper & Row.

Smith, W., editor. 1873 *A Dictionary of Greek and Roman Biography*. Vol. 2. London: Murray.

Söder, R. 1932 *Die apokryphen Apostelgeschichten und die romanhafte Literatur der Antike*. Würzburger Studien zur Altertumswissenschaft, 3. Stuttgart: Kohlhammer.

Spencer, W. G., editor and translator. 1935 Celsus, *De medicina*. Loeb Classical Library. 3 vols. London: Heinemann, and Cambridge: Harvard University Press.

Spinoza, B. 1883 *The Chief Works of Benedict de Spinoza: A Theologico-Political Treatise and A Political Treatise*. Vol. 1. Translated by R. H. M. Elwes. 1883. Reprinted, New York: Dover Publications, 1951.

Stählin, G. 1942 "μῦθος." In *TWNT* 4, 769-803.

Stein, A. 1924 "Zu Lukians Alexandros." In M. Abramič and V. Hoffiler, editors. *Buličev zbornik. Strena Buliciana. Naučni prilozi posvećeni Franu Bulicu prigodom LXXV. Godišnjice njegova života od učenike i prijatelja IV. oktobra MCMXXI*, 258-65. Zagreb et al.: Štampala Zaklada Tiskave "Narodnih Novina," 1924.

Stein, P. 1909 *ΤΕΡΑΣ: Dissertatio Inauguralis. . . .* Marburg: Cattorum.

Steinhauser, K. 1911 *Der Prodigienglaube und das Prodigienwesen der Griechen*. Ravensburg: Dorn'sche Buchhandlung.

Strauss, D. F. 1972 *The Life of Jesus Critically Examined*. Translated from the 4th German edition by George Eliot. Edited by P. C. Hodgson. Lives of Jesus Series. Philadelphia: Fortress Press.

Swinburne, R. 1970 *The Concept of Miracle*. London et al.: Macmillan.

Talbert, C. H. 1975 "The Concept of Immortals in Mediterranean Antiquity," *JBL* 94/3, 419-36.

Tambornino, J. 1909 *De antiquorum daemonismo*. RVV, 7/3. Giessen: Töpelmann.

Tarn, W. W., and G. T. Griffith. [3]1961 *Hellenistic Civilisation*. New York: World.

Tavenner, E. 1916 *Studies in Magic from Latin Literature*. Columbia University Studies in Classical Philology. New York: Columbia University Press.

Taylor, A. E. 1934 "David Hume and the Miraculous" (1927). In Taylor, *Philosophical Studies* (London: Macmillan), 330-65.

Tennant, F. R. 1925 *Miracle and its Philosophical Pre-suppositions: Three Lectures Delivered in the University of London 1924*. Cambridge: Cambridge University Press.

Theissen, G. 1974a "Soziale Schichtung in der korin-thischen Gemeinde: Ein Beitrag zur Soziologie des hellenistischen Urchristentums," *Zeitschrift für die neutestamentliche Wissenschaft* 65, 232-72.

1974b *Urchristliche Wundergeschichten: Ein Beitrag zur formgeschichtlichen Erforschung der synoptischen Evangelien*. Studien zum Neuen Testament, 8. Gütersloh: Gütersloher Verlagshaus Gerd Mohn.

1975a "Die soziologische Auswertung religiöser Überlieferungen: Ihre methodische Probleme am Beispiel des Urchristentums," *Kairos* 17, 284-99.

1975b "Die Starken und Schwachen in Korinth: Sozio-logische Analyse eines theologischen Streites," *Evangelische Theologie* 35, 155-72.

Thesaurus Linguae Latinae. 1900ff. Leipzig: Teubner.

Thimme, A. 1890 "Alexander von Abonuteichos: Ein Beitrag zur Glaubwürdigkeit Lucians," *Philologus: Zeitschrift für das classische Altertum* 49, 507-14.

Thomas, K. 1971 *Religion and the Decline of Magic*. New York: Scribner's.

Thulin, C. E. 1905 "Synonyma quaedam latina. (*Prodigium, portentum, ostentum, monstrum*)." In *Commentationes Philologicae in honorem Johannis Paulson*, 194-213. Gothenburg: Zachrisson.

Tiede, D. L. 1972 *The Charismatic Figure as Miracle Worker*. Society of Biblical Literature Dissertation Series, 1. Missoula, MT: Society of Biblical Literature.

Toland, J. 1696 *Christianity Not Mysterious: Or, a Treatise Showing, That there is nothing in the Gospel Contrary to Reason, Nor Above it: And that no Christian Doctrine can be properly call'd A Mystery*. London, 1696. Reprinted, with introduction and text-critical appendix by G. Gawlick, Stuttgart: Frommann, 1964.

Trakatellis, D. C. 1976 *The Pre-existence of Christ in Justin Martyr: An Exegetical Study with Reference to the Humiliation and Exaltation Christology*. Harvard Disser-tations in Religion, 6. Missoula, MT: Scholars Press (for *Harvard Theological Review*).

van der Loos, H. 1965 *The Miracles of Jesus*. Supplements to *Novum Testamentum*, 9. Leiden: E. J. Brill.

van Winden, J. C. M. 1970 Review of N. Hyldahl, *Philo-sophie und Christentum* (1966). In *Vigiliae Christianae* 24, 307-10.

1971 *An Early Christian Philosopher: Justin Martyr's Dialogue with Trypho, Chapters One to Nine*. Philosophia Patrum--Interpretations of Patristic Texts, 1. Leiden: E. J. Brill.

Vermaseren, M. J.   1963 *Mithras, The Secret God.*   Translated by T. and V. Megaw.   London: Chatto and Windus, and Toronto: Clarke, Irwin.

Vögtle, A.   1972   "Jesu Wundertaten vor dem Hintergrund ihrer Zeit."   In G. Strube (ed.), *Wer war Jesus von Nazareth? Die Erforschung einer historischen Gestalt* (Munich: Kindler, 1972), 209-20.   Reprinted from H. J. Schultz (ed.), *Die Zeit Jesu* (Kontexte, 3; Stuttgart and Berlin: Kreuz Verlag, 1966).   E.T., "The Miracles of Jesus against their Contemporary Background," in H. J. Schultz (ed.), *Jesus in his Time*, translated by B. Watchorn (Philadelphia: Fortress Press, 1971).

Völker, W.   1926   "Die Kritik des Celsus am Leben Jesu und die Korrekturen der Gnostiker," *Theologische Blätter* 5, 25-39.

1928 *Das Bild vom nichtgnostischen Christentum bei Celsus.*   Halle (Saale):   Buchhandlung des Waisenhauses.

de Vogel, C. J.   [2]1964 *Greek Philosophy: A Collection of Texts with Notes and Explanations.*   Vol. 3, *The Hellenistic-Roman Period.*   Leiden: E. J. Brill.

von Campenhausen, H.   1963 *Kirchliches Amt und geistliche Vollmacht in den ersten drei Jahrhunderten.*   Beiträge zur historischen Theologie, 14.   Tübingen: J. C. B. Mohr (Siebeck).

von Wetter, G. P.   1916 *"Der Sohn Gottes": Eine Untersuchung über den Charakter und die Tendenz des Johannes-Evangeliums.*   FRLANT, 26.   Göttingen: Vandenhoeck & Ruprecht.

1921 *Altchristliche Liturgien: Das christliche Mysterium.   Studien zur Geschichte des Abendmahles.*   FRLANT, 30.   Göttingen: Vandenhoeck & Ruprecht.

Waitz, H.   1904   "Simon Magus in der altchristlichen Literatur," *Zeitschrift für die neutestamentliche Wissenschaft* 5, 121-43.

Walzer, R.   1949 *Galen on Jews and Christians.*   Oxford Classical and Philosophical Monographs.   London: Oxford University Press.

Waszink, J. H.   1950   "Basilides."   In *Reallexikon für Antike und Christentum* (q. v.) 1, 1217-25.

1963   "Some Observations on the Appreciation of 'The Philosophy of the Barbarians' in Early Christian Literature."   In *Mélanges offerts à Mademoiselle Christine Morhmann*, 41-56.   Utrecht: Spectrum.

1964   "Bemerkungen zu Justins Lehre vom Logos Spermatikos."   In A. Stuiber and A. Hermann (eds.), *Mullus: Festschrift Theodor Klauser.   Jahrbuch für Antike und Christentum*, Supplementary Vol. 1, 380-90.   Münster: Aschendorff.

1965   "Bemerkungen zum Einfluss des Platonismus im frühen Christentum," *Vigiliae Christianae* 19, 129-62.

Watson, G. 1971 "The Natural Law and Stoicism." In
A. A. Long (ed.), *Problems in Stoicism*, 216-38. London:
Athlone, and New York: Oxford University Press.

Wax, M. and R. 1962 "The Magical World View," *Journal for
the Scientific Study of Religion* 1, 179-88.

1963 "The Notion of Magic," *Current Anthropology* 4, 495-
503. Comments (pp. 503-13) by 13 scholars. Response by
the Wax's, pp. 513-18.

Webster, H. 1948 *Magic: A Sociological Study.* Stanford:
Stanford University Press, and London: Cumberlege
(Oxford University Press).

Weinreich, O. 1909 *Antike Heilungswunder: Untersuchungen
zum Wunderglauben der Griechen und Römer.* RVV, 8.
Giessen: Töpelmann.

1914 "Typisches und individuelles in der Religiosität
des Aelius Aristides," *Neue Jahrbücher für das klassische
Altertum, Geschichte und deutsche Literatur* 33, 597-606.

1919, 1969 *Neue Urkunden zur Sarapis-Religion.* Sammlung
gemeinverständlicher Vorträge und Schriften aus dem
Gebiet der Theologie und Religionsgeschichte, 86.
Tübingen: J. C. B. Mohr (Siebeck). Reprinted in his
Ausgewählte Schriften I: 1907-1921. Edited by G. Wille
and U. Klein. Amsterdam: Grüner, 1969.

1921 "Alexandros der Lügenprophet und seine Stellung in
der Religiosität des II. Jahrhunderts n. Chr.," *Neue
Jahrbücher für das klassische Altertum, Geschichte und
deutsche Literatur* 24, 129-51. Reprinted in his
Ausgewählte Schriften I: 1907-1921, 520-51. Edited by
U. Klein and G. Wille. Amsterdam: Grüner, 1969.

1929 *Gebet und Wunder: Zwei Abhandlungen zur Religions-
und Literaturgeschichte.* Stuttgart: Kohlhammer, 1929.
Also printed in *Genethliakon Wilhelm Schmid.* Tübinger
Beiträge zur Altertumswissenschaft, 5. Stuttgart:
Kohlhammer, 1929. Reprinted in Weinreich, *Religionsgeschichtliche Studien.* Darmstadt: Wissenschaftliche
Buchgesellschaft, 1968. Cited in the text from the
separate edition of 1929, with the *Genethliakon* page
numbers in parentheses.

1933 *Menekrates Zeus und Salmoneus: Religionsgeschichtliche Studien zur Psychopathologie des Gottmenschentums
in Antike und Neuzeit.* Tübinger Beiträge zur Altertumswissenschaft, 18. Stuttgart: Kohlhammer. Reprinted in
his *Religionsgeschichtliche Studien.* Darmstadt:
Wissenschaftliche Buchgesellschaft, 1968. Pp. 299-434.

Wellman, M. 1928 *Die ΦΥΣΙΚΑ des Bolos Demokritos und der
Magier Anaxilaos aus Larissa.* Part 1. Abhandlungen der
preussischen Akademie der Wissenschaften, 1928, no. 7.
Berlin: Verlag der Akademie der Wissenschaften.

Wendland, P. 41972 *Die hellenistisch-römische Kultur in
ihren Beziehungen zum Judentum und Christentum.* Handbuch
zum Neuen Testament, 2. Tübingen: J. C. B. Mohr
(Siebeck).

Wey, H. 1957 *Die Funktionen der bösen Geister bei den griechischen Apologeten des zweiten Jahrhunderts nach Christus.* Wintherthur: Keller.

Wifstrand, A. 1942 "Die Wahre Lehre des Kelsos," *Bulletin de la Société Royale des Lettres de Lund,* 391-431.

Wikenhauser, A. 1939 "Die Traumgesichte des Neuen Testaments in religionsgeschichtlicher Sicht." In T. Klauser and A. Rückert (eds.), *Pisciculi: Studien zur Religion und Kultur des Altertums. Franz Joseph Dölger zum sechszigsten Geburtstage dargeboten. . . . Antike und Christentum,* Suppl. Vol. 1, 320-33. Münster: Aschendorff.

Wilken, R. L. 1970 "Toward a Social Interpretation of Early Christian Apologetics," *Church History* 39, 437-58.

1971 "Collegia, Philosophical Schools, and Theology." In S. Benko and J. J. O'Rourke (eds.), *The Catacombs and the Colosseum: The Roman Empire as the Setting of Primitive Christianity,* 268-91. Valley Forge, PA: Judson Press.

Wilkinson, L. P. 1961 *The Georgics of Virgil: A Critical Survey.* Cambridge: Cambridge University Press.

Williams, G. H. 1974a "Baptismal Theology and Practice in Rome as Reflected in Justin Martyr." In *The Ecumenical World of Orthodox Civilization: Essays in Honor of Georges Florovsky.* Vol. 3, *Russia and Orthodoxy,* 9-34. Edited by A. Blane and T. E. Bird. The Hague and Paris: Mouton.

1974b "Justin Glimpsed as Martyr Among his Roman Contemporaries." In A. J. McKelway and E. D. Willis (eds.), *The Context of Contemporary Theology: Essays in Honor of Paul Lehman,* 99-126. Atlanta: John Knox.

Williams, M. G. 1902 "Studies in the Lives of Roman Empresses: I. Julia Domna," *American Journal of Archaeology* 6, 254-60.

Wilson, R. M. 1962 *The Gospel of Philip.* New York: Harper.

1968 *Gnosis and the New Testament.* Philadelphia: Fortress Press.

Wissowa, G., et alii, editors. 1893- *Paulys Realencyclo-pädie der classischen Altertumswissenschaft.* Stuttgart: Drückenmüller.

Witt, R. E. 1937 *Albinus and the History of Middle Platonism.* Cambridge Classical Studies. Cambridge: Cambridge University Press.

Wittgenstein, L. 1972 *On Certainty.* Edited by G. E. M. Anscombe and G. H. von Wright. Translated by D. Paul and G. E. H. Anscombe. New York: Harper & Row.

Wittmann, W. 1938 *Das Isisbuch des Apuleius: Unter-suchungen zur Geistesgeschichte des zweiten Jahrhunderts.* Forschungen zur Kirchen- und Geistesgeschichte, 12. Stuttgart: Kohlhammer.

Worsley, P.   [2]1968   *The Trumpet Shall Sound: A Study of 'Cargo' Cults in Melanesia*.   New York: Schocken Books.

Wülker, L.   1913   *Die geschichtliche Entwicklung des Prodigienwesens bei den Römern: Studien zur Geschichte und Überlieferung der Staatsprodigien*.   Leipzig: Glansch.

Young, M.   1971   "The Argument and Meaning of Justin Martyr's Conversion Story."   Th.D. dissertation, Harvard Divinity School, Cambridge.

Ziegler, K.   1949   "Paradoxographoi."   In PW 18/3, 1137-66.

Zirkle, C.   1936   "Animals Impregnated by the Wind," *Isis* 25, 95-130.

INDEXES

1. GENERAL INDEX[1]

[1] Sources, ancient and modern (including names of modern scholars),
are included in the index only insofar as they supply more than documentation for the text of the study.

---

[1]Some transliterated Greek words are indexed in the General Index.